The US, the EC and World Trade

The US, the EC and World Trade

From the Kennedy Round to the Start of the Uruguay Round

Giuseppe La Barca

Bloomsbury Academic
An imprint of Bloomsbury Publishing Plc

BLOOMSBURY

LONDON • OXFORD • NEW YORK • NEW DELHI • SYDNEY

Bloomsbury Academic
An imprint of Bloomsbury Publishing Plc

50 Bedford Square
London
WC1B 3DP
UK

1385 Broadway
New York
NY 10018
USA

www.bloomsbury.com

BLOOMSBURY and the Diana logo are trademarks of Bloomsbury Publishing Plc

First published 2016

British Library Cataloguing-in-Publication Data
A catalogue record for this book is available from the British Library.

ISBN: HB: 978-1-4742-5782-4
ePDF: 978-1-4742-5786-2
ePub: 978-1-4742-5785-5

Library of Congress Cataloging-in-Publication Data
Names: La Barca, Giuseppe, author.
Title: The US, the EC and world trade : from the Kennedy round to the start of the Uruguay Round / Giuseppe La Barca.
Description: London ; New York : Bloomsbury Academic, 2016. | Includes bibliographical references and index.
Identifiers: LCCN 2015047332 | ISBN 9781474257824 (hardback) | ISBN 9781474257862 (epdf)
Subjects: LCSH: International trade—History. | United States—Commercial policy. | United States—Foreign economic relations. | Europe—Commercial policy. | Europe—Foreign economic relations. | BISAC: HISTORY / Europe / General. | BUSINESS & ECONOMICS / Economic History. HISTORY / Modern / 20th Century.
Classification: LCC HF1379 .L3353 2016 | DDC 382/.30973—dc23 LC record available at http://lccn.loc.gov/2015047332

Typeset by RefineCatch Limited, Bungay, Suffolk
Printed and bound in Great Britain

Contents

Introduction

Trade and trade policy in the years 1967–86 showed a variety and complexity unmatched by other decades in the last century, even if occurrences in those other periods lent themselves to a less controversial assessment. No doubt we can find numerous trade disturbances, either with an endogenous or an exogenous root, that affected the economy of industrial countries and which had no less severe an impact. Yet, the number and complexity of the measures adopted to cope with trade problems in the years in question is not easily paralleled in other periods. In particular as regards barriers to foreign products, the list was no longer dominated by tariffs and quotas but involved a host of measures whose protectionist bias was often disguised under the cloak of bilateral agreements or as a form of reaction against allegedly trade-distorting practices. Likewise, the complexity and scope of multilateral discussions involving international trade went well beyond previous negotiations. It is also difficult to find in previous periods, both at national and international levels, so marked a dialectic between free trade tendencies, legacy of the spirit prevailing in the post war years, though with limits and safety valves, and the protectionist tendencies gaining strength under the impact of the deteriorating economic climate.

Trade decline and trade barriers, mostly as tariffs, import quotas and exchange controls, had a role in bringing about and prolonging the plight of most countries during the great depression, although they were not its main cause. Yet, these measures overall lacked the sophistication of those enacted in the period under consideration. Apart from the ill-fated 1933 London Conference, which, however, was prevalently focused and founded on 'currency stabilization', there was no relevant multilateral dialogue on trade. There is no denying the fact that the international achievements of the years from the final phase of the Second World War to the end of the decade were and still are of paramount importance for international trade. Yet, the trade environment in the years under review was not only more difficult but also more complex. The liberalization success of the 1940s and its aftermath were the upshot of the hegemonic position of the United States which was able to impose its trade philosophy with the consensus of countries ready to see the benefits of taking part in the scheme. The process became more uncertain when the US started to lose some of the assets on which that hegemony was based.

The 1947 General Agreement on Tariffs and Trade (GATT) was basically a statement of broad principles to which substance had to be given. In a first stage a set of negotiating rounds aimed at tariff, and the Kennedy Round was the most successful of them. Yet, by the time the Kennedy Round was drawing to a close, after long and laborious negotiations, the scenario had started to shift towards greater uncertainty. In the US imports, at constant prices, had for long been moving ahead faster than exports, but the process, after a pause between the mid-1950s and the mid-1960s was giving sign of accelerating. A growing trade gap was emerging with West Germany and Japan. The pegged exchange rates regime whose roots dated back to the 1944 Bretton Woods agreement had come under pressure and the efforts to stabilize the value of the dollar at the centre of the system appeared insufficient. The US was complaining that Western Europe was not doing enough in bearing the burden of a political and economic fabric of which it was a main beneficiary, from military expenditure to 'upward' currency realignment. A growing number of industries in both the US and the Western European economies were starting to feel the heat of the competition from the Asian countries, among which Japan was prominent but not exclusive. If the close of the Kennedy Round was the apex of the liberalizing process based on the dismantling of tariff barriers that had characterized the previous two decades, it also highlighted the limit of the process. The success in tariff cutting meant that they would no longer be the main obstacle to the opening of the world market. The tariff concessions, in areas where the predominance of the transatlantic trading partners was rapidly declining, were modest and foreboded the adoption of new kinds of restrictions, as was the case for steel and textiles. In sectors like agriculture concessions were limited in scope. The attempt to tackle new topics, i.e. non-tariff barriers (NTBs), limited as it was, had modest results.

The years from 1971 to 1973 witnessed the readjustment of the parity grill based on the Bretton Woods agreement and finally the repeal of the fixed but adjustable parity regime itself. Economists and historians prevalently look at the 1971–3 turmoil from the currency angle. However, the deep changes in the currency regime should also be looked at from the trade perspective as trade worries in the US were the main factor that triggered the process and, in a first stage, the threat of tariff barriers was prominent among the weaponry employed by the Americans. During those years the strains in economic relations between the US and the European Community became more pronounced. The two transatlantic partners decided to counter the threat of trade frictions not by relying only on bilateral talks but in the context of a new round of multilateral negotiations in the GATT in which not only tariff reductions but also the abolition or reduction of NTBs were on the table.

The first oil crisis changed by 180 degrees the role that trade had played in fostering growth in the Western economies during the previous decades. Although impact and responses differed across the Atlantic and among the Community's member states, it ushered in a depression of the economy that for length, depth and number of industrial countries involved had no precedent in the previous twenty years. The aftermath of the 1974–5 slump, in spite of a recovery which was more uncertain in Europe, left many key sectors of the Western economy like steel, textiles, cars and shipbuilding in a weaker condition. Both sides of the Atlantic reacted by introducing measures aimed at protecting these sectors from foreign competition through import restrictions or, especially in Western Europe, through subsidization, the latter being also employed to foster the development of emerging sectors of the economy.

In the multilateral forum the questions facing the negotiators became more complex, ranging from which topics were to be included in the negotiations to the balance for each of the selected topics between liberalizing concessions in view of trade expansion and the need to protect various areas of the domestic economy. After an uncertain start during the presidencies of Nixon and his Republican successor, the breakthrough came under President Carter. The Tokyo Round started to transform GATT principles in more detailed regulations relating to domestic and international procedures. However, overall the various codes on NTB measures drawn up in the round turned out to be rather limited in scope for fear of allowing foreign competition in sectors that were considered pivotal to national economies or, anyway, could attract effective lobbying. The rate of tariff cuts agreed at the end of the Tokyo Round was quite impressive, but its effectiveness was moderate as cuts were applied on duties that had been strongly reduced in previous rounds of negotiations.

In the second oil crisis the price hike all in all hit the economies across the Atlantic less severely and less rapidly than the previous shock. However, as it rekindled inflation, the renewed pressure of key imported products led to the adoption of restrictive monetary policies which were joined by more prudent fiscal policies, in a first moment also in the US. The second oil crisis was soon followed by a third shock, which, according to the prevailing view, was engendered by discrepancies in the US fiscal and monetary policies resulting in a gaping trade deficit for the US, which, however, did not help make recovery on the other side of the Atlantic speedier or more robust. The shocks of the first half of the 1980s further hit those industries that were still suffering from the decline in the previous decade and increased their number. The call for protectionist and interventionist policies did not abate.

The Reagan administration on the one hand answered the call of part of the American industry through a series of trade agreements limiting the expansion of competing products from US trading partners, including the EC, in the US and in the world market. On the other hand, the US executive pressed for a radical reshaping of GATT rules, including the opening of negotiations on new subjects like services, investments and intellectual property rights and a review of the Tokyo Round arrangements, which it judged unsatisfactory. The European Community focused on enhancing the integration of its member states' market as a way to get out of the doldrums in which it seemed to be stuck. It partially agreed with the US call for a reform of the GATT system, but resisted some of its key proposals, among which those concerning agriculture. After a five-year uneven journey, in September 1986 the multilateral talks resulted in a consensus on the agenda of a new round, the Uruguay Round, which lasted for over seven years and whose results, given the standstill in the following Doha Round, are still the main source of international trade regulation.

The facts outlined above dictate the approach of this book in tackling the role of international trade in the twenty years above mentioned which are the focus of this study, with particular attention to US and EC economies and policies. The word 'trade', thus, must not only be understood as a component of the world economy, but also as regulation of foreign commerce, both at national and international level. The survey is three-pronged, and in this can claim to tackle, from an historical perspective, the trade issues in a more comprehensive way than earlier research has done. First, it looks at the interrelation between domestic economies across the Atlantic and international trade in a period marked by 'shocks', to use an expression dear to contemporary observers. In particular the book will address questions such as the direction of the causal process during the numerous phases of economic turmoil, the macroeconomic measures adopted to cope with it and their outcome. Secondly, the measures adopted by the EC and the US to tackle the predicament of a growing number of industries within their borders will be examined. What were the similarities in the policies adopted across the Atlantic? In which areas did they differ and to what extent? The third component is the stance of the two transatlantic trading partners in multilateral negotiations, particularly, but not exclusively, the GATT rounds. Here the underlying questions are whether cooperation prevailed over differences in attitude; how agreement could be reached; and what its limits were.

A series of specifications must be made. The three sectors of analysis exclusively focus on the similarities and differences that the international trade had on the economy of the two main economic areas across the Atlantic; on the similarities and differences between the two areas in dealing with foreign competition; on the cooperation and differences in attitude in dealing with trade problems in multilateral forums. The fact that this research deals primarily with international trade rather than international economy results in greater prominence given to certain issues than would otherwise be the case. For instance, agriculture, whose share of the economy in the transatlantic areas was low and declining, will have particular prominence because it was paramount in trade conflicts and trade negotiations. The EC and the US are not comparable international entities and this is reflected in their organization and their place in international trade. The EC was not a state but a supranational organization and the establishment of a common market among its member states could be labelled as a work in progress. If a customs union with a common external tariff was in place by the beginning of the period under consideration, there were no provisions for a common fiscal policy, or the establishment of a common body unifying monetary policy. This implies that neither international trade nor its impact on domestic economy was uniform among member states.[1] If there was a body, the Commission, charged with conducting trade negotiations, final power institutionally remained in the Council of Ministers of the member states. The interests and attitudes of member states towards both domestic and international issues were not always uniform.

As regards the EC, further explanation of a legal and terminological kind is needed. In the period under review there were three Communities: the European Coal and Steel Community (ECSC), the European Atomic Energy Community (Euratom), and the European Economic Community (EEC). They remained legally separate, but the Treaty of Brussels of 8 April 1965, known as the Merger Treaty, combined the administrative bodies of the three Communities into a single institutional structure. The treaty came into force on 1 July 1967. In 1970 the administrative merger was supplemented by the introduction of a single operative budget. Thus, it is logical and, above all, simpler to adopt the term prevalently used by most sources: European Community (EC). However, a distinction will be made when referring specifically to one of the three Communities, chiefly the EEC and the ECSC, and to the period prior to the merger, as is the case for the conclusion of the Kennedy Round in June 1967.

1

The Setting of International Trade as it Emerged from the End of the Kennedy Round and its Aftermath

The year 1967, in particular its first half when the Kennedy Round drew to a close, could be described – though with no pretence to mathematical rigour or time precision – as a function maximum, where the first derivative is zero and the second one is negative. In the United States the measures adopted the previous year to check the overheating of the economy resulted in a contraction of the growth rate to a meagre 0.6 per cent in real terms, followed by a rapid recovery that ushered in a succession of peaks and troughs, in contrast with the prolonged and sustained growth of the preceding five years. The US current account balance, though remaining positive, went on declining while capital outflows accelerated. On the other side of the Atlantic, responding to pressure from the international trading community, in November Great Britain devalued the pound from $2.80 to $2.40 and the devaluation of the British currency prompted speculators to focus on the greenback. The majority of the EC member states went on growing in top gear in 1967 but West Germany, by then their economic leader, had a setback.

The term 'curve maximum' fits especially the conclusion of the Kennedy Round. It was the highest point of a trade-liberalization process beginning in 1947, which was mainly based on the curtailment of tariff barriers. The Kennedy Round was even more successful in pursuing this goal than the preceding negotiating rounds, but its very success meant that the instrument till then adopted, tariff cuts, was destined to become less effective in the future. Secondly, the approach adopted in the Kennedy Round proved of little use for sorting out growing problems in main trade areas like agriculture. Finally, the round's attempt to address a limited number of non-traditional issues, i.e. non-tariff barriers at the margin of the main stream of negotiations, was not productive, at least in the short-run.

Industrial products

The agreement that put an end to the round after over four years of tough negotiations, which seemed to have reached an impasse just a few months before its close, was signed on 30 June 1967. Concessions affected an estimated $40 billion trade volume representing about 40 per cent of the imports of industrialized countries and about 80 per cent of their products available for concessions, that is, those not already bound free.[1] Number and level of tariff concessions varied according to product sectors, the main distinctions being between agricultural and non-agricultural products. The concessions were to be fully implemented by 1 January 1972, either by five equal annual instalments, starting on 1 January 1968, or by cuts equal to 40 per cent of total reduction, starting from 1 July 1968, and the rest in three equal instalments beginning 1 January 1970.

In the industrial sector the Kennedy Round produced a remarkable 35 per cent reduction of duties, with about two-thirds of the cuts reaching 50 per cent and even more for a wide range of products. This success can be ascribed to the implementation of the 50 per cent objective agreed as a working hypothesis by the 'linear negotiating countries'. The approach followed in the previous five rounds had been that of item-by-item tariff negotiations but by the end of the Dillon Round it became clear that a more comprehensive approach was needed. The participants to the ministerial meeting of May 1963, in deciding that a new negotiating round should start the following year, agreed, among other things, that tariff negotiations should be based upon a plan of substantial linear tariff reductions, with a bare minimum of exceptions that had to be subject to confrontation and justification.[2] In May 1964 the participants to the new round agreed that negotiations should start on the basis of offers of a 50 per cent linear reduction, with the proviso, however, that initial offers could be modified if in the course of the negotiations a country deemed it necessary to obtain an overall balance of advantages with the other participants.[3] Actually, the new approach was followed by the US, Japan, the Nordic Countries and the EEC and the ECSC. Instead, Australia, Canada, New Zealand and South Africa, which claimed to belong to the category of countries with a special economic or trade structure, were allowed to negotiate their tariff reduction through the item-by-item method.

Overall, the cuts reflected the logic that major concessions could be made where there was a comparative advantage.[4] Non-electrical machinery was the sector where the major cuts were made by both the EEC and the US, 42 per cent and 50 per cent respectively. Almost equivalent percentage cuts (48 per cent) were made by the US on electrical machinery. The cuts made by the EEC were lower as it opted, under French and Italian pressure, to except business machines and electronics which it did not want to subject to American competition. On transportation equipment, the cut rate for the United States slightly exceeded 50 per cent, while the EEC cut the Common External Tariff (CET) by half but did not make concessions on commercial vehicles and tractors.

Deep cuts were also agreed on chemicals at the end of the round. Yet, the apparently significant concessions were the result of two different packages, one of which was conditional on the abolition of the American Selling Price (ASP) valuation system, which later failed to get approval from Congress. Actually, the ASP package did not only concern tariff cuts but also related to one of the two non-tariff barrier issues addressed in the round. The ASP was the basis of valuation used by the US to determine the duty applicable to imports of certain benzenoid chemical products, as well as rubber-soled footwear and canned clams. The *ad valorem* duty on these imports was applied to the wholesale price of the similar domestic product rather than the usual basis of valuation, which was usually the value of the imported product at the time of exportation from the foreign country. It resulted in a higher final duty, just because of the method of import assessment. Consequently, it was not a simple, traditional question of tariff rates, but also involved the elimination of a non-tariff barrier.

Although the chemical products subject to the ASP were limited, coinciding with benzenoid products, the Community decided to make the removal of the system for tactical and economic reasons a priority issue.[5] The ASP valuation system was seen as a way to balance US pressure on the EEC to eliminate or modify its Common Agricultural Policy (CAP). Some member countries, France and West Germany in particular, deemed that their unfavourable balance of trade in chemicals could be moved more to their favour by expanding the American market for EEC benzenoid. Thus the Community insisted that a reduction in US chemical duties should be accompanied by the abolition of the ASP system. The American delegation believed that the ASP repeal was a separate issue from simple tariff reductions over which the executive already had authority, being instead subject to Congress approval, which, correctly, it deemed neither easy nor forthcoming. Consequently, the repeal had to be compensated by further concession from the US trading partners in tariff and non-tariff areas. Thus the US in the last phase of the negotiations pushed for a 'decoupage', as the issue was labelled, into conditional cuts subject to the removal of the ASP and unconditional cuts to be made in the general negotiations. The US proposal was initially unfavourably received by the European Economic Community but was finally accepted by the EEC Council also because the Commission made it clear to the representative of the member states in Brussels that also in this area, concessions had to be made to allow the conclusion of the round.

In the first package, the so-called Kennedy Round package, the United States agreed to duty reductions on most dutiable chemical imports, cutting tariffs by 50 per cent on most items with rates above 8 per cent and 20 per cent on items not higher than 8 per cent. The commitments resulted in a weighted-average duty reduction of 43 per cent in US chemical tariffs on $325 million of dutiable imports from the EEC, UK, Japan and Switzerland. The combined tariff reduction made by these countries averaged 26 per cent on nearly $900 million of US chemical exports. In particular the commitments made by the European Economic Community resulted in a weighted-average reduction of 20 per cent in EEC tariffs on chemical imports from the US, estimated at $460 million in 1964. The UK commitments resulted in a weighted-average reduction of 24 per cent in imports of more than $100 million from the US.[6]

In the ASP package further concessions were contingent on the elimination of the ASP valuation system by the US. Initially the United States was requested to replace rates based on ASP with rates to be applied on the valuation as normally calculated for other US imports, but yielding the same revenue. The converted rates would be reduced by stages. The reduction would have resulted in a combined weighted-average cut on US chemical tariffs in the Kennedy Round and ASP packages of about 48 per cent on $325 million of imports in 1964. In turn the EEC would agree to additional cuts so as to achieve a combined Kennedy Round-ASP package reduction of 46 per cent. Belgium, France and Italy would also modify road use taxes so as to eliminate discrimination against American automobiles. The combined weighted-average reduction in the level of British chemical tariffs would be approximately 47 per cent on $170 million of imports from the United States.[7]

Modest cuts were agreed by the trading partners on both sides of the Atlantic on iron and steel, an industry whose items were prevalently excepted from the 50 per cent across-the-board cut rule. As noted by Curtis and Vastine, iron and steel negotiations reflected the problems faced by the steel industries of many industrial nations.[8] Excess capacity, costly raw materials and poor profits were affecting the steel industry in Continental Europe. The UK stance in the Kennedy Round was influenced by the impending nationalization of its steel industry and by a dispute with the ECSC. However, it was the United States that was facing the main problems under the growing pressure of Japanese competitors which were outperforming the American steel industry in terms of productivity and average costs. Total factor productivity in the sector rose more slowly than in Japan as well as in the rest of the US economy and, although after the hike of the 1950s the wage growth rate showed a lower gap with the whole American manufacturing sector rates, other input costs increased. The US steel industry also failed to keep pace with technical innovation despite the investments carried out in the second half of the 1950s to increase productive capacity, which consequently remained partially unutilized.[9] In contrast, Japanese producers constantly improved their productivity and were able to find nearer sources of ore supply in Australia and Brazil, thus cutting transport costs relative to those borne by their American competitors in getting raw material to the Midwest steel heartland.[10]

The ECSC agreed to reduce rates to an arithmetic average of 5.7 per cent and the EEC agreed to reduce steel rates within its jurisdiction correspondingly so as to maintain a tariff relationship between its more highly-fabricated steel items and the ECSC's less-fabricated items.[11] The cuts agreed by the two Communities averaged 23 per cent on the previous rates. At the end of the round the Communities could claim to have achieved two objectives, the first with an inner projection and the second with an external projection. The first goal was a unified external tariff that replaced the tariffs that were previously applied by the member states. The second goal was the mutual approximation of the duties applied by the main producers of steel.

The United States agreed on reductions averaging 7 per cent on 1964 imports and harmonized its tariffs with those of its transatlantic trading partner. The United Kingdom reduced most of its rates by 20 per cent. Japan, which was becoming increasingly competitive, made a 50 per cent concession except for a few alloy steel items.

Moderate as they were, the concessions made by the transatlantic partners started from a basis that was not comparatively high at the opening of the round, and the barriers to imports could be overcome by low prices and better quality. In the United States in particular, despite the concessions made in the negotiations, even before the end of the round the question for the steel industry had become no longer how much or how little to liberalize, but how to stop the inflow of foreign products as the ratio of steel mill product imports to US domestic consumption rose from about 5 per cent in 1961 to 16.7 per cent in 1968.[12]

In February 1967 the steel industry called for a tariff surcharge on steel imports. The proposal did not receive any response from US Congress or from the executive, possibly because it ran afoul of US multilateral commitments, but more likely because it was viewed as ineffective. In Congress, however, the idea of imposing quotas was gaining ground. The problem was solved not by legislation but by diplomacy. In 1968 the State Department negotiated a series of voluntary export restraint (VER) agreements with foreign exporters, nominally Japanese and EC member states steel industries. The VERs were not intergovernmental agreements but were signed with steel industry organizations which undertook to limit their exports to the US until 1971 and to maintain the same product mix and geographic distribution as prevailed in 1968. Thus the EC Commission could claim, rather hypocritically but formally correctly, that there was no engagement on the part of the Community. In May 1972, Japanese and EC producers, as well as the British, considered it prudent to renew their VERs for three further years and with some additional provisions, in particular a reduction of the annual growth rate of shipments from 5 per cent to 2 per cent. Actually the US was not alone in soliciting VERs by foreign producers: the EC negotiated a VER with Japan in 1967.

No substantial reductions in existing tariff protection on textiles were conceded by the industrialized countries given the difficulties faced by their industry. Actually, the Kennedy Round negotiations confirmed the far from free-trade structure of the textile world market and foreboded further restrictions.

The cotton textile industry, which had long been one of the trademarks of the countries that were deservedly labelled industrialized, had entered a declining trend already in the 1950s. Despite the structural and technological decline of a great part of their traditional textile industry, the EEC member states were initially able to keep imports from non-European countries at a low level (5 per cent of domestic consumption) because of their tariff barriers and quantitative restrictions. The United Kingdom's industry was not less hampered than its continental partners by a legacy of outdated equipment and an ageing labour force. However, in contrast with the EEC member states, the UK, although able to severely restrict imports from Japan, had to maintain an open door for imports from Commonwealth countries, which benefited from zero tariffs and unlimited access. Only in 1959 were inter-industry agreements signed with Hong Kong limiting cotton exports from the colony. By 1960 import of cotton textiles constituted 35 per cent of the United Kingdom's domestic consumption.[13] The US cotton textile industry, although maintaining after the Second World War a productivity level higher than that of its Western European competitors, was hindered by governmental policy. Low depreciation allowance for taxation purposes discouraged modernization of productive plants and a two-tier system of raw cotton pricing, under which US manufacturers had to pay up to 25 per cent more for raw cotton than their foreign competitors, placed them at a severe disadvantage. As early as 1955 the Eisenhower administration had signed a bilateral agreement with Japan, then the main exporter, under which the latter agreed to restrict the volume of exports to the United States for various cotton textile products. Quite soon, however, the decline in Japanese exports was offset by the inflow of cotton textiles from Hong Kong.

In 1961 the Kennedy administration sought a multilateral agreement under the GATT aegis, in which the European industry was requested to take part. A short-term arrangement entered into force in October 1961 for a period of twelve months and on expiring was replaced by the Long Term Arrangement Regarding International Trade in Cotton Textiles (LTA) for an initial period of five years. The parties to the Arrangement were divided basically into two groups. Group I included the industrialized countries, among which the United States, the United Kingdom and the EEC member states, that is the importing countries. Group II included fourteen developing countries. Japan and Poland were treated separately. Some important net-exporting countries, such as China and most East European countries did not accede.

The LTA provided for the progressive relaxation of the quota restrictions that existed at the time the Arrangement was signed and established strict rules for new restraints that could be initiated by importing countries. In particular, any new action had be justified on the basis of proved disruption within the cotton textile market of the importing country and had to be preceded by consultations between the importing and exporting countries. However, the LTA also envisaged the possibility of mutually acceptable bilateral agreements regulating the import of a wide range of cotton textiles as long as they were not inconsistent with the basic aim of the Arrangement, that is, the orderly expansion of cotton textile trade. Bilateral agreements, whose lifespan varied from one to five years, were thus the alternative usually followed by the parties to the Arrangement. Therefore, the LTA functioned as an umbrella to a wide set of bilateral agreements, whose consistency with the general principles of the GATT is rather doubtful. Certainly, the importing country had to meet some of the demands of the exporter, at least not curtailing the inflow of its products. However, the 'mutually acceptable' agreements quite often turned out to be a 'shotgun' wedding as the alternative could involve the unilateral imposition of import quotas by the importing country.[14]

During the Kennedy Round the main interest for the industrialized countries was the renewal of the LTA, while the developing countries hoped for substantial tariff reductions, being reluctant about the renewal of the Arrangement, which, however, seemed preferable to the threat of unilateral measures taken by the importers outside multilateral regulation.

The final agreement was based on a proposal put forward by the GATT Director-General, Eric Wyndham White, for an overall settlement for the cotton textile trade, which envisaged the broadest possible tariff cuts, negotiated undertakings to improve the LTA administration and the continuation of the safeguards against real or apprehended market disruption as embodied in the Arrangement. The principal concession by the exporting countries was their agreement to the extension of the LTA till 30 September 1970, which was subsequently extended for a further three years. In return, the importing countries agreed to enlarged access under LTA and tariff reductions, which, as was to be expected, were more limited the more processed the product. The United States made a 21 per cent weighted-average reduction. Cuts were higher for yarn, less high for fabrics and lower for apparel. The EEC tariff concessions were of the order of 10–20 per cent with validity limited to the period of extension of the LTA. The United Kingdom made only token reductions to countries other than Commonwealth members.

The tariff concessions agreed by the industrial countries on non-cotton textiles were more modest. In particular the United States agreed to a weighted-average tariff reduction of 15 per cent on imports of man-made fibre textiles and of 2 per cent on wool-textile imports. This reflected the fact that the cotton textile industry was being increasingly subjected to the fierce competition of man-made fibres. In particular the share of synthetic fibres in world production grew from 5 per cent in 1961 to over 23 per cent in 1970. By 1969 clothing imports manufactured from synthetic fibres constituted 35 per cent of all imports from industrialized countries. Clothing manufactured from man-made fibres, including cellulose fibres, formed 46 per cent of their imports. The bulk of trade in man-made fibre textiles was concentrated among the Western European countries which were net-exporters but also large importers. The United States' imports came from Western Europe but especially from Japan and three emerging Asian countries – Hong Kong, Taiwan and South Korea. The US industry thus started to claim protective measures covering man-made fibres and eventually a replacement of the Cotton Textile Arrangement and found a sympathetic ear both from Congress and the executive. The Nixon administration persuaded the principal Asian suppliers to voluntarily restrict exports of wool and man-made fibre textiles to the US, but there was also the possibility of analogous requests for Western European producers. In December 1973, fifty countries signed the 'Arrangement Regarding Multilateral Trade in Textiles', better known as the Multifibre Arrangement (MFA), which covered cotton, wool and man-made textiles. The new agreement, which came into force on 1 January 1974 and was valid for four years, recognized the need for industrialized countries to protect their textile industries while acknowledging the importance of the textile sector for the economic progress of the developing world. Overall, the arrangement was free trade oriented providing that new restrictions should be permitted only in case of market disruption to be determined according to a detailed list of criteria. It envisaged that bilateral agreements between importing and exporting countries should provide a base level, i.e. the annual level at which the quantity of the export of a particular product is restrained, and future growth rates.[15] The base level of exports in the first year of the restraint could not be lower than the annual level that it had already achieved. As for restrictions of over one year, the 1973 MFA provided for a minimum growth rate of 6 per cent. In limited cases the growth rate could be lower than 6 per cent, but even in such cases it had to be positive.

Substantial cuts across the board entailed a significant reduction in dispersion of rates which varied considerably from one country to another, the sharpest contrast at the outset of the Kennedy Round being between the widely dispersed US tariff, which included several hundred rates above 30 per cent, and the largely uniform Common Market tariff.[16] The estimates provided by Preeg show that as regards dutiable non-agricultural products before the Kennedy Round, 85.6 per cent of EEC rates fell in the tariff range of 7.6–20 per cent and only 0.3 per cent were above 25 per cent, whereas 61.4 per cent of the United States tariffs fell in the 7.6–20 per cent range and 16.3 per cent exceeded the 25 per cent rate.[17] The United Kingdom also had a significant share of its rates – 13.6 per cent – above the 25 per cent level. At the end of the round 83.3 per cent of the EEC tariffs, 68 per cent of the US tariffs and 63 per cent of the UK tariffs were at a level of 10 per cent or less. Well over 90 per cent of rates in all the industrial countries no longer exceeded the 20 per cent level.[18] Yet, the reduction in the gap did not mean its elimination. Over 6 per cent of US tariff rates still exceeded 20 per cent versus just 0.2 per cent for the Community.

Agriculture

The limited achievements in the farming sector were the upshot of differences in goals and perspectives between the two main parties in the negotiations, the United States and the EEC. Safeguarding and possibly improving its share in the agricultural market of Western Europe was the main US objective. The threat was posed by the unpromising shape that the CAP was taking, with its variable levy which could insulate the Common Market from foreign competition. Two years before the opening of the round, Kennedy, remarking that American farmers had 'a tremendous stake in expanding trade', stressed that 'they are particularly dependent upon the markets of Western Europe' as 'our agricultural trade with that area is four to one in our favor'. New and flexible trade authority to the executive was, therefore, required 'if we are to keep the Common Market open to American agriculture, and open it wider still'. [19] Consistent with the declared goal of opening up the West European Market, the United States, backed by Canada, Australia and New Zealand, initially proposed that agricultural produce like industrial products be subjected to a 50 per cent across-the-board reduction. Such an approach was considered unrealistic by most observers of the Kennedy Round as it required the Community to relinquish a regime, based on the variable levy, considered a cornerstone of the CAP.[20] It had also the disadvantage of coming at a time when the CAP regime had not been fully implemented.

The European Economic Community's proposals presented a completely different philosophy. Even before the official opening of the round the EEC, arousing US misgivings, expressed the view that all factors affecting the equilibrium of agricultural markets should be kept into account.[21] For the Community, the incidence of the variable levy, which was attracting the criticism of the United States and other main exporters, was itself influenced by the extent to which trade partners produced and exported at prices determined by factors other than free-market forces. The CAP, therefore, could not be singled out as the only culprit, since the orderly functioning of the market depended on a comprehensive approach to all forms of government intervention in agriculture and, therefore, not only on levies, but also production subsidies, price support and export subsidization to which all main parties used to resort. The proposal, called Mansholt II, presented by the EEC commissioner for agriculture, Sicco Mansholt, centred on the freezing of the 'montant de soutien' (support margin), encompassing all forms of direct support provided by any country to its farmers.[22] The 'montant', to be evaluated for all farm products marketed by parties to the GATT, was determined by the difference between a reference price and one obtained by farmers in their respective countries, plus any direct subsidy to producers. The reference price could be either the average world market price during a reference period, or, if a representative world market price could not be established, a price negotiated between GATT members. The margin of support would remain bound for three years thereby preventing GATT parties from raising their level of protection, but would be automatically increased if the reference price fell, thus providing an immediate response to world price depressing effects of subsidization practices. The binding of the support margin would be accompanied by agreements on food products like cereals, sugar, vegetable oils and fats, and dairy products, based on internationally agreed reference prices and the control of supply to avoid surplus.

Mansholt's proposal had the advantage of providing an all-encompassing, and rather unbiased, approach to the gamut of farm supporting practices. It had a further advantage, at least in the eyes of Mansholt, who himself was rather worried about the prospective distorting tendencies of the CAP in the domestic market: the EEC was aware that 'by binding its own amount of support, it would limit considerably for the future the existing scope of its levy mechanism, and consequently would slow up the natural tendency to expansion of its production, due in particular to the rapid technological development of an agricultural system which has frequently been acknowledged to be backward'.[23] The proposal was not, however, directed to the curtailment of the practices in question, but aimed only to cap them and for a limited period. It also had the disadvantage of relying on a benchmark particularly difficult to assess, even more so as the EEC had not yet completed the implementation of its CAP regime.[24]

The exporters, led by the US, rejected the proposal arguing that, rather than providing for reductions in existing trade barriers, it would actually introduce new restrictions and that the proposed implementing system was exceedingly cumbersome.[25] The US suggested a new approach, which the US Special Trade Representative, Christian Herter, labelled 'pragmatic' to contrast it to the Community's 'dogmatic' approach. Recognising the inevitability of the EEC's variable levy, it divided agricultural products into three groups: duty-free products, like cotton and soybeans should be bound at zero rate; products protected only or mainly by tariffs should have them cut; for products subject to ongoing or prospective commodity arrangements like grains, which would fall under the variable levy regime, the level of protection freezing as proposed by the EEC might be applied, subject to provisions for assuring continuous market access and the opportunity to share demand growth.[26] The 'pragmatic' American approach was followed, in different forms, in the subsequent phases of the negotiations.

In the following stage the negotiations focused on grains. The EEC quite laboriously established its position in mid-May 1965 and submitted its proposal to the GATT Committee on agriculture on 17 May. The proposal was based on the assessment of the support margin for the sector and on the establishment of a base reference price for the different cereals that was to be remunerative for the exporters, while keeping into account the expectations of the importing countries.[27] The proposal received an icy reception both from the big exporting countries and from the major importing countries.[28] The exporting countries led by the US did not see in the EEC project an instrument likely to secure them better access to the Community market. In its proposal the US stated that 'the price range should not be such as would induce uneconomic and excessive production, but should yield a remunerative return to efficient producers', that is, the big exporting countries. It also made it clear that 'importing countries should so arrange their domestic policies as to maintain imports at least equal to the average levels of a recent base period adjusted for growth proportionate to the increase in their total grains consumption'.[29] Importing countries like the UK and Japan were faced with the prospect of a steep increase in the cost of agricultural supplies and balance of payments problems.[30]

After considerable internal discussions the EEC accepted to limit its grain output to an agreed percentage of domestic consumption, thus maintaining its self-sufficiency below 100 per cent and leaving the remaining share to the exporting countries. Production above the agreed self-sufficiency ceiling was to be stored or disposed of as food aid to developing countries.[31] Disagreement, however, soon emerged when principles were translated into practice, as the Community offered a 90 per cent self-sufficiency rate, well above both the exporting countries' demand for an 86 per cent rate and the actual level attained by the EEC. The exporters also complained that the undertaking to withdraw from the market was contingent on a global surplus of grains and that the bounding of the production level was related to a period of only three years.[32]

In the last stage of the round both the issues of guaranteed access and margin of support were left out. The final agreement on agricultural products, reached after a negotiating marathon in May 1967, bore modest results. According to Preeg, tariff reductions on dutiable imports of non-tropical products other than cereals, meat and dairy products averaged approximately 22 per cent, a substantial cut but somewhat lower than those agreed on non-primary products.[33] Moreover, with regard to the main importer, the EEC, many products like grains and dairy were not subject to tariff cuts.

Cereal trade was handled by a Memorandum of Agreements on Basic Elements for the Negotiation of World Grains Arrangement, signed 30 June 1967 within the framework of the Round's final act.[34] The Arrangement, signed three months later, had two components: the Wheat Trade Convention and the Food Aid Convention. The former increased the floor and ceiling price for wheat and modified certain benchmarks previously used in price assessment. No provisions for access market sharing and price support were adopted. The United States, having been unable to secure its export share in the Common Market, finally agreed with its European counterpart on minimum prices well above the previous five-year average. This agreement was certainly inconsistent with a free trade perspective but at that time seemed to boost US wheat exporters' revenue. Indeed it was supported by most farm associations, though with the remarkable exception of the powerful Farm Bureau.[35] On the EC side the viewpoint of France, already a net exporter, prevailed on those of other members, which, being net importers, were reluctant to accept the prospect of a price hike. The Food Aid Convention committed the signatories to provide 4.5 million metric tons of wheat or other grains suitable for human food to developing countries, the US supplying 42 per cent of the total commitment and the EC covering 23 per cent of the shipments.[36] The convention had the merit of combining aid to famine-hit countries with the reduction of wheat stocks overhanging world markets, but failed to provide a link between food donations and the defence of the wheat floor price set in the Trade Convention. No progress was realised in the negotiation of general arrangements in the beef and dairy products sectors, and only specific concessions were agreed by the participants.

The Grains Arrangement was soon under pressure. An unexpected abundance of wheat caused by favourable weather conditions and a contraction of international demand in 1968–9 resulted in a decline of prices below the minimum level set by the Wheat Trade Convention. After the collapse of the arrangement a new international wheat agreement was established in 1971. Like its predecessor it included wheat trade and food aid conventions, but the former lacked the price provisions and merely provided a statistics gathering operation and a forum for discussion.

Although the tariff concessions agreed at the end of the Kennedy Round on balance favoured the United States, the main result of the negotiations was the absence of any significant constraint to the coming into effect of the CAP with its trade-distorting mechanism, and with it to the exploits and problems of the farm sector in the Community. The CAP inherited the main features of the farm policies of EEC member countries and balanced their goals. When the common price for grain in the EEC was laboriously agreed in 1964, Germany had to accept a curtailment of the high price previously guaranteed to its growers but the established price, whose adoption was postponed until 1 June 1967, was somewhat higher than the price prevailing in France which was close to the world market price due to the devaluation of 1959.[37] The result, therefore, was a mixed blessing for French farmers, as they obtained higher proceeds from their sales within the Community, but, in the absence of corrective mechanisms, would be made uncompetitive vis-à-vis producers outside the EEC. The logic that informed the grain agreement extended to price fixing for the whole range of produce covered by the CAP. In short, the domestic price system in the Common Market allowed marginal producers to survive but principally benefited big, competitive producers guaranteeing higher prices than those warranted by the market, whatever the supply. In turn, this mechanism fostered an unprecedented production growth not so much through effective modernization of farms, but through the widespread use of more chemicals together with the introduction of higher yield seed, brought about by technical progress.

The preservation of the system was obviously conditional on barriers that could only allow foreign products to fill the gap between EC demand and domestic supply. The mechanisms of the CAP varied for different products but prevalently relied on the administration of three prices. The 'target price' represented the desired price in the EC, agreed yearly by the Council of Agricultural Ministers. The 'threshold price' was the minimum price for imports and was set below the target price to reflect some notional cost of transport from ports of entry to national markets. The difference between the CIF (cost, insurance, freight) and the threshold price was bridged by a variable levy, calculated on a daily basis. This levy, therefore, contrary to import duties, constantly varied according to world prices and never allowed import prices to fall below the supported price of EC products, thus guaranteeing Community preference. Finally, every year the Council established the 'intervention price', which was the minimum price that the Community guaranteed to domestic producers. It established a floor to the Community market, as intervention agencies had to buy in at that price any product supplied by farmers on condition that required minimum quality standards were met. The mechanism ensured a welfare increase for EC farmers as they could place more produce in the EC market at higher prices to the detriment of both domestic consumers and foreign competitors facing high and flexible barriers to their exports to the Community. There was no burden on the Community budget as long as domestic demand was large enough to absorb domestic supply. However, when the Community reached self-sufficiency, the EC budget was bound to face soaring expenditure in the farm sector as intervention agencies had to buy farm products at fixed minimum prices and had to dispose of them at a loss. Sometimes agricultural commodities were resold when there was less pressure on the market; alternatively they were distributed as grants or at subsidized rates to disadvantaged people within the Community or as development aid to foreign countries. A more sophisticated way of disposing of farm products (known as restitution payments) was to sell them abroad at subsidized prices, thus allowing EC producers to effectively compete on the international market despite higher domestic prices.

The misgivings of foreign exporters proved correct. The Community still continued to be a net importer but the intra-EC import to extra-EC import ratio soared from a modest 32 per cent in 1966 to 67 per cent six years later and 77 per cent in 1975. Extra-EC exports more than tripled in the same years.[38] It must be noted that the figures for temperate zone farm products were much higher and the Community reached self-sufficiency for most of them by the middle of the 1970s.

If the defenders of the CAP found it hard to deny that it insulated the EC market from foreign competition (after all, the Community preference was a stated CAP standard), they were able to claim that the new farm policy had brought about a really unified market for both farmers and consumers in contrast to the fragmentation marking the agricultural policies inherited from each of the member states. It was not for long because of the cracks appearing in the fixed exchange rate regime and its final unravelling.

The Community had adopted a unit of account (UA) for budgetary and other purposes, which had the same gold content and, therefore, the same value as the dollar. Agricultural prices were converted into national currencies when intervention prices were paid and variable levies collected. This was easily done when the fixed exchange rate regime was in place. However, only two years after the establishment of common prices within the CAP, in August 1969, the French franc was devalued by 11.11 per cent and in October the Deutschmark was revalued by 9.29 per cent. The conversion rate from the UA should have equalled the French and German currencies' new exchange rate, but that would have rekindled inflationary pressures in France, while entailing a decrease of the income guaranteed to German farmers. The solution was found in the split between the UA conversion rate for agricultural products, known as the green rate, and the new official exchange rates of the French and German currencies. Thus the green rate was allowed to diverge from the market rate, initially as a temporary device limited to Germany and France. In turn, the divergence between the official rate and the agricultural conversion rate would have led to trade distortion, as the country with the higher intervention price, Germany, would have been flooded with farm goods from its EC partners, while exports of French producers would have skyrocketed, their revenues being repatriated at the actual exchange rate, with an extra profit. To avoid such disequilibria, monetary compensatory amounts (MCAs) were introduced which depended on differences between the central and the green exchange rates. The French government was, therefore, requested to place temporary subsidies on food imports from EC member states, and levy taxes on exports to the Community members. This was called 'negative MCA'. Germany, on the other hand, introduced positive MCAs, subsidizing its exporters, while imposing import levies of 11 per cent on all CAP products.[39] The arrangement, supposedly only temporary, became a permanent feature of the CAP fabric with the definitive collapse of the Bretton Woods fixed parity regime. The permanent and generalized adoption of green money signified splintering the common market for agriculture in terms of national prices, causing divergences between producers' receipts in member states higher than in the period preceding the implementation of the common price regime.[40]

Domestic and export subsidies as well as import quotas were also present within the US farm regime. Since the New Deal Agricultural Adjustment Act, the US had adopted a price support system based on non-recourse loans – giving farmers the option of either paying the loan back at concessional interest rates or defaulting and forfeiting the produce pledged as collateral for the loan – along with forms of direct payments and bolstered by production limits on a voluntary basis. Import quotas, due to a waiver granted by the GATT members in 1955, were applied on quite a few products including dairy products, flax, peanuts and peanut oil, increasing price and marketable production for American farmers. Since 1964 quotas could be imposed on fresh, chilled or frozen meat when estimated imports exceeded trigger levels based on the relationship between imports and domestic production. In addition to direct price and income support, US farmers benefited from other measures such as processing, marketing and consumer aid. The United States also implemented a series of programmes to boost farm exports. Export payments, either in cash or in kind, helped exporters to sell US agricultural products at world prices when US prices were higher and to counter the effects of competitors' export subsidies. Export credit and credit guarantee programmes assisted foreign buyers with liquidity constraints and balance of payments problems in purchasing US agricultural products. However, in the 1950s the Republican administration adopted a more flexible support price, while curbing the various crop limitation schemes inherited from the previous executives. Also the Democratic administrations of the 1960s kept loan rates at world market equilibrium and income support was mainly achieved through direct payments to producers who participated in authorized production control programmes.[41]

Non-tariff barriers

It is arguable that, if things had gone differently, farm trade would have offered ample scope for discussion on NTBs. The EEC proposal of binding the 'montant de soutien' implied dealing with non-tariff measures. The US, while rejecting the EEC approach, made it clear that 'where non-tariff devices and domestic agricultural policies affect trade, these can and should be dealt with in the negotiations', an opinion that was staunchly asserted by the American negotiators in the following rounds.[42]

The trade ministers, deciding to launch a new negotiating round in 1964, stated that 'trade negotiations shall deal not only with tariffs but also with non-tariff barriers'.[43] However, no real progress was made and quite soon the attempt was abandoned. Indeed, not only were NTBs difficult to assess but their international regulation was harder to achieve than tariff cuts. Unlike tariffs, approaches to the reduction of NTBs were difficult to embody in the delegation of negotiating authority, as in most cases they had their roots in domestic concerns only indirectly related to foreign trade and were subject to domestic laws. Only two agreements were signed: an antidumping code and an engagement to eliminate the ASP system in the US along with equally discriminatory measures in the EEC. The latter crashed on the shoals of the US Congress which refused to repeal the ASP legislation and the Community put its concessions on hold. This happened in spite of the efforts of the US administration. Johnson, pleading for the repeal, argued that the ASP system was both unfair and unnecessary: unfair as it diverged from the provisions of the GATT, gave to a few industries special privileges available to no other American business and imposed an unjustified burden on the consumer; unnecessary because the new industries that it covered no longer needed government protection.[44]

The consistency of US law with the Kennedy Round 'Agreement on the Implementation of Article VI' was also open to dispute. Although in signing the antidumping code the executive claimed that nothing in its provisions ran counter to existing US law, many in Congress and the US Tariff Commission argued that there were several inconsistencies between the two rules. In particular, while the code provided that an injury determination could be made only if the dumped imports were demonstrably the principal cause of material industry, the US administrative practice identified material injury with any injury that was more than '*de minimis*'. Also the parameters set by the Kennedy Agreement to determine regional industries affected by the influx of dumped products were viewed as much more restrictive than those applied by the US. Thus, Public Law 90–634 implementing the Kennedy Round antidumping code in the United States allowed its application but only to the extent that it did not conflict with existing US law and did not infringe on US practice based on such law.

Following a proposal of the Director-General Eric Wyndham White in November 1967, the GATT Contracting Parties agreed to draw up a list of non-tariff measures by April 1968, which was to be submitted to the newly established Committee on Industrial Products.[45] Both the United States and the Community agreed to the proposal of the GATT secretariat but their readiness appears to have differed. The US, acknowledging the importance of an inventory of NTBs, argued that a further step was to determine which barriers should receive priority attention and stressed that the GATT parties should deal not only with traditional NTBs, but also with subsidies and related measures.[46] The Community representative just noted that 'an inventory of these various measures suggested by the Director-General would be an initial realistic step' but that 'on the other hand, one can hardly envisage that further action in this field could be undertaken in the near future with concrete results'.[47] Differences in tariff nomenclatures and tariff valuation, that is, issues complementary to tariffs, were mentioned as useful items for the inventory.

The reserve of the Commission representatives on the issue can be explained by their awareness that not only were NTBs a more complex subject to tackle than duties, but that the task of achieving unity in the EC stance could prove difficult. The establishment of the CET by 1970 was provided by the Treaty of Rome.[48] The multilateral negotiations were viewed by the Commission, entrusted to conduct the talks on behalf of the Community, as an occasion to assert its authority in setting the CET and thus to avoid, at least partially, the frustrating task of brokering an agreement among the member states. The boundaries between national and

Community competences in trade relations with foreign countries were much more uncertain. Art. 113 of the Treaty of Rome concerning the common commercial policy after the transitional period listed, as falling under uniform principles to be followed by the whole Community, along with changes in tariff rates, the conclusion of trade agreements, the achievement of uniformity in measures of liberalization, as well as export policy and antidumping or countervailing duties. Yet, as noted by Pelkmans, the article had two drawbacks: it remained open-ended with respect to border measures other than tariffs; it was silent about a host of domestic measures, such as preferential public procurement, public aid to sectors or enterprises and standards, which might have an impact on trade outside the Community's borders.[49] In short, for the EC the issue was not only the selection of non-tariff measures to be subjected to prospective multilateral discussions, but also whether such measures fell within the scope of the common commercial policy and might, therefore, be dealt with by EC bodies. It also left open the question whether such measures were to be implemented by each member state or were to be replaced by measures whose implementation was to be entrusted to the Community's bodies themselves. Actually, as shown in following chapters, protective measures from foreign competition were concurrently applied by the Community and by its member states even after the close of the Tokyo Round.

Assessments of the Round and changes in attitudes

Several issues, therefore, were left beyond the scope of the Kennedy Round or, if dealt with, could not attract a real consensus. Five months after the close of the round, at their 24th session, the Contracting Parties to the GATT agreed on a rather vague work programme directed at achieving further progress in trade liberalization and expansion. A committee on trade in industrial products was charged with examining the tariff situation when all the concessions agreed in the Kennedy Round would be implemented and, as noted above, with drawing up an inventory on NTBs. Another committee was created to examine the problems in the agricultural trade sector. The parties also agreed to entrust the committee on trade and development with examining a number of topics of special interest to the developing countries.

An attempt to assess ex-post the results of the Kennedy Round and in particular the balance of benefits among the parties to the negotiations would render a moot judgement also because it would posit the *ceteris paribus* of a plurality of factors, which is made impossible to establish by the multifaceted turmoil that marked the following years. It is, perhaps, more useful to report the, quite often contradictory, assessments made by the parties themselves. The Special Representative for Trade Negotiations, William M. Roth, reported to the president that 'the principal free world trading nations have succeeded in negotiating a balanced and mutually beneficial reduction of trade barriers', adding that 'concessions made by the other major participants … compare favourably with those of the United States'.[50] And as regards agriculture Roth stated that 'we obtained concessions that are significant in terms of aiding U.S. exports and that compare favourably with the concessions the United States is granting for imports of foreign agricultural products'.[51] Johnson, the cunning politician, did not fail to point out that the agreements accomplished the objective of safeguarding 'domestic industries that were especially vulnerable to import competition'.[52] Other members of the administration were more critical and especially with regard to agriculture pointed out that the results of the round had disappointed the US hopes as, rather than fostering American farmers' exports, they were not able to reduce the protectionism of the CAP, which was not offset by token tariff cuts in products other than grains and by the sharing of food aid for cereals. The executive was also doubtful that the tariff agreements, in industrial and farm sectors, were sufficient to achieve a trade balance improvement that could offset the payments deficit.

The reception by US Congress and industry was lukewarm and often critical. Both shared the view that the curtailment of tariff barriers on manufactured products agreed on during the Kennedy Round might not prove enough to opening foreign markets due to the growing importance of NTBs and that, in any case, a moderate export improvement was not a decisive factor given export's limited weight in the economy. What worried many American industries and their representatives in Congress were imports, which had moved ahead much more rapidly than exports (Tables 1 and 4). By the end of 1967 no fewer than 729 bills in the House of Representatives and 19 in the Senate proposed quotas on over twenty imports.[53]

The administration reacted vigorously arguing that the imposition of quotas was bound to backfire especially for a country like the US that still had a positive trade balance and a comparative advantage in many sectors.[54] The Secretary of State, Dean Rusk, also argued that protectionist pressures in Congress would affect the whole US foreign policy, undermining the good faith and credit of the US abroad and strengthening anti-American sentiment in Europe.[55] Yet, the end of the Kennedy Round was a watershed in the US attitude towards the European Community and signalled a reassessment of the EC's position and role in the American policy. According to Warley, the Kennedy Round underlined the shift in political power in the post-war world 'as the United States, which previously set the tune of trade negotiations, was unable to prevent the European countries from realizing and even strengthening in the course of the negotiations a policy it disapproved'.[56]

The US had encouraged the establishment of a 'community' among the states of Continental Europe to secure political stability and to accelerate the economic recovery of the Eastern pillar of the transatlantic bloc. To achieve this goal it had accepted the likelihood of trade diversion against its own industries. The question of whether the establishment of a customs union and the abolition of tariffs among the six founders of the Community was trade-creating or trade-diverting has been widely debated. A trade creation effect occurs if the removal of trade barriers between customs union's members results in concentration of production in lower-cost producers and in increased exports to other members of the union. But, if with the establishment of the customs union a member country switches from low-cost external sources of supply to high-cost sources within the union, the latter has diverting effects.[57] Trade among the EC members soared during the 1960s. Intra-EC imports grew by over 320 per cent between 1960 and 1970, while total imports grew by less than 200 per cent and the share of the former swelled from 34.3 per cent to 48.7 per cent (Tables 12 and 16). Constraint to trade diversion was a major by-product of multilateral negotiation. Preeg pointed out that a major objective of the Kennedy Round was to reduce trade diversion resulting from the formation of the EEC and EFTA (European Free Trade Association) and that it was reasonable to estimate that the GATT negotiations had prevented a third to a half of the anticipated trade diversion resulting from European integration. This did not apply to the agricultural sector.

What marked, therefore, the change in attitude of the United States towards its European trading partner was, in a first stage, the hostility to EC initiatives that were supposed to have trade-diverting effects. President Johnson at the Punta del Este summit of the Organization of American States in April 1967, declaring the US willingness to explore with other developed countries the possibility of adopting a system of generalized tariff preferences for the developing countries, censured the proliferation of special trading arrangements which discriminate among developing countries. Johnson mentioned as an example of such arrangements the Yaoundé Convention between the EEC and eighteen African countries, former colonies of some of its member states.[58] Subsequent history bears out that the United States ended up adopting a rather selective application of the Generalized System of Preferences (GSP) and was not the first to apply it. The GATT Contracting Parties in June 1971 approved a waiver of Article 1 of the GATT to allow developed contracting parties to implement a system of generalized tariff preferences for the products of developing countries.[59] The EC and Japan put their preferences systems into effect in 1971, whereas the US delayed its action adducing the unsatisfactory state of its balance of payments.

However, the main culprit for both US executive and Congress was the 'reverse preferences' in favour of EC exports that were envisaged by most of the agreements with the Mediterranean countries, in view of the prospective establishment of a free trade area. The US argued that since the Mediterranean countries would never be able to completely dismantle their tariff barriers, as would be required in a free trade area under Article XXIV of the GATT, the likely result was a trade benefit for the Community to the detriment of US and other industrial countries' exports. The Community rejoined that such provisions were part of its policy to promote stability in a particularly volatile area, thus fulfilling its tasks as US political ally. The United States remained unconvinced. By the end of 1967 the special group on trade with the developing countries, created within the Organisation for Economic Cooperation and Development, was able to reach a consensus on all the main topics, but the thorny question of 'reverse preferences' remained unresolved.[60]

In a later stage, as shown in detail in the following chapter, the United States, though still supporting the idea of a common market in Europe, and thus the enlargement of the EC, became less tolerant of its impact on American interests.

On the other side of the Atlantic, in spite of the official satisfaction for the results of the round, apart from agriculture, there were complaints that the balance for tariff binding was still in favour of the United States as both the arithmetic average and weighted average of the EC were lower than those of the US and that the linear cut system prevalently adopted in the Kennedy Round made the problem of tariff disparities worse since an equal reduction on either side would leave the protective effect of the high tariff substantially untouched while considerably reducing that of the lower tariff.[61]

Multinational corporations around the period of the Kennedy Round

Did the Kennedy Round influence the behaviour of what lay outside the conceptual border of trade among nations but nevertheless was having a growing weight in world trade: multinational corporations (MNCs) and in particular US multinational corporations in Europe and in the EC? It goes without saying that at this stage research can offer only a 'qualitative' ascertainment, nominally because MNCs were not a subject of GATT negotiations.

Investment in Europe was part of the swell in US outward investments that marked the decades following the Second World War. US foreign direct investments (FDIs) grew six fold between 1951 and 1970.[62] By 1973 American corporations were investing about one dollar abroad for every three they invested in the United States.[63] Within Europe, the EC in particular was the fastest growing and finally was the main destination for US investments. In 1958 Europe's share of American FDIs was 16.7 per cent, just half of Canada's share and the EC accounted for 7 per cent (Table 6). In 1973, the year of the first EC enlargement Europe's share was 37.8 per cent and that of the EC was 30.5 per cent, while that of Canada had fallen to 25 per cent and that of the other countries of the Western Hemisphere had plummeted to 16 per cent from almost 31 per cent fifteen years earlier. Dunning's research illustrated that, at least with reference to the 1954–64 period, those European countries that most improved their competitive position in the export of research-intensive products relative to the US attracted the greatest share of American FDIs. Moreover, the increase in US investments in Western Europe was in general concentrated in those industries that recorded the most impressive increase in exports.[64] In other words, US MNCs helped to close the technological gap between the US and the Western European countries and to boost their exports in a phase in which exports from the United States were slowing down.

Among the theories put forward to explain the reasons for the spread of multinational corporations, the so-called 'eclectic theory' seems to offer the best explanation for the explosion of American investments and the proliferation of US subsidiaries in Europe. According to this theory, there must be the concurrence of three factors: firstly ownership-specific advantages, such as organization, structure, financial and human resources over firms in the host countries; secondly these advantages are best exploited by the firm itself rather than by selling them to foreign firms; and thirdly location-specific advantages must be present that make it profitable to exploit the ownership-specific advantages in the foreign country rather than in the domestic market.[65] The establishment of the so-called Common Market presented at the same time a carrot and a stick: the promise of a large and growing market on the one hand; discrimination against third-party imports on the other.

Gross Domestic Product (GDP) in the EC area grew by about 5 per cent in the 1960s and intra-EC exports rose at high speed in the years following the Treaty of Rome (Table 15). Discrimination against third-party imports was foreseen to be the result of a 'common external tariff', which had to be in place by 1970. Certainly, the prospect of the distorting effects that such discrimination would exercise on the American firms' choices and by them on the US economy worried the US executive. Kennedy himself contended that 'the European Common Market has attracted

American capital, partly because American businessmen fear that they will be unable to compete in the growing European market unless they build plants behind the common tariff wall' and it was, therefore, necessary to 'negotiate down the barrier to trade between the two great continental markets so that the exports of our industry and agriculture can have full opportunity to compete in Europe'.[66]

Yet, statistical evidence does not bear out that the tariff barrier stick was the major contributory factor in the choice of American firms to establish subsidiaries in the Community. In the first place, American FDIs in the EC were only part of the US investments in Europe, averaging 45 per cent of the latter until the first EC enlargement. The UK was by far the main destination of American investments, accounting for an amount equal to or even higher than that of France and Germany together. The UK had long been a traditional outlet for US capitals. Moreover, in the case of the UK, foreign investments might have been directed at jumping tariffs, with effects not circumscribed to British soil as Britain was the main EFTA member. As noted by Balassa, the theory at the basis of FDI attraction exerted by the existence of tariff discrimination, or by its expectation implies that its lessening through multilateral tariff reductions would lead to a reverse flow of capitals.[67] In the 1958–68 period, during which the CET was put into being, American FDIs in the Community grew by a dazzling 17 per cent yearly. From 1968 to 1972, the period in which the Kennedy Round tariff cuts were implemented, American FDIs grew by a less dazzling, but still massive 14 per cent, starting, however, from a higher base.

It can therefore be argued that the carrot of a large and dynamic market had much greater sway on the decisions of American firms. This was so during the completion of the CET, during the multilateral negotiations and after them during the 1970s. But cost factors too were at play as decisions on the location of production facilities would respond to cost differences which often favoured European plants. In the 1960s wage costs in the manufacturing industries of the EC member countries and in the UK were less than half those in US manufacturing industries.[68] Besides, at least until the onset of the 1970s, the overvaluation of the dollar made it economical for American firms to invest in the European market.

Overall, in Europe the reception of American FDIs and multinational corporations was far from hostile. No doubt that in the UK some Labour members complained against the alleged threat of foreign capital dominance to the British economy. In France Servan-Schreiber argued that, in the absence of offsetting policies directed at enhancing the competitiveness of domestic firms in the European Community, the settlement of American subsidiaries would be the Trojan horse for economic colonization.[69] However, the Western European countries, with very few and non-lasting exceptions, refrained from hindering inward investments, aware that a more restrictive policy than their partners' only helped their competitors at their own expense.

The attitude of the US economists and of the US executive towards outward investments was not unreservedly favourable. Some economists argued that investments abroad and the establishment of foreign subsidiaries were necessary tools to defend and enhance American firms' competitiveness in the world market, and that MNCs overall had a positive impact on the US balance of payments. This was because the long-term capital outflow, which quite often was only the trigger of much larger total investment, was more than offset by its return, which improved the current account balance. Those criticizing foreign investments stressed that even if for an American company the net return of an investment abroad were higher than the combined return from a comparable investment in the US, the latter would have a more beneficial effect. It stimulated technological change and other so-called externalities, whereas FDIs transferred to the recipient country abroad not only resources but also improved technology and technical skills.[70] The Democratic administration, both under Kennedy and Johnson, cannot be said to have encouraged FDIs, at least those in manufacturing and towards Europe. Kennedy tried to tackle tax dodging by MNCs through accounting manipulation and repatriation of revenue postponement. Subpart F of the Revenue Act of 1962 taxed US shareholders on the income of controlled foreign corporations in the fiscal year in which income accrued to the subsidiary, considering it for fiscal purposes as distributed dividend. Johnson introduced voluntary controls on direct investments abroad in 1965 and made them temporarily mandatory in early 1968. The government policy also reflected changes in the attitude of one of the Democratic Party's major supporters. With the end of US economic supremacy the trade unions changed their free trade orientation to protectionist attitudes and to wariness of investments abroad accused of curbing employment at home.

2

International Trade in the Years of Monetary Turmoil from the Close of the Kennedy Round to the Opening of the Tokyo Round

The relationship between monetary and trade developments in the years preceding the 1971 currency realignment

The US balance of payments deficit, and with it the pressure on the dollar and finally the demise of the $35 gold parity, had their roots mostly in factors outside the trade account. The outflow of capitals took various forms. Government spending overseas had a prominent role. It included spending for the military machine and aid programmes. In the second half of the 1960s interest payments to foreign holders of US government liabilities constituted a further source of the drain on government accounts. Much of capital outflow took the form of direct investment to Europe and elsewhere. Annual outward direct investment increased from $2.9 billion in 1960 to $10.2 billion in 1970.[1]

As noted by Eichengreen, events during the dollar exchange standard ran counter to the international adjustment mechanism described by textbook theories, according to which 'with reserves flowing out, US monetary growth should have slowed and with it domestic spending', whereas 'money and spending should have risen faster in countries gaining reserves'.[2] Political and economic factors prevented the international adjustment mechanism of the gold standard from working. In the first place, the cause of the reserves outflow was not centred on the trade balance, which remained in favour of the United States with the remarkable exceptions of West Germany and Japan. Secondly, deflation in the United States would have had negative reverberations on the economy of its 'satellites' across the Atlantic and the Pacific. It is also common knowledge that most of the US trading partners had made it clear that a devaluation of the greenback would be hailed by a prompt realignment of their own currencies. The United States, therefore, acted as international liquidity provider by creating liquid dollar reserves for others to hold and investing in plant and equipment abroad.[3] During most of the 1960s the system was accepted by almost all the US trading partners who were wary of its tenability rather than its equity. France was the remarkable exception, but though the criticism of Jacques Rueff, economic adviser to Charles de Gaulle was grounded on economic theory, the attack of the French government against the system was political and had its root in the French president's desire to create a European alternative to the American hegemony.

During the 1960s the trade balance was conspicuous by its lack of role either in causing the depletion of US reserves or in offsetting the factors that caused it. Up to 1970 both the trade balance and the current account balance were positive and if the basic balance, i.e. the current account plus long-term capital movements went into the red, the former component was not part of the process. In the first half of the 1960s trade and current accounts even showed a significant improvement relative to the previous decade, when the current account often slipped into the red.[4] In particular the trade balance with the EC member states was in favour of the US, and remained so, although with the exception of West Germany from 1966. The balance with Japan had become negative a year earlier. However, several weak points were already detectable in the American industry's performance relative to the US trading partners from the beginning of the decade and even before (Tables 3 and 4). Prominent among them were iron and steel and consumer goods excluding automotive. The negative trend of textile and clothing did not change course despite arrangements under the GATT aegis.

The trade surplus waned in the second half of the decade, almost petering out in the last two years, as the US economy started to overheat (Table 2). Federal expenditures grew by 16 per cent and 14 per cent in 1966 and 1967 respectively and the fiscal deficit reached 2 per cent of GDP in 1967 (Table 8). Inflation jumped. The consumer price index (CPI) annual growth rate, which averaged 1.6 per cent between 1960 and 1965 reached almost 4 per cent in the following four years (Table 23). Labour cost in manufacturing, which had decreased in the first part of the decade, grew slightly faster than that in Japan, Germany and even France (Figure 4). This did not help close the gap as unit labour cost in West Germany and Japan was respectively 80 per cent and less than 50 per cent of that in the US as a result of still lower labour productivity, offset, however, by much lower wages.[5] The US trade deficit with Japan, which in 1965 amounted to just $334 million became four times as great four years later (Table 5). The surplus with Canada turned into deficit in 1968 and rapidly accelerated. The deficit with West Germany grew to almost $500 million in three years.

In 1968 and in the following year the overall US balance of payments for the first time in a decade was positive due to a marked improvement in the capital accounts. Several factors contributed to this result that briefly stopped the addition to world reserves through the US balance of payments: a substantial increase in foreign purchases of US stocks because of the attraction of the US market in years of turmoil in both Eastern and Western Europe; the inflow of foreign short-term capital attracted by high interest rates induced by tighter monetary policy; and above all the set of controls on outflows of capital by American business, banks and other financial institutions that were introduced in January 1968 to withstand the pressure on the dollar and the heavy gold sales in late 1967 following the devaluation of the pound.[6] The temporary measures adopted in January 1968 included restrictions on travel abroad by US citizens, the tightening of the monetary authorities' programme to restrain lending by banks and other financial institutions to foreign customers, and the reduction of government expenditures overseas, nominally in Western Europe. The main item was the compulsory curtailment of American FDIs, which in 1965 had been subject to a voluntary restraint programme. New direct investments to countries in Continental Western Europe were stopped in 1968, while new net investment in other developed countries were limited to 65 per cent of the 1965–6 average. Solomon noted that the European officials 'accepted the discriminatory capital controls in good grace'.[7] The episode bears witness to the fact that the Democratic administration, either to strengthen capital investment in the US or for balance of payments reasons, did not offer unreserved support to American business's decision to invest abroad, while the European countries, the EC member states in particular, in spite of some intellectual exercises regarding the need to protect national industrial policies from the interference of foreign capital, were not unhappy to be the goal of American investments. If the decision of the US executive did not cause an outcry it was just because the inflow was to be temporarily cut.

The relationship between trade and current accounts and the capital account and changes in foreign exchange reserves followed the opposite direction in those countries like West Germany and Japan which based a large part of their post-war booms on the penetration of foreign markets, prominent, but not exclusive among which was the US market. In these countries the trade account was the hub of the positive balance of payments, which was joined in a later stage by the inflow of short-term capital, either speculative, that is, betting on revaluation, or attracted by interest rate differentials.[8]

The export surge was among the main engines of the economic miracle of the Federal Republic. By the mid-1950s merchandise trade accounted for about 20 per cent of Gross National Product (GNP) and continued to rise. The West German share of international trade in goods rose from less than 4 per cent in 1950 to 12 per cent twenty years later. A fixed parity of 4.20 Deutschmarks to the US dollar, only slightly revalued to 4 Deutschmarks in 1961, stimulated German exports in the 1960s, supported by a significant increase in world trade, lower transport costs, high demand for capital goods in which West Germany specialized, a very elastic labour supply and a relatively low average rate of inflation.[9] At the same time the exchange rate constrained foreign competition in the domestic market. The ability to expand of German industries enjoying constantly growing demand, such as mechanical engineering, motor vehicles, electrical and chemical engineering, enabled them to successfully compete with the United States in the European and world markets and to conquer a growing share of the American market.

The positive performance of the trade balance, despite the weakness of the service sector, entailed a balance of payments surplus and with it upward pressure on the Deutschmark from the mid-1950s onwards; the level of reserves nearly doubled between 1960 and 1970.[10] The continued inflow of capital was bound to cause inflationary pressures, but this was an unacceptable prospect for a country that had entrusted its central bank with the task of preserving monetary stability and to this end had legally sanctioned its independence from the executive. The alternative would have been to allow the Deutschmark to revalue but such a choice would have hindered exports, which by themselves accounted for a large part of GDP, without considering their multiplier effect on the whole economy. To square the circle, the Bundesbank resorted to restrictive monetary measures to sterilize the inflow of foreign funds, thus keeping bank liquidity in line with a moderate rate of inflation. This monetary policy was not without difficulties. Indeed, the attempt to reduce money supply increased interest rates, which in turn induced further inflows of foreign funds. Restrictive monetary measures could only be effective as long as the higher interest rates they generated remained below those of other major countries, which was not always the case. Things were made more difficult by the attraction of portfolio investments for the German market, viewed as a hedge against inflation, and because of the likelihood of a revaluation in the near future; to prevent this happening a series of administrative control measures had to be adopted.[11] The foregoing meant that German foreign reserves went on rising along with exports. In 1969 the Deutschmark was revalued by 9.3 per cent, but this did not reverse the trend.

Things became difficult for the Nixon administration in 1970 as the restrictive measures adopted during the last years of the Johnson administration to put the brakes on the overheating economy, and not repealed by the new president in 1969, began to curb demand. This caused a mild recession (Table 1) marked by a contraction of industrial production and an increase in unemployment, which, however, were not accompanied by the abatement of inflation (Tables 22 and 23). In the same year there was a reversal in fiscal and monetary policy. The 10 per cent tax surcharge introduced in March 1968 expired in the first half of 1970, while expenditure rose. The fiscal balance which had been positive in 1969 turned into a fiscal deficit. Monetary policy began to shift away from restraint in February 1970. Short-term interest rates declined gradually in the first half of 1970 and more rapidly in the second half when they were joined by long-term rates. The surplus on current transactions increased somewhat, but this was a temporary phenomenon associated with the recession. The overall balance of payments turned into deficit, the main element in the reversal from 1969 being the switch from borrowing by US banks to repayment.

Matters came to a head in 1971 when the recovery of the US economy was accompanied by the going into the red of the current account balance and, for the first time since the Second World War, of the merchandise trade balance. This signified that, all other things being equal, overall US industry was no longer competitive relative to its trading partners in the international market and that the trade balance not only was far from offsetting capital outflows but was contributing to the balance of payments predicament. The room for manoeuvre left to the government was not large as severe monetary discipline to reverse the growing outflow of capital could jeopardize recovery in the months immediately preceding the presidential election year. The Secretary of the Treasury, John Connally, made it clear that the United States was no longer prepared to bear disproportionate economic costs and that the other members of the Western bloc had to share the burden by more effectively opening their markets to US products.[12]

The US New Economic Policy, the Smithsonian Agreement and the advent of the floating rate regime

The benign neglect policy followed by the Nixon administration made the expectation of a future realignment of the dollar a self-fulfilling prophecy for both the monetary authorities of the main trading partners of the US, which ended the defence of the American currency, and the traders in the foreign exchange market, who had been launching attacks against the greenback since the beginning of 1971.[13] In turn the flight from the dollar put renewed pressure on the currencies of countries with a positive balance.

The end of the Bretton Woods monetary system, established by international agreements in July 1944, was the result of a set of unilateral measures implemented by the US executive seventeen years later. In his 'Address to the Nation Outlining a New Economic Policy' on 15 August 1971, Nixon claimed that his success in creating what, in his opinion, was a more favourable environment for ending the hot war in Vietnam, offered the opportunity to give the American economy a new start, for which it was also necessary that the Western allies took their fair share of the burden in the management of the international economy.[14] The measures announced by the president can be divided into two groups. On the domestic side, Nixon announced a series of initiatives to stimulate the economy, keeping employment at a high level and fighting inflation. Among the fiscal measures were a tax credit on new equipment to increase productivity and generate new jobs, the repeal of excise tax on automobiles and the acceleration of income tax exemptions whose pressure on the budget were to be offset by a $4.7 billion cut in government spending through a postponement of pay rises and a 6 per cent cut in government personnel. To balance the budget, but not without effects on the economy of many developing countries, the president also ordered a 10 per cent cut in foreign economic aid. The only measure directed at contrasting the creeping inflation – the implicit price deflator grew by 6.1 per cent in 1969, 5.4 per cent in 1970 and 5 per cent in 1971 – was a freeze on all prices and wages for a period of 90 days accompanied by a call for a voluntary freeze on all dividends payable by US corporations.

The second array of measures directly affected international trade and currency relations. Nixon announced a temporary suspension of convertibility of the dollar into gold and other assets in order to protect the reserves of the United States from further draining and to let all other countries take note of US desire to achieve significant improvements in its position and of the need for a reform of the international monetary system.[15] The temporary suspension was presented as the result of speculative attacks on the dollar. Indeed, net short-term capital movements had jumped to over $10 billion in 1971 and were the main negative item in the balance of payments. However, the president did not mention any specific monetary measure to attract foreign capitals or to curb the drain from the US. On the other hand disguised de facto inconvertibility of the dollar had marked the monetary history of the previous decade. Suspension of convertibility, which was in force for a temporary but indefinite period, was aimed at forcing the US main partners in the international monetary system to give up the defence of their existing pegs, as the dollars they acquired were made inconvertible into gold and thus less desirable to hold. Concurrently, the US government imposed an additional tax of 10 per cent on goods imported into the United States to be in force, like the inconvertibility, for a temporary but indefinite period. The surtax covered about half of US imports, applying only to products on which duties had been reduced under reciprocal trade agreements with the exception of items subject to mandatory quota restrictions. The import surcharge was evidence of a link between monetary and trade problems as it was clearly directed at improving the trade balance by making foreign goods less competitive. In Nixon's words, it was 'an action to make certain that American products will not be at a disadvantage because of unfair exchange rates'. The president added that 'when the unfair treatment is ended, the import tax will end as well'.[16] The administration's objective was to achieve a $13 billion improvement in the basic balance (comprising current transactions and long-term capital movements) substantially through a surplus in the trade balance that could more than offset the negative tendency in capital movements.

The measure by itself was neither extraordinary nor unprecedented. For instance, a temporary surcharge on imports was introduced by the British Labour government when the pound came under pressure in late 1964. What was different was the weight of the two countries in the post-Second World War international economy and the way the measure was justified. The UK government claimed that the surcharge had a defensive goal, aimed at avoiding devaluation. The US made it clear that the repeal of the surcharge was conditional on a parity realignment whose burden had to be borne prevalently by its trading partners.

The United States hoped that the realignment could be achieved through a revaluation of the US trading partners' currency. A devaluation of the US dollar could be carried out unilaterally but was difficult to justify politically. The West European countries indicated, however, that the United States should raise the price of gold as part of a prospective multilaterally agreed exchange rate adjustment and this approach was supported by the International Monetary Fund (IMF).[17]

After the shock announcement of a new policy for the United States and, therefore, for all the industrialized nations in August 1971, faced with the prospect of a 10 per cent surtax on about 87 per cent of EC exports to one of its primary trading partners, the European Commission argued that the measure would threaten a stable upwards trend in trade between the two areas, whose balance had increasingly been in favour of the United States. It also contended that the surcharge, which threatened to wipe out most of the concessions negotiated in the Dillon and Kennedy Rounds, was not in conformity with GATT rules and that it was inappropriate, given the nature of the United States' balance of payments problems and the undue burden of adjustment placed on the import account with serious effect on the trade of other GATT parties.[18] A GATT working party was set up, of which both the United States and the EC member states were parties along with other countries. The working party, obviously with the contrary view of the United States, urged the US to repeal the 10 per cent surcharge as soon as possible. However, the IMF representative testified that, although a corrective adjustment in the pattern of exchange rates would be preferable, given the low level of US international assets and the high level of its reserve liabilities, in the absence of other appropriate actions the import surcharge could be regarded as being within the bounds of what was necessary to prevent a serious deterioration in the United States balance of payments position. Moreover, the US did not fail to point out that, given the findings of the IMF, it was 'entitled under GATT Art. XII to apply quantitative restrictions to safeguard its external financial position but had chosen instead to apply import surcharges, which were less damaging to world trade.'[19]

The stand-off between the United States and its West European partners was ended by a meeting between Nixon and his French counterpart, Georges Pompidou, in the Azores. Pompidou rejected the idea of a floating system, an alternative already keenly considered by the US, but declared he was prepared to help establish new parities provided they reflected relative economic strength.[20] The French president also insisted that the new parities should be defended.[21] The meeting was followed by negotiations within the Group of Ten that led to the Smithsonian Agreement of 18 December 1971. In return for the repeal of the 10 per cent surcharge, revaluation of currencies ranging from 7.5 per cent to 17 per cent was agreed.[22] The US price of gold was raised from $35 to $38 per ounce, but the dollar remained inconvertible.

The Smithsonian Agreement not only established a new set of parities but also widened the trading bands surrounding the new central rates from 2.25 per cent to 4.5 per cent. This meant that a European country's currency could fluctuate from ceiling to floor by 4.5 per cent against the dollar, but that the currencies of two European countries would fluctuate by 9 per cent against each other if one rose from floor to ceiling while the other fell from ceiling to floor. [23] This ran counter to the scheme of the Werner Report of October 1970 according to which the EC central banks had to restrict the margin of fluctuation between Community currencies and subsequently from 1974 would progressively exclude autonomous parity changes. In April 1972 the EC members inaugurated a regime, known as the 'snake in the tunnel', by which their currencies would jointly fluctuate against the dollar by 4.5 per cent (the tunnel) while the fluctuation between member countries' currencies was to be kept within the narrower limit of 2.5 per cent (the snake). The three prospective members of the European Community, Denmark, Ireland and the UK, joined the arrangement, along with Sweden and Norway, but the UK retired in June, followed by Ireland. Italy left the snake in February 1973.

In March 1972 the US Congress passed the law authorizing the Secretary of the Treasury to implement the dollar devaluation agreed at the Smithsonian meeting. However, soon after tensions on the greenback started again and on 29 July the Federal Reserve Bank of New York sold about $32 million in foreign currencies to support the Smithsonian rate and thus withstand a first assault on the dollar. As noted by Tew, the absence of a firm commitment to defend the Smithsonian Agreement and the knowledge that many in the US administration and banking were ready for a transition to floating, while others believed that larger currency changes were needed to restore equilibrium, led the market to expect another devaluation of the American currency.[24] Actually, in 1972 an improvement in the balance of payments was registered but it was not brought about by a return of the trade balance to the black. On the contrary, in January 1973 the Department of Commerce announced that in the previous year the merchandise trade deficit had soared to $6.4 billion from $2.3 billion in 1971, that is, an increase of more than 175 per cent. The European Economic Community could now boast a surplus of 996 million ECU in its trade with the United States (Tables 13 and 14). The worsening of the US merchandise trade in spite of the devaluation could be at least partially explained by the J curve effect which determined a soaring import bill in US dollars. This was because the US demand for foreign products did not adjust speedily enough to their new price, while US exports failed to rapidly attract foreign demand in spite of their lower price in terms of other currencies. The consequent lack of confidence in the permanence of the Smithsonian central values triggered a run on the dollar. In the first ten days of February 1973 the West German Bundesbank bought $6.1 billion and the Japanese central bank $1.2 billion. On 10 February the Japanese authorities closed the exchange market and suspended their support for the dollar. After a series of secret rounds of consultations of the Undersecretary for Monetary Affairs of the US Treasury, Paul Volcker, in Bonn, Paris and Tokyo, the US changed the dollar's par value from $38 an ounce to $42.20 an ounce, while the gold value of other main currencies was left unchanged. This meant a devaluation of 10 per cent of the dollar relative to the currency of its main trading partners. Seven months later the US Congress ratified the rise of the official price of gold. Yet, in February and March 1973 a further run on the dollar occurred, which resulted in the abandonment, wrongly thought to be temporary, of pegging on the dollar. After two meetings in Paris, France, Germany, the Benelux countries and Denmark agreed to proceed with a joint float in which they were joined by their snake partners, Sweden and Norway, while the other EC members continued to float individually as did Canada, Japan and Switzerland. None of these currencies was pegged to the dollar.

The events from August 1971 to the middle of 1973 showed a clash of perspectives and approaches in which the US viewpoint prevailed. For the United States the first cause of the US deficit lay in the desire for surpluses in the rest of the world rather than in the budget deficit and the relaxation of monetary policy in the early 1970s.[25] The United States, therefore, did not believe that severe domestic fiscal and monetary measures were urgently necessary to restore competitiveness to the American economy so as to rebalance its trade and financial relations with its main trading partners. Instead, the burden of readjustment had to be borne by the surplus countries. For instance, at the 1972 annual meeting of the IMF the Secretary of the Treasury, George Shultz, proposed a reserve indicator system under which countries would be obliged to adjust when their reserves passed certain specified points. The alternative approach, regarded with growing sympathy in Washington, was to accept floating rates through which the value of a currency was to be dictated, at least partially, by the market. Both approaches were looking for an automatic mechanism which could remove the currency undervaluation that allowed some countries to constantly achieve a trade surplus which, in turn, entailed hoarding of international reserves.

The European countries, whether in surplus or deficit, resented the monetary dependence implied by the dollar standard, while viewing the growing volatility of the international monetary market as a threat to their integration goals. The 'snake in the tunnel' was a tentative response to that perceived threat. However, their position was far from monolithic. The main concern for Germany was to prevent the inflationary bias inherent in the current system. Thus the Federal Republic's main aim was to establish effective control over the volume of global liquidity, which, in turn, also meant the creation of a system of asset settlement that could neutralize the pressure generated by future US deficits. France was a strong advocate of fixed parity, which, however, did not necessarily coincide with a dollar-centric system. It is likely that in France's eyes adherence to fixed exchange rates would compel the United States to share the burden of economic adjustment. Besides, the volatility of the main reserve currency was bound to affect the stability of the European currencies. On the other hand, it cannot be said that the French were unsympathetic to the aim of ensuring that countries in surplus played a proper part in the adjustment process, as shown by the disputes on the adjustment process with West Germany and by the fact that the French tabled a proposal for a reserve ceiling beyond which reserves would have to be deposited in a special account with negative interest rate in the IMF.[26] Nor was French allegiance to the fixed exchange principle unconditional as borne out by the fact that the franc was allowed to float out of the snake when market pressure developed in January 1974. By June 1972 Britain was converted to the idea that floating was the best available option. Although the June 1972 float was described as temporary, the government showed no hurry to re-peg and declined to participate in the joint float against the dollar operated by other EC partners.[27] Initially the pound was allowed to find its own level but in May 1973 the Bank of England started to intervene in the market, at first to moderate upward pressure on the British currency and later to support it. Analogous interventions were carried out by other central banks and by the end of the year a managed floating regime was the rule, one way or another, in the industrialized countries. In 1976, at the annual meeting of the member countries held in Jamaica, the IMF Articles of Agreement were amended to give official recognition to the system of floating rates.

Growth in GDP and trade and inflation build-up

Despite the currency turmoil, both 1972 and 1973 were marked by a very strong GDP growth rate in the Organisation for Economic Cooperation and Development (OECD) countries and by a sustained increase in world trade, accompanied, however, by accelerating inflation. After the slump of 1970, the US economy started its recovery in the second half of 1971 and strengthened in the following two years, reaching its peak in the first half of 1973. While in France 1973 marked the fifth year of increase in general demand, in West Germany, Japan and the UK the acceleration in growth rate started only in the second half of 1972. In the United States and France investments in manufacturing plants and equipment represented the main driving force in the expansionary phase, while the growth of the West German economy was provided by the external component. The continuous increase in West German exports, despite the appreciation of the Deutschmark, could be explained by the fact that relative price rises in the period were far smaller than the cumulative revaluation of the Deutschmark and by the characteristics of German exports heavily weighted in favour of machinery often sold in fairly monopolistic markets.[28] In the other OECD countries demand was mostly boosted by domestic consumption.

The recovery coincided with and contributed to an upsurge in international trade that grew by approximately 19 per cent in 1972 and 38 per cent in the following year, compared with a 9.5 per cent average in the 1960s. This growth can be attributed to a large increase both of trade volume and of international prices, estimated at around 11 per cent and 25 per cent respectively in 1973. Various factors contributed to this expansion: the high rate of economic growth, coupled with the coincidence of the boom phase of the cycle in most industrial countries, at least since the second half of

1972; the distribution of income in favour of a number of developing countries; greater participation of socialist countries in world trade. The price rise was preceded and accompanied by monetary expansion, as the combined growth of the nominal money supply (M1) in eleven major industrial countries almost doubled between 1970 and 1972. On the other hand, the acceleration of inflation increased the demand for international liquidity, while the US decision to sever the link between gold and the dollar eliminated the principal factor limiting the supply of liquidity.

The parity changes that had taken place since December 1971 fully manifested their influence on the pattern of world trade in 1973. The growth rate of United States exports, in real terms, was roughly twice as large as that of imports. With the exception of Germany, the trade balance with the EC member states and the whole of Europe, which was negative in 1972, showed a substantial credit for the US. A particularly dynamic sector was agriculture.

The early 1970s also witnessed a shift in the terms of trade between the industrialized countries and developing countries that exported raw materials. The international prices of raw materials started to rise in 1968 but they gathered considerable speed in the second half of 1972. The hike was due not only to the faster growth of economic activity in the main industrialized countries, but also to structural factors such as the increasingly oligopolistic nature of the primary products market occasioned both by the growing number of multinational corporations and by agreements among producer countries. However, the attempt of the countries exporting raw materials was also a defensive move, as is borne out by the price acceleration in 1972. Primary products, including oil, were generally priced in US dollars, a currency whose value was falling. The developing countries' reserves were in US dollars or British pounds. Their imports were affected by an accelerating inflationary process and were quite often from countries whose currencies were appreciating against the greenback. The hike in one essential import, food, was particularly strong as the United States had difficulties in coping with soaring demands for its farm products.

The year 1973 was the *annus mirabilis* of American agriculture, ushering in nine years of farm products export boom. In 1972 exports had already grown by over 20 per cent rising to $9.4 billion and the Secretary of Agriculture, Earl L. Butz, confidently predicted that they would reach $11 billion by 1973.[29] His forecast was dwarfed by the accounts: in 1973 exports grew by 88 per cent, reaching $17.7 billion (Figure 15). About 60 per cent of the increase was caused by increased volume, the remainder coming from higher prices. The $9.4 billion positive farm trade balance showed an improvement of over 25 per cent. In the following years it remained the strong point of the US trade balance, while the fortunes of manufactured goods declined. Net farm income, already on the rise in 1972, jumped by 76 per cent in current dollars and by 66 per cent in real terms to $34.4 billion and $69.4 billion respectively. However, this success was short-lived as growing production expenses started to erode the earnings from the following year onwards.

With the exception of the Second World War, US agriculture had been marked by excess capacity even before the slump of the 1930s, to deal with which government restrictions on farm outputs were adopted. By 1973, however, the higher level of exports had eliminated almost all excess capacity and the government accelerated the implementation of policies encouraging all-out production. The reasons for this change were several. Backstage there was a slight gap, which had however a cumulative effect, between production and consumption that was traced back to the 1950s. World food production outside the US grew by 2.95 per cent per annum between 1950 and 1972, whereas in the same period consumption grew by 3 per cent per annum.[30] The gap was particularly wide in certain key food products like wheat and coarse grains where the US was the dominant producer. According to the International Wheat Council, in the market year 1972–3 wheat production fell to 337 million tons, contracting by over 7 million tons relative to the previous year.[31]

In the early 1970s demand for food produce in the international market also increased in response to contingent factors like shortages in the Central Plan economies, in particular the USSR and China which were affected by bad weather. In the summer of 1972, following a poor harvest, the Soviet Union entered the American market and purchased some $750 million worth of wheat and feed grains over a three-year period. The July 1972 deal bolstered the policy of détente which the two blocs were pursuing at that time. In the years preceding the Afghan crisis, exports to Eastern Europe and the USSR increased by 41.9 per cent annually. Also contributing to the pressure on the market was the growing need for food products in some fast-growing economies in East and South East Asia and the hike in world population which grew by 75 million in 1972 alone. The depreciation of the dollar, whose multilateral trade-weighted value fell by 21 per cent between 1970 and March 1973, also contributed to encourage demand for American produce, first preceding and then partially offsetting the price hike.

In this favourable context the administration pursued a policy aimed at making US agriculture more respondent to market signals.[32] The Agriculture and Consumer Protection Act of 1973 allowed farmers to plant any crop they chose on the acres outside the portion of the base acreage they had to keep fallow if they agreed to participate in farm support programmes. Loan rates for non-recourse loans administered by the Commodity Credit Corporation (CCC) were fixed well below the foreseeable market price, having, therefore, only a safety net function. This made 1974 the first year in which a farmer was not assured of direct payment regardless of the market price level. On the other hand, the 1973 Act added an income support regime to the price support mechanism for crops and cotton, based on target prices related to changes in production costs adjusted for yields. According to the new regime, a deficiency payment would be made if the average market price during the first five months of the marketing year were below the target price. The new regime was not as market-neutral and budget cost-effective as one might have expected. Indeed, it was bound to increase budget costs, at least in times of low average market prices, since, in contrast to a pure loan rate regime, the burden on the taxpayer was not shared by domestic consumers forced to buy agricultural produce at higher prices. Besides, it did not reduce the incentive to overproduce, as target prices could result in total returns for farmers above those provided by the equilibrium market price and, because of the expansion of local production, would interfere with international trade.[33] As noted by the Deputy Director of the Cost Stabilization Program, deficiency payments applied to portions of the crop required for domestic and export use would result in a more direct subsidy to exports. It was, therefore, to be expected that: 'Such a program would invite criticism from those countries whose producers would be affected by this competition. This could seriously impair our posture in upcoming GATT negotiations'.[34]

On the other hand, the export expansion and the consequent disappearance of excess capacity in agriculture brought about strains for the domestic food market. In 1973 the food component of the CPI rose by over 19 per cent accordingly reducing the purchasing power of American consumers. The large exports of feed grains and oilseeds raised the cost of livestock production. Beef producers, whose profits were squeezed first by the ceiling price on red meat and then by the general freeze on food prices, were no longer able to pay world prices for the available supplies of soybean products and started to slaughter breeding animals.[35] On 27 June the government imposed export embargos on soybeans, cottonseed and their derivatives. A month later the embargos were replaced by export licences, which were also applied to other farm commodities, livestock feed, edible oils, peanuts and animal fats. By October the restrictions were lifted but the incident provided ammunition to the advocates of a special treatment for agricultural trade, particularly numerous in the European Community and Japan. Indeed, the embargos were evidence of the danger of unconditionally relying on free imports from countries allegedly endowed with a comparative advantage and of the wisdom of actively pursuing a policy of self-sufficiency.[36]

The first EC enlargement and its impact on internal and international trade relations

The accession of the UK, Ireland and Denmark in 1973 enhanced the position of the EC as the central economic grouping in Western Europe and as the main trading partner of the US. As regards the United Kingdom in particular, although at the end of the day the Heath government's decision to join the Common Market was made on political grounds, economic factors and political economy considerations also had a salient role.

In spite of the cuts agreed in the Kennedy Round, industries outside the EC tariff wall had to compete with opponents able to offer their products at zero duties in the growing market of the Community. This was the case of the British automotive industry which found itself more and more excluded from the market of the six EC members, once a secure outlet, and later was not able to recover lost ground.[37] For Britain the effects of exclusion from the expanding European economic market were made more acute by the changing economic trend of British trade. In 1955, 39.8 per cent of the United Kingdom's imports came from Commonwealth members and 40.6 per cent of its exports were directed to those countries. Imports from and exports to the six countries that would form the EC accounted respectively for 12.6 per cent and 14.1 per cent; those from and to the EFTA countries for 11.5 per cent and 11.8 per cent. Imports from and exports to the United States amounted to 10.9 per cent and 6.6 per cent respectively. By 1972 the Commonwealth's share of imports and exports had more than halved. The share of imports from the EC doubled, while the share of exports to the Six increased by 62 per cent. EFTA's share substantially increased while that of the United States remained almost unvaried.[38] Thus, the European Community had become Britain's largest market, albeit in a period during which Britain's share of exports to major industrial countries had fallen from almost 21 per cent in 1955 to less than 12 per cent. Full integration into the Common Market was, therefore, seen as an occasion that, as had happened for the six member states, would force numerous sectors of British industry to compete and raise efficiency and reduce costs. This would also provide new opportunities for industries like computers, chemicals, automobiles and textile machinery which were believed to enjoy a competitive edge. Besides, there was the perceived risk that British industry could find itself overtaken, along with firms in the EC member states, by American transnational corporations. A way to avoid this predicament was to take an active role in the interpenetration of capital within an enlarged European Economic Community, which, however, was conditional on acceding to it.[39]

Observers, however, agreed on pointing out that the possible positive dynamic advantages were contingent on a series of factors whose occurrence was not automatic. They comprised the replacement of the existing stock of capital which was relatively old as compared to other countries, as well as changes in working conditions and methods of production. They also included changes in the UK's economic policy and a solution to the long-running balance of payments problems marked by the inability of growing without triggering an excess of imports over exports.[40] The potential dynamic advantages had to be weighed against likely static effects of the accession. For instance, joining the CAP was bound to increase imports from EC member states, and food prices as well, although it might also boost British production and thus export capacity. The adoption of the CAP regime was linked to the looming issue of the contribution to the EC budget and, above all, of its repartition, as the UK was looking for a curb on agricultural expenditures and an enhancement of the European Regional Development Fund (ERDF). On these issues the Heath government was not able to negotiate a settlement favourable to Britain.[41]

The attitudes of Ireland and Denmark in negotiating the accession were prevalently determined by economic interest factors and their options were less open to controversy than in Britain's case. For Ireland, accession to the EC meant securing an outlet for its booming farm products and a share in the CAP bestowments. Germany and the UK were the main export markets for Denmark and it had to follow them.

After de Gaulle's 'Non' in 1963, on 10 May 1967 the Labour government formulated an official application for accession to the Community, soon followed by the applications of Denmark, Ireland and Norway. In September the EC Commission addressed a preliminary opinion to the Council which stressed that the accession of the four applicants, whose political and economic structures were very close to those of the EC member states, would strengthen the Community. It underlined, however, that applicants had to accept the basic principles of the common policies implemented by the Community, its customs tariffs in their entirety and EC contractual obligations towards third countries. Once again the French general announced that he did not see the UK as being ready to join the EC. The application was renewed at a summit meeting in The Hague in 1969, but progress towards an agreement proved difficult and long. It was only on 30 June 1970 that negotiations were officially opened and were completed in nineteen months. In January 1973 Denmark, Ireland and the UK formally joined the European Community, while Norway opted to stay out. The Accession treaties provided that tariffs on trade with the EC were to be abolished in five equal stages beginning on 1 April 1973 and ending in July 1977, and that the acceding countries' tariffs on imports from the rest of the world were to be brought in line with the common external tariff over the same period. The Common Agricultural Policy (CAP) system, based on domestic intervention prices and minimum import prices and levies for major products, would be extended to the three new members. The new members would accede to the association and preferential trading agreements between the Community and the Mediterranean countries. As regards Britain in particular, a guaranteed but diminishing market at guaranteed prices was ensured for New Zealand butter and cheese during the transition period, while the Commonwealth sugar agreement was to remain in force until 1974, to be subsequently replaced by special arrangements within the framework of association or trading agreements with the enlarged Community. Independent Commonwealth countries in Africa and the Caribbean might choose between association under a renewed Yaoundé Convention or a more limited form of association like that already enjoyed by Kenya, Uganda and Tanzania under the Arusha Convention, or a straightforward trade agreement.

The main British difference with the Community of the Six lay in agricultural policy since the United Kingdom's support system was based on deficiency payments rather than domestic support prices and non-tariff barriers to foreign farm products which imposed a burden on the budget but did not affect consumer prices. However, food policy in the UK had already undergone substantial changes that made accession to the CAP easier. The Conservatives, back in office in 1970, developing a pattern already partially implemented by the Labour government, contemplated replacing the existing deficiency payment regime, considered too heavy a charge on the budget, with a minimum import price regime, implemented through import levies, despite the foreseeable hike in the cost of living. In short, to participate in the common external tariff and the CAP, the new members had to undergo on average slight reductions in their tariffs on manufactured goods, while accepting higher and more cumbersome trade barriers in the agricultural sector.

In 1974 the British Labour government demanded the renegotiation of accession terms to the EC for Britain. In particular the Wilson government called for major changes in the CAP 'so that it ceases to be a threat to world trade in food products, and so that low-cost producers outside Europe can continue to have access to the British food market' and called for fundamental changes in the Community budget accused of increasingly imposing a burden on the UK that was not commensurate with its lower income per head and growth rate.[42] The new British administration also rejected the idea of fixed parity among the member states and asked for guarantees against prospective interferences from the Community with British state aids to industry and regions. Also the question of access to the EC for the products of Commonwealth states was a subject of the renegotiation demands.

The renegotiation of the terms of accession, concluded in February 1975, did not bring remarkable changes. The question of access of developing Commonwealth members' products was favourably dealt with in the framework of the 1975 Lomé convention, whose negotiation was already in progress when Labour returned to power. To Harold Wilson's great pride, the free entry of New Zealand butter into the Community was extended beyond 1977. In contrast to Labour's worries, curbing and regulation of domestic subsidies, as shown in the following chapter, did not become a major concern in the EC during the 1970s. On the other hand, no CAP reform was carried out and the non-substantial amendments of the rules on British contribution to the EC budget did not alter its destiny as net payer. The budget and CAP issues were exhumed, with a vengeance, by the 'Iron Lady' in the following decade.

Despite the defection of its main member, the EFTA countries remained the main trading partner of the EC. During the last phase of the accession talks for the UK, Ireland, Denmark and Norway, the EC started negotiations for a special trade arrangement with the EFTA countries. The idea of a customs union between the two trade areas was ruled out because decisions on the common external tariffs would have to be shared with countries that were not members of the EC. The solution that was thus worked out took the form of a series of bilateral trade agreements with each EFTA country for the establishment of free trade areas for industrial products. The agreements with Austria, Iceland, Portugal, Sweden and Switzerland took effect from 1 January 1973. The free trade agreement with Norway, which had opted not to join the EC, took effect from 1 July 1973, and that with Finland from 1 January 1974.

The US executive's stance towards EC enlargement reflected the changes in attitude in both administration and Congress that marked the years following the close of the Kennedy Round as regards the EC place in the US policy scheme and the transatlantic partner's growing political and economic strength. The US objective was no longer exclusively the strengthening of the Western European economies even though this could entail some costs for the American economy. Nixon, in his reports to Congress and in correspondence with his top representatives, was keen to emphasize that 'we wish our friends in Europe well in their efforts toward economic and political unity and will watch their steps toward this end with sympathetic interest – remaining alert, however, to the need for respect for our commercial interests'.[43] Indeed, according to the US president, if the United States had always supported and still supported the strengthening and enlargement of the European Community, European unity would 'also pose problems for American policy, which it would be idle to ignore', and as regards the trade area major hindrances to a satisfactory balance of reciprocal interests might be found in agriculture.

In the negotiations, which formally opened in January 1973, the EC initially argued that the tariff reductions implemented by the three acceding countries outweighed the tariff increases and, therefore, little or no compensation was due. The United States, along with other exporters, maintained that since it had bargained and paid for the lower tariff rates previously applied by Denmark, Ireland and the UK, it was entitled to receive compensation through EC tariff reductions on items of interest to its exporters. In December 1973 the Community made a global offer of tariff reductions on items of interest to many countries, which, however, was found to be insufficient. The April 1974 decision of the EC Council of Ministers to be open to further settlement efforts resulted in an intensification of the dialogue between the Community and the United

States which led the following May to a bilateral settlement. The US obtained concessions not only on some industrial products, but also on a number of agricultural products like tobacco, oranges and grapefruits.[44] No concessions, however, were obtained on the item of main interest for US farmers, cereals, and the two parties agreed to continue discussions with a view to seeking agreed solutions to the problems of international trade in grains through international negotiations.[45]

The road towards the Tokyo Round and the stance of the EC and the US

The 10 per cent surcharge applied by the US on imports was repealed on 20 December 1971 soon after the Smithsonian Agreement. However, in the course of the talks on currency realignment, the American representatives, probably aware that the prospective currency arrangement was not enough to secure the hoped-for reversal of the current account deficit, made it clear that the resolution of the international monetary crisis had to be complemented by trade negotiations. During the Rome G-10 meeting on 30 November 1971, the Secretary of the Treasury, John Connally, pointed out that the areas for discussion had to be (and were): currency realignment, burden sharing (of defence expense) and trade, the latter topic to be addressed by negotiations between the United States and Canada, Japan and the European Community.[46] The demands on the European Community concerned in particular several aspects of the EC agricultural policy and the Community preferential arrangements with third countries. The Special Trade Representative, William Eberle, was sent to Brussels in December for preparatory talks. The Community agreed to start prompt negotiations on specific trade topics with its transatlantic partner, once the parity realignment had been put in place and the 10 per cent surcharge repealed and on the basis of reciprocity and mutual advantage, that is, concessions were not to be unilateral. On the other hand, the parties agreed that, in line with the issue of monetary realignment, where a multilateral approach had been preferred to bilateral deals, by 1973 a full-scale review of the entire trading system was to be set in motion.[47] The bilateral talks ended on 11 February 1972 with limited concessions by the European Community, mostly addressing American grievances on transatlantic farm trade.[48] No engagement was made with regard to the thorny reciprocity issue in the preferential agreements with the Mediterranean and ex-colonial countries. The really noteworthy result of the talks was a joint declaration by which the United States and the Community recognized the need for a comprehensive review of international economic relations with a view to negotiating improvements in the light of the structural changes which had recently occurred. These covered '*inter alia*' all elements of trade, including measures which impeded or distorted agricultural, raw material and industrial trade.[49] The multilateral negotiations which, within the GATT framework, were to begin in 1973 – subject to the required internal authorizations – had to aim at the expansion and ever greater liberalization of world trade and improvement in the standard of living of the people of the world, paying special attention to the needs of the developing countries, goals that could 'be achieved "*inter alia*" through the progressive dismantling of obstacles to trade and improvement to the international framework for the conduct of world trade'.[50]

Thus the transatlantic trading partners acknowledged that their conflicts could be properly and lastingly solved only within the context of multilateral negotiations aimed at curbing obstacles to trade and improving the rules of the world trade game. It seems, however, that the parties to the declaration, and in particular the European Community, saw these two objectives as part of a greater puzzle in which variables other than trade liberalization were to be taken into account. This wider context – with reference to which the term '*inter alia*' could be explained – was also likely to include the reshaping of the world monetary system on more stable bases.

The 'declaration' along with a Japan–US statement[51] having similar content was hailed by the GATT Council at its 7 March meeting.[52] However, the EC–US Joint Declaration had a jarring note. On agriculture the Community stated that 'in appropriate cases' the conclusion of international commodity agreements was also one of the means to achieve expansion of world trade and improvement in standards of living. The United States dryly answered that 'such agreements do not offer a useful approach to the achievement of these aims'. In other words, the viewpoints of the United States and the Community on how to achieve a better environment for farm trade seemed to be irreconcilable and, therefore, on one key point of the talks the two parties had to agree to disagree.

Trade authority request in the US

His standing and room for manoeuvre boosted by a sweeping endorsement by the electorate in the 1972 presidential election, on 10 April 1973, Nixon proposed a Trade Reform Act to Congress and asked for wide negotiating authority in view of the approaching GATT round.[53] The bill had the following goals: negotiating for a more open and equitable world trading system; strengthening the US ability to deal with unfair competitive practices and rapid increases in imports which threatened the disruption of the US market; managing more efficiently the US trade policy and using it effectively to fight inflation and improve the balance of payments; enhancing the contribution of trade to the development of poorer countries.

With particular regard to the issue of negotiating authority, in contrast with the previous requests, the bill did not set a limit in the percentage change of the tariffs subject to negotiation, thus maintaining full freedom to raise a duty to any level the president wished or eliminate it altogether. As regards non-tariff barriers the main problem lay in the fact that the elimination of such barriers quite often required changes in domestic laws, whose uncertain implementation would make foreign governments reluctant to accept concessions subject to congressional delay and opposition. The president asked for a prior mandate to negotiate the repeal of non-tariff barriers, giving Congress the option, in some cases, of a negative veto within ninety days.[54] The authority would be granted for five years on both tariff and non-tariff barriers. On agriculture, Nixon stressed that the executive expected the round to achieve the expansion of agricultural trade, arguing that the concerns of all nations for farmers and consumers could be best met by greater reliance on free-market forces. He also made it clear that he did not believe that agriculture should have a separate place in the negotiations as barriers to agricultural trade were either tariff or non-tariff in nature and could therefore be dealt with under a general framework which would encompass other primary products as well as manufactured goods. Finally, Nixon called for presidential authority to extend Most-Favoured Nation (MFN) treatment to any country when he deemed it in the national interest. MFN status was a condition for the implementation of the US–Soviet trade agreement of October 1972. The agreement was the cornerstone of the détente policy with the Soviet Union which was not a party to the GATT. Moreover, if the agreement did not enter into force the USSR would not have to repay its Second World War lend-lease debt of $722 billion.

However, the request for negotiating authority was made at a moment in which Nixon's personal authority was shaken as his administration was embittered over the so-called Watergate scandal while the country was heading for economic turmoil. On 11 December the House passed the government bill with amendments.[55] It rejected the president's request for unlimited authority to raise or lower tariffs, setting limits to his power according to the tariff rate to be reduced. It adopted the procedure for prompt consideration of non-tariff barrier agreements briefly outlined above, but rejected Nixon's request for advance authority on matters concerning customs valuation practices and rules of origin. However, a main reservation, the so-called Vanik Amendment, was made with regard to the authority to give MFN trade status to the Soviet Union. Although the president was given authority to grant MFN status to countries that were not GATT parties, particularly Communist countries, for the Soviet Union the status was made conditional on the relaxation of its policies discouraging Soviet Jews from emigrating to Israel, actually preventing the coming into force of the US–Soviet trade agreement. In turn, the Senate postponed any decision on the governmental bill until 1974. Thus, because of an issue unrelated to the GATT negotiations, the American executive could not enter the round it had helped to launch with the full authority it had requested and with definite terms of reference.

The European Community's stance

In October 1972 the European Summit requested the Commission to work out an overall approach of the Community to the coming trade round in the GATT, establishing 1 July 1973 as the deadline for its submission to the European Council.

A first Memorandum was sent by the Commission on 4 April.[56] In keeping with the Summit communiqué, the Commission expressed the view that the imminent negotiating round had to have two general goals. The first was the pursuit of trade liberalization on the basis of reciprocity and mutual advantage for all parties. The second was greater participation of the developing countries in international trade and the achievement of better economic equilibrium with the industrialized world. The Commission, however, was careful to stress that the participation of the Community to the negotiations would not jeopardize the advantages already enjoyed by those countries with which the EC had special relations. In other terms, their margin of advantage in trading with EC member states relative to the generality of developing countries was to be preserved.

As regards the main aspects of the negotiation, the Commission did not consider the complete elimination of all customs duties as a realistic approach. There were two main obstacles: the role of customs duties in protecting sectors that in quite a few countries were experiencing difficulties in withstanding foreign competition; the lack of harmonization of national policies concerning taxation, social security and measures to stimulate economic development. On the other hand, every tariff reduction method had to take into account the differences between average customs duty levels in the developed countries as well as their different structure, since some countries applied tariffs of a roughly homogeneous level to all products while others applied very high tariffs to some products and much lower ones to others. What was to be worked out, therefore, was a mechanism that could at the same time reduce the overall level and level off the differences. However, the general scheme should not prevent the parties from seeking, on a reciprocal basis, greater concessions on individual items, which could even imply the abolition of customs duties.

The Commission's approach to non-tariff barrier negotiations was less specific, since negotiators would be confronted by a set of problems wider than those concerning tariff barriers. Firstly, the existence of a great variety of different kinds of barriers, classified by a GATT committee under nearly thirty chapter headings, rendered a solution for all the listed measures problematic and made it preferable to select a restricted number of non-tariff barriers on which the negotiations should be focused. Secondly, reciprocity was harder to assess and this made it necessary to come up with a wide range of solutions to make up a well-balanced package of concessions, while there was the possibility that not all the negotiating parties would be willing to or could take part in the agreement. In this context, before entering negotiations the Community and its member states had to fulfil two tasks. The first was to select those non-tariff barriers whose suppression or regulation was in the Community's best interest. On the other hand, as such measures were in most cases imposed and administered by the member states rather than by the Community itself, it was necessary that the former agreed as soon as possible on a sufficient number of negotiable measures so as to offer adequate reciprocity in return for concessions by the trading partners. Finally, in order to secure the greatest possible participation of the GATT parties to such agreements and to prevent the worsening of the existing imbalance it was to be made clear that the advantages derived from solutions comprising obligations going beyond the existing GATT rules would be reserved to those countries which in practice abided by those solutions. In short, the Commission was suggesting, as was the case for the US Congress, the conditional application of the MFN clause.

On agriculture the Memorandum reiterated the Community's stance that, although the objectives of the negotiations were to be in keeping with the general approach of the round, that is, trade expansion and barrier reduction, they also had to take into account the sector's specific characteristics: the universal existence of support policies and the instability of world markets. In the Commission's view, the condition for expanding trade was stability of world markets and the best way to achieve this objective was a code of good conduct on export practices, aimed at introducing market discipline. Within the domestic sphere governments should intensify structural reforms so that marketing policies and price policies were based to a greater extent on economic considerations. On the other hand, for products such as cereals, dairy products and sugar the Commission suggested the negotiation of international arrangements, which should provide a price mechanism and adjustment of supply including measures of storage. The Community was to pledge to apply the instruments of its Common Agricultural Policy in a way consistent with its multilateral commitments. However, taking into account the criticism of the Economic and Social Committee and some member states, the Commission amended its draft, stressing that 'the principles of the Common Agricultural Policy should not be called into question'. Thus, on agriculture the Memorandum seemed to meet French farm market philosophy and policies. France, which in the 1960s had carried out structural reforms aimed at transforming peasant farming into modern agriculture, in the 1970s was eager to secure its present and prospective share in the world market, while guaranteeing its role as main supplier in the EC market. These objectives made it favour forms of multinational cooperation and orderly trade conduct rather than the elimination of trade barriers and the retreat of government from the domestic market.

Like the United States, the Community was concerned with the upsurge of imports that could cause market injury to the domestic industries of its member states. The Commission suggested that the provisions of GATT Art. XIX should be kept in force, but, given the difficulty of their effective implementation, that they be accompanied by a complementary mechanism, which should especially allow selective application of safeguard measures and suspension of the affected trading partners' compensatory rights.

Specific advantages had to be provided to the developing countries through improvements to the GSP, with the inclusion of a greater number of processed agricultural products and the widening of duty-free quotas, and through a more flexible application of the rules to be established on non-tariff barriers.

The Commission was careful to stress that its memorandum was based on the assumption that parallel machinery would be developed in the monetary sector to guarantee its long-term balance and stability, the absence of which would jeopardize the effectiveness of any wide-ranging agreement in the field of trade.

The launch of a new trade round

During the run-up to the Tokyo Round as well as during the initial stage of the negotiations, neither the US administration nor the EC executive had a definitive mandate on the specific items to negotiate. Actually, the American executive had no trade authority and this was particularly problematic with regard to non-tariff barriers.

As regards the EC, Art. 113 of the Rome Treaty entrusted the Commission with the task of conducting negotiations on trade matters. However, the power of the EC executive was not open-ended. Article 113 of the Treaty of Rome provided that when agreements with third countries were to be negotiated in order to implement the Community's Common Commercial Policy, the Commission should make recommendations to the Council, which should authorize it to open the necessary negotiations. The article also stated that the Commission should conduct the negotiations in consultation with a special committee appointed by the Council to assist it in the negotiating task within the framework of directives issued by the Council, the so-called Article 113 Committee, which was composed of senior civil servants (or their assistants) from the interested ministries of the member states. Thus, although formally an advisory body, the Article 113 Committee, whose members were national representatives, acted as a link between the Commission and the Council and, as its recommendations were often regarded as a preview of Council position, the Commission complied with them.

The Commission modified its Memorandum in May before submitting it to the Council for its final approval, which is indicative of a complex process of redaction that had to balance the not always reconcilable directives of the member states. Actually, the Memorandum outlined the negotiating objectives of the Community, without, however, entering into the details. By approving the document the Council simply countenanced the line of action submitted by the Commission. On the other hand, as noted by the Commission itself, the 'overall approach to trade' was not a mandate to negotiate, nor did it provide specific negotiating directives on the various items of the forthcoming talks.[57] Besides, while the 'overall approach' was quite specific on items such as tariff reduction and harmonization, the safeguard clause and, in particular, agriculture, it postponed the outline of the EC negotiating stance on non-tariff barriers to a subsequent stage.

Yet, the foregoing did not prove to be an insurmountable hindrance during the preparatory stage. In the absence of negotiating authority to the president which would have helped define the United States' scope and approach to the GATT talks on tariff and non-tariff barriers and in the absence of any directive to the Commission on what the non-tariff barriers negotiations should be concerned with, in the run-up to the opening of the Tokyo Round there were only two areas of open disagreement between the US and the EC: trade in agriculture and the link between the prospective multilateral talks and the ongoing upheavals and negotiations in the monetary sector. A third potential area of disagreement concerned the manner and extent of tariff cuts, but it was to be expected that differences on this topic would be left to a later stage of the negotiations.

During the July meeting of the Preparatory Committee, the EC delegation circulated a 'Statement by the European Economic Community on the General approach adopted by the Council of Ministers on the forthcoming multilateral trade negotiations', which addressed, among other things, the question of the relation between trade negotiations and developments within the monetary system.[58] The text of the Statement on this point had previously been debated in the European Council where the Commission had suggested a reference to the need for parallel efforts to set up a monetary system shielding the world economy from the shocks and imbalances which had recently occurred and to the necessity that progress in the monetary field should be borne in mind by the Parties to the Agreement, both at the beginning and during the course of the negotiations. France proposed a harder and more pressing statement which labelled the actual start of trade negotiations as unrealistic until the necessary steps had been taken to allow the exchange market to reflect the parity grid agreed during the last official currency realignment. A compromise was finally reached, adding a paragraph stating that there were prospects for the establishment of a fair and durable monetary system based on fixed but adjustable parities, the general convertibility of currencies, effective international regulation of the world supply of liquidities and a reduction in the role of national currencies as reserve instruments.[59] The United States remarked that an efficient monetary system was conditional on the adoption of trade measures which would facilitate the adjustment process as well as upon concurrent efforts to provide for trade liberalization and an improved framework for trade relations.[60]

In spite of the various differences in attitude there was no clash between the transatlantic parties. On the contrary, one senior member of the Commission delegation in Geneva related that in the last phase of the preparatory talks to the September ministerial meeting in Tokyo, the American delegation showed a strong desire to smooth over the points of dispute with the Community, avoiding any criticism of EC trade policy, and the CAP in particular, as it had done in the previous stages.[61] Thus, with regard to the agricultural trade and monetary system issues the Declaration approved by the Ministers at Tokyo on 14 September 1973 was a compromise in which the Community did not have to make any significant concessions.[62] Regarding agriculture, the Declaration called for an approach to negotiations which 'while in line with the general objectives of the negotiations, should take account of the special characteristics and problems in this sector'. As regards the link with international monetary arrangements, the Ministers recognized that the policy of liberalizing world trade could not be carried out successfully without parallel efforts to set up a monetary system shielding the world economy from the shocks and imbalances which had previously occurred, but also acknowledged that the new phase in the liberalization of trade, which it was their intention to undertake, would facilitate the orderly functioning of the monetary system.

The Tokyo Declaration did not make any reference to the elimination of tariff barriers suggested by Japan and the Scandinavian countries, but in line with the Community's perspective simply referred to negotiations on tariffs based on appropriate formulae of as wide application as possible. On non-tariff barriers the Declaration pledged to reduce or eliminate non-tariff measures or, when this was not possible, their trade-distorting effects. However, the measures in question were not listed. The Ministers also agreed that the negotiations could concern the coordinated reduction or elimination of all barriers to trade in selected sectors. As requested by the European Community, the adequacy of the multilateral safeguard system under GATT Art. XIX was to be examined.

A Trade Negotiations Committee (TNC) was established with the task of elaborating detailed plans for the negotiations, working out appropriate procedures and supervising the progress of the negotiations. The Committee whose membership was open to all governments taking part in the talks and to the European Community had to begin work by 1 November 1973. The deadline for the negotiations was set in 1975, a date that turned out to be overly optimistic. To avoid delays the parties agreed to concentrate their work in this first phase on the analytical and statistical aspects of the negotiations. The Commission decided not to table for the moment any substantive proposal not to allow the American negotiators to change their position on the pretext of new conditions attached to their mandate by the US Congress. On the other hand, the Commission suggested that the EC negotiators should be given specific directives which had to take into account the discussions on the trade bill in the US Congress, nevertheless avoiding the risk that they be left behind by the Americans in establishing their negotiating stance.[63]

Thus the spirit of the Tokyo Conference reflected the favourable but increasingly overheated climate of the world economy in which income and trade were strongly growing and there was a close correlation between the two. This meant that the voices of those calling for fewer barriers to trade were not drowned out by the complaints of import competing industries. Moreover, import liberalization began to be seen as an antidote against inflation by increasing the availability of goods at better prices and by generating major pressure for production efficiency. The performance of American farm trade made the United States consider the idea that the dismantling of CAP was still a priority but a less immediate one. On the other hand, the hostility of many European countries against the floating rate regime was waning as the West European countries, including the hardliners in the EC were, willingly or unwillingly, accepting a floating system as the normal course of currency management. The attitude changed when only a month later the so-called oil crisis ushered in a period in which inflation was no longer the unwelcome companion to growth but went hand in hand with recession.

3

The Oil Shock, the Partial Recovery and their Impact on Trade Policies Across the Atlantic

The onset of the oil crisis and the disparate responses of the industrial countries

The years 1974 and 1975 witnessed an unprecedented slump on both sides of the Atlantic which had its impact on trade relations between the United States and the EC member countries, as well as between the two areas and the rest of the world. Contrary to previous slumps in the nineteenth and twentieth centuries, the reversal of the upwards phase that had marked most of the 1950s and 1960s was accompanied by an inflation upsurge that hit the EC member states and the US. Indeed the years following 1973 are remembered as the years of stagflation. The 1974–5 slump was triggered by an exogenous factor, the so-called oil crisis set off by events that took place in the last quarter of 1973. Triggering, however, is not synonymous with cause, or even main cause, of a process. Besides, although its impact on the economies of both sides of the Atlantic was broadly similar, the crisis took partially different features in the US and the EC member states, as context and constraints were not the same in the United States and in the Western European countries, and thus gave rise to different responses in political and economic terms.[1]

Two lines of thought compete in explaining the causes of the oil crisis. The first perspective emphasizes the distortive impact of the oil import bill, which concurrently pushed up domestic prices and subtracted resources for domestic demand, and the ineffectiveness of the response of the monetary and fiscal authorities.[2] The second one places the stagflation in a wider context in which the oil price hike was not the main causal engine. A Marxist commentator claims that 'the 1974–75 recession was a classical overproduction crisis and the outcome of a typical phase of decline of the rate of profit', which pre-dated the leap in oil prices following the Yom Kippur War.[3] With reference to inflationary pressures, Aldcroft argues that the leap in oil prices cannot be regarded as the initial cause of acceleration of inflation or as the main contributor to its perpetuation in the 1970s and that instead 'a secular upward trend in inflation from the mid-1960s had superimposed on it a cyclically or partly cyclically generated price boom in the early 1970s'.[4] Rostow points out that overall the Organisation for Economic Cooperation and Development (OECD) countries suffered total output declines in 1974 and 1975 twice the level that could be directly attributed to the rise in the oil price, while the inflation rate after 1972 was greater than what could be directly attributed to the rise in food and energy prices. However, the scholar adds that the effect on GDP of the rise in the oil bill was compounded by policies of fiscal and monetary restraint, while the inflation leap caused by the hike in basic commodities was also the outcome of the attempt of the labour unions to protect the real wage of workers from explosive increases in the price of basic commodities.[5] Armstrong, Glyn and Harrison note that the price increase imposed by the Organization of Petroleum Exporting Countries (OPEC) would not have been possible in the absence of the surge in raw material prices that accompanied the short synchronized recovery of the early 1970s and that, on the other hand, 'the basic problems of over accumulation in relation to the labour supply and sharp decline in profitability preceded the oil crisis and would not have evaporated in its absence'.[6] The report of the Italian central bank (Banca d'Italia, BI) for 1974, making an implicit distinction between the causes of the stagflation, pointed out that 'the recent cyclical turn-around is dependent not only on the oil crisis but also on other structural factors which gained importance between the end of the 1960s and the beginning of the 1970s.' According to the BI the latter had taken the form of an increasingly short duration of the upwards phase of the cycle, and from the end of the 1960s onwards, of strong pressure on enterprises' profit margins in most industrial countries, as was confirmed by the drop in the enterprises' self-financing and by growth of indebtedness.[7]

The outlined perspectives focus on the possible impact of a particular import item, oil, on the economy of one or several countries. In keeping with the general subject of this research, this chapter follows a different approach, looking firstly at the effect of the oil bill hike on the trade balance of the US and the EC member countries, and secondly on its impact, as part of the trade balance alteration, on domestic developments in the two areas, without overlooking other causal factors that might have been at play in the slump and inflation process. It must be noted that the duration of the effects of the oil price increase on the US and EC trade balances went beyond the so-called oil crisis.

The events that characterized the oil shock in 1974 and in the following years reflected the relative self-sufficiency in energy sources across the Atlantic and, consequently, the relative dependency on energy suppliers. The EC member states were traditionally heavily dependent on foreign oil supply. Only the UK, Germany and Belgium had a sufficient alternative source of energy in coal, whose exploitation, however, was becoming increasingly expensive relative to oil imports, while the Netherlands had good gas reserves. Although the United Kingdom had the medium-term prospect of becoming an important oil producer itself, at the time of the crisis it was no exception, its problems being exacerbated by a lengthy dispute between the Heath government and the National Union of Miners which had curtailed supply of its alternative energy source, coal. The United States, the main oil producer, but at the same time the dominant oil consumer, after 1970 had passed rapidly from a position of relative oil supply independence to a position of relative oil supply dependence. In spite of new discoveries on the North Slope of Alaska and on the Outer Continental Shelf, oil production slowed down in the 1960s and early 1970s, also hampered by a variety of environmental restrictions and governmental controls, while no significant progress took place in the development of alternative sources of supply. In contrast, demand for fuel kept growing, stimulated by oil and gas prices which remained below the market clearing price.[8] In April 1973, the system of import quotas adopted in 1959 to limit dependence upon foreign sources supply was definitively abandoned in favour of a flexible import fee. Imports of crude oil and refined products in the US rose from 22 per cent of domestic consumption in 1969 to 36 per cent in 1973.[9] Thus the US could no longer be relied on as a source of fuel and related materials.

The EC member states deemed it unwise to throw in their lot with the United States and to follow its leadership in a coalition of importing countries against OPEC, and even less with the Organization of Arab Petroleum Exporting Countries (OAPEC), given the long-lasting political relations with many OAPEC members. They chose instead to assert their independence in deciding their energy policy, relying on a cooperative relationship with the oil producing countries by which long-term security of fuel imports should be balanced, at least in the mid-term, by growth in demand for European products, especially in the area of capital goods. It must be noted that the same policy was promptly adopted by Japan. The EC member states were made more determined in their economic strategy by the fact that the country that had summoned them to take part in a coalition of importers was itself strengthening its trade relations with its traditional suppliers in the Middle East and was far from being keen on pursuing the conservation policy it had advocated.

The year 1974 marked a systemic alteration in the composition, direction and value of the external trade of the EC member states as a whole. It must be remembered that extra-EC trade accounted for about 50 per cent of the EC member countries' merchandise trade and that imports and exports had a greater weight in the West European economies than in the United States. In the years 1971–3 extra-EC fuel products imports were slightly higher than imports of raw materials and food products, and lower than imports of manufactured goods other than machinery and transport equipment (Figure 8). From 1974 onwards the value of imports of fuel products dwarfed those of other commodities and from 1974 to 1976 it was as high as imports of raw materials, food products and chemicals taken together.

Correspondingly, imports from OPEC countries, which in 1973 were slightly below those from EFTA, from 1974 onwards exceeded by a large margin those from other areas and in 1974 even went beyond those of the US and EFTA taken together. In line with the hopes of the member states, EC exports to OPEC strongly increased but the deficit remained high (Figures 5 and 6).

The merchandise trade balance of the EC as a whole, positive in 1971 and 1972, showed a deficit of over 4,000 million ECU in 1973, which swelled to over 15,000 million ECU in 1974 and in 1976, after a brief respite during the 1975 slump. After the 1973 peak the following three years witnessed a decline in intra-EC trade (Tables 15 and 16), which can be explained by the need to reorient EC trade towards oil-exporting countries. The Community trade gap with the United States almost quintupled between 1973 and 1976 (Tables 13 and 14). The share of exports from the EC member countries to the United States over their total exports declined from 7.5 per cent in 1973 to 5.5 per cent in 1976 while the share of imports remained constant at just over 8 per cent. Conversely, the share of US imports from the EC declined from 22 per cent in 1973 to 15 per cent three years later, while the share of exports did not change (Table 5).

Obviously the picture was not uniform. The Federal Republic of Germany, although its exports contracted in 1975, was always able to keep a positive trade balance and the Netherlands improved its own thanks to its energy exports, while the other EC countries saw their trade gap worsen in spite of the growth of their exports. Countries with sources of oil and gas like the UK and the Netherlands suffered much less than the other Community members from the burden of the energy bill or even benefited from its rise.

Taking also into account intra-EC trade, the share of fuel products rose from 12 per cent of the whole of commodity imports in 1973 to 21 per cent in 1974, but gradually decreased to 17 per cent on the eve of the second oil shock (Table 18). This was due to the conservation policy of the EC member states, which, in turn, was helped by the slump and the slackening of the economy after the 1976 recovery. Petroleum consumption in West Germany, France and the UK declined respectively by 3.6 per cent, 6.4 per cent and 14.7 per cent.[10] Thus in the EC, in keeping with economic theory, the price rise was accompanied by lower consumption of the relevant product. However, the success achieved by the EC member states was not the result of a unified policy entrusted to a supra-national entity. Although the Commission reviewed the overall energy position in the Community, the individual members maintained full control of their domestic and foreign policy in pursuit of their national energy interests, nor was there any pooling of energy sources.[11] In particular, the United Kingdom quite soon made it clear that it was not willing to surrender control over North Sea oil. France used state-owned or controlled companies to exploit foreign oil resources and developed a domestic nuclear energy programme.

A partially similar trend can be found in the US trade balance. The merchandise trade balance, which was positive in 1973 because of the effect of the dollar depreciation, went back into the red a year later. The deficit in the industrial supplies and materials class, which had been growing at a yearly average of about $800 million since 1965, reaching $8,187 million in 1973, jumped to $24,300 million in 1974 (Table 3). The soaring value of import of mineral fuels and related materials was the chief culprit, in 1974 being over three times as great as in the previous year (Table 4) and accounting for one-fourth of the US import total, entirely as the result of the steep price increase.[12]

The US merchandise trade deficit turned shortly into a surplus in 1975, mainly because the slump brought about a contraction in imports, but with the recovery the balance became negative again and the deficit increased in the following years, the dominant cause being industrial supplies and fuel in particular. This time it was no longer a question of price hike but of growing imports of crude and refined oil. In November 1973 Nixon declared that by the end of 1975 oil imports would be reduced by one million barrels per day through energy conservation and enhanced domestic energy supply. Things turned out differently. With the aim of preventing windfall gains for domestic oil producers and curbing the inflationary impact of the increased cost of energy, the oil policy measures that were actually adopted ended up by implicitly taxing domestic producers and subsidizing consumers and importers. The result was lower levels of production, more consumption and higher imports, thus increasing the bill paid to the OPEC countries.[13] In stark contrast with the EC, US oil consumption between 1973 and 1978 grew from 17,308 thousand barrels per day to 18,847 thousand barrels per day and total imports grew from 6,256 thousand barrels per day to 8,363 thousand barrels per day.[14] Imports as percentage of demand grew from 36.1 per cent to 44.4 per cent, whereas in 1970 they had accounted for only 23.3 per cent.

In particular, the share of imports from the Middle East grew considerably, but the share of American export to the region showed a corresponding increase mainly due to the demands of Saudi Arabia and Iran, strategic allies of the US, for infrastructural investments and military equipment. Until 1978 the United States often managed to achieve a trade surplus with the Middle East countries, though American trade diplomacy was much less successful with the African exporters (Table 5).

Economic recession and recovery with different speeds and strengths across the Atlantic

The quadrupling of oil price affected the OECD members' economy in a plurality of ways, although their impact was not uniform. No doubt, domestic prices had doubled on average in the course of the 1972–3 recovery, the hike occurring under the pressure of food and raw materials, among them oil (Tables 23 and 24). Besides, as regards oil the dollar depreciation in early 1973 was an incitement for OPEC members to demand higher prices as oil, along with other raw materials, was quoted in US dollars. Yet, it is the statistics for 1974 that reported an explosion of import prices, triggered by the events of the last quarter of 1973, which dwarfed the rise of the preceding year. The swell in fuel prices was accompanied by the decline in the other factors that had stoked inflation in the previous biennium as minerals and metal prices fell by 30 per cent between May 1974 and the end of the year and an equivalent decline in food prices was recorded from November 1974 to June 1975.[15]

A primary distinction should be made between the direct effects of the price rise and consequent changes in the economic environment and economic policies that were brought about by the oil shock. Firstly, the quadrupling of the oil price caused a diversion of expenditure in the oil-importing countries from domestically produced goods to imported petroleum products, whose immediate result, in the absence of an equivalent decline in the price of other classes of goods, was a reduction in the available income. The worsening of the terms of trade compelled oil consumers, manufacturing industries in particular, to pay higher prices for equal or even declining quantities, and in order to foot the bill the industrial countries had to withdraw resources from the domestic economy. In short, the fuel price hike acted as a tax loaded onto importing countries.[16] The analogy, however, has a caveat. The tax was not collected by importing countries' governments that could use the revenue to increase their purchases to stimulate the economy: it was collected by developing countries that had to adjust their expenditure programmes to the bonanza. Thus the increase in the price of oil led to a deficit in the current account of the oil-importing countries, or increased it while creating a matching surplus in the current account of the oil-exporting countries. The latter, however, in the short-run, were precluded from significantly increasing their demand for imported products by the restriction of income gains to narrow segments of their populations, or by the long lead time in developing major projects needing imports from industrialized countries. The OPEC countries' trade balance surplus amounted to $102 billion in 1974, compared with $22 billion the previous year, while the industrial countries' deficit more than tripled. On the other hand, the constraints for the importing countries, and for the industrial countries in particular, were not equal. Their weight depended on the amount of their currency reserves and on the impact of the oil bill on these reserves, as well as on their capacity to attract unspent oil producers' proceeds. Thus countries like the US and the UK which were recipients of surplus oil funds were better off than countries like Italy whose dependency on oil imports was particularly strong and was not a likely destination for idle funds from oil-exporting countries. Only for countries in the second group can the origin of the slump be explained by the Thirlwall model according to which, if a country gets into balance of payments difficulties before reaching its short-term capacity growth, then demand must be curtailed, thus discouraging investment and slowing down technological progress.[17]

Soaring oil prices also had an indirect impact through the price increase for other goods of which oil was an input, and the higher price for oil heightened the demand for substitute sources of energy driving up their costs. This, combined with a lack of compensating increases in productivity and real wage resistance, resulted in lower profits and hence fewer investments, which, in turn, led to a fall in output and productivity growth.[18] Thus, even though the cut in profit margins preceded the oil crisis, the oil shock accelerated their decline.

Finally, the perception of inflation as the starting and main cause of the economic plight of the oil-importing countries prompted their fiscal and monetary authorities to continue the restrictive macroeconomic policies that had been adopted since 1972 to curb the overheating of the economy, although such policies were not designed to tackle the problems of a producer dominated market during the oil shock years.

In the United States, the country in which stagflation was first experienced, the crisis was not brought about by current account constraints. After the recovery of 1973, the US merchandise trade balance went back into the red in 1974, but the losses caused by soaring oil import expenditures were partially offset by fast growing exports boosted by the dollar devaluation. The US slump was caused by its inability to fight inflation without compromising growth and employment. As noted by Matusow, American authorities had analysed the economy in terms of aggregate demand, whereas the primary source destabilizing it in 1974 was supply rather than demand.[19] As the United States had to rely on the usual instruments of 'total' demand management, while the causes of its troubles were several, it was not able to achieve a satisfactory balance between price stability and growth and unemployment reduction.

At the beginning of the recession inflation was perceived as the most acute problem. The US consumer price annual growth rate had already increased from 3.5 to 5.4 per cent between 1972 and 1973 but it ballooned to double figures the following year (Table 23). The wholesale price for manufactured goods hit 19 per cent. In addition to disruption of economic activity, the energy crisis erased all hopes of controlling inflation through wage and price control programmes. In turn, inflation curtailed real purchasing power as real wages fell by 5 per cent during the year. It is arguable that the Nixon administration saw the oil shock as an extension and worsening of the overheating of the economy that had marked the previous two years and, therefore, went on adopting the contractionary monetary and fiscal measures introduced in 1973. Actually, the boom of 1972–3 had already ended. The Economic Report of the president for the year 1973 relates that as early as the second and third quarters of the year there were signs of deceleration in the growth of output and demand.[20] According to Matusow, real GNP, which had grown at an annualized rate of 8.8 per cent during the first quarter of 1973, increased at a rate of only 1.4 per cent during the last three quarters. This would entail the end of the upward pressure on commodity prices, both domestic and imported, as actually happened with the remarkable exception of oil.[21] Initially, the Ford administration had a similar perspective and adopted analogous policies. Presenting his programme to check inflation and encourage growth, President Ford exhorted the nation to 'whip inflation now' (WIN) as a scourge threatening to destroy the American way of life.[22] The rate of growth of money sharply declined in the second half of 1974 and the M1 growth rate actually became negative in the first quarter of 1975, just when the US economy was reaching the trough of the cycle.

The slump first hit housing and then spread to other sectors, prominent among which were automobiles and clothing. In 1974 GNP declined by 0.6 per cent and GDP by 0.8 per cent (Table 1). Industrial production fell by over 12 per cent in the last quarter of the year and unemployment rose to 7.2 per cent in December, reaching 8.5 per cent by March 1975. In 1975 GDP and GNP declined respectively by 0.9 per cent and 1.2 per cent. During the months of the recession the capacity-utilization rate dropped to 68 per cent from 83 per cent at the beginning of the period. Nominal unit labour costs added to inflationary pressures as the growth of compensation per hour exceeded the growth of output in the two recession years. Finally, however, rising unemployment curbed the labour cost.

In January 1975 President Ford called for tax reductions to fight the recession and Congress backed him. In December 1975 the tax cuts were renewed. As government expenditures also increased, the federal budget deficit jumped from $11.5 billion to $69.3 billion, thus rising from a modest 0.8 per cent of the GDP to a conspicuous 4.5 per cent (Table 8). In 1976 a robust recovery (4.8%) seemed to be firmly established, due to the recovery of fixed investment and consumer expenditure, while consumer prices abated to 1973 levels under the effect of the recession, the monetary squeeze and the end of the oil hike in the previous two years. Yet, inflation was still high and the unemployment rate stood at a high 7.8 per cent, not far from the trough rate of the previous year. Meanwhile the merchandise trade balance had markedly returned to the red under the impact of growing imports, oil in particular, even though the current account balance was still positive (Table 2).

The legacy of Gerald Ford's short reign was not inconspicuous. Apart from a recovery that was not ephemeral and whose end, obviously, cannot be blamed on Nixon's successor, two events must be noted. Ford's presidency saw the start of the summits which would bring together the heads of state and government of the major economic power of the Western world. The initiative came from the European side as the proposal was officially made by Giscard d'Estaing in agreement with the then German chancellor, Helmut Schmidt and the gathering was held at Rambouillet castle, near Paris. But the start of summitry was only made possible by the acceptance of the proposal by the American president, who overrode the misgivings of members of his administration.[23] Although the effectiveness of the economic summits might be doubtful, they helped to smooth over disagreements between the perticipants and to work out initiatives of common interest. On the domestic side Ford broke the impasse on the grant of negotiating authority that had marked Nixon's last years in office, thus making the actual start of the Tokyo Round possible, although disagreements prevailed during his presidency. On the other hand, the same legislation sharpened the teeth of the defence of American industry from foreign competition, and the improved weaponry was to be largely adopted in the years that followed.

The onset, duration and severity of the slump were not uniform among EC member countries, which suggests that the causes of the recession were not identical.

West Germany managed to escape the balance of payments constraint that affected most other EC member countries. Its trade balance remained healthy in spite of an export decline in 1975 (Tables 11 and 12). The slowdown in 1974 can be primarily attributed to the restrictive monetary policy adopted by the Bundesbank till the end of 1973 in the wake of the breakdown of the Bretton Woods system to combat inflation which in that year had already hit 6.9 per cent.[24] The restrictive policy sustained the appreciation of the Deutschmark vis-à-vis the US dollar, thus curbing the oil bill and with it inflation. However, investment contracted by almost 10 per cent in 1974 ushering in a slowdown which turned into recession in 1975 when the spreading slump caused exports, the engine of German economic strength, to decline for the first time in over twenty years. Thus, it was not the constraint imposed by the surge of import value in the balance of payments but the decline of main components of demand, nominally investments and exports, that brought about the slump. In 1975 the German monetary authority adopted a cautiously expansionary stance, while the fiscal authority continued the countercyclical course already adopted in 1974 and the fiscal deficit reached an unprecedented high of 5.8 per cent of GDP (Table 19). In 1976 the economy recovered fully with a 5.1 per cent growth rate no lower than the 1960 average (Table 9), fuelled by the resurgence of exports and the recovery of investments. However, the expansionary momentum slowed down quite soon.

There was greater volatility in the course of events in Italy, the UK and France which, in turn, showed many similarities. In particular, the Italian economy, in spite of the oil crisis, went on growing in 1974, although at a rate lower than the previous year: 4.1 per cent and 7 per cent respectively (Table 9). Industrial production also continued to grow (Table 21). Inflation, however, jumped to over 19 per cent and the trade gap widened at an unprecedented rate (Tables 11, 12 and 23). Thus, in line with the model developed by Thirlwall, the gaping current account deficit, which in 1974 exceeded $8 billion, forced the Italian central bank to tighten credit conditions to reduce private demand.[25] The credit squeeze helped reduce the trade deficit and abate inflation, though not significantly nor durably (Tables 10 and 23). At the same time the Italian GDP plunged by a stunning 3.6 per cent (Table 9) while the fiscal deficit soared to over 10 per cent of GDP under the combined pressure of lower revenues and higher expenditure to subsidize declining industries and contain unemployment (Table 19). To redress the current account balance without penalizing growth, the Italian authorities tried to boost exports by resorting to devaluation. At the beginning of 1976, after a 40-day suspension of the foreign exchange market, the lira depreciated by about 30 per cent on average. The manoeuvre raised the competitiveness of Italian products despite the continued rise of the cost of labour (Figure 4) and in the short term the Italian GDP recovered by a robust 5.9 per cent, while the import bill and inflation remained high. In the following three years the GDP growth averaged 3.2 per cent and inflation started to abate, but unemployment went on rising (Table 22).

The recession started earlier in the UK than in Italy but was less severe, while the 1976 recovery was less pronounced (Table 9). Inflation, whose average was 5.1 per cent in the years 1961–73, ballooned to 16 per cent in 1974 and hit 24 per cent in 1975 and did not fall below 16 per cent the following year, thus remaining well above the EC average along with Italy (Table 23). The initial impact of the oil crisis on the trade balance was even more severe than in Italy, but in 1975 the import bill went down, partly because of the prolonged slump and because North Sea oil began to flow (Table 12). Oil production helped to convert the balance of payments deficit into a surplus by the end of 1977. Correspondingly, the pound, which had depreciated by over 25 per cent vis-à-vis the US dollar, strongly recovered (Figure 1). Throughout the years 1976–9 GDP grew by an average of 2.6 per cent (Table 9). The pace of the recovery was initially set by exports and a high rate of stockbuilding, but from 1978, as the government adopted a reflationary policy, the main engine was consumer spending with some support from fixed investments and expenditure of public authorities, while exports declined and imports grew, worsening the trade balance.[26] On the other hand, the rate of unemployment that had reached 5.3 per cent in 1976 did not decline.

The first impact of the oil shock on France was to accelerate the overheating of the economy stimulating in the first semester of 1974 both the demand for consumer goods and investments, but the monetary and fiscal squeeze carried out in June 1974 drastically altered the economic environment hitting both above-mentioned components.[27] On a yearly basis GDP grew by 3.2 per cent, while inflation jumped to 13.7 per cent (Tables 9 and 23). Exports grew by a robust 33 per cent but imports soared by 47 per cent (Tables 11 and 12). In 1975 the GDP growth rate was almost nil and import value declined slightly but inflation remained above 10 per cent. In September 1975 a plan was adopted to boost the demand by public investments, by the reduction of fiscal pressure and interest rates to stimulate private investments and by social aids. The outcome was not convincing as there was a strong recovery, but at the price of a rate of inflation higher than the EC average, and the worsening of the trade balance, which forced the French government to abandon for the second time the European Snake.[28] In September 1976 the new French government introduced a plan, known as the Barre Plan, primarily directed at stabilizing the economy and curbing inflation. The set of measures helped to improve the trade and current account balances but the GDP growth slackened, the rate of investment decreased and unemployment remained high relative to the years prior to the oil crisis, while inflation did not significantly abate.[29]

When the new president, Jimmy Carter, took office in January 1977, he inherited an economy that had fully recovered from the slump of the previous two years. Yet, the rate of unemployment was 7.4 per cent, a level of joblessness that the Democratic executive could not but consider unacceptable, being only one point below the 1975 peak. The Tax Reduction and Simplification Act, passed in May 1977, increased the personal standard deduction and provided additional funds to states and localities. Later the administration increased spending on public works and on public service employment. The fiscal deficit of the two previous years was not curtailed (Table 9) but the economy kept growing and by 1978 the rate of unemployment was reduced to a still high but more acceptable 6.1 per cent. From 1977 onwards, the favourable picture was marred by the worsening of the balance of payments. The merchandise trade deficit soared by 228 per cent relative to the deficit of the previous year, which, in turn, was much higher than in 1972, that is, the year in which the effects of the dollar devaluation had not yet been felt, while the current account balance, positive for the last four years, turned into a deficit of $14.5 million in 1977 and $15.4 million the following year (Table 2). The deficit with Germany, which had been cancelled in the previous year, reappeared in 1977 and further grew in 1978, but overall the negative balance with the Federal Republic remained a modest portion of the US trade deficit. The deficit with Japan more than doubled between 1976 and 1978, accounting for over a third of the US merchandise trade deficit (Table 5).

A cursory analysis of the causes of the deficit, that is, without considering its various components, does not point to the non-competitiveness of American products in terms of costs. On the contrary, it appears that the competitive edge provided by the 1971–3 devaluation of the greenback had not been eroded. For instance, the unit labour cost in manufacturing of the main US trading partners, estimated on a dollar basis, rose much more quickly than in the United States (Figure 4). It is, therefore, arguable that at least part of the deficit was the result of the discrepancy between the speed and extent of the recovery in the USA and in the other OECD countries. Indeed, if in 1976 the economy was fast recovering in all OECD countries, from 1977 it was characterized by a divergent tendency in the industrialized countries as, while the United States continued to grow in the two following years at approximately the same rate as in 1976, the growth rate in the EC member states markedly slowed down, with the exception of Ireland and Luxembourg (Tables 1 and 9). Japan also experienced a deceleration of its rate of growth.

The path to a sustained, non-inflationary growth in all industrialized countries, also capable of avoiding dangerous gaps among their balance of payments, was seen in the coordination of their policies, in particular those of the United States, Japan and West Germany. The 'Locomotive' approach, which was the official G7 philosophy, was that a satisfactory pace of global recovery could be achieved only if the major industrialized countries, that is, initially Germany, Japan and the United States adopted a stimulative stance in their domestic stabilization policy. In turn, such a policy would not only bring about export-led expansion in the weaker countries but would also loosen domestic policy constraints linked to balance of payments deterioration risks. The apparently rational picture was spoiled by the fact that the three engines forming the locomotive had different levels of inflation and above all of unemployment, which was higher in the United States than in the other two countries, and their priorities in fighting the two ills were different. Both Germany and Japan were wary of relying on domestic stimuli to the economic recovery, also because, as in the past, their recovery, modest though it was, was export-led. The German monetary authorities, in particular, were worried about measures that could rekindle Germany's traditional bogeyman: inflation. The May 1977 Downing Street Summit committed the G7 governments 'to targets for growth and stabilization which vary from country to country but which, taken as a whole, should provide a basis for non-inflationary growth worldwide'. The Summit declaration also stated that the governments of countries pursuing stabilization policies, designed to provide growth without inflation, would continue to pursue those goals, whereas countries that had adopted reasonably expansionist growth targets would keep their policies under review and, if needed, adopt further measures to contribute to the adjustment of payments imbalances. It seems, therefore, that Japan's and West Germany's policies received full endorsement while the United States was required to implement adjustments in case of worsening of its balance of payments.

Attitudes substantially changed at the time of the Bonn Summit in August 1978 as the pace of recovery had not shown any significant improvement in most EC member countries where the unemployment rate was approaching that of the United States, which in turn was declining. The Bonn declaration pointed at unemployment as the main evil, to combat which the G7 governments would build on the progress already made in curbing inflation, pursuing, however, higher economic growth. In this context West Germany's chancellor, Helmut Schmidt announced that his government would propose to the German parliament additional fiscal measures of up to 1 per cent of GNP. Actually, the German government's fiscal stimulus had already been pledged to its EC partners as the Summit held in April at Copenhagen had called for a growth rate of 4.5 per cent throughout the EC by 1979, while the GDP growth of Germany, by definition the Western Europe Locomotive, in 1978 was not expected to exceed 3 per cent.[30] The Japanese Prime Minister Takeo Fukuda stressed his government's efforts to increase by 1.5 percentage points the growth rate of the previous year, mainly through the expansion of domestic demand, and pledged to increase imports through the same channel. The US president announced that his government had already taken measures to prevent its fiscal stimulus from re-igniting inflation by reducing expenditure projection for 1978 and 1979, while a very tight budget was prepared for 1980. Carter also committed the US executive to introduce measures directed at curbing US dependence on imported oil by the end of the year. Actually, the programme, whose cornerstone was the decontrol of oil prices, had been hailed at the Downing Street Summit, but was soon bogged down on account of opposition in Congress and in the administration as well, as some of Carter's political and economic advisers deemed that such a measure could rekindle an inflation that had abated but did not give any sign of disappearing. In any case, price deregulation was bound to stir up resentment from the average American who had long taken cheap consumption of oil for granted. The renewed pledge in Bonn offered Carter the international backing that enabled him to push through the reform, also assisted by the announcement that, during the European Council held in Bremen the previous week, the EC member states had agreed to reduce the Community's dependence on imported energy to 50 per cent by 1985. Although with a delay of five months from the deadline indicated at the G7 Summit, price decontrol in the US began on 1 June 1979, with all controls to end by October 1981. It must be noted that the administration was careful enough to schedule the final stage of the alignment to world prices well after the November 1980 presidential election.

The commitments made in the various summits, including the one held in Bonn, did not significantly alter the present trend in the trade balance of the participants. Only Japan briefly made its surplus with the United States less conspicuous. Reflecting the worsening of the current account balance the dollar steeply depreciated vis-à-vis the currency of its main trading partners, thus making its exports more competitive and constraining its imports (Figure 1). The downward trend of a devaluating dollar changed course in 1980 when changes in US monetary policy began to be felt.

Decline and growth in old and new industries across the Atlantic and measures adopted to buoy and boost them

The recovery, whose strength was different in the United States and in Western Europe, concealed areas of decline and expansion bound to have an impact on their economic policies and on the multilateral negotiations. The sectors experiencing grave difficulties were shipbuilding, in particular in the European Community, textiles and steel, while agriculture and the aircraft industry acquired growing importance in the expansion of US and EC trade. In line with the teaching of international political economy, the crisis that affected the first three sectors fostered protectionist tendencies on both sides of the Atlantic. Yet, the sheer fact that the success of the latter two sectors was inextricably linked to public support both in the US and in the EC, although with different levels and different kinds of intervention, hampered trade liberalizing agreements and only postponed the confrontation between the two areas, for agriculture until the early 1980s and for aircraft until the twenty-first century.

Shipbuilding

As noted by Lindert, the United States shipbuilding industry was never able to effectively compete with the United Kingdom shipbuilding industry and the chance to gain ground on the British was seized by other European nations and later by Japan. The United States, therefore, satisfied itself with isolating a non-competitive industry from foreign onslaughts.[31] Thus, there was no question of any new difficulties for the American industry in the 1970s. A serious decline was, instead, experienced by the EC industry, unable to withstand competition, not only from Japan but also from some newly industrialized countries in a global environment dominated by overcapacity. Order books in the international market swelled unprecedentedly between 1960 and 1973 as a result of optimistic forecasts of the world economy and of speculative demand. To meet orders received in 1972–3, annual world production in the period 1974–6 grew to approximately 20 million cgrt (compensated gross registered tons).[32] Production in the EC countries had not kept pace with the buoyant world market, as its share had steadily declined from 70 per cent in 1955 to 23.3 per cent twenty years later, while that of Japan had jumped from 12 per cent to 50.6 per cent.[33] The 1974–5 slump, although not the only cause of the decline, put an abrupt end to the rosy expectations. By 1977 new orders had fallen to 14 million cgrt and had started to cause overcapacity problems even to Japan. A year later they plummeted to just 10.8 million cgrt (–23% relative to 1977 and –32% relative to 1976). Production fell from 22.1 million cgrt in 1976 to 16.5 million cgrt in 1978 (–25%).[34] The recession was forecast to extend well into the following decade. The EC shipyards were hit more than their competitors as their share of world newbuilding completions declined to 21 per cent by 1978. Already in 1975 the decline was affecting 8.3 per cent of the workforce in the shipyards of the EC member countries. In 1978 employment in new shipbuilding fell to 155,840 units, with a 25 per cent decline relative to 1975 and a similar trend characterized all other sectors of shipyards.[35] The member states at national levels reacted by supporting their shipyards, i.e. placing orders for naval vessels and, above all, through financial intervention aimed at overcoming the price advantage of Japan and of the Newly Industrialized Countries (NICs). These efforts, however, ended up keeping afloat an industry affected by overcapacity but without effectively tackling this problem.

The European Community intervened by issuing directives aimed at harmonizing state intervention in the sector and reducing the level of aids which were damaging intra-Community competition. The stated aim of the Community was to make the EC shipyards more competitive in the world market, thus providing a more significant proportion of the member countries' fleets. Since demand for shipping was declining, because of the continuous impact of the oil crisis, the European Commission suggested that financial measures should be taken to stimulate demand and to orientate it towards local production. Nevertheless, restructuring and curtailment of production potential had to be accepted. The European Regional Development Fund provided financial support to the regions, prevalently located in France, Germany, Italy and the UK, where there was a high concentration of shipbuilding to create or preserve jobs and to assist the execution of industrial infrastructure projects. Obviously, the Community's efforts to buoy up, restructure and render its shipbuilding industries more competitive were open to the accusation that reorganization of the shipyard industry would interfere with the market, distorting competition with other producers. Under the auspices of the OECD 'general guidelines for government policies in the shipbuilding industry' were agreed by the EC member states together with the other members of the Association of West European Shipbuilders (AWES) and by Japan, with the stated aim of pursuing the reduction of production capacity so as to restore in the medium term the balance between supply and demand, while maintaining fair competition. The OECD agreement was made more effective by pressure on Japan to bear a satisfactory share of the consequences of the crisis under threat of unilateral protective measures. Japan agreed to raise its export prices by 5 per cent and introduce a series of measures of voluntary restraint vis-à-vis some EC member states, which, however, was far from bringing balance back into the market.

Steel industry

Similar problems were experienced by the US and EC steel industries in the period ushered in by the oil crisis. The predominance of the American industry in the world steel market had already waned in the previous decades. The US, which accounted for 53 per cent of world production in 1950, accounted for 21.1 per cent twenty years later, while Japan, which accounted for only 2.6 per cent of world output in 1950, accounted for 16.1 per cent in 1970.[36] By 1960 the US had become a net importer and by 1970 its net imports amounted to 6.3 million tons of steel products. Japanese net exports soared from 0.4 million tons in 1950 to 22.3 million tons in 1970. The European Community remained a net exporter but its share of the world product, after climbing to over 29 per cent in 1960, declined to less than 18 per cent twenty years later.[37] The changing production pattern of steel trade flows is primarily explained by changes in relative costs in favour of Japan and the NICs vis-à-vis their competitors in the United States and Europe.

The years 1973–4 witnessed a strong expansion in steel demand which entailed major expansion projects as producers were forecasting an upwards trend for the following decade. After a decline in 1975, world consumption slowly recovered in the second half of the 1970s until it exceeded its 1973 level by a meagre 3.7 per cent in 1980. However, the overall trend masked more ominous developments for the industrialized countries, the US and the EC in particular, whose industry lost further ground to their foreign competitors. As a result the steel industry on both sides of the Atlantic experienced significant losses and overcapacity. In 1977, crude steel production declined in the United States by 14 per cent relative to 1974; capacity utilization contracted by 29 per cent; employment fell by 59,407 units.[38] The industry's difficulties were exacerbated by imports which, during 1977, rose 35 per cent by volume and covered 17 per cent of domestic consumption. It was, therefore, natural to claim that in a sluggish world market, foreign competition was taking the form of major price reduction which was quite often bound to result in sales below production costs.[39] In September 1977, an interagency task force, headed by Treasury Undersecretary Anthony Solomon, was established to examine the steel industry's problems. The task force recommended measures to encourage modernization of steel-making facilities; assistance to firms and workers in adjusting to import competition; review of the environmental regulations applying to the steel industry; and above all the establishment of a trigger price mechanism for monitoring imports into the US and initiating expedited antidumping investigations. The Trigger Price Mechanism (TPM) was approved by Carter at the end of 1977 and was formally initiated the following February in the investigations on the 32 categories of steel products marketed in the US. It was based on the full cost of production by the most efficient foreign steel producer, Japan, plus the cost of bringing the imported products into the United States. The TPM was not considered a minimum price system as the importers were free to sell steel in the United States below the trigger price as long as they were selling above 'fair value' as defined by the Antidumping Act. It indicated, however, when an imported product was likely to be sold at less than fair market value, thus automatically opening an investigation unless the exporter had received a preclearance. In other words, importers of foreign steel at better prices than increasingly costly US products were warned that they were embarking on a dicey adventure. It was, therefore, much more consistent with prudence to buy American products.

Things became comparatively worse for the EC member states as the downturn meant the inversion of a phase of expansion culminated in 1974. In 1977 the Community's production of crude steel amounted to just over 126 million tons, compared with 134 million in 1976 (–6%) and 155.6 million in 1974 (–19%). The rate of utilization of production capacity was approximately 60 per cent and the rate was even lower in Germany, Belgium, Denmark, Luxembourg and Ireland. Employment declined by 73,151 units. Steel imports increased by 67 per cent compared with 1974 and the proportion of consumption covered by imports jumped from 5.8 per cent to 10.4 per cent.[40]

The measures adopted by the Community were even less consistent with the principles of free trade and free market which, after all, was the philosophy to which both sides of the Atlantic claimed to adhere. The EC steel industry set up a cartel, which fixed minimum prices and quotas of production and exports within the Community. Derogating the General EC rules on competition, the steel cartel was allowed under the 1951 European Coal and Steel Community Treaty. The effectiveness of a cartel depends on two factors: its comprehensiveness and unity; and its ability to prevent the entry of foreign competitors into its market. Within the EC the effectiveness of the cartel was put into question by competition from the so-called Bresciani firms (from the name of a town in the industrial north of Italy). These small and efficient firms were able to produce at much lower costs than big German and particularly French steelmakers and, therefore, were threatening their markets. The growing inflow of steel products from a wide range of countries was even more dangerous.

As the system by which steel producers could voluntarily undertake to limit supplies of certain products did not prevent the deterioration of the market, in March 1977 the Commission, endorsed by the European Council, adopted a set of guidelines for steel policy which were further expanded in December, to reorient and reshape the steel industry and to protect it from foreign competition. These measures, known as the 'Davignon Plan', after the commissioner for Industrial Affairs, provided for mandatory minimum prices for products under stiff competition (concrete reinforcing bars, hot-rolled wide strips and merchant bars) and called for guidance prices for other products, combined with voluntary production quotas. Concurrently an import control programme was initiated. Like the TPM in the United States, the programme employed a system of basic prices reflecting the lowest production costs in the exporting country in which normal conditions of competition prevailed, but went further than the American regime, as it provided for the levy of provisional duties on imports below basic price without need for prior enquiry.[41] Steel-exporting countries were, however, exempt from the basic import price system if they negotiated voluntary export restraint (VER) agreements. Fifteen countries providing about 75 per cent of EC imports, including EFTA members and Japan, agreed to a VER as of 1 January 1978.

One of the declared objectives of the plan put forward by the Commission – whose policy, unlike the United States', along with protectionism, was also characterized by a high degree of dirigisme – was to bolster the profitability of the EC steel industry by a severe curtailment of its capacity in order to achieve balance between offer and prospective demand.[42] This would have required a restructuring policy involving the reconversion of industrial plants and workers to other sectors to be financed by the Community budget and stricter rules on subsidies provided by member states as they would distort competition and hinder the capacity cut process.

If the measures adopted by the Community were definitely inconsistent with the GATT provisions, they did fit with the understanding worked out in the OECD where, at the initiative of the United States, an Ad Hoc Group on Steel was formed to identify structural problems of the sector on a worldwide basis and to provide a forum for discussion. The Group, which in late 1978 was replaced by a standing Steel Committee, focused on three main areas: steel trade, steel prices and longer-term structural changes in the industry. At a meeting in November 1977 the Group agreed on a number of principles to guide governments in dealing with the steel sector's problems: worldwide rationalization of the sector was needed and the burden of adjustment was not to be shifted from one producing nation to another either in the short or the long term; immediate measures to keep domestic firms afloat had to be consistent with the longer-term need to rationalize the industry while maintaining free and fair flow of trade and, therefore, 'unilateral' quantitative restrictions were to be avoided; in spite of slack demand, the parties to the understanding were to refrain from cut price competition that could affect the industry of the other parties, which was a warning not to exploit cost advantages under threat of countervailing measures.[43] To render the commitment more effective and to prevent freelancing, a monitoring mechanism was established which aimed at identifying incipient problems and facilitating 'rational investment decisions through increased transparency'.

The dealings in the OECD were obviously influenced by trilateral talks held by the US with its EC and Japanese counterparts. This may explain why the United States, while pressing foreign exporters with quasi-judicial antidumping proceedings, refrained from large-scale actions involving presidential decisions. For instance, President Carter decided in January 1978 to discontinue the review of a complaint filed by the American Iron and Steel Institute under section 301 of the 1974 Trade Act alleging substantial diversion of Japanese steel to the US market as a result of a voluntary restriction agreed with the European Community. The president noted that there was no sufficient evidence of significant diversion of Japanese steel towards the US and that, at any rate, adequate relief could be obtained through the antidumping complaints filed by the steel industry.[44] However, there is no evidence that the activities in the OECD and the tripartite talks resulted in or aimed at the establishment of an international steel cartel. The Americans, for instance, were not prepared to impose a curtailment of capacity on their industry. No deal on market shares is traceable. The EC steel producers looked favourably to the rebirth of the voluntary restraint arrangement expired in 1974, which would have provided a limited but not threatened share of the US market, but this policy was not followed by the Commission. On the other hand, the absence of a stable outlet in foreign markets, and the United States was a main importer of EC steel products, meant that the forecast of excess capacity made by the Commission could prove optimistic and that, therefore, more severe rationalization measures were needed.

Textile and clothing industries

The aftermath of the first oil crisis also witnessed a surge in import restricting policies within the textile and clothing industries. The new trend was the outcome of the worsening condition in Western European countries, although the US was not coy to exploit the advantages offered by the EC call for greater control over developing-country exports. While the United States had actively pursued bilateral agreements during the first period of the Multifibre Arrangement (MFA), the EC had not implemented a consistent textile trade policy and was paying the price.[45] In 1977, the United States had agreements with 18 countries, covering approximately 77 per cent of its imports of cotton, wool and man-made fibre textiles and apparel and was actively negotiating new bilateral agreements. The European Community had been slow in exploiting the room for manoeuvre offered by the MFA, as most of the voluntary restraint agreements signed with developing countries did not come into force until 1976, that is, two years after the MFA took effect. Moreover, the quantities stipulated in many bilateral agreements were relatively large and numerous concessions had to be given to those countries with which the EC had signed preferential agreements. The EC trade surplus for manufactured textiles and clothing of over $900 million in 1971 turned into an $846 million deficit in 1975, and in terms of tonnage this deficit rose from 163,000 tonnes in 1974 to 383,000 tonnes in 1975 and 600,000 tonnes in 1976.[46] Between 1971 and 1977 530,000 workers left the textile and clothing industries, while over 700,000 workers were either unemployed or working part-time.[47]

The negotiations for the extension of the MFA offered the industrial countries an opportunity to curb textile and apparel inflows. The 1973 Multifibre Arrangements, though imposing import limits on all kinds of textile products, provided for a 6 per cent annual rate of growth for individual countries that was in line with the normal increase of their exports. When the Arrangement was renewed in 1977 with reference to the 1978–82 period, although it still envisaged the above-mentioned growth rate, it did allow the importing countries to set lower limits through bilateral negotiations. The European Community, at the behest of France and the United Kingdom in particular, required that the exporters of the largest developing countries reduce their 1978 exports of textiles and clothing to the Common Market below the 1976 level. Likewise, the United States reached agreements with Hong Kong, Korea and Taiwan to freeze their 1978 exports of textiles and clothing at the 1977 level and then to increase the exports of a number of sensitive items at a rate substantially less than 6 per cent.

The difficulties of the sector contributed to worsen the prospect in the EC member states of the synthetic fibres industry which was affected by the economic decline triggered by the first oil crisis and by the consequent explosion of overcapacity, estimated at around 30 per cent in 1977. The EC Commission urged the member countries not to provide aid which would create new production capacity. In turn, the main producers in the Community resorted to the establishment of a semi-official cartel similar to the regime in place in the steel industry. This informal understanding, which was based on a concerted reduction of production capacity and production quota allocations, was tolerated by the Commission in spite of its dubious conformity with EC rules on competition.

Civil transport aircraft

The US predominance in the civil aircraft market continued throughout the 1970s, but the EC industry gradually increased its presence in the market. The orders and deliveries of American jet aircraft up to December 1974 outshone their European competitors by a ratio of 5.3 to 1.[48] However, between 1970 and 1975 the American market shrank from 64 per cent of the world market to about 46 per cent, while the EC market rose from 14.7 per cent to 17.6 per cent and that of the other Western European countries from 6.3 per cent to 8 per cent. On the other hand, the share of European products on the various markets fell substantially: from 33 per cent in 1970 to 22 per cent five years later and from 2 per cent to just 0.3 per cent of the US market.[49]

Nonetheless, prospects for the EC industry started to become brighter in the second half of the decade without direct involvement of the European Community, but thanks to cooperation among the industries and governments of some member states. The first main example was Concorde which entered service in 1976. This new aircraft was the product of an Anglo–French government treaty, combining the manufacturing efforts of Aerospatiale and the British Aircraft Corporation. The main enterprise was, however, the Airbus. Airbus Industrie was formally established as a Groupement d'Interêt Économique (Economic Interest Group) in December 1970 as a result of a government initiative between France, Germany and the UK that dated back to 1967. The members of the Group were Aerospatiale, Deutsche Airbus, Hawker Siddeley and Fokker-VFW, joined in October 1971 by the Spanish company CASA. In January 1979 British Aerospace, which had absorbed Hawker Siddeley, acquired a 20 per cent share of Airbus Industrie. By the early 1980s the European Industry led by Airbus had become a main competitor of the American giants, Boeing, McDonnell Douglas and Lockheed.

Both the United States and the European states involved in the Concorde and Airbus projects were lavish in providing financial aid, but the means of support were different. In the United States the federal government intervened primarily by means of military purchases and military research and development contracts which provided a basis for many large-scale civil engineering projects. In the Community, government support was given through purchases and R&D contracts, later followed by reimbursable launch investments. In case of a legal conflict involving governments on both sides of the Atlantic, it would have been easier for the US to deny that it was financially supporting its civil aeronautical industry as the aid it received was just a by-product of military contracts. The European member states could reply that their support was only the result of ordinary purchases and that, at any rate, subsidies bestowed on their national industries were domestic subsidies that were not aimed at distorting competition in world trade.

Agriculture

The aftermath of the 1974–5 depression saw the continuation of the farm products export boom in the US, although at a growth rate lower than in the years between 1971 and 1974 (Figure 15). Exports, which as expected, showed a very strong correlation

(0.99) with gross farm income, in 1978 accounted for over one-fourth of a fast growing gross income while, on average, they had made up just one-eighth of it in the 1960–70 years. The scenario was less bright for the net farm income in constant dollars. Indeed, after reaching a $69.4 billion peak in 1973, with an over 100 per cent increase relative to 1971, the net income of the whole sector constantly fell and in 1977 was much lower than in 1966, totalling less than $30 billion. The decline was the upshot of the faster growth of the non-farm components of the gross product such as wages paid to farm workers, rent on land owned by non-farm operators and inputs provided by other sectors. On the other hand, the net farm operator income per farm significantly improved compared with the previous decade, due to the continuing decline in the number of farms, from almost 4 million in 1960 to about 2.7 million in 1977.[50] However, in 1977 also the net farm income per farm was somewhat lower than four years earlier as the 1973 bonanza slowed down the exodus from agriculture and the prices paid to non-farm sectors were biting. In other words, the export boom was not enough to prevent the malaise of farm operators, or at least a number of them, as borne out by the numerous demonstrations of protest, which manifested striking similarities with those organized on the other side of the Atlantic.

It is in this context, less positive than the one in which the 1973 farm law was drafted, that the Food and Agriculture Act of 1977 was approved. As for the 1973 statute, the loan rates, that is, the support prices provided by the Commodity Credit Corporation, were kept below market prices and, therefore, were not destined to impinge on the export propensity of US farmers. However, target prices, introduced in the 1973 legislation to determine the amount of direct support of farmers' income whenever necessary, were fixed by the 1977 Food and Agricultural Act, as amended by the Emergency Agricultural Act of 1978, at a level higher than market prices and loan rates, in particular for wheat, thus entitling farmers to an integration of their income. As the Food and Agricultural Act stipulated that deficiency payments – i.e. the difference between target prices and market prices or loan rates – be proportional to production rather than tied to allotments fixed on a historical base, they were likely to increase supply on a greater scale than set-asides and acreage diversions designed to reduce production. Therefore, as predicted by agricultural experts, the new income support programme left the United States open to the charge of dumping, thus weakening its call for reform of the EC Common Agricultural Policy that it was accusing of trade distortion through subsidization. Besides, as it was a form of direct income support, it increased the pressure on the budget when the prevailing policy called for the curtailment of fiscal deficit.

Yet, there is no denying that the CAP was bound to raise the worries of the United States as, assisted by scientific progress enhancing productivity, the Community was fast reaching self-sufficiency in main farm products sectors and by 1979 sugar and butter exceeded self-sufficiency by 20 per cent (Figure 13). Surpluses entailed the need for storage and disposal in markets outside the EC. The CAP mechanism started, therefore, to cause costs that were no longer exclusively borne by consumers but by the tax payers, straining the limited budgetary resources bestowed on the European Community by its member states. But progress towards self-sufficiency was not uniform in all member states, some of which reached and exceeded self-sufficiency in most products covered by the CAP long before others which remained net importers. France, in particular, by far exceeded self-sufficiency in all kinds of grains, especially wheat, along with sugar, cheese and butter by the early 1970s. The aim of achieving balance in farm trade, underlying the 'Loi d'Orientation Agricole' (Law of Agricultural Development) of 1960, by the mid-1970s was replaced by the goal of becoming a net exporter.[51] This objective was made possible by membership of the European Community within which France had a positive farm trade balance while it was still a net importer vis-à-vis the countries outside the Community which, however, also provided many products that France was unable to grow. Therefore, for France it was not just a question of successfully competing in the world market but of safeguarding the non-tariff barriers that prevented third-country competitors from displacing it in its preserve, the European Common Market. France was not the only great farm product exporter in the Community. In 1972 the Netherlands exceeded self-sufficiency in butter by over 200 per cent, in cheese by over 100 per cent and in veal by a modest 1,700 per cent. Germany in 1978 exceeded self-sufficiency only in rye (6%), sugar (29%) and butter (35%). As West Germany was the main exporter of industrial products in the EC it would have been foreseeable that the Federal Republic might be inclined to sacrifice the preservation of the CAP to favourable deals in other areas of the multilateral negotiations that could enhance its predominance in manufacturing exports. Yet, the German farmers had a staunch ally in the Minister for Agriculture, the liberal democrat Josef Ertl and were among the main beneficiaries of the European Agricultural Guidance and Guarantee Fund (EAGGF). Besides, if it is true that manufactured exports dwarfed the agricultural exports of the Federal Republic, to deduce that the latter were irrelevant would be misleading. If intra-EC exports are included, West Germany numbered among the main farm product exporters of the 1970s and by 1977 it had outstripped traditionally big exporters like Australia and Canada.

An overall assessment of trade-distorting measures

The foregoing shows that the measures in question could be divided into two strands: those aimed at hindering the inflow of foreign products and those aimed at boosting domestic production, which in so doing could prevent imports of foreign like products or could outcompete them in foreign markets, including the market of importing countries. The first class, in turn, could be divided into tariff barriers, which had been on the decline due to the various rounds of GATT negotiations, and non-tariff barriers.

The years under review witnessed a decline in the implementation of safeguard measures in the US. Both GATT Art. XIX and US legislation gave relevance to safeguard measures (also known as escape clause). This form of temporary protection was originally designed only to protect against import surges causing economic dislocation in excess of what had been anticipated by trade negotiators in offering concessions. Subsequently, however, these measures were increasingly used to protect domestic industries against increased import competition regardless of previous tariff concessions.[52] In particular, in US legislation, the link between serious injury or threat of serious injury had become increasingly weak: the 1951 trade law provided that imports had to cause or threaten serious injury; the 1962 Trade Expansion Act provided that imports had to be the major factor in causing or threatening to cause serious injury; the Trade Act of 1974 only required that the increased import be a substantial cause of serious injury. Yet, no relevant increase in the use of such measures can be detected in the years following 1974. Not only had serious injury to be proved but the remedy had to be applied in line with the Most-Favoured Nation principle, i.e. it had to be applied to all exporting countries rather than the main exporter and in the absence of compensation retaliatory measures would be applied. Above all, the final decision on adopting the remedy was for the president who had to balance the interest of the industries affected by foreign competition with those of other industries interested in expanding their trade or acquiring cheaper inputs and with the need not to cause undue strains in relations with US trading partners. At the close of 1977 the US had in effect escape clause relief on just five products and three other safeguard measures were authorized the following year.[53] The trend was different in the European Community where the number of safeguard actions soared from 2 in 1974 to 36 three years later, though declining to 23 and 19 in the following years.[54]

Conversely, quota restrictions were rapidly increasing following the oil crisis. As is well-known, quotas, which were the trademark of Orderly Marketing Arrangements (OMAs) and VERs, were prohibited by GATT Art. XI, with the exception of clearly circumscribed cases in agriculture, and were only allowed by GATT Art. XII to safeguard the balance of payments, a provision that was never invoked by the United States nor, after the 1950s, by the EC member states. Yet, quota restrictions became current currency in the 1970s under the cloak of a deal between importer and exporter, thus falling, with the exception of the textile arrangements, into a grey area outside the GATT purview. As related in Chapter 1, import quotas were doubtless already applied in the 1960s, but after a pause in the first half of the 1970s they soared in number and value during the stagflation years. The rise does not seem to be directly linked to the general state of the economy, but to the declining health of some particular sectors, encompassing not only textiles and clothing or iron and steel products, but also chemicals, machinery and transport equipment as well as footwear and domestic appliances like TV receivers.

At EC level so-called bilateral trade agreements jumped from 3 in 1973 to 14 in 1975, 11 in 1976, 19 in 1977, 11 in 1978 and 15 in 1979.[55] However, in measuring the impact of such measures it should also be remembered that analogous restrictive measures could be taken by each member state. Apart from 13 safeguard actions authorized by the EC, Italy between mid-1976 and mid-1979 established 29 import quotas and twice as many autonomous surveillance measures. The most important restraints imposed by France were quotas on automobile imports from Japan in 1977, on umbrellas from Singapore in 1978 and footwear from Taiwan and Korea in 1979.[56] The UK negotiated a VER with Japan to stem the inflow of cars. Also there was a surge in the imposition of quotas on the other side of the Atlantic. Apart from the quotas established within the framework of the Multifibre Arrangement, orderly marketing agreements were signed in 1977 with Japan on colour TV receivers, a sector in which the US had been the world leader until recently, and with South Korea and Taiwan on footwear. In the first instance, imports were limited to 60 per cent of the 1976 level until

1980. Regarding South Korea and Taiwan, quotas would apply until 1981, curtailing imports to a level below the 1976 value despite annual increases. In 1978, when imports of colour TV receivers from Japan were replaced by an inflow from Taiwan and Korea, voluntary restraint agreements were promptly negotiated with both countries. Following the expiration in 1974 of voluntary restraints on Japanese and European steel imports a series of orderly marketing agreements was negotiated in 1976 on specialty steel with Japan, the EC, Sweden, Spain and many Latin American countries.

Trends and features are even more clearly detectable in the upsurge of antidumping and countervailing measures. Antidumping measures are duties imposed on products exported at less than their normal value in the exporting countries. There was and still is controversy among economists on whether this practice should be condemned. After all, price discrimination, i.e. the ability to identify separate markets for a product and to charge a higher price in the market attaching greater utility to the product, is usually tolerated by competition law when the markets in question are located within national borders. Dumped products sold in a foreign market can benefit domestic consumers except in limited cases, such as predatory dumping, e.g. when differential prices are charged with the aim of driving domestic producers out of the market in order to ultimately raise them to monopolistic levels. On the other hand, dumping damages domestic producers of like products and it was the interest of the latter that was upheld by Art. VI of GATT in 1947. The article provided that products are exported at less than their normal value if their export price is less than the comparable price in the ordinary course of trade (a concept that the article failed to define) when destined for consumption in the exporting country or, in the absence of such domestic price, is less than the cost of production plus a reasonable addition for selling costs and profit.

The US antidumping statute provided that antidumping duties could be applied if imports occurred at less than fair value. The concept of fair value substantially coincided with the concept of normal value as outlined in the GATT. Although the US statute only provided for injury caused by dumping, whereas GATT Art. VI required material injury, affirmative decision in antidumping cases could not be taken for granted and resort to antidumping procedures was limited to individual cases of allegedly unfair competition from foreign firms. In other terms, it was not the main defence to protect declining domestic industries against foreign competition. Things, however, started to change in December 1974 when, in the middle of an unprecedented recession, the president was granted trade authority no longer limited to tariffs but incorporating the unexplored areas of non-tariff barriers. A trade-off was expected between the granting of authority and the strengthening of the defence for domestic industries that had to compete with inflows of foreign products or could not find outlets abroad. One trade-off was the introduction of antidumping rules which were stricter and more favourable to domestic firms, including a shorter deadline for determinations in antidumping proceedings, the right of judicial review of negative findings and, in ascertaining 'fair value', the possibility to disregard persistent sales of the investigated merchandise in the home market at prices below cost of production. Tightening the net allowed the US to accuse of unfair trade those foreign industries whose main fault was that they were able to successfully compete with US firms and to impose extra duties onto their exports. Thus, although the legal objective of antidumping and countervailing measures differed from that of safeguards, the former being directed against unfair trade, their economic objective tended to coincide, boiling down to protection from foreign competition through import restriction. However, antidumping did not have the limits of an escape clause: safeguards could only be implemented for limited periods, whereas antidumping had indefinite length once there was a positive finding. And whereas safeguards were subject to the executive's discretion, the quasi-judicial character of antidumping proceedings – in which the petitioner was a domestic entity and the defendants were foreign firms – ensured a binding result in case of positive findings.[57]

Apart from more favourable rules, a factor that increased the use of antidumping petitions was the depreciation of the dollar vis-à-vis other currencies and in particular the yen, which accelerated between 1976 and 1978 (Figure 1). In spite of the yen appreciation, which entailed a rise of the Japanese unit labour cost on a dollar basis (Figure 4), the merchandise trade gap with Japan soared between 1975 and 1978 (Table 5). Ito provides a convincing explanation pointing out that the yen appreciation was partially offset by the lower cost of imported components and, in particular, of raw materials most of which were priced in dollars, as well as by the adoption of partial pass-through practice in determining the price charged on export products. In order to keep the retail price constant in foreign markets so as not to lose market share, many Japanese firms lowered their profit margin for exports while maintaining or even increasing their profit margin on domestic sales.[58] The pricing to market system, which resulted in different prices in the domestic market and in the export market, unfortunately fell under the purview of the antidumping law whenever it injured domestic industries, which was not difficult to claim in a moment in which Japanese competition was becoming particularly effective not only in steel and motor vehicles but also in industrial plants and electronics. Thus, the rise in antidumping proceedings in the US was at the same time a by-product of the dollar devaluation and its complement, which made life harder to those foreign exporters who were disposed to pricing to market whenever their products effectively competed with domestic industries.

In 1976 nine antidumping investigations were initiated on automobile imports from Canada, France, West Germany, Italy, the UK, Belgium, Sweden and Japan, involving over $7 billion of imports. However, the investigations were discontinued after receipt of satisfactory price assurances from foreign manufacturers. Twenty-nine investigations were in progress at the end of 1977 involving trade for over $1,960 million. Almost two-thirds of them, involving $1.7 billion, concerned steel products, 70 per cent of which were from Japan.

In the European Community antidumping rules were first introduced by Council Regulation n. 458/68 of 5 April 1968, amended in 1973 and 1977. Some sixty antidumping proceedings were initiated under the mentioned Regulation, of which only five resulted in the imposition of antidumping duties as in most cases exporters subject to investigation signed price revision undertakings, that is, increased their export prices. In 1977 the Commission adopted antidumping rules specifically directed to products covered by the Treaty establishing the European Coal and Steel Community by introducing its Recommendation 77/320/ECSC, later modified in December to allow the imposition of provisional duties on steel imports not falling within a basic price system. Recommendation 77/320 and its amendment brought about a spate of self-limitation agreements with iron and steel producing countries. The foregoing seems, therefore, to indicate that also in the European Community antidumping measures were nothing but a disguised tariff or a threat of one, successfully transforming protection from unfair competition into a protectionist instrument.[59]

Within the import hindering class, four other kinds of measures came to the attention of the GATT parties during the Tokyo Round: customs valuation of imported goods, standards, import licensing and public procurement. Customs valuation, as exemplified by the ASP, could increase the assessed value of imported goods, thus leading to the imposition of higher duties. Standards, i.e. rules drafted to ensure that particular products possess certain physical, technical and health requisites to be marketed in a country, could be bent to exclude foreign products. Import licensing is the legal permission of import merchandises from foreign suppliers, either to implement trade restrictions or for statistical purposes. Although it did not prevent the entry of foreign goods, it could have a delaying effect. In the EC, Italy and later France were particularly keen on using it to make imports more difficult, thus rendering imported goods less marketable. Finally, the awarding of contracts for public works and for the purchase of goods and services by public authorities usually excluded tenders from foreign firms, resulting in a trade barrier. On the other hand, public procurements also provided a surreptitious means to subsidize domestic firms. The issue was not only an international trade problem. Within the EC, although the abolition of national restrictions in public procurements was already envisaged in the 1962 General Programmes and Directive 66/683 prohibited rules requiring the use of national products and the ban on foreign products in public procurement, it was only Directive 77/62 that, ten years later, adopted general rules that effectively made tendering across member states possible.

Up to this point the United States and the European Community seemed to be treading similar paths with regard both to the kinds of measures adopted and the objectives pursued. They parted company, however, as regards countervailing measures and subsidies. Along with antidumping investigations, the number of countervailing duty proceedings in the US increased in the stagflation years during which on the other side of the Atlantic the number and value of subsidization measures stepped up. In 1974 in the US four countervailing duty orders and a negative determination were issued. Five countervailing investigations were launched. In 1977 12 petitions were filed and 14 final determinations were made, 8 affirmative and 6 negative while 11 other investigations were in progress covering trade for $57.2 million. In 1978 18 final determinations were issued, 11 positive and 7 negative, while 20 investigations were pending. However, a relevant percentage of countervailing duties was temporarily waived in the course of multilateral trade negotiations until January 1979 under section 331 (a) of the Trade Act of 1974.

The increase in the number of investigations and affirmative decisions does not necessarily mean that countervailing measures had turned into a protectionist tool. It could be argued, as the Americans did, that countervailing measures were a necessary means to prevent unfair pressure on US industries as a result of more and more frequent trade-distorting practices adopted by other countries. On the other hand, American industries confronted by foreign competition, with the aid of the US trade courts, were able to expose to the countervailing authorities certain practices not condemned at the time by GATT rules. This was in particular the case of domestic subsidies. The first general US countervailing duty statute, the Tariff Act of 1897, only provided for the imposition of countervailing duties whenever a foreign government bestowed, directly or indirectly, any bounty or grant upon the exportation of any article or merchandise. The Tariff Act of 1922, however, widened the scope for countervailing measures covering any bounty or grant 'on manufacture or production as well as on exportation'. From 1922, therefore, subsidies that had no export-related performance requirements could also be considered countervailable. Until the 1960s the US administering authority had refrained from imposing duties to offset public support not related to exports. Things changed radically a few years later. In 1974 countervailing measures were imposed on rubber tyres produced by a French company, Michelin S.A., in a factory located in Nova Scotia, Canada, so as to benefit from a series of incentives offered by the provincial government. In this case, although most of the products would ultimately compete in the US market, the Canadian statutory provisions that allowed the countervailed subsidies in question provided no requirement of export capability for programme eligibility. Thus, the rationale for this kind of countervailing measure was that what is relevant is not the destination of the subsidy but the impact of subsidized export on the US market. And this test was made more severe for foreign exporters by the absence of a material injury requirement in the US statute.

Some import competing American industries tried to extend the boundaries of the US countervailing legislation without, however, receiving governmental endorsement. This was the case with consumer electronics, in particular colour television receivers, a sector targeted for export growth by the Japanese government in the 1960s, which made heavy inroads in the US market in the following decade. American firms petitioned for countervailing duty proceedings arguing that rebates of commodity tax on exports allowed by the Japanese authorities constituted subsidies. An analogous petition was made against EC rebates of the value-added tax (VAT) for steel exports. The Treasury Department issued a negative determination in line with a long-established practice in the US and in the GATT. However, US legislation was ambiguous on this issue and a leading American firm, the Zenith Radio Corporation, successfully appealed the negative determination in the Customs Court in 1976. In a rare instance, Japan and the EC joined forces claiming that classifying indirect tax rebates on exports as subsidies ran counter to GATT Art. VI. The message did not go unheeded and in 1977 the Court of Customs and Patent Appeals reversed the Customs Court decision. That same year the Committee to Preserve the American Television Industry filed an Escape Clause petition arguing that Japanese exports caused injury to the American domestic industry. The president agreed with the claim of injury with regard to colour televisions but did not deem that 'safeguard' was the appropriate remedy, directing instead the Special Trade Representative to negotiate an orderly marketing agreement with Japan, which, as noted above, was duly signed.[60]

The EC had a system under Articles 92 and 93 of the Treaty of Rome to monitor and eventually prohibit subsidies bestowed by its member states, which at that time was applied quite leniently, but had no regime to countervail subsidized imports from third countries comparable to that in force on the other side of the Atlantic.

The United States in its heavy use of countervailing proceedings could claim, in contrast to most of its trading partners, that it was not a subsidizer. Subsidies amounted to only 0.5 per cent of US GDP in 1970 and declined to 0.3 per cent in 1975 and 0.4 per cent five years later, although it is extremely likely that the United States did not include its public support to industries like civil transport aircraft and did not take into account the numerous measures offered by state and local authorities to attract investments.[61] Conversely, the EC member states not only started from a much higher basis but showed a marked upwards trend in their degree of subsidization: the EC average, which was 2 per cent of GDP in 1970, jumped to 2.9 per cent in 1975 and 3.2 per cent in 1980; in France and Italy the rate grew respectively from 2 per cent and 1.5 per cent in 1970 to 2.5 per cent and 3 per cent in 1980; in the UK the rate soared from 1.7 per cent in 1970 to 3.5 per cent five years later, declining to 2.3 per cent in 1980.[62] The Federal Republic was on the lower echelon with a rate of 1.7 per cent of GDP in 1970 and 2 per cent in 1975 and in 1980. German scholars, however, contend that after the first oil crisis public subsidization took on a new qualitative dimension amounting to 4–5 per cent of German GNP as subsidization, which before had concentrated on sectors of the economy traditionally considered as needing assistance, like mining and agriculture, now extended to many other sectors including shipbuilding and to a lesser degree, steel.[63] The same scenario characterized the other main Western European economies. In the UK the declining nationalized steel industry and the motor vehicle industry, where British Leyland was effectively state-owned though technically not nationalized, were heavily subsidized. In Italy, where the capital of most import-competing industries such as those in the steel, chemical and shipbuilding sectors was directly or indirectly controlled by the state, government-controlled firms would receive financial support from the owner. In France automobile, data-processing, pulp and paper, steel and watch industries received various forms of government aid.

The amount of domestic subsidization was in inverse relation with the competitiveness of the firms receiving subsidies, with their numbers and with the level of EC tariff protection.[64] This does not imply that government support policies necessarily reduced non-tariff protection. On the contrary, most of the cases described above indicate that financial support to industries hit by foreign competition was part of a scheme in which import restraints played a large role, whether through quotas, antidumping proceedings or licences. In some cases the granting of subsidies was not linked to the displacement caused by competing foreign products, as the subsidies were granted to encourage investments in underdeveloped areas by offsetting the greater cost of the investment, or were granted to compensate for extra costs brought about by stricter requirements imposed on some industries. Likewise subsidies were bestowed to prevent firms from having to resort to laying-off their employees. All these kinds of measures could always be accused of artificially expanding production and by so doing impinging on the normal play of the market. The accusation, therefore, could be easily made that whatever their avowed purpose, most public aid 'would shore up, and hence protect, weak industries or weak firms that found it difficult to face foreign competition'.[65]

The fact remains that, whatever their political persuasion, West European governments of the second half of the 1970s found it impractical to stop financial support to manufacturing industries and agriculture at a moment in which recovery could not steadily take off and unemployment was still high. When a few years later governments like those of Margaret Thatcher and Helmut Kohl came to power, though officially committed to freeing the economy from state interference or to balancing the budget, they found it difficult to reverse policy.

In short, though it may be precipitate to state that the increase in antidumping and countervailing proceedings on one side of the spectrum and in subsidies on the other was by itself clear evidence of rising protectionism, the foregoing demonstrates that there was an upwards trend in their use. The number of antidumping and countervailing proceedings increased and there is no denying that in many cases such proceedings were adopted to constrain imports regardless of their fair or unfair nature, stretching the boundaries established by GATT Art. VI. In Western Europe, though it is doubtful that the trend was limited to the eastern side of the Atlantic, public authorities intervened more frequently and more generously to buoy up industries that in the aftermath of the oil crisis were experiencing financial strains and were losing ground to foreign competitors.

4

The Tokyo Round

Following the Tokyo Declaration, three phases can be distinguished in the talks.

The first phase, which did not register any substantial progress in the negotiations went on until the signing into law of the Trade Act of 1974. A second phase, during the presidency of Gerald Ford, was marked by the conflicting perspectives of the US and EC on most main topics under discussion. The third stage saw the breakthrough and apparently satisfactory conclusion of the round during the Carter years.

The granting of negotiating authority to the US president under the Trade Act of 1974

The multilateral talks launched by the September 1973 Ministerial Conference in Tokyo were kept in a preparatory stage awaiting Congress's grant of negotiating authority to the US executive. The negotiating mandate was expected to provide a clear signal of the American stance in the negotiations as well as of the room for manoeuvre allowed to the executive. Fifteen months after the launch of the round and three months after Nixon's resignation, Congress cleared the bill on 19 December 1974, just before the end of the second session of the 93rd Congress and the bill was signed into law by Gerald Ford on 3 January 1975. The delay was formally caused by a peripheral controversy over restriction on Jewish emigration by the Soviet Union to which the administration wanted to grant MFN status, but actually it was the result of the declining authority of a presidency crippled by impeachment and by the deterioration of the American economy. It also concealed substantive issues of trade authority allocation on which the Senate's attitude was less compromising than the House's. The legislation, entitled the 'Trade Act of 1974', has been labelled as 'essentially liberal'.[1] This judgement can be accepted only with some caveats. The Act is divided into six Titles of which only the first, dealing with negotiating authority, can be labelled as 'essentially liberal', although its provisions were far from being unconditionally free-trade oriented and many of the administration's preferences to secure room for manoeuvre in the multilateral negotiations did not meet with unconditional Congressional acceptance. Many other Titles contained provisions aiming at unilaterally opposing alleged unfair trade practices by foreign competitors or directed to providing more protection to those sectors of the economy allegedly hit by foreign competition or to make quasi-judicial remedies already in force, like antidumping and countervailing measures, stricter, more effective and more easily accessible.[2] Indeed, although openly protectionist proposals, such as the Hartke and Burke bill were rejected, the legislation was adopted in a moment in which the economy was hit by the second recession in just four years and unemployment was increasing. The Senate Report pointed out that during the 1960s and early 1970s US pre-eminence in the world economy had declined as compared with Western Europe and Japan. It was then arguable that much of world economic history in the years following the Trade Expansion Act of 1962, considered the climax of the US drive to secure a freer and fairer world trade, 'has been unfavourable to this country, largely because of the antiquated rules of the international trade and monetary systems and the related lack of genuine cooperation and reciprocity in international economic relations'.[3]

Negotiating authority to the president was granted for tariff cuts, following the long-established rule of allowing the executive to negotiate cuts and implement them by self-executing presidential order. The Trade Act authorized the president to eliminate tariffs on goods carrying duties of 5 per cent or less and to reduce higher tariffs by as much as 60 per cent, subject to commensurate actions by other countries.

Things were much less simple with regard to non-tariff barriers, as in this area future international deals would overlap with often quite complex domestic rules, which, in most cases, till that moment had not been affected by international commitments, whereas domestic interest groups had swayed their draft.

The administration had proposed an arrangement, accepted by the House of Representatives, under which the president would give notice in advance to Congress of his intention to negotiate an agreement so as to allow lawmakers to express their views. After the negotiation the agreement would be submitted to Congress along with the implementing legislation, entering into effect if not rejected by a majority vote within 90 days. In short, Congress would have been given an advisory function plus a power of veto to be exercised in a short span, but no positive approval of the agreements was envisaged. This approach would have satisfied the other parties to the negotiations, afraid that the NTB agreements could be blocked or deprived of content by the US Congress in the ratification stage. The lot of the limited number of non-tariff issues dealt with in the Kennedy Round, the American Sale Price system in particular, did not bode well. Formally Congress maintained veto power, but this would have cast on it full and, even worse, open responsibility for scuttling a deal laboriously worked out by the United States and its trading partners.

The Senate was not satisfied with the arrangement as the quasi-automatic implementations of multilateral trade agreements would impinge on its power to regulate, and to regulate in detail, matters that had often quite a weight on the domestic economy. The implementation of a tariff barrier agreement would simply require the lowering of a duty. The implementation of an NTB agreement would often entail a complex grafting on the legislation already in place. On the other hand, it was clear that Congress could not have an autonomous role in negotiating with foreign countries. The compromise worked out envisaged a greater voice for Congress in shaping an international agreement that could satisfactorily be implemented in the domestic legislation, but no power of amendment or deferral. The Trade Act of 1974 thus required the president to notify Congress at least ninety days in advance before entering into an NTB agreement and, following such an agreement, to transmit a copy of it along with the draft of the implementing bill and a statement of the reasons as to how the agreement served the interests of the United States. Congress had ninety days (sixty for non-revenue bills) to decide on the legislation, but could not introduce amendments. This in practice meant that the Special Trade Representative had to work closely with the House Ways and Means Committee and the Senate Finance Committee during the transmittal phase. To this end delegates of both the House and Senate were accredited to the US delegation to the trade negotiations and the chairmen of the Ways and Means and Finance Committees were authorized to designate members to be official advisers of the delegation in Geneva.

The Trade Act also gave a direct role to interest groups in the NTB negotiations by creating a system of private sector committees to supply advice and information for US negotiators. The Act provided for the creation of an Advisory Committee for Trade Negotiations (ACTN) composed of forty-five members appointed by the president, representing labour, industry, agriculture, small business, consumer interests and the general public. The ACTN, presided over by the US Special Trade Representative, would convene in Washington and in Geneva as well. At a level below the ACTN the legislation called for the creation of general policy advisory committees for industry, labour and agriculture and for a series of advisory committees to be established at a sectoral level. Thus, the reform relieved Congress of the pressure of interest groups and arguably diminished the lawmakers' power as mediators of such interests in drawing up statutes. Conversely, the interest groups were now able to make their voice heard directly, becoming a major interlocutor of the executive, and of the Special Trade Representative in particular, in the course of the multilateral negotiations.

The stated overall objective of the trade negotiations was to obtain more open and equitable market access and the harmonization, reduction, or elimination of devices that distort trade in every area. The Senate Report stressed that, as far as was feasibly possible, the process of harmonization, reduction or elimination of agricultural trade barriers should be undertaken in conjunction with industrial trade liberalization.[4] This meant that in contrast with the EC perspective, although certain particular features of the farm sector could be recognized, this should not entail separate negotiations for agricultural trade. On the other hand, for some industrial sectors, such as steel, aluminium, electronics, chemicals and electrical machinery, sectoral negotiations could be carried out which should result in equivalent competitive opportunities for the developed countries within each sector. The Senate also made it clear that benefits and obligations of non-tariff barrier agreements should be limited to the parties of such agreements in order to encourage all trading nations to commit themselves and to avoid freelancing in the hope of obtaining benefits without reciprocal engagements.[5] Finally, the Trade Act directed the president to seek reform of the GATT to promote the development of an open, non-discriminatory and fair world economic system. Among these principles particular attention was given to the revision of the decision-making procedures of the GATT, the establishment of international procedures for consultation among countries on trade issues and for the resolution of commercial disputes, the reform of GATT Art. XIX on safeguard measures with the view to making it more flexible. In response to the particular difficulties of the economic situation in 1974, Congress also called for strengthening of the rules directed to assure access to supplies including procedures governing imposition of export controls and sanctions on those countries that denied fair and equitable access to supply sources. However, the Trade Act of 1974 and the reports of the Ways and Means Committee and of the Finance Committee were silent on issues such as customs valuation, public procurement, import restrictions and technical barriers to trade, which would figure prominently in the negotiations in Geneva.

Along with the draft of the US goals and strategies in the multilateral negotiations, the Trade Act set a series of domestic measures nominally directed at strengthening the protection of the US economy and of its industries against the pressure exerted by the international economic environment, whether its causes were labelled as unfair or otherwise.

As requested by the executive, the legislation relaxed the criteria for industries to be allowed relief from import competition, providing for an affirmative determination wherein the International Trade Commission (ITC) found that increased imports were a substantial cause of injury rather than a major cause as in previous laws.[6] The Act, under Section 122, also required the president in case of large balance of payments deficit to proclaim for up to 150 days corrective action, including import surcharges of up to 15 per cent and temporary quotas, unless he determined that such measures were contrary to the national interest.

Under Section 301 of the Act the president was given authority to retaliate against 'unjustifiable or unreasonable' foreign countries' policies or practices that burden or restrict US commerce, both in goods and services, or access to supplies, whether through high tariffs or non-tariff barriers, including subsidies and import and export quotas. The section offered no definition of the mentioned terms. However, the committee reports explained that the term 'unjustifiable' referred to restrictions which were illegal under international law or inconsistent with international obligations, while the term 'unreasonable' referred to restrictions which were not necessarily illegal but which nullified or impaired benefits accruing to the United States under trade agreements or which otherwise discriminated or burdened US commerce. Thus the meaning given by Congress to the word 'unreasonable' opened the door for affirmative findings even if no treaty or international law provisions were violated. The section allowed the president to suspend trade concessions, impose new higher tariff rates on a selective basis, or take other retaliatory actions, including the imposition of antidumping duties or countervailing measures or even exclusion orders which barred a product from being imported into the United States. Although any decision on unjustifiable or unreasonable restrictions was the executive's responsibility, the procedure of ascertainment could be initiated by the petition of individual parties seeking recourse against foreign actions adversely affecting their interests.

The Trade Act introduced a host of amendments – examined in the preceding chapter – to the 1921 Antidumping Act, which were directed to make the remedy more effective.[7] Time limits were also established for countervailing duty proceedings, thus preventing the Treasury Department, considered by the lawmakers as too soft in opposing foreign subsidization, from stretching out or shelving countervailing duty investigations.[8] On the other hand, the Trade Act of 1974 introduced a temporary provision that allowed the Treasury Department to waive countervailing duties during the trade negotiations. However, the House bill was amended by the Senate making the Secretary of the Treasury's discretionary authority conditional on three requirements aimed at acting as stick and carrot for other participants to the multilateral negotiations on subsidies: the foreign government had taken steps to reduce substantially or eliminate the adverse effect of the bounty or grant; there was a reasonable prospect that an NTB agreement would be negotiated; and the imposition of duties would be likely to jeopardize the satisfactory completion of the negotiations.

The Trade Act also tightened the rein in applying the Generalized System of Preferences in favour of developing countries. The statute contained several exclusions some of which were opposed by the administration. The exclusion from receiving generalized preferences concerned Communist countries as well as any country which entered into a cartel to withhold supplies of vital materials or to charge monopolistic prices, including first and foremost the OPEC members. The exclusion also applied to those countries that expropriated the property of US nationals and to those that applied reverse preferences to imports from other developed countries; that is the developing countries that had entered into a preferential agreement with the European Community.

Subjects of discussion in the initial stage of the Tokyo Round

The bestowal of negotiating authority on the US president signalled the effective start of the discussions but was far from entailing a breakthrough. On the other hand, as noted by Winham, despite the lack of overall progress, the early period of the Tokyo Round opened up a large range of areas for formal negotiations, as some of these areas had already been the subject of talks in the GATT even before the launch of the Tokyo Round.[9]

In February 1975 the Trade Negotiation Committee created six specialized subcommittees which conformed to the negotiating areas outlined in the Tokyo Declaration:

- group on tariff negotiations
- group on reduction or elimination of non-tariff measures and their trade-distorting effects
- group for the examination of the sector approach as a complementary negotiation technique
- group for the examination of the multilateral safeguard system
- group on agriculture negotiations
- group on tropical products negotiations.

Later in the year the non-tariff measures group was subcategorized into five subgroups: quantitative restrictions; technical barriers to trade; customs matters; subsidies and countervailing duties; government procurement. The agriculture group was subdivided into three subgroups: grains; meat; dairy products.

In most topics there were differences in attitudes between the two transatlantic trading partners. In others there was open disagreement that resulted in stalemate in the talks.

Many EC industries complained that a host of non-tariff measures on government procurements, quantitative restrictions, antidumping and countervailing proceedings as well as on product standards and customs assessment, had been lowering their foreign market share. The main target was the United States whose domestic legislation was accused of imposing undue burdens on foreign exporters. The directives issued by the EC Council for the GATT multilateral negotiations in February 1975, though, as admitted in the document introduction, did not aim at predefining a line of action on the detailed aspects of the negotiations, stressed the Community's stance on a series of negotiating issues.[10] In particular, for industrial customs tariffs the Council's objective was a significant lowering of duties which, however, was to lead to their harmonization, that is, resulting in the levelling of the differences between the maximum and the minimum rates in the various tariffs. As regards non-tariff barriers the directives stressed the need for a case-by-case approach concentrating on the measures likely to create the greatest obstacles to international trade. The directives also made clear that, at least in some cases, the Most-Favoured Nation principle should be made conditional on the participation in the agreements.

With specific reference to countervailing measures, the EC Council stressed that such measures should be applied by all GATT parties, including the United States, only when they were fully justified in terms of already existent GATT rules and consistent with the injury criterion established by GATT Art. VI. In exchange of a satisfactory agreement on countervailing duties the Community was willing to negotiate rules on direct export subsidies for industrial products other than basic materials. Reading between the lines it meant that the Community was not disposed to a deal on agricultural subsidies or on domestic subsidies even if applied to manufactured products. On agriculture the directives emphasized that the tensions of the previous two years had turned a period of surplus characterized by increasing competition among exporters into a period of scarcity marked by concern over security of supply, which showed the need for an expansion of trade based on stable world markets. This goal was to be achieved through a set of multilateral agreements covering the main commodities, i.e. wheat, maize, sorghum, barley, rice, sugar and dairy products, and involving the major producing and consuming countries. For dairy products the agreements had to be based on the establishment of minimum and maximum safeguard prices and on preferential purchase and sale obligations, while for the other products, price arrangements were to be accompanied by coordinated national stockpiling policies. For products other than those subject to international agreements, the expansion of trade had to result from coordinated actions from importers and exporters directed at securing the orderly functioning of the market.

For the United States the real problem was dumping and subsidization and therefore, alleged inconsistencies of its regime with GATT rules would become irrelevant once a satisfactory solution to the mentioned trade-distorting practices had been found. In contrast to the European Community, the US negotiators called for stricter regulation not only of export subsidies but also of domestic support measures, even prohibiting those able to significantly distort trade. In the US view the CAP was unquestionably trade-distorting and had to be reformed. The US was also interested in starting multilateral discussion on standards. The US interest was spurred by the conclusion in the late 1960s of a European arrangement for the harmonization and certification of electronic components – the European Electrical Standards Coordinating Committee (CENEL) agreement – which, according to the American electronic industry, constituted a non-tariff barrier as there was no way for firms of states not parties to the agreement to obtain the mark of conformity. Although a conference held in London in June 1971 gave American electronics producers the opportunity to participate in the CENEL arrangement, the US was afraid that similar regional arrangements might hinder its exports, in particular to Western Europe. For their part, the Europeans held the view that the United States was unwilling to adopt international standards. The negotiators, however, took advantage of the existence of a draft code prepared before the start of the Tokyo Round, which was used as a starting point for discussions.

As regards duties the US and the EC differed on the weight to give to tariff cuts relative to tariff harmonization. Proposals for a general approach to tariff reductions were tabled in 1976. The United States, which had the highest and most frequent tariff peaks, had gradually accepted the idea of a formula aimed at duty reduction and harmonization but was recalcitrant to accept a significant curtailment of its highest tariffs. The tariff-cutting formula proposed by the United States envisaged that the percentage tariff reduction (Y) should be equal to one and one-half times the initial tariff rate (X) plus 50, but with a ceiling of 60 per cent of the previous duty rate: $Y = 1.5 X + 50; Y \leq 60\% X$.[11] This reflected the limit imposed by the Trade Act of 1974 which allowed the president to reduce duties over 5 per cent by a maximum of 60 per cent of the 1 January 1975 rate.

The US proposal was not welcomed by the other parties in the negotiation. The European Community in particular noted that, although the formula suggested by the US delegation contained an element of harmonization, the 60 per cent ceiling considerably limited its effectiveness.[12] Indeed, if it was undisputed that the formula nominally cut the highest tariffs deeper, the gap with average or low rate duties remained. For instance, applying the 60 per cent maximum reduction rate, a 25 per cent duty would be reduced to a still high 10 per cent but a 6 per cent duty would be reduced to a modest 2.5 per cent, ineffective in discouraging imports. The Community, therefore, contended that the formula put forward by the United States, particularly with regard to industrial products, would impact prevalently where, as in the case of the EC, a high concentration of moderate tariffs could be found, that is, on those sectors that had already attained a non-negligible level of liberalization. It would be much less effective where, as in the case of the US, there was still a high proportion of protective duties and consequently international trade could not achieve its potential. What was needed in the EC view was a formula aimed at significant tariff reduction and harmonization but not fixed at a level where it would lose credibility being, consequently, eroded by a host of derogations and exceptions.[13]

For its part the Commission suggested a formula based on a reduction rate equal to the initial tariff ($Y = X$) repeated several times. However, by the beginning of 1977 most European countries, including the EC member states, were showing preference for the proposal put forward by the Swiss delegation which was based on the following formula: $Z = 14 \times X/(14 + X)$, where Z is the final duty and X is the initial duty.[14] The Swiss formula had a series of advantages. It was simple and direct as it determined the new tariff rate rather than the reduction rate and above all it was very effective in achieving harmonization since the reduction rate rose steadily as the initial duty increased. For instance, applied to an initial 5 per cent duty the formula gave a 3.68 per cent final duty, with a 26.32 per cent reduction rate, while applied to a 21 per cent duty it gave a final 8.4 per cent duty, with a 60 per cent reduction rate. On the other hand, the formula ensured that for very high initial duties, i.e. those above 100 per cent, final duty would not fall significantly below a 14 per cent ceiling.

The US and the EC were initially at variance on the methods to be used for determining the value of imported goods for the purpose of imposing duties. GATT Art. VII required customs valuation to be based on the 'actual value of imported goods', i.e. the actual price at which the product is offered for sale in the ordinary course of trade under fully competitive conditions, but it did not shed light on the methodology to be followed for the assessment. The EC member states followed the Brussels Convention on valuation of goods and, along with most participants in the Tokyo Round, assessed imports according to the Brussels Definition of Value (BVD). Under this method, the value for customs purposes should be the normal market price, defined as the price that goods would fetch on sale in the open market between a buyer and a seller independent of each other. Other countries, among which the United States, followed different systems. The United States accused the BVD of being based on a notional approach, focusing on what the value would or should be rather than on what it was.[15] However, the US regime was not an example of administrative simplicity as it allowed for a multitude of assessment criteria according to needs and products, which could be basically grouped in five methods of valuation in order of preference: export value (actual export price of freely offered goods); foreign value (price in the exporting country's market); United States value (price of comparable imported products in the US); cost of production (estimated cost of production plus profit); and American sale price (price of comparable goods produced in the United States). As previously noted, the US executive had on many occasions called for the repeal of such a method, but Congress had denied its assent. However, by 1975 the main beneficiary of the method, the chemical industry, had signalled its willingness to accept the repeal of the American Selling Price (ASP) in exchange for higher duties and the US customs authority was arguing that life would be easier if a simplification of the existing methods were carried out. Also the EC Commission had started to view a multilaterally agreed customs valuation reform as an opportunity for strengthening its grip on the functioning of the customs administration in the Community. Indeed, although a common tariff regime was already in place, its administration continued to be carried out by the customs services of the member states and the BVD appeared to give them discretion in following their traditional paths on evaluation.

Both the United States and the European Community, as major exporters of finished and semi-finished products, had an interest in an agreement that could secure outlets in a new main section of the developed countries' economies: public procurement. Negotiations on public procurements were already carried on in the Organisation for

Economic Cooperation and Development and many member states believed that they could be continued in the OECD in parallel with the GATT talks. The prospective agreement would then be included in the Tokyo Round final package and would be opened for accession by the GATT parties that were not members of the Paris Organization. The major aim of the European Community in the negotiations had been, long before the start of the Tokyo Round, the abolition of the 1933 Buy American Act which provided that goods purchased with federal funds for government use or for construction of public works must be of domestic origin as long as the American firms' bid did not exceed their competitors' offered prices by a given percentage (originally 25 per cent and later 6 per cent, except for Department of Defense procurements). The European Commission and the EC member states also feared that the United States would try to limit its commitments appealing to national security reasons, or arguing that many groups of potential buyers were not under federal jurisdiction or belonged to the private sector even though they exercised public functions, while many American firms could bid for public procurements within the European Community through their subsidiaries in the EC member states. On the other hand, the Community was handicapped in its negotiating position by the lack of a general discipline on public procurement bids among its member states. It was only in December 1976 that a draft Directive submitted by the Commission was finally approved by the EC Council, with an effective date in 1978.

As was to be expected, most of the skirmishes concerned agriculture. Here, the European Community contended that agriculture had a unique position in the world market and that multilateral negotiations should focus on the stabilization of the market for the main farm products. Conversely, the United States, though recognizing that the sector had its peculiarities and trade stabilization was important, argued that in the long run market equilibrium would be brought about by liberalization of world trade and, therefore, by the elimination of protective barriers and distorting subsidies.[16] The creation in February 1975 of an 'agriculture' group within the Trade Negotiations Committee (TNC) was a favourable starting point for the Community. There was, however, the problem of the relationship of this group with the other groups in the TNC and in particular with the group on non-tariff measures, whose jurisdiction would also cover import restrictions and subsidies. Before the formal establishment of the 'agriculture' group, France, the main producer and exporter in the Community, had requested that the EC negotiators should make a declaration on the role of the prospective group, stating that it should have 'responsabilité globale et exclusive' (global and exclusive responsibility) on farm issues. However, a softer statement proposed by the Commission, to be circulated by 'note verbale', was finally agreed by the EC member states which assigned to the group 'responsabilité globale et principale' (global and main responsibility).[17] The position of the United States was that negotiations on agriculture should take place primarily in the groups on tariff and non-tariff measures and other functional groups, on the assumption that the objective of the negotiations in agriculture and industry alike was liberalization of trade restraints and that this task could best be accomplished through an across-the-board approach to these issues. In May 1976 a compromise seemed to have been reached according to which the agriculture group would treat tariff and non-tariff measures relating to agriculture in conjunction with the work in the groups on tariff and non-tariff measures.[18] The United States interpreted the compromise as allowing any participant to the round to raise a matter relating to agriculture in other groups, thus ruling out exclusive jurisdiction for the 'agriculture' group. As expected, the EC rejected such an interpretation. Subsequent attempts to break the deadlock through a compromise agreement did not succeed.

The same kind of problem about objectives and relations with other negotiating instances emerged in each of the three subgroups on grains, meat and dairy products. The disagreement was particularly manifest in the grains subgroup where the Community proposed the negotiation of a comprehensive international grains agreement that would stabilize prices within a wide band by means of stocks operated by the participating countries, whereas the US along with the other main producers saw trade expansion and liberalization as the major goal.[19]

The relaunch of the multilateral negotiations under the Carter administration

The defusing of the agriculture controversy

The advent of the Carter administration and the nomination of a new Special Representative for Trade Negotiations, Robert Schwarz Strauss, an accomplished lawyer in fields not directly related to international trade, but also a cunning politician with long-standing good relations with Congress members, meant the relaunch of the multinational negotiations. It also meant an agreement with the European Community that involved the US renouncing its efforts to significantly liberalize trade in agriculture by opening up the EC market and dismantling the CAP. Various factors can explain, also from a rational viewpoint, this turn in US strategy. Firstly, if the United States wanted the commitment of its main trading partner to the 'Locomotive' approach to sustain growth without trade disequilibrium and consequent currency instability, progress towards a mutually satisfactory deal on trade issues, based on perceived reciprocity, was a cornerstone in fostering wider cooperation. By the same token, prolonging the round stalemate on an issue to which the other main party in the negotiations appeared to give paramount importance, thus risking non-cooperation on other areas, was something to be avoided. Secondly, the need for improvement of the trade balance and for greater opportunities for those sectors with higher competitive capacity did not involve, or at least no longer involved, an enhanced contribution from agriculture. Certainly, as noted after the completion of the round by the Secretary for Agriculture, Bob Bergland, in contrast to the non-agricultural trade balance which had been in deficit for most of the decade, agricultural trade had posted a surplus for over 15 years and this surplus had been rocketing since 1973.[20] The share of US agricultural exports over world farm exports grew from 12 per cent in 1971 to over 16 per cent six years later.[21] But all this was due to the high productivity of American agriculture, assisted by a set of favourable circumstances, including the devaluation of the dollar, and so the achievement did not appear to be conditional on a legal environment guaranteeing trade liberalization and the curbing of trading partners' protection and support policy. Besides this, room for further expansion was predictably not unlimited. From the 1950–4 base period to 1977 world production of all goods, agricultural and non-agricultural, had more than tripled in volume, while the volume of farm production had grown 75–80 per cent. During the same period world agricultural trade had nearly tripled in volume, but the volume of American farm exports had almost quadrupled.[22] No doubt, less than 6 years later the scenario would have completely changed and with it the US attitude, but in 1977 the main problems concerned industrial trade and it was there that substantial gains had to be speedily sought.

In April 1977 during the talks that Strauss had in Brussels with Wilhelm Haferkamp and Finn Olav Gundelach, vice-presidents of the Commission respectively responsible for External Relations and Agriculture, agreement was reached on the need to conclude the GATT negotiations as soon as possible on the basis of an overall compromise embracing all the areas of the negotiations. A month later the heads of state and government participating in the Downing Street Summit stated that continuing economic difficulties made it essential to achieve the objectives of the Tokyo Round negotiations and 'to negotiate a comprehensive set of agreements to the maximum benefit of all'. As regards agriculture, the participants committed themselves to a mutually acceptable approach that would achieve increased expansion and stabilization of trade and greater assurance of world food supplies. The commitment made no further explicit reference to liberalization. In June and July the United States and the EC tabled convergent proposals.

The new terms of negotiations agreed upon by the two parties relied on an offer and request approach, covering both tariff and non-tariff barriers, with reference to single farm products. Lists of requests had to be submitted by 1 November 1977, but they could be modified and additional lists could be submitted as the negotiations proceeded. Offers had to be tabled by 15 January 1978.[23] The formula simply meant that concessions, mostly in the form of tariff reductions and quota increases or repeals, should concern single products of interest for the parties involved in the negotiation. No agreement implying the general framework of agricultural trade was scheduled. Thus, no general reform of the various kinds of support, either in the United States or in the Community, was required. There was certainly the possibility that the negotiations on subsidies and countervailing measures could also address agriculture, but, given the rather vague GATT provisions concerning farm subsidization and the resistance of the Community negotiators to an agreement going beyond the border of trade in non-primary products, there was no likelihood that any significant provision on farm trade could be agreed.

On the other hand, discussions for a comprehensive arrangement of the market continued in the three product areas covered by the subgroups on grains, meat and dairy products, although relevant negotiations were conducted outside the Tokyo Round framework. In particular, negotiations for a new International Wheat Agreement (IWA) were conducted in the International Wheat Council (IWC) under the auspices of the United Nations Conference on Trade and Development (UNCTAD) between late 1977 and the early weeks of 1979, during which period the GATT subgroup suspended discussions on this topic. As the Wheat Trade Convention negotiated during the Kennedy Round had soon collapsed when in 1968–9 contraction of demand, coupled with unexpected abundance of supply, resulted in a decline of price below the minimum level set by the arrangement, a new IWA was established in 1971, but with no pricing provisions.

The negotiations in the IWC under the aegis of the UNCTAD offered the advantage of more active participation of the developing countries than in the GATT and the presence of important members of the wheat market like Russia which were not GATT members. China, however, did not take part in the negotiations.

The Carter administration, which was more willing to explore an arrangement on wheat than its Republican predecessor, saw the IWC as an appropriate forum in which to negotiate an arrangement with stabilization, food security and burden sharing, leaving the issues of subsidization and access to the GATT negotiations.[24] In spite of these favourable premises, the IWA Conference, whose work officially started in February 1978, soon got bogged down in a multitude of issues on which the participants were not able to find practical trade-offs.[25] A consensus was quite soon reached that the operative mechanism for the Wheat Trade Convention should be a system of nationally held reserves whose accumulation and release should be triggered by the movement of price indicators specified in the convention. Accumulation of reserves would occur when the indicator fell to a pre-agreed low level and release would occur when the indicator rose to a high level. However, disagreements soon emerged on the level of reserves and on the minimum price for their build-up. Thus the IWA Conference concluded unsuccessfully in February 1979. For a moment the US and Canada together with Argentina considered an arrangement which would have excluded the importers but the Carter administration, hostile to an agreement that could be seen as a cartel by consumer nations, among which developing countries were the majority, abandoned the proposal.[26]

As regards dairy products, in late 1977 two proposals were put forward by the EC and New Zealand which led to a draft arrangement. The draft originally included such areas as maximum and minimum prices, but such provisions were dropped in 1978. On bovine meat the discussions were based on proposals put forward by Australia and the EC in late 1977. In particular the EC proposal called for a multilateral framework arrangement which would provide for an information and surveillance system, multilateral consultations in crisis situations and consensus recommendations for joint action by all meat traders. The proposal also envisaged a framework of bilateral or plurilateral agreements between exporters and importers, including commitments on both export behaviour (i.e. voluntary restraints and export price agreements) and import behaviour (i.e. actions to improve conditions of import). The idea, however, was abandoned.

The removal of one of the main stumbling blocks in the negotiations paved the way to negotiating achievements in some other sectors of the Geneva talks, although in others progress was slower and more uncertain.

Industrial tariffs and customs valuation

During the talks with his counterparts in the EC Commission Strauss made a prudent but clear reference to the need for substantial tariff reduction with a sufficient degree of harmonization, thus making it implicitly clear that the US was willing to improve on its 1976 proposal. By 1978 only two main issues remained: which items were to be excluded from the application of the Swiss formula, and whether a parameter other than 14 – for instance, a parameter resulting in a lower level of approximation – should be adopted. But these issues turned out to be thorny.

By the beginning of 1978 substantial progress had been achieved on the customs valuation issue. During 1976 and the first half of the following year, in the course of a series of visits from European Commission officials to Washington and debates within the Commission and among the member states, the EC gradually changed its stance in favour of the 'positive' concept, that is, the price at which imported goods are in fact sold under specified conditions, which was at the basis of the US customs system. The problem was that the 'positive' concept was at the basis of just one of the measurement criteria followed by the US customs statute which provided nine methods of valuation, some of which, the ASP in particular, were notoriously used as a protectionist device. In November 1977 the European Community submitted a draft customs valuation code which, as the EC negotiators did not fail to point out, was based on a 'positive' rather than a 'notional' approach.[27] The proposal put forward by the EC, which actually was a compromise between the two systems, adopted the price paid or payable for imported goods as the primary base for evaluation, even if the buyer and seller were related so long as such a relationship did not give rise to a non-allowed price reduction. If this method could not be applied, the proposal provided for a set of subsidiary criteria (price of identical goods; price of similar goods; price of the imported goods sold to an independent buyer less commissions and various costs) to be applied hierarchically. The draft also carefully listed the methods that should not be applied: the cost of production of the goods; the selling price in the country of importation of similar or comparable goods produced in that country; the price of identical, similar or comparable goods on the domestic market of the country of exportation; and the price of identical, similar or comparable goods sold to another country. It is to be noted that some of the forbidden methods were part of the array of valuation criteria envisaged by the US legislation. The draft also stated that valuation procedures should not be used for antidumping purposes.

The EC proposal was favourably received overall and became the basis for the following negotiations.[28] However, sources of disagreement remained in areas like the need for separate rules for developing countries and methods for dispute settlement and a particularly thorny issue was found in the area of transactions between related parties.

Government procurement

The negotiators in the 'government procurement' subgroup were able to make substantial progress also because a lot of preparatory work had been done in the OECD where the negotiations involved the individual countries of Western Europe and America plus Japan. The United States supported the transfer of the negotiations to the Tokyo Round deeming that a larger forum would provide greater opportunities for trade-offs and settlement, while some EC member states, in particular France, opposed the move.[29] The EC Commission supported the transfer, firstly because it was the Community negotiator in the GATT forum, whereas the OECD negotiations were conducted by the single EC member states and secondly because its role in the GATT negotiations provided it with a better opportunity to push through a Directive for the coordination of public procurement procedures all over the Common Market.[30]

A first draft of the code was circulated in December 1977, followed by a second draft in July 1978. Progress was made on the issues of transparency, tender procedure and the value threshold for the application of the code, although some differences were not settled. During the negotiations efforts were made to establish a threshold low enough to accomplish the goal of opening up the market but high enough not to cause difficulties to the authorities in the signatory countries. The United States favoured a low value threshold deeming that American companies could benefit from the fact that foreign procurement contracts tended to be much lower in value than those in the United States. Other industrialized nations, among which the European Community, which had set a minimum threshold of approximately $250,000 in its good procurement Directive, favoured a higher value threshold.[31] Tender procedures remained a difficult issue till the end of the negotiations. The US proposal provided for two types of tender, 'public' (formal) bidding and 'informal' (negotiated or sole-sourced) bidding.[32] The EC along with Japan, in line with their domestic practice, favoured a tripartite system with 'open', 'selective' and 'single' tenders.[33] The open tender allowed all interested parties to bid, while in selective tenders only invited suppliers could do so. In single tendering procedures, permitted only in few cases, governmental bodies could deal with single suppliers. The disputes over transparency were resolved quite quickly. The United States pressed on this issue feeling that its procurement procedures were more open, and therefore fairer, than those of other industrialized countries, among which the EC member states and Japan. The thorniest issue remained the determination of the entities subject to the code. The EC was not disposed to make commitments on international tendering in areas such as energy, transportation and telecommunications. The United States, in turn, was not willing to extend the agreement to state and local government bodies many of which had enacted their own 'Buy American' laws. The July 1978 draft overcame the problem by adopting a system of offers and requests whereby each country would notify the others of those entities in its own country that would be subject to the code and those entities in other countries it would like to see covered.[34]

Standards and licences

The negotiations on technical barriers to trade went quite smoothly and the draft code tabled in May 1977 was similar in content to the text finally approved two years later also because the subject was rather technical and did not have a direct impact on sensitive issues. The negotiations, which covered such areas as testing and certification by governmental bodies, packaging, labelling and marking of origin, resulted in the basic agreement that signatories to the code would refrain from using standards as obstacles to trade. Substantial progress was also made on drawing up a code directed at preventing licences from being used as a non-tariff barrier.

Subsidies, countervailing duties and antidumping measures

Progress in subsidies and countervailing measures was slow, but by the end of 1977 the United States and the European Community were able to draw up a heavily bracketed 'outline of an approach' in which, although reiterating their viewpoints, some common ground was found.[35] The United States aimed at extending subsidy regulation to domestic support to non-primary products and at clarifying the rules on agricultural export subsidies in a way that could rein in their use. Although the US had already accepted the idea that causation of injury was necessarily to be part of an agreement on countervailing measures, it was not disposed to allow that subsidization should be the main, or even worse, the sole cause of injury and if the prospective code were not to reform the provision of GATT Art. VI, according to which injury was to be 'material', this term should be interpreted restrictively. The European Community was wary of commitments that could endanger its own and member states' policies to support industry in a presumptively limited period of difficulty, or in need of restructuring and policies to encourage business to locate to depressed regions. This had been even more necessary since 1975 because the recession had been followed by slow recovery and the unemployment rate remained high. After all, the adjustment assistance provided by the US government to industries and communities hit by foreign competition could be considered a form of subsidization and state authorities were not loath to offer incentives to attract business. On the other hand, the Community judged that, as material injury was already required by GATT Art. VI for the imposition of antidumping and countervailing duties, there was no reason to view it as a bargaining chip in the negotiations, nor had it any sympathy for a watered-down interpretation of the requirement lest it allow leeway to the US authorities in their investigations against imported products accused of being dumped or subsidized.

The 'outline of an approach' did not explicitly mention domestic subsidies, but confined itself to state that agreement should be sought not to use export subsidies on non-primary products and that an updated list of prohibited subsidies should be drawn up. The provisions on agricultural subsidies proposed by each delegation were bracketed by the other as the negotiators did no more than restate the traditional positions of the United States and the European Community. As reported by two former high-ranking officers in the US delegation, the United States proposed a Supplementary Understanding on Internal Subsidies which stated that signatories would 'seek to avoid the use of subsidy practices in a manner that causes serious prejudice to the interests of other signatories' and provided an illustrative list of subsidies that could have an impact on the interests of other countries.[36] The proposal was not accepted by the other negotiators in the group. However, during the run-up to the Bonn Summit a new 'outline of an arrangement' was put forward by the US and EC delegations together with the delegations of Canada, Japan and the Nordic countries.[37] The new outline recognized that subsidies other than export subsidies were widely used as important instruments for the promotion of social and economic objectives of national policy and recognized the right of signatories to implement such subsidies, but contained in an Annex a list of internal subsidy practices which might have an adverse effect on the trade and production of other signatories. As was to be expected, the list was in brackets. On the other hand, as regards countervailing measures, requirements that subsidized products should be a principal cause or an important contributing factor of injury were also presented in brackets.

Aircraft

A late arrival in the negotiations was a proposal tabled by the United States for the elimination of tariffs and substantial reduction of non-tariff barriers on aircraft between the US and its main competitors on aircraft exports, i.e. the EC, Japan, Canada and Sweden. Although the United States was the leader in the market, competition from the above-mentioned countries, quite often providing strong financial support to their national companies' production and export, was starting to make itself felt. The US was convinced that tariffs were not a serious obstacle to a continued high level of exports but non-tariff barriers could represent a threat. In return for the elimination of its 5 per cent duty on aircraft it called, therefore, for effective discipline on non-tariff measures going beyond the general agreements under negotiation in the round. The kind of measures the United States wished to subject to strict discipline included government-directed procurements, governmental subsidies, licence restrictions and mandatory subcontracts.

Naturally, the United States failed to notice that major manufacturers of aircraft like Boeing could receive a boost from their governments if their activities also embraced military equipment through sole-sourced bidding for high value contracts and R&D financing.

On 13 July 1978 the delegations of the main trading nations issued what they called a 'framework of understanding on the major elements of a comprehensive package for the Tokyo Round', which was to be 'a reasonable basis for completing a mutual agreement in the weeks ahead'.[38] The document was endorsed three days later at the Bonn Summit by the heads of state and government who also set a deadline for the conclusion of the negotiations on 15 December 1978. The deadline, designed to add further impetus to the talks, proved too optimistic. The 'framework of understanding' took stock of the progress achieved but also of the work that was yet to be done. The main differences concerned the prospective codes on subsidies and countervailing duties and on safeguards where the proposals on actions against individual countries put forward by the EC were facing stark resistance from the developing countries. As regards industrial tariffs, though the delegations agreed on the approach to achieve a substantive harmonized reduction of tariffs, generally following the Swiss formula, they were still negotiating reciprocal adjustments in their initial offers involving improvements as well as exceptions.

Within the European Community, France feared that the articles of the subsidy and countervailing measures code on the exportation of primary products could result in curbing farm exports which had an increasingly important role in improving its merchandise trade balance. France, with various degrees of support from the other member states, was not prepared to accept stricter discipline on domestic subsidies and in particular on a list of domestic subsidization measures that were likely to cause serious prejudice to the trade interest of other GATT parties. The British Labour government shared the French misgivings while Germany, though not reluctant to provide financial help to those industries that most suffered from the sluggish economic recovery, favoured a more flexible approach.

On the other side of the Atlantic, at a moment in which imports were by far exceeding exports, despite the ongoing devaluation of the dollar, Congress felt that concessions on countervailing measures should be subject to commitments to avoid any kind of subsidization, either domestic or export oriented, that could hinder US trade or impair American industries. In its view it seemed that other parties to the multilateral negotiations, nominally the EC, were dragging their feet on accepting a fair deal. The Trade Act of 1974 authorized the Secretary of the Treasury to waive the imposition of countervailing duties for a four-year period ending on 2 January 1979, one year prior to the expiration of the president's overall negotiating authority. Congress simply refused to renew the authorization. The imports found to be subsidized amounted to about $600 million and were mostly agricultural products from the European Community.

The move provoked a firm response from the EC side. Wilhelm Haferkamp, vice-president of the Commission, in a letter addressed to Robert Strauss in September made it clear that the imposition of countervailing duties on EC exports would precipitate a commercial war of considerable dimension that would prevent the Community from concluding the Tokyo Round.[39] Since the threat of pending countervailing measures was not removed, despite the goodwill pressure exerted by the US executive on Congress, the Commission's step was followed by an apparently more conciliatory public statement from the president of the Council of the Community announcing that 'in spite of the serious decision taken in Congress', the Community would continue the talks to prepare the way for the conclusion of the negotiations on the understanding, however, that 'the continued application of the waiver, even after 3 January 1979, is guaranteed'.[40] The US Special Representative managed to keep the negotiations on track. In November, in a series of visits to European capitals and meetings in Geneva, Strauss convinced his European counterparts that the US executive would introduce legislation in the opening days of the new Congress session and would take any appropriate measure to avoid the disruption of normal trade flow. The law temporarily extending the executive's authority to waive countervailing duties was signed by Carter on 3 April 1979.

In its report submitted to the Council of the Community in late December 1978, the Commission argued that the conditions for signing a comprehensive agreement on the various negotiating items had not yet been established.[41] Although most codes, including customs valuation and standards, could be signed and significant progress towards the EC position had been secured in the negotiations on subsidy and countervailing measures, further talks were needed in other areas. Apart from safeguards, where there was no prospect of a prompt deal, on government procurements there were still differences on both the government purchasing entities and the value level of contracts to be covered by the code. As regards the Aircraft Agreement, if a deal on zero import duties seemed near, the US desire for a series of additional clauses governing the degree of government involvement in the manufacture and sale of aircraft was regarded with suspicion by the Commission.

As regards tariffs, the Commission related that progress had been made in securing possible improvements of US offers on textiles and chemicals, but that a full additional evaluation of the offers had not been completed and pending further discussions both parties had agreed that reaching a satisfactory overall balance was not yet possible. On the other hand, in the case of Japan, even though additional offers were forthcoming, they did not include significant concessions in areas of interest for the Community, such as textiles, leather goods and processed agricultural products. Since the additional offers were accompanied by a number of possible withdrawals, there was no prospect for real improvement at that stage.

It was only in a subsequent communication sent to the Council of Ministers at the end of February 1979 that the Commission claimed that conditions were ripe for a GATT agreement as, viewing the negotiating package as a whole, it was equitable and balanced and overall was advantageous for the European Community.[42] According to the Commission, the agreement on tariffs would offer much greater access to new markets for EC producers, while the EC concessions were moderate and would be gradually introduced over a long span of years. As regards non-tariff barriers, a series of gains was to be achieved, from the repeal of the ASP and of the Wine Gallon Assessment method to the curtailment of the Buy American Act in those sectors covered by the Government Procurement Agreement and to the acceptance of the 'material injury' principle in countervailing measures proceedings by the US authorities. After a delay of over a month, the Council gave the Tokyo Round Agreements its green light in April.

The US executive, which in mid-December had reached a comprehensive understanding with Japan on issues under negotiation in the Tokyo Round, had to appease Congress on sensitive tariff issues. Indeed, if Congress was barred from introducing amendments on the agreements to be signed in Geneva, nevertheless it had the definitive word on any non-tariff agreement. If there was no hope for a comprehensive settlement on agriculture satisfying the expectations of the powerful farm lobby, and if the outcome of the negotiations on subsidies only partially met the expectations of key areas of American industry, no ground was to be given on tariff and quota protection for sectors threatened by foreign competition or on countervailing measures. The US government by the end of December felt that the balance of concessions and achievements negotiated in Geneva would not meet with opposition from the lawmakers and on 4 January notified Congress of its intention to enter into MTN agreements, according to the procedures envisaged by the Trade Act of 1974. In the event, in the following three months the executive had to appease some interest groups with powerful lobbies in Congress, textiles and steel industries in particular. An agreement, made public on 15 February, was reached with the unions and employers of the textile industry in which the administration pledged to control disruptive import surges, to negotiate bilateral agreements with new emerging suppliers like China, and to continuously monitor textile imports on a global basis. Although no comparable overt arrangement was made with the steel industry, the administration had to be particularly attentive to the industry's insistence on a minimal injury test and on stricter rules on antidumping and countervailing proceedings. The executive had also to take heed of the chemical industry's call for more moderate tariff cuts on some of the products in the list negotiated in Geneva.

The results of the round

On 12 April 1979 the heads of key delegations accepted the documents embodying the results of the negotiations, thus concluding the round in substance. Two protocols containing tariff concessions were signed in June and November. By December the main parties to the negotiations signed or ratified the codes or agreements on subsidies, antidumping, licensing, product standards, meat, dairy, government procurement, customs valuation and civil aircraft. For each of the codes a committee was established with the task of ascertaining their correct implementation and solving disputes and as a forum wherein the contracting parties could discuss amendments and negotiate enlargements of the scope of the agreements.

Industrial tariffs

The tariff reductions negotiated in the Tokyo Round were apparently impressive. According to GATT estimates, the schedules of concessions annexed to two protocols signed in the second half of 1979 affected a total value of trade of over $155 billion measured on MFN imports in 1977.[43] Concessions by the European Community, the United States, Canada, Japan and five EFTA members covered imports for $141 billion. Those agreed on industrial products covered about $127 billion, 90 per cent of the industrial trade among the major developed countries in 1977. The weighted-average tariff on manufactured products of the industrialized countries was bound to decline from 7 per cent to 4.7 per cent, amounting to a third of tariff collection. The adoption of the Swiss formula as a general criterion to establish reduction rates meant that the deepest cuts were mostly made on the highest tariffs. Most of the tariff reductions were scheduled to begin on 1 January 1980, to continue with equal annual cuts until 1987.

The average US tariff on total industrial products (dutiable plus duty-free), excluding petroleum, was cut by 32 per cent from 6.2 per cent to 4.2 per cent.[44] The US applied the Swiss formula with the 14 per cent coefficient, subject to the 60 per cent maximum imposed by the Trade Act of 1974, as well as to a set of exceptions for individual products. This allowed the United States to reduce the duty on products exposed to foreign competition such as textiles and apparel or iron and steel by much less than the average 40 per cent trade-weighted cut rate under the Swiss formula. On the other hand, the number of duties exceeding 20 per cent was greatly reduced.

The tariff concessions of the European Community were slightly less generous overall than those of its transatlantic partner.[45] A report on the final results of the Tokyo Round somewhat candidly stated that 'the Community's aim was to keep the Common Customs Tariff at a significant level and, at the same time, to obtain a reduction of tariff from its main trading partners to increase the degree of harmonization'.[46] The EC along with the Scandinavian countries applied the Swiss formula, however, using a coefficient of 16 rather than 14 as in the US and Japan. It must be noted that the smaller the coefficient the higher the tariff reduction. The EC also made a substantial number of exceptions to the general formula to protect industries particularly sensitive to import competition, such as motor vehicles, television sets, fertilizers, shoes and cutlery.[47] Overall, the Common Customs Tariff on industrial goods, excluding duty-free imports, was reduced from an average of 9.8 per cent to an average of 7.5 per cent. Thus most of the EC duties lay in a range between 5 per cent and 10 per cent with the exception of only 180 duties exceeding 10 per cent and one (on lorries) exceeding 20 per cent.[48] Including duty-free imports, the average tariff was cut by 27 per cent from 6.3 per cent to 4.6 per cent. The areas where tariff reductions offered the greatest opportunities to Community exporters included chemicals, ceramics and mechanical engineering, while the areas opened to increased competition from foreign producers were paper, plastics and non-ferrous metals.[49] The customs reductions were spread out over a period of eight years from 1980 to 1987, but the Community reserved the right to review the situation after the first five years before deciding whether to proceed to the final three stages of reduction.

The concessions made by the US and the EC to each other exceeded their average level of reduction as they made a depth of cuts of about 35 per cent on their reciprocal trade. The United States obtained gains on certain chemical items, certain paper items, printing machinery, electrical machinery, scientific instruments and photographic equipment, while it made important concessions to its trading partner in certain textile, leather, glassware, chemical and machinery items. The tariff concessions benefiting US products also made it possible to narrow the gap with the EFTA countries and those Mediterranean and former colonies which had preferential arrangements with the Community that allowed most industrial and some agricultural items to enter the European Common Market duty-free.

The impact of tariff reductions was, however, watered down from the outset by the concessions already made in the previous rounds. For instance, a 30 per cent reduction on tariffs not exceeding 10 per cent would result, at most, in a 3 per cent cut. The cut, perhaps, could have been significant under fixed exchange rates but it was easily offset by currency movements in a floating exchange regime. Besides, as the tariff cut was to be completed in eight years, it would amount to a reduction in import prices of one-half of one percentage point a year, not to mention the fact that the tariff concessions agreed in the Tokyo Round might be nullified by antidumping or countervailing duties imposed on imported items and, as we shall see, the Tokyo Round codes did not prevent such measures from being adopted more and more frequently as a weapon against competing products which were performing too well.

Customs valuation

On the other hand, the modest impact of the tariff reductions agreed at the end of the round was balanced by the harmonization of the systems designed to assess the import value for the imposition of *ad valorem* duties and by the consequent elimination of assessment methods that unfairly distorted such a value. The Customs Valuation code established five valuation methods – applicable on either a FOB or a CIF basis – ranked in hierarchical order. The first and primary method referred to the transaction value as expressed by the invoice price. The second and third methods relied on the transaction value of identical or similar goods exported to the same country. Under the fourth method the resale price of the imported goods was used as the starting point for calculation. The fifth value was based on the computed value of the imported goods which comprised material and manufacturing costs plus general expenses and profits. If none of the above listed methods could be applied, the customs value was to be determined using any reasonable means consistent with the principles and general provisions of the code and of Art.VII of the GATT. The methods provided by the code largely reflected the US practice, but the code also meant the abrogation of the ASP system as well as the special valuation system for what were known as Final List products which together accounted for about 20 per cent of customs entries. On the other hand, the United States secured agreement on higher tariff binding for some of the products protected by the eliminated systems, such as benzenoid chemicals and rubber-soled footwear. There was thus a trade-off between concessions in different, though related, areas of negotiations which left the actual tariff protection for some specific sectors almost unchanged.

Subsidies, countervailing measures and antidumping duties

The Subsidies and Countervailing Measures (SCM) code reinforced the ban on export subsidies on non-primary products and the prohibition was supported by an illustrative list of prohibited export subsidies. The code also introduced a four stage dispute settlement procedure providing for consultation, conciliation by a newly established committee on subsidies and countervailing measures, investigation by a panel and countermeasures. This procedure applied both to export subsidies and domestic subsidies allegedly causing or threatening to cause serious prejudice to other contracting parties. The foregoing met the US goal of achieving stricter discipline on subsidies. However, there was no definition of what constitutes an export subsidy, even less a subsidy, and as regards domestic subsidization a compromise was reached between the United States and the European Community which was aimed to satisfy everybody but was not destined to be very effective. Indeed, the code started by claiming that non-export subsidies can be a means for achieving desirable social and economic policies, such as eliminating regional disadvantages, restructuring particular sectors, encouraging R&D and maintaining employment and encouraging retraining. But it added that domestic subsidies may cause adverse effects to the interest of other signatories in several forms: injury to the domestic industry of another signatory; nullification or impairment of previous benefits; serious prejudice or threat of serious prejudice in the export market. The question was where to draw the line between commendable goals in the domestic market and adverse effects on other signatories. In particular, there was no clear definition of what could cause serious prejudice. Nor, contrary to the hopes of the United States and unlike export subsidies, was there a list of domestic measures likely to cause prejudice. Thus, the United States claimed that the code resulted in 'an explicit recognition of the needs for limits on domestic subsidies', while its transatlantic counterpart argued that 'the Community's freedom of action in the matter of internal subsidies (regional ones for instance) will not be fundamentally affected'.[50] If, as claimed by the United States, the code introduced stricter discipline also for domestic subsidies, there was more ground for confrontation than conciliation.

On the countervailing duty side, the code embodied the principle of material injury but here too it failed to provide a definition of what the term actually meant. Thus, the effectiveness of the code in preventing protectionist abuse would depend on the implementing legislation of the countries adhering to it. In ratifying the code the US Congress was likely to adopt a restrictive interpretation as prospects for industries like steel, facing competition from abroad and capable of conducting effective lobbies, were getting increasingly bleak.[51]

Substantially analogous rules were agreed on antidumping. Therefore, here too, particularly with regard to implementation in the United States, the question of what was meant by 'material injury' remained hovering and the code failed to prevent or at least effectively restrict the use of antidumping duties as a protectionist tool for import competing industries.

Public procurement

The Government Procurement (GPR) code, which came into force in 1981, contained detailed rules on the way in which tenders for government purchasing contracts should be invited and awarded to ensure they did not protect domestic products or suppliers or discriminate against foreign products and suppliers. The agreement applied to contracts worth more than 150,000 Special Drawing Rights (SDRs), equivalent to about $197,000. In line with US hopes and contrary to the European Community's wishes, the agreed minimum amount was below the threshold set by the EC Directive on good procurement within the Community. On the other hand, the 150,000 SDR threshold eliminated access to many smaller contracts frequent in the developing countries. In any case, the code had some relevant limitations. In the first place, its scope was not abreast with the widening areas of government procurement at the end of the 1970s. It did not apply to the purchase of services. This was in line with the purview of the General Agreement which referred only to trade in goods, but did not take into account the growing demand for the supply of services from public authorities. Neither did the agreement apply to construction contracts or to defence-related purchases. Secondly, procurements by states and local governments (with or without federal funds) and by important government entities were not covered. The United States, for instance, excluded the Department of Transportation and the Department of Energy and certain quasi-governmental organizations. This entailed that, although the Buy American Act could no longer apply to some federal procurements, buy-American or buy-local law proliferated among states and local governments within the US.

Aircraft

The Aircraft Agreement abolished customs duties and similar charges not only on complete aircraft but also on engines and components as well as on their maintenance and rebuilding. It also prohibited import and export restrictions unless justifiable under the provisions of the GATT and, with a sentence which sounds quite vague, provided that no obligation or unreasonable pressure should be imposed to persuade prospective aircraft buyers to choose from a particular source. As regards subsidies, the signatories noted that the code on subsidies and countervailing duties also applied to civil aircraft but qualified the statement by stressing that special factors applying to the aircraft sector, and in particular the widespread governmental support in this area, had to be taken into account. Thus domestic subsidies were left aside but even in the export subsidies area, export credit subsidization, one of the major instruments in promoting civil aircraft sales, was not covered by the agreement. Certain agreements on export credits were concluded under the aegis of the OECD, but at that time they did not prove very effective. The fact that just over twelve years later the United States and the European Community would sign a bilateral agreement with the specific goal of solving a dispute by regulating their respective industry support measures is clear indication that the Tokyo Round Agreement on civil aircraft was far from establishing an environment free from state interference as was claimed at that time.

Agriculture

In keeping with the request and offer process agreed in mid-1977, both the United States and the European Community made and obtained some important concessions on agricultural export. The United States obtained concessions on tariff reductions and quota liberalization on products representing about 16 per cent of its farm exports. The trade coverage of the concessions received from the EC, measured on a 1976 basis, was about $1 billion. The major concessions by the Community involved beef, tobacco, rice, poultry and certain fresh and canned fruits.[52] The most significant US concessions to its transatlantic partner concerned the increase of the quota allocation for cheese, the removal of certain retaliatory duties imposed as a result of the chicken war of the 1960s and the elimination of the so-called 'wine gallon' method of duty assessment.[53] This system assessed taxes and duties on all bottles containing less than one gallon as if they were 100 per cent proof. Instead domestic producers generally only paid excise tax on the proof gallon method, i.e. the actual alcoholic equivalent of one gallon of spirits at 100 per cent proof. The different method of assessment resulted in a classic non-tariff barrier penalizing foreign alcoholic beverages as they entered US customs already bottled.[54] In return for the removal of this system of assessment, the US received various concessions from other countries, including a pledge from the EC to ensure that its member states would eliminate any measures resulting in discrimination against US distilled spirits.

As regards the regulation of particular commodity markets, the round produced an International Dairy Arrangement (IDA) which provided for minimum export prices for butter, powdered milk and certain cheeses, and established a mechanism for information exchange and policy consultations. However, the agreement had neither enforcement mechanisms nor provisions for stock and production adjustments. The Bovine Meat Arrangement created a council with the task of monitoring the sector and a mechanism of consultation and settlement of differences, but had no economic or regulatory provisions. As regards wheat the only result, after the failure of the IWA Conference, was a decision to extend the 1971 International Wheat Agreement which contained no economic provisions.

Regarding farm export subsidies, limited progress was achieved by the code on SCM whose Article 10 referred to primary products. The code provided a more precise interpretation of the expression 'equitable share of world export trade' and extended the ban to export subsidies that resulted in the acquisition of a non-equitable share 'in a particular market' and in cut price competition in that market.[55] However, these precisions proved to be ineffective when applied to actual cases of export support. Nor did the code provide any effective discipline on domestic mechanisms of farm price or income support. Thus Finn Olav Gundelach, vice-president of the Commission with special responsibility for agriculture, could claim with justified relief, at least for the time being, that the Uruguay Round agreements meant the acceptance 'of the principles and mechanisms of the Community's common agricultural policy' and 'had brought an end to the "trench warfare" and "religious wars" that had so often characterized discussion of agriculture in the past'.[56]

Developing countries

In line with the stated objectives of the Tokyo Round, formal steps were made towards more favourable treatment to developing countries. In particular, the so-called 'enabling clause' provided that notwithstanding the MFN provision of GATT Art. I, 'contracting parties may accord differential and more favourable treatment to developing countries without according such treatment to other contracting parties' with regard to both preferential tariffs and non-tariff measures. However, in keeping with the policies adopted by the United States and the European Community during the decade, the provisions in favour of the developing countries contained a 'graduation clause' which made it clear that their capacity to accept obligation under the GATT and to benefit from preferential treatment would respectively increase and decrease according to their economic development. In short, countries like Hong Kong, Taiwan and South Korea and many other newly industrialized countries could not expect to be entitled to special treatment and had to play by the rules, which were prevalently established by the industrialized members of the General Agreement.

Safeguards

The most conspicuous absentee among the agreements signed at the end of the round was the code on safeguards. The main stumbling block was selectivity. The European Community backed by the 'Nordic Countries' group had been trying to push through a reform of GATT Art. XIX which would have allowed selective actions against individual countries, subject to subsequent review by a GATT committee. The strongest opposition came from the developing countries which, having had to accept that they would not be entitled to any general exclusion from safeguard measures, argued that such measures should only be applied according to the MFN non-discrimination principle. The EC proposal also presented a fundamental strategic difficulty: it impinged on the network of voluntary export restraints agreed outside the discipline of the GATT, which were in fact selective safeguards adopted with the sometimes quite reluctant countenance of the exporting country. If a radical reform of

GATT Art. XIX had been agreed extending the power of Western industrialized countries to curtail, though temporarily, the inflow of products from the NICs or other emerging countries, not to mention Japan, then it was to be expected that the vast array of so-called 'grey-area actions' was to be dismantled or at least conducted within the scope of the GATT. At the end of the round it was clear that it was impossible to bridge the gap between the European Community and the developing countries, whatever their industrialization progress. Differences also remained in the negotiating stance of the main industrial participants as the call from the EC for unilaterally actionable safeguard measures was received with caution by the United States and with suspicion by Japan.

Did the agreements secure a freer and fairer trade environment and to what extent?

As expected, opinions on the results of the negotiations are not uniformo. Many political economy experts were sceptical. Curzon Price argued that, 'although worse cases could be cited', the Tokyo Round was characterized by 'protracted negotiations which by any normal input/output measure have been extraordinarily unproductive and disappointing'.[57] This was because the negotiations were doomed by the steady advance of protectionism which was the natural result of a declining economic environment marked by a high rate of overcapacity which both the main parties were unable to redress. The European Commission stated that the conclusion of the Tokyo Round brought 'results which exceed appearances' not only with regard to tariff negotiations but above all to the non-tariff issues and that 'protectionism and world crisis were held in check', an outcome even more significant as it was 'achieved at a time of international economic recession'.[58] The EC statement can be read as an admission, with an undertone of satisfaction, that the round had achieved the maximum level of 'cooperation' that was acceptable by the parties in the negotiations, also taking into account the unpromising economic environment. More cautiously, the Report of the President of the United States argued that 'in their entirety, the Tokyo Round Agreements represent a new beginning to achieve and maintain an open and fair trading system'.[59] The Special Representative for Trade Negotiations, Robert Strauss, commenting upon the results of the Tokyo Round with specific reference to NTB codes said that 'we should be realistic about the significance of these agreements, neither overstating nor understating their importance. They are no more and no less than the first new chapters on a new book of rules for international trade'.[60]

Actually, the upshot of the Tokyo Round was a settlement to which the parties had come at a moment in which they hoped to strengthen a recovery that delayed taking off. In particular, the two transatlantic partners saw the favourable conclusion of the round as part of a wider economic equilibrium. Therefore, if they could not be overcome, differences had to be papered over. Agriculture was a glaringly obvious example. In other areas like customs valuation and standards and, to a certain extent, public procurement, progress towards a freer and fairer world trade was made, but in most cases it did not shake the entrenched interests of the parties concerned. In some cases the observer might come to suspect that some Tokyo Round codes, nominally those on antidumping and countervailing measures, rather than encouraging freer trade, lent themselves to protectionist ends, as better explained below.

As was foreseeable, the round provided a good occasion to cut tariff rates but the results were not impressive, especially because the impact of tariff cuts had been pre-empted by concessions in previous rounds and also because, as was to be expected, import competing sectors managed to obtain greater tariff protection than the average. No agreement could be reached on safeguards while the question of surreptitious imposition of quotas though VERs and OMAs was not given any significant degree of attention, despite the claim that the round was aimed at improving the condition of the developing countries.

The negotiations were concluded when the first signs of an imminent deterioration of the economy were beginning to be seen. The implementation of the agreements was carried out when the threats, in particular with regard to some basic industries, gained substance. As regards agriculture, the US accommodating attitude towards the CAP changed drastically when the success story of American farm exports was replaced after 1981 by an export plunge made worse by rising EC competition. Less than two years after the conclusion of the round, in a more volatile economic environment, a more ideologically committed Republican administration argued that although the Tokyo negotiations had achieved agreement on new codes covering a wide range of non-tariff barriers and on substantial reduction in tariffs, there were 'a number of issues that were not adequately resolved . . . or were not addressed in these negotiations'.[61]

Putting the agreements into practice

Similarities and differences in perspective among the parties of the round influenced both the level at which the measures agreed upon were applied and the cooperation in the committees that had been established to follow up the agreements.

All the industrialized countries, with the exception of Japan, eagerly applied antidumping measures, although such practices might be directed to protectionist ends. Indeed, exploitability for protectionist goals helps explain why antidumping proceedings became widely adopted, apart from the US and the EC, not only in other industrial countries like Canada and Australia but also in some fast-growing developing countries. As illustrated by the reports of the Committee on Anti-Dumping Practices, the United States was prominent among the users of antidumping measures, with 192 proceedings initiated and 118 definitive duties applied between July 1980 and June 1985.[62] In the same period the EC initiated 187 proceedings and applied 45 definitive duties. Canada started 154 proceedings and applied 89 definitive duties. Australia in spite of its much smaller economy, boasted 203 new proceedings and 86 definitive duties. Things went differently for countervailing measures.[63] Here the EC, for the reasons explained in this and previous chapters, was far from being able or willing to cast the first stone; rather the EC along with its member states was one of the preferred targets of US countervailing proceedings. From July 1980 to June 1985 the US initiated 199 countervailing duty actions and imposed 60 definitive duties. In the same years, the EC started 5 proceedings and imposed 3 definitive duties. Rather surprisingly, Chile initiated 114 actions, but did not impose definitive duties.

The EC approved the Tokyo Round codes in November 1979 and subsequently conformed the legislation of the Community and its member states to the international rules, in most cases reproducing their wording. Things were more complex in the case of the United States whose Congress was called by the 1974 Trade Act at the same time to approve, without passing any amendment, the multilateral NTB agreements signed in Geneva and to implement them by amending and, if necessary, establishing the relevant US statutes.

The main expert on the Tokyo Round negotiations, Gilbert Winham, argued that in passing the Trade Act of 1974 'Congress removed itself from a major role in writing legislation or representing constituencies in connection with the MTN'.[64] This may be true as regards the course of the negotiation, but it does not imply that Congress was ready or willing to cut itself off from the dialogue between lobbies and administration in the final stages of the round. The dialogue was trilateral as Congress was empowered to approve or to reject the agreements worked out in Geneva and above all to preside over the consequent adaptation of domestic law. Thus, if Congress was certainly not prepared to scupper the international deals in which it had had a role, it was far from willing to allow such agreements to entail the weakening of the domestic system of defence against foreign competition it had inherited or had itself built over the last few years. On the contrary, the Trade Agreements Act of 1979 turned out to be an opportunity to render the domestic rules stricter and exploitable for protectionist ends.[65]

Thus, the Act approved the Tokyo Round codes, stressing, however, that no provision of any trade agreement would take precedence over domestic law in the event of a conflict. The Act also provided that the NTB agreements would not come into force in the US until each major industrial country also completed its domestic implementation procedure. The president, however, could accept a particular agreement if only one industrial country had not accepted it and acceptance by that country was not considered essential. As stated in the Senate Report, the intent of the provision was 'to assure that the United States would not commit itself to new international rules that could only be effective and beneficial to the United States if accepted by all major Western industrial countries'.[66]

As regards measures directed to counter so-called unfair trade practices, i.e. subsidies and dumping, the Act further shortened the investigation period and imposed more severe obligations on importers of subsidized or dumped products. In antidumping proceedings the 1979 Act allowed the Customs service six months to assess the duty and during the assessment period importers had to pay estimated antidumping duties. In countervailing procedures importers were forced to deposit a bond or cash in less than three months if a preliminary investigation should find that imports were subsidized.

As regards countervailing measures in particular, the Trade Agreements Act tightened the reins relative to the preceding statutes in two ways. Firstly, by codifying a practice dating back to the Michelin case, the Act made it clear that countervailable subsidies included not only export subsidies, prohibited by the MTN code, but also a number of domestic subsidies, which, unsurprisingly, coincided with the list of domestic subsidies allegedly causing serious prejudice to other trading partners proposed by the American negotiators during the Tokyo Round but not accepted by the other parties. Secondly, it was a long-established rule that US countervailing duties should be applied to so-called 'net subsidies' and a somewhat open-ended set of factors could be considered in arriving at their value. 'Gross subsidy' was the value of the subsidy provided, while 'net subsidy' was assessed by deducting from the gross subsidy one or more offsetting costs. The 1979 Act limited the allowed deductions to three: payments made to qualify for the subsidy; losses in the value of the subsidy resulting from its late receipt; charges levied on the export of the merchandise specifically intended to offset the subsidy received. As the Senate Report on the Trade Agreements Act of 1979 pointed out, the reform wanted 'to place clear limits on offsets from a gross subsidy'.[67] Therefore, it was no longer recognized that subsidies are often granted to offset certain negative effects that government measures can have on an industry, such as interference in the location of new plants, closure of old installations in the context of industrial sector restructuring, or policies to buoy up employment and prevent lay-offs. All these policies were widely followed within the European Community. The combination of the statutory extension of countervailing duties to domestic subsidies and the marked curtailment of allowed reductions in assessing net subsidies helps explain why the American steel firms, after prevalently relying on antidumping duties until the beginning of the 1980s, in 1982 shifted the emphasis of their attacks to the countervailing duty provisions of the Trade Agreements Act of 1979 so as to coerce their European counterparts into a comprehensive pact to regulate production and exports.[68]

The Trade Agreements Act, in keeping with the Tokyo Round codes, made the imposition of both antidumping and countervailing duties conditional on proof of material injury or threat of it to an industry in the US or material retardation to the establishment of such an industry. The new provision, however, was much less innovative than could appear at first sight. In the first place, the material injury requirement applied only to countries that had enacted the two Tokyo Round codes and to countries that had assumed substantially equivalent obligations. Even more important was the fact that both the statute and the executive's Statement of Administrative Action defined 'material injury' as 'injury which is not inconsequential, immaterial or unimportant'. The term 'material' is commonly considered equivalent to important, substantial and significant. Certainly, the definition of 'material injury' adopted by the US lawmakers might be in line with the ordinary meaning of the term, but it could also mean something less and it was for the US administrative authorities and subsequently for the US trade courts to decide where to draw the line.

Thus, on the one hand, the Trade Agreements Act of 1979 marked the approval by the US of a multilateral regime aimed at better preventing trade distortion and improving the environment for solving potential dispute. On the other hand, with regard to domestic rules directed at countering imports of allegedly dumped or subsidized products, the Act meant not only the confirmation of practices that could carry protectionist effects, like the imposition of antidumping duties even though the export price was not lower than the price of like products in the exporting countries, but made new legal instruments exploitable for protectionist ends available to import competing firms. To render the implementation of the new rules more effective the

Carter administration transferred the assessment of both the existence and amount of dumping and subsidization from the Department of Treasury, considered not responsive enough to the interests of domestic industries, to the Department of Commerce.

Many importers expressed their misgivings on the stricter antidumping and countervailing regimes. The representative of the Automobile Importers of America, John Rehm, was quoted as saying that he deplored 'the fact that as the product of an international effort to liberalize trade, we now see these two statutes turned into protectionist measure'.[69] As the Act did not have to implement any Safeguard code, given the failure to reach an agreement on this subject at the close of the Uruguay Round, no amendment was made to the previous US law. It was, therefore, natural that American firms threatened by foreign competition, irrespective of whether it was fair or unfair, looked at antidumping and countervailing proceedings as the only effective method to keep imports at bay.

In other sectors too the Trade Agreements Act of 1979 did not involve the opening of the American market that the ratification of the Tokyo Round codes could have allowed. For instance, the implementation of the Customs Valuation code meant the repeal of the American Selling Price system, but converted ASP rates of duty into tariffs estimated to afford the same level of protection provided under the abrogated valuation method. Contrary to the hopes of the European Community, the implementation of the GPR code was far from bringing about a significant curtailment of the preference given to American firms by existing federal and state laws. The president was given power to waive certain Buy American Act restrictions, but the Act was not repealed. According to the Senate Report, the procurements subject to presidential waiver only accounted for about 15 per cent of federal government procurement.

Overlooking the limitations of its statute the US called in the GPR committee for an extension of the provisions of the code to government purchasing entities not covered by the Tokyo Round Agreement, but over which governments had direct or substantial control, such as government-owned companies. The attempt was resisted by the EC and analogous resistance met the attempt to extend GPR rules to the provision of services, a sector of growing interest for the United States but also one of the areas on which the EC executive focused to enhance integration within the Common Market. For instance, in the telecommunication sector the United States claimed that the end of the monopoly held by American Telegraph and Telephone (AT&T), a public company performing public functions while providing advanced R&D, was hindering US leadership in the sector. It, therefore, pressed for access to foreign countries, which had to reform their monopolistic procurement system. In contrast, in the EC the Commission was finding it difficult to start a liberalization process within the Community's boundaries where the telecommunication and postal services remained based on national legislation and were provided or supervised by public bodies that, with the exception of Great Britain, were not keen or speedy on liberalizing.[70] Finally, for over five years, the EC resisted the US call for a reduction of the threshold level above which public purchases were subject to the GPR code. It was only in 1986 that the threshold level was reduced by 20,000 SDR, but this was done on a two-year experimental basis. The European Community resisted any extensive interpretation of obligations concerning subsidies and, ignoring US complaints, for a long time failed to notify its subsidy programmes also because it only managed to make a full survey of subsidization within its borders in 1989. The unwillingness to notify may also be explained by the fact that notification of subsidy programmes was likely to be taken as evidence that the programmes were affecting trade, thus harming the trading interests of other partners; therefore, it entailed the risk of becoming the target of countervailing measures or dispute settlement actions in the GATT.[71]

5

From the Second Oil Shock to the Spread and Consolidation of the Recovery

The year 1979 ushered in a long period of turmoil in international trade, marked by a deterioration of the trade balance of most Western countries, accompanied first by a rekindling of inflation and then by persistent unemployment. The period was also characterized by wide fluctuations of the exchange rates of the main Western currencies, which, in turn, affected the trade of the countries involved.

Although divisions and subdivisions for historical analysis purposes have quite often an element of arbitrariness, and although the lack of uniformity and contextuality among the trading partners across the Atlantic, and even within the EC, was a hallmark of the period under review, two phases can be distinguished within an encompassing period from the end of the 1970s to the start of the second half of the 1980s. These were the second oil crisis and the Reagan years, i.e. the years in which international trade and capital movements were deeply affected by the upshots, not always foreseen, of innovative choices made by the Republican administration for domestic goals. This is because the second oil shock and the economic policy choices that it inspired on both sides of the Atlantic helped establish an environment without which events in the second stage would probably have taken a different turn, the main link being monetary policy and the partially related upward pressure on interest rates.

The impact of the second oil shock across the Atlantic and economic policies adopted to counter its effects

The second oil shock, which started in 1979 and accelerated in the following year, entailed rising inflation, worsening of trade and current account balances in the Western countries, although with the relevant exception of the United States. On 31 December 1978 the oil price was $12.70 per barrel. By 1 July 1980 it was around $30 and was approaching $35 at the close of the year. The volatility of the political situation in the Middle East led to widespread fears of an upcoming oil shortage for the Western world and this situation led to pressure on the market price for oil, which in turn allowed the OPEC countries to set higher prices. What was originally believed to be a looming supply crisis soon turned out to be a price crisis. No effective response to stop the rise came from the consuming countries.

As in the previous oil crisis, the new price rise had a double impact on the oil-importing countries: direct and indirect inflationary consequences, and a curtailment of domestic demand as the so-called 'OPEC tax' reduced consumer spending power, which was not offset by a prompt increase in the oil-exporting countries' demand for imported products. The gap between the transfer of resources to the OPEC countries and their capacity to absorb imports, in turn, caused strains on the ability of the international monetary system to recycle an increasingly huge volume of funds. However, the cyclical swings during the second oil crisis were less severe than those accompanying the first one. Whereas in the years preceding the first shock there had been a synchronized boom in the major industrial countries, in the late 1970s the upswing was weaker and less heavily synchronized. Likewise, the impact of the oil shock was not uniform and, in spite of the widespread adoption of restrictive monetary policies, in most industrialized countries there were offsetting factors which helped delay, with different lags, the constraints imposed on domestic demand.

The economic policy of the major industrial countries reflected these new, or more exactly renewed, challenges. The Tokyo and Venice G7 Declarations, in June 1979 and June 1980 respectively, focused on two priorities: inflation, whose reduction was regarded as the immediate top priority, replaced unemployment as the main target for the United States and the major EC member states, along with Japan; and the need to counter the threat of narrower room for manoeuvre in running the economy caused by rising oil prices, aggravated by the possibility of supply shortages.

The first goal was pursued through a prudent fiscal policy and above all through a restrictive stance in monetary policy in the main industrial countries which, following a method implemented by the Bundesbank in 1972, set targets for the growth of monetary aggregates. The downward trend of such growth targets during the biennium was accompanied by repeated increases in official discount rates and in several industrialized countries by direct control of certain monetary aggregates.

As regards the second priority, the industrial countries adopted two sets of measures, starting with the reduction of oil consumption. Already in June 1979, at the Tokyo Summit, the European Community declared its commitment to restrict 1979 oil consumption to 500 million tons and to maintain oil imports between 1980 and 1985 at an annual level no higher than in 1978. As a goal for 1985, the United States adopted import levels not exceeding either the level of 1977 or of the 1979 target of 8.5 million barrels per day. The achievement of this policy objective relied on two instruments. Firstly, curbing energy consumption in the production process; secondly the shift to alternative sources of energy like coal and nuclear power. In the second instance, the industrial countries looked at sources other than the OPEC producers for their oil import needs. The consumption of the OECD members, measured in millions of oil barrels per day, fell from 40.5 million in 1979 to 35.4 million (–12%) in 1981 and stabilized at around 34 million in the next four years. Net exports from OPEC countries declined from 28.2 million in 1979 to 20.9 million (–26%) in 1981 and 14.1 million (–50%) in 1985.[1]

The United States during the Carter administration

In the United States the long-awaited recession did not occur in 1979 but, in the words of Campagna, 'some of the old problems continued, and some new ones were added'.[2] The oil drag was estimated to reduce consumer spending power by about 3 per cent of after-tax income in 1979, wearing away 2 per cent of gross national product by the end of 1980. Relative to the size of the US economy, the new oil price increase was larger than the 1973–4 rise. During the first shock the world price of oil tripled from about $4 to about $12 per barrel, adding about $18 billion to the US bill for imported oil, roughly 1.4 per cent of the GNP. In percentage terms the 1979–80 hike was definitely more modest (about 170 per cent), but in absolute terms it meant a rise of over $20 per barrel, adding about $50 billion to the oil cost. Its impact on GDP was, however, offset in the short-run by a drop in the personal saving rate which resulted in an increase in private spending. In 1979 unemployment remained below the average of the decade, even though it was above the average of the 1960s, but inflation accelerated (Tables 22 and 23). Consumer prices soared by 3.6 points above the already high 1978. As noted by the Economic Report of the President for 1980, the 1979–80 oil price shock worsened a ratchet-like inflationary process that had characterized the American economy since the mid-1960s, accelerating from the beginning of the following decade. In this process the inflation rate only partially decreased when the cause of the previous jump in price stabilized. In particular, after the hike of the first half of the 1970s, in spite of the subsequent recession, inflationary expectations remained high and were built into demand for higher wages by employees and price setting by firms.

To fight inflation the Carter administration adopted a more restrained fiscal policy, while the Federal Reserve embraced a restrictive monetary policy directed at curbing the growth of the monetary aggregates. The Federal Reserve fixed low target ranges for M1 and M2 growth in 1979 allowing the federal funds rate to increase. However, the management of interest rate did not hit the target, and monetary aggregates exceeded their desired growth range. In October 1979 the Fed, led by the new chairman Paul Volcker, announced a policy shift to close control of money supply.[3] Under the new approach, open market operations had to supply the volume of bank reserves consistently with the desired rate of monetary growth.[4] As the growth of monetary aggregates went on surging despite the new policy announcement, in March 1980 the Federal Reserve imposed comprehensive credit controls, but in June adopted a more relaxed policy. The uncertainty caused by the persistence of inflation and the expectation of a restrictive stance from the monetary authorities resulted in rocketing interest rates which became positive in real terms too.

It was predicted that such measures would cause a recession with real GNP falling by 1 per cent. Actually, for the whole year GNP declined by only 0.2 per cent (Table 1) but in a way that did not favour the incumbent president in the run-up to the November elections. After rising in the first quarter, real GNP plummeted by almost 10 per cent, the sharpest decline in the post-war period, although it quickly recovered in the second half of the year. Unemployment jumped to 7.1 per cent, while inflation, rather than declining, went on growing (Table 23). The decline in consumption, under the strain of rising inflation in the wake of increasingly high oil prices, was accompanied by a contraction in housing and business investments. Although the current account balance markedly improved, the merchandise trade deficit remained high (Table 2). In the presidential campaign Carter tried to keep his distance from the Federal Reserve's stance, stressing its independence from the executive under American law. The president even declared that 'the strictly monetary approach to the Fed's decision on the discount rate and other banking policies is ill-advised', adding that 'the Federal Reserve Bank Board ought to look at other factors and balance them with the supply of money'.[5] The voters did not pay much attention to his remarks.

The European Community

The direct burden imposed on the Community's trade balance by the oil rise in 1979–80 was almost $70 billion compared with some $31 billion in 1974. Expressed as a percentage of the import bill in the years preceding the oil shocks, if exchange rate changes are ignored, the costs to the trade balance were quite similar: 13.4 per cent and 13 per cent respectively.[6] As a percentage of GDP they amounted to 3.4 per cent in the 1979–80 price rise and 2.9 per cent in the previous rise. However, during the second oil shock the dollar price rise was eased by the appreciation of the European Currency Unit (ECU), i.e. the basket of the EC member states' currencies, whereas during the first oil crisis the dollar price rise was amplified by the 1974 depreciation of the ECU vis-à-vis the dollar after the hike of the previous year. As a percentage of GDP the oil price rises in ECU were respectively 3 per cent for the second oil shock and 3.1 per cent for the first.[7] Obviously, the exchange rate factor varied with reference to the various currencies included in the basket: for instance in 1979 and much of 1980 the Deutschmark went on appreciating vis-à-vis the dollar, while the Italian lira continued its downward trend (Figure 1).

However, the oil drag did not bring about a slowdown in the EC during 1979 and the first months of 1980. In partial contrast to the United States, the economic activity that had shown gradual improvements in 1978 strengthened in 1979 also benefiting from the stimulus package decided by the European Councils in 1978, which had assigned the 'Locomotive' role to the Federal Republic. In 1979, the GDP of the EC member states rose on average by 3.3 per cent and industrial production grew by 5 per cent (Tables 9 and 21). Consumer spending grew by the same rate as the GDP, while gross fixed capital formation increased by 3.8 per cent, the highest rate since the early 1970s. On the other hand, there was no reduction in the unemployment rate relative to 1978 and, as was to be expected, inflation remained high. The second quarter of 1980 marked the beginning of a severe slowdown. In the Community the GDP growth rate declined to 1.4 per cent reflecting the levelling off of domestic demand. Consumption slackened under the pressure of accelerating inflation triggered by the rising oil bill. Capital formation declined in the second half of the year in the face of high interest rates and the tightening of financial conditions. Real interest rates became positive in most EC member states and membership of the European Monetary System (EMS) prevented the countries participating in the new scheme from viewing depreciation of their currencies as an easy way to boost their exports. The new EC currency system, which was established by the Brussels European Council on

5 December 1978, and entered into force on 13 March 1979, was mainly the result of a Franco-German initiative. Undoubtedly economic considerations of interest for the whole Community were at play in encouraging the initiative: the traditional European aversion to exchange rate instability; the mistrust, after the collapse of Bretton Woods, of the domestic and monetary policy of the US; the hope of achieving greater price stability; and the strains imposed on the CAP by currency volatility.[8] Yet, political considerations based on the different interests and perspectives of France and Germany, and their predominance over the other EC members, were the main factor at the origin of the EMS.[9] Indeed, the new system was the upshot of talks between Helmut Schmidt and Valéry Giscard d'Estaing, while the competent Community bodies – the monetary committee, the committee of governors and the finance ministers – played a role only after the Bremen European Council in July 1978. Likewise, the Commission was not involved in the negotiations until the essentials were agreed across the Rhine.[10] The Franco-German discussions aimed at reconciling France's desire for a more symmetrical system than the Snake, which was considered skew at the advantage of stronger currencies like the Deutschmark, with German insistence on discipline.[11] Thus the new system, which replaced the unsuccessful Snake, was also based on a parity grid and compliance with bilateral margins of fluctuation (set at +2.25% and −2.25%, with the exception of the Italian lira which was allowed a wider 6% margin). However, the new regime provided for correctives aimed at guaranteeing greater flexibility, at more rapid forms of action when strains emerged and at avoiding that the burden of readjustment prevalently fell on the weaker currency, that is, on the currency at the bottom of the fluctuation range.[12] The base of the EMS was the ECU, a basket of the currencies participating in the system, each of which was assigned a different weight. Each EC currency had an ECU related central rate – with the exception of the pound, excluded at the time from the exchange rate mechanism. When the margins of fluctuation were reached unlimited intervention on the exchange became compulsory. On the other hand, the SME also adopted a preventive intervention system, the 'divergence indicator' providing for action by the authorities responsible for the currency whose rate exceeded certain limits fixed in terms of ECU, limits which being narrower than those demarcating the bilateral margins would be reached before them. The SME also provided for a substantial increase in the volume and the duration of credits to support the weakest currencies. The actual results were quite limited.[13] A key currency, the pound, did not participate in the arrangement. The divergence indicator was flawed since it involved no obligation to intervene. The credit mechanisms were a mere swap agreement between central banks rather than the pooling of reserves. The discussions for the establishment of a European Monetary Fund (EMF) were postponed.

In spite of the attempt to harmonize one main variable in the management of economic policy the trend was far from being uniform within the EC. In 1979, West Germany's GDP grew at a 4.2 per cent rate, the best result since the 1976 recovery, due mainly to a substantial increase in fixed investments and to the steady growth of exports. Imports, however, moved ahead more rapidly than exports and for the first time in the 1970s the current account balance was in the red (Table 10). In 1980 the GDP growth rate fell to 1.4 per cent, the industrial production shrank and the value of imports almost caught up with that of exports. The current account deficit reached $17.5 billion. The 5.3 per cent consumer price growth rate was above the average of the years prior to the first oil shock, although it remained well below the average of the other EC members in 1980 (Table 23). In short, the continuous high value of the Deutschmark, in particular relative to the greenback, prevented the oil hike from stoking domestic inflation, but eroded the competitiveness of German industry.[14] Nevertheless, at the close of the year, under the impact of the deterioration of the current account balance, the German currency started to decline vis-à-vis the dollar.

In spite of the oil drag the French gross domestic product went on growing in 1979, although at a moderate 3.3 per cent rate (Table 9). The expectation of an accelerating inflation engendered speculative demand both in stocks and investments, while private consumption did not contract significantly because French consumers reacted by curbing their saving rate.[15] In 1980 the GDP growth rate fell to 1.1 per cent and industrial production declined. The inflation caused by the oil bill started to affect consumer spending power, while French firms' profit margin underwent the impact of an acceleration of salary expenditures, higher prices of intermediary products, oil in particular and this impact could not be fully transferred to final consumers because of price competition from foreign products.

The Italian economy presented some peculiar characteristics compared to most of the major members of the Community. The rate of unemployment was higher than the EC average reaching 6.7 per cent and 7.2 per cent in 1979 and 1980 respectively as the labour force grew faster than employment due to demographic reasons and a higher female participation rate (Table 22). The fiscal deficit, which since the late 1960s had been constantly higher than the EC average, amounted to 8.3 per cent of GDP and 8.5 per cent of GDP in 1979 and 1980 (Table 19). The consumer price index (CPI), after slightly subsiding from its 19.2 peak in 1974, started to accelerate again during the second oil crisis reaching 21.2 per cent in 1980. Although entry into the EMS in 1979 forced Italy to adopt a rather less free management of the currency, the depreciation of the lira helped to preserve the competitiveness of Italian products in spite of high inflation and soaring unit labour costs on a national currency basis (Figure 4). The GDP growth rate from a 1.9 per cent low in 1977 jumped to 4.9 per cent in 1979 and 3.9 per cent in 1980, well above the EC average (Table 9). Also the rate of industrial production was much higher than the EC average in the period and the most dynamic factor was exports, which, in turn, helped bolster consumer spending and stimulate a recovery in investments. However, because of the deterioration of the terms of trade, imports grew faster than exports and increased the trade deficit in 1979 by over 1,100 per cent relative to the previous year (Tables 11 and 12). The gap went on growing in 1980, jumping to 15.7 billion ECU, as imports soared under the continuous pressure of the oil price rise while exports slackened because of the weaker competitiveness of Italian products caused by the inflation differential and the slowdown in foreign demand brought about by the worsening of the international economic environment.

The year 1979 witnessed an acceleration of inflation in the UK as the CPI jumped to 13.4 under the combined pressure of a wage explosion consequent on the refusal of the TUC to further endorse the social contract at the centre of the Labour government income policy, the increase in VAT decided by the incoming Conservative government and the impact of the oil bill (Table 23). The latter, however, was not as strong as in most other EC members, as North Sea oil came on stream in 1976 and by 1980 the direct contribution of domestic oil and gas to GDP reached 4.4 per cent. The Thatcher government, which came into office in May 1979, made fighting inflation its main priority, duly stressing its commitment to the issue, whereas the previous administration had shown a commitment to both tackling unemployment and price stability.[16] And in the words of the Iron Lady, 'inflation was a monetary phenomenon which it would require monetary discipline to curb'.[17] In keeping with its declared monetarist approach, the new Conservative government's strategy was to reduce the growth of monetary supply. Already in 1979, the first moves were taken to curb the demand for bank credit by raising interest rates. To lend more credibility to its monetarist policy, in 1980 the Thatcher administration introduced a medium-term financial strategy, establishing targets for periods of up to four years for both monetary growth and Public Sector Borrowing Requirement, the latter no longer seen as an instrument of demand control but as a source of monetary base and hence as an inflationary factor. In the short-run the new policy was not very successful as inflation continued to rise reaching 18 per cent in 1980. On the other hand, the squeeze resulted in a marked GDP slowdown in 1979 which turned into a slump the following year, pushing the unemployment rate up. In contrast to Italy, the deficit of Britain's trade balance did not result in a steady depreciation of the pound. After the downfall of 1976, the UK currency went on rising from the following year, also in real terms.[18] Various factors explain this trend. If the trade balance was constantly in deficit, the current account, including the invisible balance, turned positive in 1978 and after a slightly negative figure in 1979, yielded a surplus a year later. The sharp rise of interest rates in the first years of the Thatcher government attracted capitals from abroad because of the rate differential and also because the rise indicated the willingness of the new administration to curb inflation and consequently to avoid the weakening of the currency in the exchange rate market. After the widening of the gap in 1979 the trade deficit shrank in 1980 as demand for imports was curtailed by the recession and North Sea oil replaced imports from the OPEC and other developing countries. On the other hand, the strength of the pound made it difficult to cushion the rising unit labour cost of manufactured products. By 1980 the differential between the unit cost increase measured on a dollar basis and on the national currency basis, allowed by the slide of the pound in 1976, petered out (Figure 4).

The trade balance across the Atlantic

In spite of the impact of the sharp rise in oil price, coupled, to a lesser extent, with the increase in the price of other raw materials, the gap in the US merchandise trade balance narrowed and the current account approached the balance in 1979 and reached it in the following two years (Table 2). Despite a 20 per cent decrease in the volume of the US energy imports between 1979 and 1980, rising prices led to a 25 per cent increase in the US energy import bill.[19] On the other end, the marked slowdown of the US economy in 1979 and its decline in 1980, short and limited as it was, entailed a contraction in imports. In other words, by 1979 the United States had ceased to be an engine of the international locomotive, a role that, instead, was still played by West Germany. The real, i.e. adjusted by changes in consumer prices, multilateral trade-weighted value of the dollar slightly recovered in the two years following 1978 (Figure 2). But the appreciation was the result of divergent trends vis-à-vis the currencies of the main trading partners. The dollar was still declining relative to most European currencies, though at a lower rate than in the years immediately following 1975, but was appreciating vis-à-vis the yen (Figure 1). Thus the United States curbed, although for a short while, the deficit with Japan, while largely increasing the surplus with the EC and with the other Western Europe states (Table 5). In 1980 the surplus with the EC was enough to offset the deficit with Japan and the Middle East countries. The balance of the current account and then its surplus were helped by the performance of the service sector. The balance on goods and services, negative in 1977 and 1978, again turned positive in 1979 and in 1981 reached $14.3 billion (Table 2). Net investment income rose from $20.6 billion in 1978 to $31.2 billion a year later and reached $34 billion in 1981. The current account recorded a $6.9 billion surplus in 1981.

The combination of a strengthening current account and rising interest rates started an appreciation of the dollar since the third quarter of 1980. Thus both the appreciation of the American currency and the rise in real interest rates were already present before the explosion of the fiscal deficit, that is, when such a deficit was more moderate than that recorded in most EC countries, including Germany (Table 8 and Table 19).

The second oil shock marked a serious deterioration of the trade balance of all the EC member states as well as of their current balance with the relevant exception of the UK. The EC overall deficit soared from 2.5 billion ECU in 1978 to 43.8 billion ECU two years later. By 1980 the fuel product bill was much higher than that for food, beverages and tobacco, raw materials and chemicals taken together (Figure 8). The already high negative gap with OPEC countries quadrupled between 1978 and 1980 (Figure 5 and Figure 6). The EC deficit on bilateral trade with Japan rose from $1.3 billion in 1973 to $7.1 billion in 1979, reaching about $10 billion in 1980.[20] Japan's exports concentrated on products such as cars, television sets, electronic goods and machine tools, while the Community failed to secure offsetting outlets for its manufactures.

The total trade deficit of the nine EC member states towards the United States swelled in 1979 and 1980, although it started to narrow the following year under the effect of the income slowdown and the appreciation of the greenback (Tables 13 and 14). EC exports grew much more slowly than imports. Even Germany's positive gap shrank (or even turned into a deficit in 1980 according to the ECU data). As regards manufactures the US deficit of $1.5 billion in 1971 turned into a surplus of $5.7 billion nine years later (485 per cent).[21] In 1980, the main US export products were office machinery and computers, electrical machinery apparatus and chemicals and soybeans, while imports from the EC were concentrated in passenger cars, special purpose machinery, iron, steel and other ferrous metals, chemicals and, quite surprisingly, crude petroleum.[22] This trend reflects the depreciation of the dollar vis-à-vis the currency of its main EC partners, between 1976 and 1980 (Figure 1) and with it the increased competitiveness of the US. Indeed, as shown by Figure 4, under the pressure of inflation, incorporated in turn in the trade unions' demand for higher wages, which were not offset by sufficient productivity increase, the unit labour cost grew in most EC member states at a rate no lower than in the United States. However, the unit labour cost in the Community measured on a US dollar basis grew much faster than the equivalent cost in the United States, with the exception of Italy and, to a lesser extent, of the UK. It also reflects the fact that during the 1979–80 biennium, with the remarkable exception of the United Kingdom, the EC member states' growth rate was higher than in the US (Table 9), thus stimulating import demand more than across the Atlantic.

The worsening of the EC merchandise trade balance with its transatlantic trading partner was accompanied by rising tension in various sectors. The European Community had traditionally posted a substantial surplus in textile and apparel trade with the US, but from 1977 the United States started to close the gap as its exports to the European Community more than doubled while its imports started to level off. In 1979 the EC industry showed a deficit that widened to almost $1.4 billion the following year. The British industry was particularly affected by foreign competition and in February 1980 the European Community instituted a safeguard action under GATT Art. XIX on imports of certain synthetic yarns into the UK for the whole of 1980. The United States contested the selective nature of the safeguard action as the bulk of imports came from the US and threatened the retaliatory withdrawal of tariff concessions on imports of certain wool apparel items, mostly supplied by the UK. Finally, at the end of the year, the EC lifted the quotas on synthetic yarns while the US accepted as compensation the Community's offer of accelerated implementation of Tokyo Round tariff concessions on certain chemical products. As is usual in such cases, the Community also resorted to the antidumping lever imposing duties on imports of acrylic and polyester fibres from the United States.

In the petrochemical sector, where the US had a trade surplus with the EC, the latter had been complaining in the GATT since 1979 that growing US synthetic fibre exports to the Community were the result of indirect subsidization allowed by price control regulation on oil and natural gas combined with export controls on petroleum and naphtha, which gave American exporters a cost advantage over European producers. The United States rejoined that the rise in synthetic fibre exports was instead brought about by US competitive advantage combined with current EC structural problems in the sector and the depreciation of the dollar relative to EC currencies. In 1980 the two parties agreed to establish a bilateral government–industry group to explore on the one hand the impact of US energy controls on petrochemicals and on the other the general causes of the chemical industry difficulties in the European Community. The conflict on petrochemicals subsided in 1982 when the recession dampened EC demand for these products and the appreciation of the dollar curbed the US cost advantage.

The Keynesian bias of Reaganomics and its impact on the US trade balance

The trade scenario across the Atlantic started to change in 1982 and the trend accelerated in the following years.

From 1983 the generalized slump was followed by recovery which had, however, different speeds and strengths not only on the two sides of the Atlantic but also among the EC member states. The management of fiscal policy differed across the Atlantic as the Reagan experiment was mirrored by a more prudent management of the budget in Europe, though with the initial exception of France. Above all the period saw a swelling US current account deficit which, in stark contrast to what was to be expected in a different political and economic context, was joined and stoked by the appreciation of the greenback as the United States became a magnet for foreign capital. World exports declined in the first two years in line with the slump (in volume, 1 per cent in 1981 and –3 per cent in 1982) and then recovered in the following years (3 per cent, 9.5 per cent, 3.5 per cent and 4 per cent from 1983 onwards). It was also a period of protectionist pressures.

Before focusing on the deterioration of the US trade balance and its impact on trade relations with Japan and its transatlantic trading partner and its member states, it is appropriate to look at the evolution of the whole American economy. If one looks at 1981–6 there is no strong evidence of a real impact of Reaganomics or of its failure and, on average, leaving aside an exceptionally strong recovery after an extremely marked contraction, there is no remarkable gap between the first six years of the Reagan administration and the previous five years, in terms of both GDP and investment growth. Changes concerned, however, public deficit and the export performance.

In the year that followed the recession of 1980, which contributed to the downfall of President Carter, the recovery was modest compared to the previous decade. The omnibus Budget Reconciliation Act was passed in June 1981 and in August Reagan signed into law the Economic Recovery Tax Act (ERTA), which was supposed to lay the foundation of a permanent boost for the economy under the sign of Reaganomics, that is, by creating the fiscal environment for growth in investment as well as in savings. In 1981 the balance on goods and services as well as the current account balance were still positive even showing an improvement over the previous year and the dollar started to appreciate sharply, both in nominal and real terms. According to the Economic Report of the President, 'this movement was explained only in part by the current account surplus of the United States relative to its trading partner, another relevant factor being the shift toward dollar-denominated assets', which 'may have been a consequence of the President's economic recovery program'.[23] GDP grew by 2 per cent. This concealed, however, strong changes among the quarters of the year as products soared in the first quarter and plummeted in the final. Short-term interest rates grew in the first months of the year but substantially declined later in nominal terms, while long-term interest rates remained higher than in 1980. Restrictive monetary policy, whose priority was to curb inflation rather than promoting growth, had a severe impact on the most credit-sensitive industries, such as housing, consumer durables and business investments. The following year witnessed the deepest recession since the 1930s, with a GDP contraction of 2.5 per cent and the unemployment rate ballooning at 9.7 per cent, a rate much higher than in the 1974–5 depression. Only at the end of the year did the economy begin to recover. The GDP grew by 3.7 in 1983, a robust rate but certainly far from exceptional if compared to the years of positive performance in the preceding decade. However, the following year marked an unprecedented recovery with a GDP growth rate of 7 per cent, although unemployment remained quite high. In 1985 and 1986 the rate of growth became more moderate, averaging 3.2 per cent. On the other hand, unemployment abated to 7 per cent, a rate still high relative to the previous decades but much more moderate than the rate in most European countries, including the Federal Republic.

The components that contributed to the recovery, as shown in Table 1, were in the first place fixed investments and to a lesser degree private consumption. It is rather doubtful that the progress in these components can be attributed, at least exclusively, to the success of Reaganomics precepts. Indeed a fiscal stimulus is also a tenet of Keynesian policy; there was no increase in overall private saving as a share of national income, although net business saving grew, thus entailing greater self-financing, and the fiscal deficit, rather than contracting with GDP expansion, soared. From 1984 onwards there was also a strong increase in public expenditure. Federal deficit grew from 2.7 per cent of GDP in 1981, a percentage in line with the average of the second half of the 1970s, to 5.5 per cent a year later, reaching a 6.1 per cent peak in 1983. An analogous trend marked the total government deficit (see Table 8). In the first three years of the Reagan administration the deficit was prevalently the result of the slowdown in public receipts while expenditures, including the increasing burden of interest rates on public debt, kept on growing. Subsequently there was a hike in receipts but expenditures moved ahead even faster. In December 1985 the Balanced Budget and Emergency Deficit Control Act, promoted by senators Ernest Hollings, Phil Gramm and Warren Rudman, was signed into law by Reagan, which provided for automatic spending cuts, though with some exceptions, if the deficit exceeded a set of fixed deficit targets.

Real exports declined while imports soared (Table 1). The result was an explosion in the current account deficit, as the positive balance turned into deficit (–$8.7 billion) in 1982 and the deficit grew by over 15 times in four years totalling $141.4 billion in 1986 (Table 2). The deficit soared in automotive vehicles and consumer goods (Table 3). However, the US merchandise trade plight appears to be much worse looking at many domestic exports and imports for consumption in several prominent US industries all of which plunged into the red with the exception of chemicals, while fuels, though remaining in the red, improved their balance thanks to the abating of the oil crisis (Table 4). The weight of imports over the GDP grew by 3 percentage points from 1981 to 1985 and exceeded 14 per cent in 1986. The figure was far from exceptional especially if compared with the EC countries' average. However, import penetration swelled in sectors in growing difficulties, from steel to automotives and clothing. And these sectors had traditionally provided employment for a non-negligible share of the working population and were influential in Congress.

Which were the causes and effects of such astounding deficit? An explanation of the deterioration of the US current account might be provided by the well-known open economy identity: $CA = SP - I - (G - T)$, where CA represents the current account, investments, SP private saving and G – T is the budget surplus or deficit. Indeed, during the Reagan period the explosion of the current account deficit relative to the GDP was joined by a corresponding increase in the excess of investments over domestic private savings and by the explosion of the fiscal deficit. However, being an identity, this explanation overlooks the underlying process. At the same time, for any economics student the arrow goes from the excess of investment over private savings and budget balance to the current account deficit. But this leaves aside the role of factors like capital movements, changes in international prices and interest rate differential among trading partners which had a primary role in the process during the first part of the decade.

Contemporary US governmental sources repeatedly focused on three concurrent factors: the changed trade pattern of developing countries affected by the debt crisis; differences in economic growth among the main trading partners; and the saving-investment balance, its impact on capital flows and exchange rate movements and competitiveness.[24]

One reason for the poor US trade performance was found in the developing countries' efforts to handle their debt crisis. Credit-restricted nations had to reduce current consumption, restrict imports and increase exports. By lowering domestic demand, high-debt nations cut back their import levels. However, as the resulting import decline was insufficient in many debtor countries they enacted policies to discourage or actively restrict imports. As limiting imports saved these countries' foreign exchange, but did not actually earn them additional hard currencies, their retrenchment efforts also included a strong push to increase exports. In 1981 the United States had a $3.1 billion merchandise trade surplus with its Central and South American trading partners. As high-debt Latin American countries, in particular Argentina, Brazil, Chile, Mexico, Peru and Venezuela, slashed imports and boosted exports to counteract the drop in gross capital flows from the US and other developed countries, in just three years the surplus turned into a $18.2 billion deficit: a net $21.3 billion swing (Table 5).

However, this cause of the deterioration of the US current account is geographically limited. It can explain the shift in the trade balance with the other Western Hemisphere countries, excluding Canada, but as regards merchandise trade in particular, relations with these countries accounted for about 15 per cent of the overall US deficit while the deterioration of the US trade with Japan and the European Community was even more dramatic.

The second factor that was called on to explain the deficit was America's earlier and more robust economic recovery compared to that of its trading partners. The recovery from the 1982 slump was quite strong. From the end of 1982 through 1984 US GNP increased at an average 5.3 per cent annual rate. Its booming economy helped the US absorb increased imports while its export growth lagged as America's trading partners' economic recovery did not keep pace with its own. The US administration, therefore, argued that its booming imports helped keep its trading partners, nominally the European countries, from sliding into a worse economic situation. Yet, a gap between speed and rate of American recovery and that of Europe was also present in the previous decade without resulting in so gaping a trade and current account deficit. In 1985 and 1986, despite the convergence of the rates of growth of economic activity among industrialized countries, the US current account deficit went on increasing. In any event, the soaring deficit with Japan, which grew at a 4.3 per cent annual rate between 1982 and 1985, and other Asian countries could not be ascribed to significant disparities in income growth.

The main culprit was thus found in the effect of the high dollar in real terms on the price competitiveness of US industry in international markets. The price-adjusted weighted-average exchange value of the dollar rose by over 50 per cent against a basket of major foreign currencies from the beginning of 1980 through February 1985, when the dollar peaked. The appreciation of the dollar overwhelmed the other determinants of international cost. For instance, by 1985 unit labour costs in the United States rose to 111.2 per cent on a 1980 base while rising by over 116 per cent in the eleven largest foreign industrial countries during the same period. Yet, in dollar terms foreign unit labour costs fell nearly 20 per cent. Instead of experiencing a 5 per cent improvement in US international cost competitiveness, the strong appreciation of the dollar boosted the ratio of US unit labour costs to foreign unit labour costs by 39 per cent.[25]

The main, though not unique, cause of the rise of the greenback was found in the positive differential between US long-term real interest rates and the average of comparable foreign interest rates and the consequent inflow of foreign capitals.[26] This differential, in turn, was associated with monetary restraint exercised by the Federal Reserve since the end of the Carter era and subsequently with an expansionary US fiscal policy. Tax cuts and subsequent high public expenditure reduced public savings and fuelled budget deficit. The Fed's anti-inflationary policy meant that the deficit had to be financed by selling bonds rather than printing money and higher interest rates were needed to induce investors to absorb the additional debt. The excess of real domestic demand over real domestic output, linked to the excess of real domestic investments over real domestic savings was covered by the net inflow of foreign capitals in a variety of forms, such as direct and portfolio investments, purchases of US government securities and deposits in banks in the United States. In short, the open economy identity theory can be accepted, but in this particular instance the gap between domestic savings and investments did not have a direct impact on the current account deficit but was mediated by pressure on the currency put by capital movements attracted by the positive interest differential. The inflow of foreign investments thus prevented the fiscal deficit from crowding-out private investment and to a certain extent curbed the rise in interest rates. The European partners were far from happy with the results of the US economic policy since the pressure of high interest rates inhibited their economic recovery, while capital flew out of Europe to the other side of the Atlantic. On the other hand, the appreciation of the dollar entailed for all the EC member states a positive trade balance with their transatlantic partner.

However the inflow of foreign capitals was not only the result of real interest rate differentials. During the first half of the decade capitals were also attracted by the prospect of a high ratio of revenue over capital invested, linked to the favourable tax treatment and to the expectation of higher economic growth. Actually, as illustrated by Table 7, in 1980 foreign direct investments, in nominal terms, were six times as high as in 1970; just five years later they were almost fourteen times as high. The bulk came from Europe, in spite of the higher cost of the investment in national currencies, and in particular from the United Kingdom, the Netherlands, West Germany and Switzerland. FDIs from Japan, negligible till 1975, soared in the 1980s and by 1984 overcame Canadian investments. The net transfer of financial wealth from abroad rapidly eroded the long-standing US position as a net creditor and by 1985 the US became a net debtor for the first time since the First World War. With hindsight it appears that the Reagan years, still seen as years in which the United States was able to reassert its predominance in the world economy, marked the emergence of problems like fiscal and trade deficits that, with various levels of intensity, are haunting it through to the present time.

Recession and slow recovery in the EC member states and their reflection on international trade

In the first years of the decade, the EC member states, although with remarkable differences among countries, overall experienced a more protracted decline and a slower and less vigorous recovery than the United States. Sectors that had a main role in the European economy less than ten years earlier, such as textiles and clothing, iron and steel, shipbuilding and automotive, saw the deepening of the decline triggered by the first oil crisis or an unforeseen slowdown. European countries were forced to maintain a restrictive monetary stance and high interest rates to defend their currencies against the dollar, while they adopted a much more prudent fiscal policy than in the previous decade, also to prevent a crowding-out threat on private investment. Investments declined in the first three years under the pressure of rising real long-term interest rates and plunging net rate of return on fixed capital. They started, however, to pick up from 1984 onwards, helped by the recovery in profitability. Unemployment rose at levels higher than in the previous decade and, on average, did not significantly decline in spite of the recovery.

The main European economy, West Germany, contracted more moderately than the United States in 1982 but its rate of recovery was much slower (Table 9). Particularly evident was the growth rate gap in 1983 and 1984. Only in 1986 did the growth rate of the Federal Republic come close to that of its transatlantic trading partner. The unemployment rate doubled between 1980 and 1982 and from 1984 was higher than in the United States. The current account, which had turned into the red during the second oil crisis, became positive once again in 1982; in 1985 its annual average surplus was 2.2 per cent of GNP and the following year it reached 4.1 per cent. In line with the dominant trend in the German economy, the positive current account results were largely driven by the merchandise trade balance. Various factors can explain the performance of the trade and current account balances. In spite of the hike in the international price of oil in 1979–80 and the subsequent appreciation of the dollar, the currency in which oil prices were quoted, the oil bill for Germany declined from 4.6 per cent of GDP in 1981 to 3.8 per cent in 1985. Although both the United States and Germany followed an anti-inflationary policy, in contrast to its transatlantic counterpart, the German government tightened its fiscal stance even before the arrival of the Khol administration. As a result gross saving exceeded gross investment from 1982.[27] As regards trade with the US, the gap in the two countries' GDP growth rate along with the appreciation of the dollar also presented German exporters with excellent opportunities. After a brief reversal in 1980 and 1981 the traditional trade surplus soared in the following year, reaching over 33 billion ECU in 1985 (Tables 13 and 14). At the same time German savings found an outlet across the Atlantic attracted not only by the interest rate differential but, above all, by the favourable prospect of high revenues in an economic environment that after 1982 seemed to be more promising than in Germany. Thus German FDIs in the United States grew by 56 per cent between 1981 and 1985.

The slump of 1980 and 1981 in the United Kingdom was much more severe than the average of the other member states, but in the following year the recovery was more vigorous (Table 9). Industrial production in 1982 was still lower than three years earlier but afterwards showed a marked acceleration (Table 21). Significant improvements were achieved in the fight against inflation that declined from over 15 per cent in 1980 to just 2.4 per cent in the summer of 1986, though thereafter there was a gradual rise. The major factor in bringing down inflation was the severity of the recession of 1980–2 and, as in other OECD countries, the fall in commodity prices, apart from oil, which in turn, was the effect of the decline in demand experienced in that period. Unemployment cut wage pressure on the cost of products and on their prices. On the other hand, unemployment went on rising even after the 1983 recovery reaching a peak of 12 per cent in 1985. In spite of the Thatcherite rhetoric, the UK fiscal deficit as percentage of GDP did not decline in the first half of the 1980s and the same went for public expenditure, which actually increased in constant prices during the Thatcher years.[28] The current account position remained positive during the period under review, while the merchandise trade balance showed a negative trend (Tables 11 and 12). Oil played an important role in the process, as the UK went from being a net importer of mineral fuels by around £1.8 billion in 1979 to a net exporter of these products by just over £6 billion six years later. The UK also became less dependent on food imports and actually could be counted among the world's largest food producers reflecting the boost to British farming by the much criticized Common Agricultural Policy. On the other hand manufacturing exports showed a deep decline: in 1983 Britain ran a deficit in manufactured goods, the first since the Industrial Revolution.

France paid the price of trying to follow an expansionary policy when most other countries were adopting a deflationary stance, although with the exception of the United States and Italy as regards fiscal policy. Actually, the reflationary measures adopted by the French Socialist government that came to power in May 1981 were overall moderate.[29] Besides, their sustainability relied on forecasts that were shared by the OECD and the European Community: a moderate 2 per cent GDP growth, higher than in most other industrial countries, and an increase in the volume of world trade which would partially offset the impact of growing imports. The reflationary policy relied on both budgetary and non-budgetary measures. The former were rather balanced. The budget deficit in 1981 did not exceed 2 per cent of GDP, although in 1982 it neared 3 per cent. The main budgetary measures included investment by government departments, housing subsidies and subsidies to industries. Several banks and some high-tech industries were nationalized. Raising the minimum wage was the main non-budgetary reflationary measure along with a modest reduction of the working week and the retirement age. Several of these measures were not hailed by French employers. Pressures on the balance of payments gained momentum in 1982 when the expected world trade recovery failed to materialize and the slump hit many countries, including the United States. The current account balance, which had been in equilibrium and even positive in the previous two years, went into the red in 1981 and by 1982 showed a deficit totalling 3 per cent of GDP. From the start of the Socialist government a certain lack of confidence generated large capital outflows which over the two years 1981 and 1982 more than doubled the current account deficit and increased the external borrowing requirement. The combined pressure of current account deficits and exits of capital led to an external debt which in francs had increased four times between 1980 and 1983 and doubled in dollar terms.[30] A first devaluation within the EMS was decided in October 1981, partly as a result of the previous overvaluation of the franc under the Barre government, partly due to capital flights and partly as a result of the new government's plans for reflation. The French franc and the Italian lira were devalued by 3 per cent, while the Deutschmark and the Dutch guilder were revalued by 5.5 per cent. In June 1982 the Deutschmark and the guilder were revalued by 4.25 per cent, while the franc and the lira were devalued respectively by 5.75 per cent and 2.75 per cent. A third realignment took place in March 1983 when the Deutschmark was revalued by 5.5 per cent along with the guilder, the Danish krone and the Belgian franc, but by a lower rate, while the French franc and the lira were devalued by 2.5 per cent and the Irish pound by 3.5 per cent. A further devaluation of the franc occurred in 1986 at the start of the 'cohabitation' of François Mitterrand with the Conservative cabinet of Jacques Chirac.

March 1983 marked the so-called 'tournant de la rigueur' (austerity turn), based on an increase in taxes, which mainly affected households, and a reduction in spending in government services. The austerity turn affected investments in both the private and public sectors and caused a slowdown of the economy whose growth rate, though still positive, remained below the EC average (Table 9). The decline of demand helped improve the current account balance. However, the merchandise trade balance, with the exception of relations with the US, which, on average, only accounted for 6.5 per cent of French total exports and 7 per cent of total imports, remained in the red despite the depreciation vis-à-vis the dollar and realignment in the EMS. Farm trade, previously in balance, became positive in the 1980s, but deficit in trade of manufactured goods was more than double the agricultural trade surplus during 1980–5, leaving a huge trade deficit. Exports towards Africa and the Middle East, a traditional preserve of French exports, declined due to the end of the oil bonanza in those countries and the free-trade orientation of the Common Market in manufactured goods resulted in large and growing deficits in France's intra-European trade.

The aftermath of the second oil shock witnessed a prolonged overall worsening of the main sectors of the Italian economy. After a marked slowdown in 1981 the Italian GDP growth rate further declined in the following two years, starting to recover in 1984 at a level slightly higher than the EC average. The growth rate, however, remained below the Italian average in the second half of the preceding decade and the moderate recovery did not stem the surge of unemployment which exceeded 13 per cent in 1986. The constraints imposed by EMS membership, in spite of the realignments in 1982 and 1983 did not leave room for manoeuvre to an expansionary policy. The interest rate rise, which from the United States had spread to most industrialized countries, also affected the demand for investments which were prevalently directed to re-equipment and restructuring. On the other hand, success was achieved in curbing inflation which from a peak of over 21 per cent in 1980 fell to 6 per cent six years later, although it remained above the average of the other member states. The Bank of Italy took the main role in managing deflation, its autonomy being boosted by the so-called 'divorce' between the Treasury and the Central Bank lifting the obligation for the latter to purchase bonds the government was failing to option. However, the 'divorce' did not force any significant adjustment in fiscal policy and the deficit went on rising from 1981 onwards, reaching 12.3 per cent of the GDP in 1985. Total expenditures soared from 39.4 per cent of GDP in 1979 to over 50 per cent six years later (Table 19). The deficit was bloated by the growing burden of interest rates which were also the results of upward international pressure and, to a certain extent, of the 'divorce' itself. On the other hand, the primary deficit (that is, excluding interest payments) started to slow down.

The current account balance remained mostly in the red, although the deficit declined from a peak of 2.2 per cent of GDP in 1980 to 0.9 per cent in 1985. Trade continued to show a wide negative gap as exports grew faster than imports (Tables 11 and 12) but from a much lower basis. Exports consisted mainly of traditional consumer goods like textiles, clothing and leather goods as well as engineering goods of low or intermediate technological content, but also more sophisticated products such as machinery tools showed particular dynamism. The growth of imports continued to be fuelled by food, chemicals and fuels and it was only in 1986 with the concurrent fall of the oil price and the depreciation of the dollar, the currency in which most commodities were quoted, that the trade balance showed a detectable improvement.

The trade balance of the Community as a whole showed a marked improvement relative to the second oil shock years, although it remained in the red till 1984 (Tables 11 and 12). In particular, there was significant improvement in the trade balance with the United States, which from an $18,217 million deficit in 1980 turned into an $18,985 million surplus five years later (Table 5).Yet, the US, though as a single state the main trading partner of the Community, as an economic area accounted for less than 10 per cent of EC exports and imports. Much of the shift was undoubtedly due to the appreciation of the dollar against the European currencies and this might have given a competitive edge to the EC industries in third markets. Thus, the American authorities could say that the appreciation of the greenback was a windfall for Europe which was not able to exploit this opportunity to achieve a fully-fledged economic recovery because of the rigidities inherent in its market, that is, to use a term that became common in economic and political parlance, 'eurosclerosis'. However, the appreciation of the dollar also entailed some disadvantages for Europe with regard to imports, in particular of commodities, most of which were valued in the US currency. In particular, despite the curtailment on oil consumption and a drop in the dollar price of oil, the value of fuel products remained by far the main item among the extra-EC imports and although it did not increase after 1981, neither did it show signs of declining up to 1985 (Figure 8). The main subject of complaint by the Community and its member states, particularly vociferous among which was France, were the constraints imposed on the money market by contradictions in the US monetary and fiscal policies: the upwards pressure on interest rates. Indeed, the European countries were facing a dire dilemma.

They did not want their exchange rates to depreciate further, because this raised the cost expressed in their own currencies of oil and other dollar-denominated imports, thus worsening inflation. To avoid such an occurrence they had to keep interest rates high. On the other hand, as rates of return on industrial capital were driven down by adverse terms of trade, high labour costs, decline in factor productivity and weak final demand, they dropped below real interest rates thus discouraging new investments, which in turn delayed the recovery.[31] High interest rates also contributed to curb exports to developing countries which were forced to adopt strict policies directed at servicing their foreign debt. For countries like France that had to take up foreign loans to cover the current account deficit, high interest rates along with the strength of the dollar made the service of the debt more demanding, thus adding to the constraints on domestic demand.[32]

New attitudes across the Atlantic on currency management since 1985

During its first four years, the Reagan administration, in line with its official philosophy of bowing down to the invisible hand of the market, preferred not to oppose the appreciation of the dollar, claiming instead that it was a sign and consequence of the healthy state of the American economy.[33] This does not necessarily imply that the US Treasury was indifferent to the excessive strength of the dollar. Though not directly intervening in the market, it is arguable that the US was not averse to putting pressure on other countries. Some experts argue that the main reason for bringing up the issue of financial liberalization in Japan in 1983 was to help US manufacturers by strengthening the yen relative to the dollar, whereas opening the Japanese market to American financial institutions was a secondary goal. In this perspective the best way to realign the two currencies was to open up Japanese capital markets and to internationalize the yen.[34] If this was the case, the result was not up to the American hopes.

Things changed in early 1985 with the replacement of Donald Regan at the head of the Treasury Department by James Baker whose nomination marked the end of the 'hands-off' (from the dollar) policy previously followed by the executive. The change in attitude was encouraged by the choir of complaints, not so much from foreign partners, but from US industries threatened in both the foreign and the domestic market by foreign competition, and by undeniable evidence of a rocketing trade deficit.

After reaching a peak in the first quarter of 1985 the dollar started to decline. In their June meeting in Tokyo the finance ministers of the Group of Ten discussed ways to make the international monetary system more stable and effective. On 22 September 1985 the finance ministers and central bank governors of the Group of 5 (France, West Germany, Japan, the UK and the US), meeting at the Plaza Hotel in New York, declared that 'recent shifts in fundamental economic conditions among their countries, together with policy commitments for the future, have not been reflected fully in exchange markets', hence gainsaying the view that the market's assessment should be trusted.[35] According to the Plaza statement, the exchange misalignment had 'contributed to large, potentially destabilizing external imbalances among major industrial countries' whose main outcome was the United States' large and growing current account deficit and Japan's and, to a lesser extent, Germany's large and growing current account surplus. The ministers and governors, therefore, announced that 'exchange rates should play a role in adjusting external imbalances', better reflecting fundamental economic conditions. It must be noted that the Plaza declaration did not mention a depreciation of the greenback, assuming instead that 'in view of the present and prospective changes in fundamentals, some further orderly appreciation of the main non-dollar currencies against the dollar is desirable'. The representatives of the G5 group made it clear that 'they stand ready to cooperate more closely to encourage this when to do so would be helpful'. Each participant made a statement of 'policy intention' whose implementation in his country would have helped achieve a better currency equilibrium, although no formal detailed engagement for coordination in fiscal and monetary policy was agreed on. Commitments for closer cooperation in macroeconomic policies were made at the Louvre meeting eighteen months later when the G5 finance ministers and governors plus the representatives of Canada and Italy met again to put the brakes on the apparently unstoppable fall of the American currency.[36]

By early 1986 the multilateral trade-weighted value (in real terms) of the dollar had fallen by 20 per cent back to its 1981 level. Yet, there was no apparent impact on the trade and current account balances. Among the factors explaining the absence of a prompt response was the willingness of foreign producers to cut their profit margins and maintain their shares of the US market, exploiting the room for manoeuvre provided by their widened profits during the 1980–4 appreciation of the dollar. It is also possible that American producers, who had lost market shares during the appreciation of the dollar, found it difficult to re-establish their beachhead. Besides, the dollar had not depreciated substantially against the currencies of several important trading partners such as Canada, Korea and Taiwan. Actually, both the merchandise trade balance and the current account balance further deteriorated in 1986 (see Table 2). However, by the fourth quarter of 1986, when the greenback's value had plunged by over 30 per cent, there were signs that the depreciation of the dollar was working to reduce external imbalances, while some of the main US trading partners started to worry about the prospective consequences of losing the price advantage gained in the previous years. The participants of the Louvre meeting of 22 February 1987 stated that, given the economic policy commitment they were making, their currencies were within ranges broadly consistent with underlying economic fundamentals and that 'further substantial exchange rate shifts among their currencies could damage growth and adjustment prospects'.[37]

Yet, the dollar did not bottom out soon, and neither the fiscal deficit nor the current account deficit disappeared. Figure 3 offers an explanation of the interplay of some of the main causal factors from a wider time perspective. Certainly by 1990 the current account deficit as a percentage of GDP had dropped significantly, but the deficit was still present and quite high despite the fact that the multilateral trade-weighted value of the dollar (in real terms) was almost at its 1980 level. Figure 3 shows, however, that the deficit overall followed, with a lead time, the variation of the fiscal deficit. It is feasible, therefore, to argue that from 1982 through the first months of 1985 the growing public borrowing requirements overlapped and accelerated the upward pressure on the dollar, already triggered by the rise in real interest rates caused by strict monetary policy. At the very moment in which the monetary brake was starting to relax, the two factors brought about a soaring current account deficit. When the value of the dollar fell, the current account deficit continued but gradually declined in correlation with the fiscal deficit shrinking.[38] As explained above, other factors could have also been at play. It must be noted that the administration repeatedly stated in its reports to Congress that trade-distorting practices by its trading partners had contributed to a deterioration of the US current account balance but their role had been marginal relative to the macroeconomic factors previously examined.

The increased impact of services and MNCs on world trade

Previous pages in this chapter, and in earlier ones, may give the impression that changes in developed countries' trade and trade policies occurred against a backdrop that did not undergo substantial alterations during the years covered by this research and they seem to refer dominantly, if not exclusively, to the merchandise sector. Yet the backdrop mutated and its changes help explain why the impact of the repeated crises that affected many traditional sectors, along with the difficulties faced by sectors to which both the US and the EC had entrusted their hopes of economic relaunch, was less severe than it might have been, although an accurate quantitative assessment is not available. This also helps explain why trade policy concerns of the transatlantic trading partners changed both at domestic and multilateral levels.

In the first place, the proportion of the three main sectors, services, industry and agriculture, in the GDP changed. In the advanced economies the weight of services grew from 54 per cent to 61 per cent between 1965 and 1987.[39] According to the US president report, in 1984 services accounted for nearly 69 per cent of US GDP and provided seven out of ten jobs.[40] In the 1970s the Western European service sector entered into an era of accelerated growth, in particular in terms of employment, at the expense of both the agricultural and manufacturing sectors. Its share of value added reached 65.6 per cent in 1980. The share of employment grew from 42.8 per cent in 1960 to 55.8 per cent twenty years later.[41]

Industrial countries were also the main service exporters and services had been providing a lifeline for the current account of many of them, including the United States, offsetting the negative trend in merchandise trade since the early 1970s. There were, obviously, exceptions, most of which were to be found among dominant manufacture exporters like Germany and Japan. The EC member states taken together, and including intra-EC trade, were the main exporter. As a single country the United States became the main exporter in the 1980s, having overtaken France (Figure 12). Services were also important to many developing countries. Eight of the top 25 service exporting countries were developing nations: Singapore, Mexico, Korea, Saudi Arabia, Yugoslavia, Greece, Israel and Egypt together provided $42.4 billion of exports in 1982.[42]

However, the picture showed a conspicuous incongruity, especially with regard to the developed countries which were the dominant exporters. In stark contrast with their weight in the domestic economies, world service exports totalled about $367 billion in 1980 and $383 billion five years later compared to $2,036 billion and $1,954 billion in merchandise trade. It could, therefore, be argued that full exploitation of the service sector potential in international trade was hampered by restrictive practices not less trade-distorting than those hindering merchandise trade. This applied not only to tradable services but also to services whose provision abroad relied on the establishment of a branch or a subsidiary.

The issue was of particular concern for the US, whose fortunes in manufacturing trade had steadily declined (Figure 11). Meanwhile the opportunities for foreign firms to enter the American market, which were offered by the deregulation process affecting a growing number of services from the middle of the 1970s, were not matched, in the US view, by equivalent opportunities for American firms. Measures against alleged foreign barriers to US service exports were already provided by the Trade Act of 1974 and were made more effective and extended to FDIs in the service sector by the statutes adopted during the 1980s. The EC's main concern was the establishment of an effective common market among the member states, but, given the sector's importance for the economy and the employment of the EC countries, they joined the US in pressing for the regulation of barriers to service trade and investment in international fora.

The 1970s and the first half of the following decade witnessed the strengthening of the sway of the MNCs on the international economy. In the early 1980s foreign multinationals in the UK accounted for 19 per cent of industrial output and 15 per cent of industrial employment. Foreign-owned enterprises in West Germany accounted for 26 per cent of industrial production and in France for 25 per cent.[43] In Canada foreign companies controlled about 50 per cent in manufacturing, 44 per cent in petroleum and 46 per cent in other mining. The bulk of FDIs continued to be destined to developed countries, while the share of developing countries fell, as in the 1980s the importance of Latin America for FDI flows declined, while inflows to Africa, South and East Asia remained unchanged. The FDI cross-flow among industrial countries was characterized by significant changes in the trend between the 1970s and the 1980s as the United States shifted from main source to main recipient of capital invested abroad. Having peaked in 1981, US FDIs steeply declined in the following three years but, measured in current US dollars, they recovered in 1985 (Figure 6).[44]

In particular US investments in Latin America fell precipitously in the 1980s and the share of the region, after an almost 20 per cent peak in 1978, plunged to a less than 12 per cent low six years later. American FDIs in Europe also declined after 1981 but recovered in 1985. US investments in Asia gradually increased from 1974 onwards.

In 1986, foreign investments in the United States, in current US dollars, were sixteen times as high as fifteen years earlier, the bulk being provided by Western European companies, whose share of the total stock in the period ranged from 65 per cent to 74 per cent (Table 7). Japanese investments, whose share was negligible before 1975 overtook Canadian investments by 1984 and in 1986 accounted for over 12 per cent of the total stock.

Although attempts to curb the influence of foreign corporations go back to the 1930s, nominally in Latin America, it was in the 1970s that MNCs came more and more into the spotlight of host states, whether developing or industrialized and into international fora. Naturally states' concerns and their stance towards multinational corporations varied according to their level of economic development. On the other hand, the goals and features of multinational corporations cannot be viewed as uniform, but varied according to the sector of activity and to the economic environment in which they were carrying out their activities. A first distinction can be made between extractive industries and manufacturing and service industries. For the first group the relation between host country and MNC primarily hinged on the share of rights in the exploitation of natural resources. For the second group of sectors the variables conditioning the choices of the corporations and the demands of the host countries were multifaceted. For instance, foreign firms in the United States contributed to worsening the US trade balance as being oriented to the local market would import more than what they were exporting.[45] This, however, was not necessarily true for foreign firms in the EC as they carried out their activities in one or more EC countries but also exported to other member countries or elsewhere, and within the EC, despite the aim of establishing a true common market, there was no such thing as a common balance of payments. MNCs in many developing countries quite often exported relatively more than domestic firms because they were established as export platforms. On the other hand, they had a much higher import propensity than domestic firms. Besides, the precarious balance of payments of many developing countries could be hard hit by the reverse flow of capital they had received, as the foreign plants would remit earnings and profits back to the parent company, and this reverse flow might, in time, exceed the inflow of capital. MNCs were the main source of technology for developing countries, but was the foreign technology suitable for exploitation by domestic firms? Furthermore, the commercial and technological predominance of MNCs might hinder the entry and development of local firms. In both industrialized and developing countries, not all new ventures undertaken by MNCs involved the actual transfer of capital to the host economy since some of their new investments might either be financed by borrowing in the host country capital markets or by the reinvestment of retained earnings from the foreign affiliates, not to mention the fact that local firms might be bought with local money.

The stance of the industrialized and developing countries in tackling these issues differed. Even when multinational corporations were seen as an international problem, in the West the extent of that problem was perceived as rather limited. The fear of economic costs and loss of national control was balanced by the perception of economic benefits to be gained by foreign investments. As regards the home country, the perspective of governments toward FDIs – though not necessarily of workers' organizations and of some industries – became much more favourable in the 1970s and 1980s. In the United States the executive's reservations during the 1960s era of the Democratic Party predominance gave way to a favourable attitude recognising the MNCs' contribution to the current account balance in the changed trade environment. The Republican administration stressed that United States' investment abroad had a net positive effect on US trade and on national as well as international well-being, noting that, according to the Department of Commerce, in 1977 roughly one-third of all US exports were trade between US companies and their affiliates abroad.[46] And the surplus on investment income, which reached a $34 billion peak in 1981, also played a role in offsetting the worsening of the merchandise trade balance.

The 1976 OECD Declaration on International Investment and Multinational Enterprises stressed the positive contribution of transnational corporations and was accompanied by governmental decisions to extend national treatment to their subsidiaries. At the same time it laid out a rather comprehensive set of voluntary norms of behaviour for multinational corporations on fiscal and labour issues, that is, the topics in which conflict between MNCs and industrial countries might arise. This did not mean that the national treatment principle was unconditionally and uniformly adopted. Certain sectors, such as defence and communication industries, remained closed to MNCs. Japan was repeatedly accused of obstructing the effective entry of foreign firms into its market. Canada tried for a long time to retain control on the entry and activity of foreign companies, which led to disputes with its southern neighbour.

In contrast, among the developing countries there was the perception that the global strategies of multinational corporations might conflict with the development needs of the host countries and have no coherent linkages with local industries. The developing countries tried, therefore, to assert the principle that MNCs were to be subject to the development policies of the host states as affirmed in the Declaration for the Establishment of a New Economic Order (NIEO) adopted by the United Nations in 1974. The Declaration provided, *inter alia*, that states had full permanent sovereignty over their natural resources and all economic activities, and that in this context they should be entitled to regulate and control the activities of the MNCs operating within their territories and be free to nationalize or expropriate foreign properties on conditions favourable to them.

The interests of the MNCs, with the increasingly explicit support of the home governments, went in the opposite direction. They resented the limits imposed by the host countries on the entry of new investments, with regard both to the sectors in which the activity of foreign firms was allowed and the amount of equities that foreigners might hold in local companies. They favoured unhindered repatriation of capital invested and remittance of affiliates' earnings. Both the MNCs and their home countries defended the principle of national treatment, meaning essentially equality of treatment for foreign and domestic enterprises. To this, most developing countries rejoined that non-discriminatory treatment would in practice amount to discrimination in favour of transnational corporations and would conflict with efforts to strengthen their own enterprises.[47] Though conceding that the right of states to nationalize is acknowledged, the industrial countries claimed that this right should be exercised in conformity with international law and contractual agreements, and the procedure and amount of compensation, should respect them.

In the natural resource sector, after a gradual build-up through the 1960s, there was a sharp rise in the number of expropriations in the first half of the 1970s. Later, however, their number sharply declined and takeovers were replaced by investment agreements. As regards the manufacturing sector, the relative negotiating strength of developed and developing countries changed between the 1970s and the following decade. After 1973, when the growth of manufacturing in industrialized market economies was slackening, it continued to grow rapidly in the developing countries, fuelled by increasing foreign debt. Faced with stagnating markets and rising costs in the North, a number of manufacturing TNCs turned their attention to the South. Between 1973 and 1982 the share of developing countries in world manufacturing added value rose from 8.8 per cent to 11.2 per cent while that of developed market economies fell from 72.1 per cent to 63.5 per cent.[48] The competition among MNCs to enter these dynamic markets provided the host countries with more room for manoeuvre in selecting foreign investors and in imposing on them better terms for their economies. The power shift was exploited both at national and international levels. The United Nations established a Centre on Transnational Corporations charged with monitoring the activity of MNCs and formulating a code of conduct for multinational corporations. As was to be expected, the negotiations did not prove successful given the differences in viewpoint on substantial issues between developed and developing countries. It was only in 1982 that a heavily bracketed draft code on the conduct of transnational corporations was produced, but it never managed to be adopted.

The tide turned in the early 1980s under the impact of the debt crisis. The tumbling of rates of return, particularly steep between 1981 and 1982, was soon followed by a marked contraction in investments. After a 30 per cent peak in 1982, the share of foreign direct investment inflows received by the developing countries plunged to 21.3 per cent in 1984.[49] However, the fall was not uniform. While the inflow of investments in the Asian countries did not show significant changes, the share of FDI flows directed to Latin American countries fell by half in just two years.[50] And Latin American states were among the countries that had been more assertive in calling for a new economic order and strict requirements for MNCs. At the same time, developing countries and socialist countries, faced with an acute shortage of foreign exchange resources, turned to MNCs as a possible source of resource flows and in the process resorted to bilateral investment treaties, over 100 of which were concluded, mostly with industrial countries, from 1980 onwards. Bilateral agreements, rather than addressing the conduct of MNCs, focused on the promotion and protection of FDIs. Most such agreements included both national and most-favoured nation standards as applicable to investors and activities in connection with the investment and, though not guaranteeing an absolute right of entry for investments, placed clear emphasis on facilitating the entry of investments between the contracting parties.

The United States, which, along with Western European countries, signed many bilateral investment treaties, also felt that many issues could be addressed multilaterally, but in a forum more favourable than the United Nations Conference on Trade and Development, that is, in the GATT. US attention was primarily directed to export requirements and minimum import and local content requirements. The former provided for the export of a fixed percentage of the goods produced in the host countries. The latter provided that a given percentage of the final product should be obtained from local sources rather than imports. Other requirements that, according to the US, might be the subject of prospective discussions related to size (e.g. capital invested and local employment level); location of investments; restriction of investments in certain priority sectors; limits on foreign ownership and restrictions on access to local capital.[51]

6

Trade Policies and Trade Conflicts across the Atlantic in the 1980s

The 1980s were characterized on one side of the Atlantic by the assertiveness of the Republican administration which tried to re-establish American leadership in the world economy under the ideological banner of free trade and free market, while the protectionist voices in Congress became stronger. On the other side of the Atlantic, the EC was concerned in the first place with overcoming the stagnation of the economy in member states and with establishing a real common market, thus more conducive to growth.

The interaction between trade liberalization, unilateralism and protectionism in the US Congress and administration

Reagan, or more precisely the Reagan administration, was a vocal supporter of free trade. Statements like 'Protectionism usually succeeds in increasing the income of the sector seeking protection. However, it imposes costs on other sectors that more than outweigh the benefits for the protected sector' were staple in the Reports of the President.[1] Yet, in the Reagan years the number of protective measures and bilateral agreements to regulate trade flows marked a quantitative leap relative to the previous decade. Some of these agreements were, at least officially, directed at opening up the other party's market or regulating competition in third markets; others openly aimed at restricting foreign product inflows into the US market. Examples can be found in a wide range of sectors spanning from basic industries like steel to high-tech. Does this, therefore, allow us to argue that Reagan's policies were schizoid or that his political statements were misleading? In fact, the policies pursued by the US administration could be labelled, with a high degree of confidence, as coherent, although in some cases contradictions between stated goals and objectives actually pursued can be detected. Moreover, the executive had to take into account the orientations of a Congress increasingly wary of foreign competition, whatever its form. At the same time it is arguable that the spectre of a 'protectionist' Congress might have been a useful tool in softening the stance of quite a few US trading partners.

In its 1981 policy agenda the Republican administration addressed challenges and opportunities brought about by the greater integration of the United States in the world economy at a moment in which prospects of rapid recovery were slim while foreign interventionism was becoming more pervasive and protectionist voices in the US louder.[2] According to the executive, a coherent but multiple US response combining 'more vigorous defence of US interests through the use of existing mechanisms with the exploration of new strategies and tactics' was needed. As domestic and foreign economic problems were viewed as a continuum, a major task was a better integration of the two policy arenas. For US domestic policy the challenge was to fashion programmes that might allow the nation's economy to respond to the rapidly changing technological and economic conditions. In keeping with its free-market programme, the agenda made it clear that 'resistance to change through propping up declining industries or raising protectionist barriers was not only futile but also would mortgage the nation's future to outdated, unproductive industrial sectors'. The government was to have, however, a key role in creating a healthy economic environment that would encourage the private sector to seek out new opportunities for investment.

The executive reaffirmed its allegiance to multilateralism as the central framework for the pursuit of US trade goals. In this context it pledged to tackle more assertively non-tariff barriers, in particular with regard to subsidies and problems in agriculture. Emerging issues in such areas as services, trade-related investment problems and high-technology trade had to be placed on a track for later inclusion into the GATT system. On the other hand, as GATT was 'a compromise among conflicting governmental philosophies and by itself cannot provide the means for the complete protection of US interests', other policy instruments – bilateral agreements and US internal trade law – had also to be utilized. In particular, bilateral negotiations were seen as a privileged instrument for a more precise delineation of problems between the United States and its major trading partners and for solutions better tailored to advance their reciprocal trade interests. In any case, as emerged at a later stage, deals with individual countries were presented as a viable alternative in case of absence of progress in multilateral negotiations.

In dealing with the growing trade deficit and its impact on US industry and employment, lawmakers favoured the establishment of cogent rules to defend American interests in the trade arena. Two, sometimes intersecting, strands prevailed in Congress: a more protectionist one calling for higher duties or quotas, either limited to particular products or to the whole of imports, and for stricter proceedings against unfair trade; and a second one calling for reciprocity in the face of allegedly restrictive trading partners' practices hindering American exports and investments.

Lawmakers, both Democrats and Republicans, were spokesmen for import-competing industries hit by the fast-rising inflow of foreign products. Thus, bills aimed at helping the domestic copper industry would check foreign copper suppliers' share of the US market at less than 20 per cent. As regards steel, members of the House of Representatives wanted to limit foreign steel to 15 per cent of the US market. The shoe industry requested a ceiling restricting foreign shoes to 50 per cent of the US market for five years. As the International Trade Commission turned down the industry's bid for safeguard measures, members of Congress quickly introduced a bill providing for equivalent protection. The 'fair practice in automotive products' Act, commonly referred to as the Domestic Content bill which passed the House of Representatives in

1982, required certain manufacturers to produce vehicles for sale in the United States market that included specified levels of US labour and parts. The domestic content requirement would increase according to the number of sold cars. Thus the bill allowed manufacturers to import into the United States up to 100,000 vehicles without regard to domestic content, whereas for manufacturers producing or importing over 900,000 vehicles there was a requirement for a 90 per cent domestic content ratio. This amounted to a strict import quota on foreign-produced autos and auto parts. It also meant that foreign manufacturers needed to consider relocating to the United States a significant proportion of their production, thus creating jobs in the US.[3]

Other bills, some of which were endorsed by the administration, focused on the achievement of commercial opportunities in foreign markets, for both merchandise and service trade as well as for investments, substantially equivalent to those accorded by the United States. The main contentious issues in this approach concerned the powers of the executive and of Congress in assessing and addressing barriers in foreign markets and the kind and extent of reaction to crowbar them, which could open the door to unilateralism and with it protectionist upshots.

The Trade and Tariff Act signed by the president on 31 October 1984 was an amalgam of more than 100 measures, many of which requested import relief for particular products, but whose final version was deprived of strong protectionist content. Some of its provisions, however, did attract critical reactions from US trading partners as well as from trade law experts.

The reciprocity provisions authorized negotiations, as well as the imposition of retaliatory measures, to remove or reduce barriers against trade in high-technology products, US investments abroad, US property rights and trade in services. Section 301 of the Trade Act of 1974 was amended, expanding the definition of commerce to include foreign direct investment 'with implications for trade in goods and services' and providing a definition of the terms 'unjustifiable', 'unreasonable' and 'discriminatory' which had been previously explained only by reference to legislative history. The amended section 301 also authorized the US Trade Representative to initiate investigations without waiting for a private petition or an order from the president. The president under section 301 had authority to take action without receiving a petition but had not used it. The USTR was also requested to prepare, in consultation with the House Ways and Means and the Senate Finance Committees, an annual national trade estimate (NTE) on significant barriers to the exportation of US goods and services and restriction on foreign investments and on actions taken to remove these barriers. The reciprocity provisions aimed at obtaining effective equivalence between trade and investment opportunities in the US market and those available by US firms in foreign countries.

The amendments, which were endorsed by the executive, attracted criticisms since they were viewed as a further step of the US drift towards unilateralism. Unilateralism must be conceptually distinguished from protectionism, although the two can interact. The link between unilateralism and protectionism is given by the fact that reprisal against countries unwilling to open their markets to American merchandise or services could take the form of restrictions of foreign products threatening import-competing US industries. The critics pointed out that the amended version of section 301 allowed the US to unilaterally determine which foreign measures were unfair or nullified and impaired expected US benefits under the GATT and, under threat of retaliation, demand the elimination of such measures to the exclusive advantage of American industry.[4] As a consequence, in the first place, dispute settlement would revert from the existing multilateral approach through the GATT to a bilateral settlement or otherwise would result in the imposition of unilateral restrictive measures. In the second place, the settlement would violate the fundamental GATT principle of Most-Favoured Nation treatment according to which trading rights and obligations must be equally extended to all GATT parties.[5] Thirdly, the amended section 301 interfered with the balance between industries interested in conquering foreign markets and import-competing industries. If the former wanted to expand their presence, any international settlement had to accept unhindered or less hindered access to the US market. Instead, the reformed section offered an autonomous remedy for industries affected by foreign restrictions, while industries threatened by foreign competition could resort undisturbed to the panoply of remedies offered by the US statutes.

The Act extended the purview of countervailing law to so-called upstream subsidies, also catching in the net imported products that were not directly subsidized but were made of subsidized inputs whenever these inputs bestowed a competitive benefit. It requested the administration to remove or reduce trade barriers to US wine trade. At the prompting of the Californian grape growers, a provision of the Act allowed grape growers to join wine makers in filing unfair trade complaints. This meant that petitions against allegedly trade-distorting practices (nominally subsidized exports of wine) could also be filed by an industry other than that directly injured by the practices in question. Obviously the extension, which seemed to go beyond the purview of GATT rules, did not fail to attract an irritated response from the European Community.

The Act also agreed, although partially, to some of the government's wishes. The statute extended the grant of the Generalized System of Preferences (GSP) to developing countries but for a shorter period (eight-and-a-half years) than the one suggested by the administration. The GSP had little support among US economic interests, both employers and organized labour, although exports from less developed countries accounted for about 3 per cent of US imports. The administration, however, saw the extension of the preference as a gesture towards developing countries which attached political importance to the GSP and as an incentive to negotiate on issues of importance for the US such as access to their markets and protection of intellectual property rights. Thus, Congress made the benefit conditional on developing countries' steps to open their markets to exports from the US and to honour intellectual property rights. It also denied benefits to countries with a per capita income of over $8,500.

Finally, the Act permitted administration officials to pursue talks with Israel on the establishment of a free-trade agreement between the two nations. It also approved a limited version of powers required by the administration to negotiate free-trade agreements with other countries; that is, Canada. Thus, the executive could proceed with talks with its northern neighbour, although no authorization was given to eliminate or lower trade barriers on some products in the short-run as it had hoped.

In 1985 the administration started to take a tougher stance against allegedly unfair trading practices by foreign countries, self-initiating section 301 proceedings against

Brazil, Japan, South Korea and the European Community. The stance of the executive was summarized and explained in 'the administration statement on international trade policy' according to which it was committed to pursue more open access to markets abroad for US exports and fairer conditions of trade while opposing policies at home and abroad that were protectionist. On the one hand, the statement announced that it would take initiatives 'necessary to achieve more equitable access in a number of foreign markets, particularly Japan and major developing countries', thus stepping up the use of the authority given by Congress to address unfair foreign trade practices that hindered US trade and investment. On the other hand, it promised to 'vigorously enforce US law aimed at countering foreign dumping and subsidies practices'. Reagan went even farther in emphasizing the absence of contradictions, that is, the consistency of the administration's policy in a talk given to a receptive audience, that of business and trade leaders. According to the Great Communicator 'free trade is, by definition, fair trade'. Indeed, in the US president's words, 'when domestic markets are closed to the export of others, it is no longer free trade' and 'when governments assist their exporters in ways that violate international laws, then the playing field is no longer level, and there is no longer free trade'.[6] The EC Commission scathingly observed that 'it was tempting to think that it was always the "other side" that was guilty of unfair practices'.[7]

The new posture of the executive was also an attempt to pre-empt the much more muscular policies advocated by numerous bills discussed in Congress and in particular in the House of Representatives where the Democrats had the majority of seats. It succeeded only partially as the worsening of US trade difficulties prompted Congress's activism. Many Democrats were eager to gain political advantage in the forthcoming election for the renewal of Congress while the Republicans, on the other hand, were worried about the political costs of being associated with Reagan's free trade stance.

In December 1985 Reagan vetoed a bill that would set strict import limits on exporting countries and individual categories of textile products and would limit imports of non-rubber footwear to no more than 60 per cent of the domestic shoe market for an eight-year period. Though vetoing the bill, which had also been approved by numerous GOP lawmakers especially from the textile-producing southern states, Reagan claimed to be deeply sympathetic about job lay-offs and plant closures and directed the Treasury secretary to determine within 60 days whether import levels set by previous negotiations had been exceeded. He also promised not to weaken existing import restraints under the MFA and gave assurances that the next multifibre arrangement would be no less restrictive than the ongoing one. Eight months later an attempt by the House of Representatives to override the veto failed to gather the required two-thirds majority thanks to the administration's intensive lobbying campaign towards wavering Republicans. The campaign, however, was made more convincing by the signing of pacts with South Korea, Hong Kong and Taiwan, the three primary targets of the textile bill. At the same time various bills were presented which called for the start of negotiations with foreign countries, notably Japan, to remove barriers from their telecommunications imports. One bill, sponsored by a Republican senator, John C. Danforth, provided for an 18-month negotiating period at the end of which the president would be required to impose sanctions which could include increased import tariffs, prohibition on federal government procurement on imported telecommunication products, and tougher approval standards for foreign-made equipment.

In May 1986, in spite of the administration's protests portending a presidential veto, the House of Representatives passed a heavy-handed bill addressing several aspects of trade relations. The bill, which also garnered a conspicuous number of Republican votes, would outlaw new kinds of export measures allegedly offering an edge on foreign products on the US market, as one of its provisions would approve punitive actions against foreign governments subsidizing the cost of natural resources that companies used to make export goods, while another would countervail exports from targeted industries. The commonly accepted definition of targeting included any governmental or officially sanctioned policy that sought to enhance or foreseeably would enhance the competitiveness of a particular industry or industries in the domestic and export market. Targeting practices would, among other things, be directed to subsidize R&D, reduce domestic competition, increase available capital or increase the market size. The executive's approach towards such practices was more cautious and sophisticated. For instance, in a report submitted to Congress in July 1985 the administration remarked that in several industries targeting involved subsidization and could, therefore, be countervailed. In other cases, however, targeting was carried out through measures, such as high tariffs, that did not contravene GATT rules. In other areas, as was the case for R&D, the United States had often offered a helping hand to its own industry and therefore was not well placed to cast the first stone; nor were the requirements for applying section 301 remedies always present. Consequently, in quite a few cases, if the United States wanted to stop targeting practices on the part of its trading partners, it had to seek a negotiating solution and offer some concessions.

In several other sectors, including telecommunications, the bill passed in the House would force the president to retaliate against countries that discriminated against US exports, unless he decided that retaliation would harm US economic interests. Above all the bill included an amendment, sponsored by the Democrat representative Richard Gephardt, that would force 10 per cent annual cuts in the trade surplus of big surplus countries, nominally Japan, West Germany and Taiwan, firstly through negotiations, then through higher tariffs and finally by the imposition of quotas.

The bill and its equivalent in the Senate could not reach the conference stage before the end of the 99th Congress in October. However, it bore out the mood that was gaining strength in Congress. Other bills were introduced in 1987, finally leading a year later to the 'only marginally protectionist', in Destler's words, Omnibus Trade and Competitiveness Act and the adoption of special and super 301 proceedings.[8]

The administration censured the bill contending that it contravened several GATT provisions. It also argued that it would place rigid restrictions on its ability to handle trade matters and would finally lead to retaliation against export-oriented industries in the United States. And indeed the executive had been actively negotiating and would continue to negotiate, quite often with some success, bilateral agreements to 'regulate' sensitive trade areas for the United States, or, in particular in the case of Japan, to spur comprehensive policy changes. In short, it is arguable that under the cloak of uncompromising support for free trade the executive's approach was basically pragmatic. No doubt, the administration would have liked to reach a multilateral agreement paving the way to freer trade in which US industries could affirm their competitive advantage with no hindrance. In fact, in the first two years of the 1980s it actively pursued this goal. However, at the same time it was aware that even a successful negotiating round could not secure fully-fledged free trade in all sectors and, therefore, there were areas in which bilateral talks were needed. It was also aware that there were sectors in which some US industries, at least in the short and perhaps in the medium term, needed protection from foreign competition and it realized that it could not ignore the pressure and complaints from part of the Congress in a moment in which the inflow of imports was swelling and unemployment was high. Moreover, the executive recognized that many export-oriented industries were no longer as competitive as ten or fifteen years earlier. It was, however, both strategically and tactically opposed to rigid, automatic implementation of measures against inflow of foreign products and alleged trade barriers from trading partners as such measures would provoke retaliation and, in any case, would curtail its room for manoeuvre.

The administration's pragmatism made it explore a second path to the elimination or curbing of tariff and non-tariff barriers: that of bilateral free trade areas. The US executive, however, was careful to stress that bilateral negotiations were not aimed at supplanting but rather at supplementing GATT and that the US was not interested in dividing the world into competing trade blocs. The trial balloon, possibly also for political reasons, was the agreement with Israel. Israel originally proposed the establishment of a free-trade area in 1981 but at that time the US chose not to pursue a bilateral arrangement. After the disappointing results of the 1982 GATT Ministerial meeting, the US started to consider new trade liberalization approaches. A year later Reagan and the Israeli prime minister agreed to begin bilateral negotiations, which were formally started in January 1984. An agreement was signed on 22 April 1985 which provided for the elimination of duties and non-tariff barriers between the two countries by January 1995.

In a first stage the United States and its northern neighbour opted to explore the feasibility of limited sectorial free-trade agreements analogous to the 1965 auto-pact between the two countries. However, in September 1985 the Canadian prime minister requested that the United States and Canada consider the potential for negotiating a comprehensive free-trade agreement. Bilateral negotiations began formally on 17 June 1986 and the Free Trade Agreement was signed on 2 January 1988, acting as the catalyst for the North Atlantic Free Trade Agreement (NAFTA).

Steps towards further integration of the EC market and their influence on extra-EC trade

In the European Community a series of policies was relevant with regard to international trade. The first one openly referred to trade with foreign countries; the others addressed intra-Community issues but were bound to have an impact on trading relations outside the EC market.

A French memorandum in early 1982 drew the attention of the member states to the lack of rules at EC level to combat unfair commercial practices that were not prohibited by a specific provision of the GATT or under a non-tariff code concluded under the aegis of the General Agreement. According to the French document the EC had to follow the steps of the US which had been using these legal instruments since 1974. Adoption of these measures 'would be a token of the Community's commitment to the defence of the interests of European producers as effective as that enjoyed by their chief competitors'.[9] The European Council of June 1982 stated that in the matter of trade protection the Community should act with as much speed and efficiency as its trading partners and in February 1983 the EC Commission duly submitted to the Council a proposal for the strengthening of the common commercial policy with particular regard to protection against unfair commercial practices.[10] After long debates and some amendments the Council adopted a regulation on the strengthening of the common commercial policy in September1984.[11] The objective of the regulation was to respond to any unfair commercial practice and remove the injury resulting from it, thus ensuring full exercise of the Community's rights.

However, the scope of foreign practices addressed by the regulation was less broad than in the US. Unfair commercial practices were identified with illicit ones, in turn described as any practices attributable to third countries which were incompatible with international law or the rules commonly accepted by the Community's partners regarding commercial policy. Thus the regulation was not concerned with unreasonable or discriminatory practices. On the other hand, the new rule avoided concentrating on a limited list of clearly identified measures as the Community deemed it impossible to draw up in advance an exhaustive list of all cases that might arise. The regulation gave the right to start proceedings not only to member states but also directly to Community producers and lay down a decision-making machinery within set time limits.

The first half of the 1980s witnessed significant developments with regard to state aid policy, which had been a sticking point in the Tokyo Round negotiations. On the one hand, the number of aid schemes and the quantity of state resources involved showed a rising trend for most of the period under the pressure of the worsening economic climate. On the other hand the Community, and the Commission in particular, adopted a much more severe attitude in regulating and vetting subsidization measures by member states.

In its 1984 Competition Report the Commission pointed out that in the period 1981–4 the number of state aid proposals in the industrial field rose by over 25 per cent relative to the previous four-year period when just over 500 proposals had been notified. However, in the same period the cases in which the Commission opened procedure under article 93(2) of the Treaty of Rome multiplied by a factor of three. The adoption of the above-mentioned procedure indicates that, on first examination, the plan to grant or alter aid is not compatible with the Common Market under article 92. The number of negative decisions, i.e. decisions in which the aid proposed was completely prohibited, multiplied by 12 and this figure would rise considerably if the number of proposals withdrawn after the opening of an Art. 93(2) proceeding is taken into account. In 1985 the Art. 93(2) procedure was opened in one case in three, although it did not result in an increase in the number of final negative decisions. Strict rules on the admissibility of state aid by member states were applied to several industries hit by the crisis like steel, textiles and shipbuilding. Some practices were also targeted. It was the case of the provision of capital to companies by governments for which the Commission made it clear that capital infusion by member states was allowable only if consistent with investment decisions by private investors and not as a way to buoy up ailing firms or to expand their production. In short, in the first half of the 1980s the curb on state aids, which had been advocated by the US during the Tokyo Round on account of their distorting the international market, started to be enforced by the Commission, with the (sometimes grudging) approval of the member states, as affecting trade within the Community.

Yet, public aid was still considered an essential ingredient of industrial policy in other areas prominent among which were the high-technology industries where the EC member states and the whole Community, in spite of their ambitions, were falling behind the US and Japan. In two memoranda published in 1981 and 1983 France, the most active supporter of industrial policy in Western Europe, argued that if the Community aimed to be an industrial pole in its own right rather than a subcontractor of American and Japanese firms, industrial cooperation at EC level was essential and European projects should be developed with financial assistance provided by the Community.[12] The French government also stressed that a Community industrial policy implied the freeing from national restraints of technical standards and the phased opening up of public contracts, but with access reserved to Community producers. The memoranda also called for the relaxation of competition rules to promote European champions and for the establishment of external barriers during the first stages of the relaunch of the internal market. As regards foreign investment in the Community, France maintained that it should be encouraged if it made a net contribution to employment or if it introduced new technology, but member states should not invite investment increasing production capacity in industries where there was already excess capacity. Other member countries took a more cautious approach. Germany in particular was extremely critical of the French suggestion of protecting EC infant industries in sectors deemed by politicians and technocrats as having high developmental prospects. Though in favour of support for basic research at Community level, the Federal Republic argued against financing firms for product development because it distorted competition. Britain was critical of the regulation of foreign investments. For its part, the Commission was keen to promote new technology in Europe but was wary of infant industry protection measures as they could invite reactions from the EC trading partners. It was also worried that increased intervention could blur the line between domestic policy measures and those aiming at giving an industry a competitive advantage in international trade, thus providing ammunition to those who, in particular across the Atlantic, were calling for a strong response to targeting or were arguing that also domestic subsidies might affect international trade and should, therefore, be countervailable.

Actually, the first steps at Community level preceded the second French memorandum. The ESPRIT programme was promoted in 1983 on the initiative of 12 of the EC's largest information technology companies. It covered five sectors – advanced microelectronics, software technology, advanced data-processing, office information and computer assisted production. The central phase of the programme was due to last until 1989, with half of the necessary finance of 1.4 billion ECU being provided by the EC budget and the other half coming from operations. ESPRIT was followed by other programmes under direct EC control like RACE, launched to develop the base for an integrated broadband communication network, BRITE, established to encourage the application of new technologies in traditional industries and SPRINT, which aimed at helping small firms to access specialist services. Yet, the level of resources assigned to EC technology policies was still relatively small as it amounted to 2.5 per cent of the Community's total expenditure and was only a tiny fraction of national government spending on R&D.

The goal and the approach of the EUREKA programme was different. This was launched in 1985 to coincide with presentation of the Commission's White Paper on the completion of the internal market. EUREKA functioned primarily as a matchmaking body since the Community did not provide direct financing but encouraged cooperative cross-national European research. Projects approved by the EUREKA secretariat qualified for national R&D support. The effectiveness of the programme was based on the presuppositions of real progress in market integration. Indeed, the qualitative leap in the recovery of the Community was entrusted not to widespread adoption of an industrial policy steered by the Commission, which in the following years turned out to be quite limited, but to a liberalization process across the Community which was to be based on the elimination of the remaining barriers to the free movement of goods, services, persons and capital. Already in December 1982 the European Council discussed a Commission communication that recommended the removal of NTBs, simplification of frontier formalities and liberalization of public procurement. The Summit's debate was followed by an array of parliamentary resolutions and European Council declarations. The process gained momentum with the accession of a new Commission headed by the former French Minister of Finance, Jacques Delors, in January 1985. The March 1985 EC Summit in Brussels gave the green light for the presentation of an internal market reform project by the Commission and the White Paper it submitted was endorsed by the Milan European Council in June 1985, which also summoned an intergovernmental conference for the reform of the European Communities treaties. In February 1986 the Single European Act (SEA) was signed by representatives of the 12 member states incorporating, in a wider context, the objective of the establishment of a true single market.[13]

The White Paper 'Completing the Internal Market',[14] produced in June 1985 by Lord Cockfield for the Commission, identified 279 measures which were deemed necessary to remove a host of barriers including state procurements, technical standards, taxation differences and customs and other frontier barriers. The barriers were categorized in three groups, although their demarcation is somewhat artificial.[15] Fiscal barriers comprised those distortions deriving from differences in product base and in VAT and excise tax rates. Physical barriers referred to frontier control on the movement of goods, persons and capital, from customs duties to passport and health checks. The remaining category of technical barriers included not only those arising from the lack of technical harmonization and public procurement procedures but also institutional obstacles to capital movements and the provision of services. As regards this latter category, the White Paper suggested a new approach while not completely discarding the old one based on harmonization among the member states. The Commission, therefore, proposed to apply a mutual recognition strategy placing regulation into the hands of national bodies in the member countries, but also listed numerous directives for minimal rules and standards across the EC market. With respect to public procurements, the Commission proposed improvements of the relevant directives to increase transparency and the extension of the legislation coverage to include energy, transport, water and telecommunications.

The White Paper launched the last stage of integration and internal liberalization in the Community. Yet, as Tsoukalis noted, one if its remarkable features was 'the apparent introspection manifested through the absence of any serious consideration of the external dimension of the internal market'.[16] Notwithstanding this, the implementation of the 1992 single market programme was bound to have a deep impact on merchandise and service trade with the rest of the world as well as on investments. It also affected bilateral and multilateral negotiations as it influenced the expectations and fears of the EC main trading partners of the goals and scope of the measures that were to be adopted to implement the 1992 programme. Although most of these issues emerged in the last years of the decade and therefore fall outside the period covered by this research, it is apposite to list them as they had their roots in the White Paper. In the first place, the prospective repeal of border controls necessarily entailed the end of barriers against third countries deriving from the various commercial policy measures individually enforced by member states, quotas or equivalent restraints in particular. It would have been useless to negotiate a complex VER on cars or videocassettes with Japan if the very same products could cross unchecked the frontier with another member state that had no analogous agreement in place. Was the VER simply to be repealed or was it to be replaced by another restraint managed by the Commission and, in the affirmative, was the new restraint to be applied less or more restrictively, being, for instance, enforced in the whole Community?

A second question concerned reciprocity, one main example being the liberalization of the finance sector. The approach chosen in the run-up to 1992 was to enable any bank that had received authorization from any competent authority of a member state to provide services across the border and open branches in any other member country. It would have been, therefore, possible for any subsidiary of an American bank chartered in any EC member state to operate within the whole Common Market. But across the Atlantic the Glass-Steagal and the McFadden Acts imposed restrictions on the inter-state activities and branching of US and foreign banks alike. Japan, in turn, was accused of imposing severe and highly effective restrictions on the settlement of foreign financial institutions. Was the unconditional national treatment, codified in GATT Art. III, to be applied, as the United States claimed in view of the prospective windfall offered to its credit institutions by the 1992 directives, or was the reciprocity requirement to prevail, and if so to what extent and in which form?

Public procurement liberalization among the 12 member states was a main point of the 1992 programme as around 15 per cent of the Community's GDP was accounted for by this. Was public procurement to be opened to foreign firms beyond the purview of the Tokyo Round code, especially when there was still uncertainty regarding the member states' willingness to make rapid progress in this area? Certainly, subsidiaries of foreign MNCs in the Community already had a foothold in the EC public procurement market. But what about other companies? Besides, there was also the possibility that a minimum EC local content might be imposed to tender for public procurement in the Community, and so on.

US–EC controversies not linked to specific industries

The first half of the 1980s witnessed a worsening of the economic policy cooperation between the two sides of the Atlantic and correspondingly an increase in the number and asperity of trade conflicts between the US and the EC. From a methodological point of view, we can distinguish between conflicts related to specific trade sectors, which will be addressed in the next chapters, and conflicts whose official subject had a wider scope even though their roots were actually related to the two trading partners' divergent interests in a particular industry, in most cases agriculture. This second type of conflict re-proposes issues that have already been examined in previous chapters, i.e. the position of multinational firms in the host state, enlargement and trade preferences.

Trans-Siberian natural gas pipeline

In the case of the trans-Siberian pipeline which was one of the main factors marring transatlantic relations in 1982 even before the clash at the November GATT ministerial meeting, the Reagan administration unilaterally expanded trade controls over dealings with the Soviet Union as a result of its role in repressing the Polish Solidarity labour movement and the imposition of martial law by General Jaruzelski in December 1981. Actually, the hostility of the Reagan administration to the joint Euro-Soviet pipeline project preceded the events in Poland. The worries of the executive, shared by many in Congress, went from fear of stronger links between the Soviet Union and the West European countries, which could increase Soviet influence and entail dangerous vulnerability to the interruption of supplies of natural gas from the USSR, to the availability for the Soviets of hard currency that might finance a number of developments inimical to the US.[17]

Along with other measures, the United States decreed a halt to exports from the US of material for the construction of the Siberian gas pipeline. By itself this measure was bound to affect EC firms that had legally binding contracts to provide equipment to the Soviet Union which involved components made in the United States. The severe crack in the conduct of business with the Soviet bloc by the Western partners took a turn for the worse when on 18 June 1982 the US executive announced that under a 'temporary denial order' the export limitations were also to apply to foreign entities owned or controlled by US residents, nationals or companies, as well as to transactions by licensees or distributors who were involved in the re-export of goods or technology of US origin. The US also made it clear that the new, more severe restrictions had retroactive effect.

The reaction from the EC member countries was one of unanimous outrage. Even the staunchest ally of the Reagan administration and supporter of its trade philosophy, Margaret Thatcher, states in her memoirs that 'I was appalled when I learnt of this decision', adding that '[t]he reaction of the Europeans was even more hostile'.[18] The extraterritorial measures adopted by the US and the reaction of the EC and its member states appeared to show a different perspective on the management of multinational corporations and consequently on their obligations under US and foreign law. The extraterritorial application of US restrictions implied that subsidiaries in foreign countries could be put on the same footing as domestic branches of their American parent companies. The European governments adopted a totally different stance. In many cases EC member states' courts issued orders to compel delivery of banned goods by US subsidiaries which soon after delivery to their European customers found themselves blacklisted by US authorities. The Community also sent a verbal note to the US government pointing out that the new limitations and their retroactive effects on existing contracts put in jeopardy the basic principle of the world trading system and were likely to have long-lasting negative effects on business relations between European and American firms, thus worsening the strains of the economic decline on both sides of the Atlantic. As for the legal implications, the Community argued that the extension of US legal control to companies incorporated in the EC on the grounds that they were subsidiaries of companies incorporated in the US or were controlled by citizens or residents of the US was not warranted by public international law. Likewise, no support in public international law could be found for the US assumption of jurisdiction over purely EC companies on the sole ground that they had purchased technological data from US firms to manufacture products subsequently exported to other countries.

After having inflamed courts and chancelleries across the Atlantic the conflict came to an end for natural causes because the temporary denial order was vacated as a result of the sanctions themselves being lifted in November 1982.

Citrus case

The second confrontation was the upshot of an attack launched by the Reagan administration to the preferences given by the European Community to Mediterranean countries on the imports of certain agricultural products, nominally citrus.

A central provision of the trade agreements stipulated with countries of the Mediterranean Basin provided concessions on agricultural products without which the Community would have had little to offer to the poor economies of the region. As the benefits were directed only to Mediterranean countries, they might not be deemed, in the absence of a justifying factor, to comply with the Most-Favoured Nation principle. In response to a petition under section 301 of the 1974 Trade Act, the US sought a GATT ruling on the effect of EC tariff preferences for imports of citrus products from Mediterranean countries on American citrus exports to Europe. The Community argued that the differential treatment was justified by the effect of Part IV of the GATT concerning trade and development on Art. XXIV on free trade areas. The GATT panel considered that Art. XXIV and Part IV constituted distinct sets of rights and obligations and that measures taken under one could not be covered by the other. Consequently Part IV could not be invoked as grounds for failing to conform with the strict criteria set out by Art. XXIV not to respect the MFN principle.[19] Since the EC blocked further GATT consideration of the issue, the USTR forwarded a recommendation for action to the president who, to retaliate to the EC's allegedly discriminatory measures, in June raised duties on pasta imports effective 6 July 1985. It must be noted that the US pasta producers had brought an action under section 301 complaining that EC export subsidies on pasta were injuring them and in 1983 a GATT panel had ruled the EC export subsidies inconsistent with Art. 9 of the GATT Subsidies code.[20] The EC, however, had blocked adoption of the panel's report. The new quarrel was, therefore, a golden chance to kill two birds with one stone: to give satisfaction to American pasta producers overcoming the inaction of the GATT instances and to put pressure on the EC to the advantage of US citrus producers over the issue of the Mediterranean agreements, which, though for different reasons, had often been accused by the United States of being trade-diverting.

In response, the EC increased duties on imports of American lemons and walnuts. It proposed, however, to start talks on improving access of US lemons into the Community in exchange for an engagement by the US to desist from challenging the validity of Mediterranean agreements under Art. XXIV. Thus the two armed-knights agreed on a cooling off period until 31 October 1985 before implementing the tit-for-tat measures they had promised each other. The negotiations failed and both parties raised the duties on their respective imports: the US duties were raised from about 0.25 per cent to 25 per cent on pasta containing eggs and from about 0.5 per cent to 40 per cent on pasta without eggs.

The conflict was settled almost a year later in the friendlier spirit of the run-up to the new round of trade negotiations. The new talks led to an '*ad referendum* agreement' between the USTR Clayton Yeutter and Willy De Clercq, members of the Commission with responsibility for external relations and trade policy, which was approved the following October. The settlement provided for recognition by the United States of the Community's current and renewed agreements with the Mediterranean countries; the abolition of the duties applied by the two parties on pasta and citrus products and reciprocal concessions over imports of sweet oranges, lemons, grapefruit, almonds, groundnuts and orange juice from the United States and imports of anchovies, cheeses, satsuma oranges, olives, olive oil and capers from the European Community.

Accession to the EC of Portugal and Spain

Although not lacking in problems, the entry of Greece into the EC in 1981 did not have a significant impact on intra-EC and extra-EC trade also because of the small economy of that Mediterranean country. Greece was granted a six-year transitional period for opening its industrial goods market, later extended for two years. Actually, imports from the old member states declined during the first years of Greece's membership. The accession did not arouse a strong reaction from the EC trading partners, including the US.

Portugal and Spain formally applied for membership of the EC in 1977. The treaty of accession was signed in 1985 and both countries were incorporated into EC space in January 1986. Negotiations were long and difficult. Spanish output of fruits, vegetables, wine and olive oil was destined to compete with that of other member countries. France and Italy in particular were concerned to protect their farmers from the low-cost competition offered by the applicant's farm exports. Likewise, the cost of integrating Spain into the CAP was bound to create severe budgetary strains in the absence of a prompt reform. In the fisheries sector the inclusion of Spain would magnify current problems of overcapacity and the lack of EC fisheries resources. The EC members were also concerned with the impact of low-cost Portuguese textiles. The accession of both countries also threatened to cause severe strains on the limited share of the EC budget destined for regional programmes. The accession treaty provided transition periods of up to ten years to protect EC farmers from Iberian competition, especially in the market for olive oil, wine, vegetables and citrus, while transition periods were allowed to Iberian producers against competition in the markets for cereals, meats and dairy products. As regards fishing, the two countries were granted only limited access to the fishing grounds of the other member states for a ten-year transitional period. A seven-year transitional period was established for the progressive adoption of the common external tariff and the customs union in manufacturing.

Things went much less smoothly than for Greece as regards third countries. The proportion of Spanish and Portuguese imports from the EC had declined during the 1970s while manufacturing imports from Japan and farm imports from the US had grown. The United States asked for compensation for the new barriers created on its farm exports by the accession to the EC. The legal reasoning at the basis of the position of the two parties was quite similar to that put forward in previous EC enlargements. This time, however, the United States, under the leadership of a former Hollywood action film star and the pressure of its agricultural lobby, made it clear, in words and actions, that it was poised to draw its sanction gun from its holster. The European Community replied that it was ready to take up the gauntlet, though not failing to show its perplexity and regret at having to accept the challenge.

In April 1986 the White House announced that it would impose extra duties and other measures on a still unidentified number of imports from the EC in retaliation for agricultural restrictions that could affect as much as $1 billion worth of farm exports to Portugal and Spain. As regards Spain, the alleged restrictions concerned access on the Spanish market for US cereals, mainly maize and grain sorghum and later wheat. As regards Portugal, the difficulties of access for farm products derived from quotas on soya and its products and the obligation for the Iberian country to buy from the EC at least 15.5 per cent of its imports of cereals. As on previous occasions the Community replied that disadvantages and benefits resulting for third countries from its enlargement were not to be assessed for any particular product but from an overall perspective. From this perspective the United States was destined to gain as Spain and Portugal would substantially reduce their duties, on average amounting to 15 per cent, to align them to the EC common commercial tariff and a considerable number of quantitative restrictions would gradually be abolished in line with the application of the common trade policy.

The negotiations on the consequences of the enlargement within the framework of XXIV.6 of the GATT started in May, but the same month the US executive ordered retaliatory measures against the effects of the accession of the two countries on US exports. It stated, however, that the measures would apply only if compensation was not obtained from the Community by the beginning of July. In June the EC ordered the imposition of measures equivalent in effect to those applied by the US but reaffirmed its readiness to complete negotiations under Art. XXIV.6 of the GATT. An interim solution was negotiated *ad referendum* to stave off a crisis in the run-up to the new GATT round. The solution, which was to apply from 1 July to 31 December 1986, provided for the monitoring of American exports of maize, sorghum, corn gluten feed, brewer grains and citrus pellets to the Community and for the adoption of measures to maintain the balance should American exports of the said products fall below 234,000 tonnes per month. Despite Community hopes, the talks broke down and in December Reagan announced that by the end of the following January he would impose duties of 200 per cent on a range of Community exports worth 400 million ECU, including cognac, gin and certain white wines. The EC declared that it was ready to retaliate. At the eleventh hour, the two parties, though recognizing that their different interpretation of GATT Art. XXIV.6 could not be reconciled, worked out an agreement which envisaged in particular tariff concessions by the Community on a number of American industrial and agricultural products for a four-year period and a commitment to ensure a minimum annual level of imports of 2 million tonnes of corn and 300,000 tonnes of sorghum into Spain from non-EC sources.

The European Community, the United States and their burns from the Rising Sun

While the analysis of difficulties and remedies in the main industries of both the EC and the US is left to the following chapter, the overall picture shows that in the 1980s much more than in the previous decade, the Japanese juggernaut became a main concern for both and consequently the main scapegoat for complaints and actions on both sides of the Atlantic. Japan had been the main cause of the US merchandise trade deficit since 1975 but in the period under review it became the fastest growing component of an unprecedentedly soaring deficit. In 1985 the gap with Japan was higher than the US gap with the Americas, including Canada (Table 5). According to the EC Parliament, the rate of coverage of Community imports from Japan by its exports fell from 98 per cent in 1967 to 44 per cent in 1975 and to only 35 per cent a decade later.[21] A deficit of just over 500 million ECU in 1970 turned into over 17,000 million ECU fifteen years later.

Ascertainment of the causes of the growing gap with Japan pointed to similar factors in the US and the EC: on the one hand, enormously successful production by the Asian country of manufactured products intended first and foremost for export markets, quite often with current or previous help from the government; on the other, the failure of foreign producers to penetrate the Japanese market due to distribution channels which were almost exclusively reserved for Japanese products and to restrictive regulations governing foreign establishments in the service sector and participation in public procurements. The United States and the European Community even more were both worried by the qualitative deterioration of trade with the Far Eastern partner as Japan's exports consisted largely of high added-value products, while the only exports making inroads in the Japanese markets were raw materials and semi-manufactures. The merchandise trade gap was viewed, at least partially, as a result of a supposed weakness of the yen, particularly against the dollar. Actually, in contrast to the European currencies, from 1980 to 1985 there was no pronounced downward movement of the Japanese currency vis-à-vis the greenback (see Figure 1). It seems, however, that the relative stability of the exchange rate between the two countries did not fully reflect the fact that wholesale prices in the US were increasing, even though at a low rate, whereas they were plummeting in the Pacific country.[22] On the other hand, the yen appreciated considerably against Community currencies though, as noted by the Commission in one of its reports, it was questionable whether real exchange rates were a valid measure of the general competitive strength of the Japanese economy.[23]

The low value of the yen was also seen as a consequence of the reluctance of the Japanese authorities to let their currency play its full part in the international monetary system because, although there had been progress in dismantling exchange controls for undertaking transactions abroad, the liberalization of inward investments had been slower and less extensive. Yet, the undervalued yen and capital outflows from Japan played an undeclared but pivotal role and it is arguable that, at least until the US administration's change of heart in 1985, they suited both sides of the Pacific. On the one hand, the appreciation of the dollar stimulated an export-led expansion of the Japanese economy. On the other, Japanese capitals were at the forefront in financing the US capital account and fiscal deficits and therefore helped preserve the unconstrained growth of the American economy, obviously with the exception of industries hit by foreign competition.[24] From 1986, also in an effort to prevent an excessive revaluation of the yen, the Japanese authorities adopted a monetary policy aimed at stimulating domestic demand. The result was a bubble economy marked by a speculative boom in stock and real estate, followed later by stagnation.[25]

Despite this common background, the dialogue with the Japanese colossus and its willingness to respond to the demands of its trading partners differed across the Atlantic: Japan was ready to respond to American promptings; in turn the European Community, i.e. the member states, the Commission and the Council of Ministers, were more vociferous in complaining against the alleged flaws of the Japanese economy. Certainly, the US deficit with its trans-Pacific partner in 1985 was almost five times larger than in 1980 (Table 5), while the EC deficit had not even doubled (Figures 5 and 6). This would suggest that the main difficulties should be concentrated in relations with the United States and indeed the deficit repeatedly attracted the attention of Congress. Yet, the differences in the widening of the gap were offset by other factors. From a political angle the United States was the main ally of Japan and the guarantor of its security. The Community member states were only allies with the US intermediate. From an economic policy angle, imports by the US accounted for 24.5 per cent of total Japanese exports in 1980 and for 37.6 per cent five years later while imports by the EC accounted for 14 per cent and 11.9 per cent in the same span of years.[26] The fact that imports from Japan had risen from 13 per cent of US imports in 1980 to 20 per cent just five years later, equalling those from Canada and overtaking those from the EC, while exports to Japan were growing slowly and unsteadily (Table 5), might only increase Japan's willingness to promptly find a *modus vivendi* with its main trading partner; this in a period in which Congress was debating bills envisaging the imposition of quotas against countries whose trade surplus exceeded a given threshold and when existing statutes were requesting the US executive to take action against unjustifiable trade practices. Likewise, it is arguable that the Reagan administration could more easily ask for cooperation from Japan if it were to succeed in its declared endeavour to hold the rising tide of protectionism in check.

Conversely, the European parliament could label Japan as 'the thorn in Europe's side',[27] but the fact remains that imports from the Asian country, though growing at the alarming speed of almost 16 per cent per year, accounted for less than 7 per cent of extra-EC imports in 1985, being dwarfed by imports from the United States, from the EFTA and Mediterranean countries and from OPEC (Figure 6). Merchandise exports to Japan remained slim but did not worsen: 2.7 per cent of total extra-EC exports in 1985 against 2.6 per cent in 1970. Restrictions against Japanese exports had long been implemented by several member countries. A hard stance could, therefore, improve the position of the EC in its relationship with the Asian partner without the risk of compromising previous achievements.

Thus the Reagan administration could boast some diplomatic success like the 1981 offer by the Japanese Ministry of International Trade and Industry (MITI) to restrain auto exports in order to give the American industry breathing space to become more competitive, or the 1986 Semiconductor Trade Agreement. Both these agreements were contested by the Community which complained they were diverting Japanese exports to its market. Above all the United States was able to obtain flexibility in managing the yen. Indeed, the appreciation of the Japanese currency was a key factor in the Plaza declaration process.

In 1982 the EC Council, in a declaration smacking of dirigisme, solicited the Asian trading partner 'to provide tangible assurances' that it would pursue a policy of 'effective moderation' as regards exports whose increase could cause significant problems to the Community as a whole, as well as to ensure 'determined and swift action by the Japanese government positively to promote imports, e.g. through guidance to public and private sectors'.[28] These requests were repeatedly made during encounters between members of the Commission and their Japanese counterparts. More effectively the Community requested Japan to start negotiations under GATT Art. XXIII claiming that its reasonable expectations on benefits arising from GATT negotiations had not been fulfilled with respect to its trading partner because Japan thus far had shown little propensity to import European manufactured products. The pressure produced some results. During the talks held in Tokyo in February 1983 EC negotiators obtained assurances that Japan would moderate exports of ten 'sensitive products', including cars, vans, motorcycles, fork-lift trucks, numerically-controlled machine tools, colour television sets, cathode tubes and video recorders. The pledge, however, was only partially fulfilled. Exports of video recorders, colour television tubes and television sets declined, but exports of cars and numerically-controlled machine tools did not moderate and new products like office equipment and electric generators made inroads into the EC markets. Meanwhile Japanese imports from the Community continued to stagnate. In the second half of the decade the Japanese partially changed strategy.

Under the perceived menace of a Fortress Europe and the perceived opportunities of a real single market, by 1992 investments from Japanese corporations rose vigorously, mainly in car production but also in an array of other sectors. The main recipient, the UK, was accused of being a Trojan horse for the exploitation of the Single Market by Japanese firms, but many of the accusers, including France, were not coy in letting Japanese capital and technology in.

7

The Decline of Key Industrial Sectors in the US and the EC and Policies Adopted to Stem it in the 1980s

The unfavourable environment of the first part of the 1980s accentuated the difficulties of many industries in the US and in the EC. Despite the Tokyo Round, or, perhaps, because of the contents and limits of its codes, the array of protectionist and trade-distorting measures across the Atlantic did not shrink, but grew in number and sophistication. According to the US Council of Economic Advisers in major industrialized countries the proportion of total manufacturing subject to non-tariff barriers rose to 30 per cent in 1983 up from 20 per cent just three years earlier.[1] The difference in emphasis between the measures chosen by the United States and those adopted by the EC did not significantly change from the 1970s, although they were applied by both transatlantic partners. In the US emphasis was on import restrictions. The main instruments, as seen in Chapter 3, were antidumping and countervailing measures, while between 1980 and 1986 there were only 28 escape clause cases. Their effect was to increase duties well above the level agreed in the multilateral negotiations. However, in many cases they were instrumental to the submission of foreign countries to voluntary export restraints. According to Finger's estimates, almost half of the 774 antidumping or countervailing duty cases completed from 1980 to 1988 were superseded by VERs.[2] Most of the agreements aimed at restricting exports to the US market. However, in the semiconductor trade case the agreement with Japan had a wider, more complex scope.

Although across the Atlantic governments under intense budget pressures increasingly turned to import restrictions, in most cases under the jurisdiction of the Community, to support their industries against foreign competitors and although the Commission tried to keep a tight rein on subsidization viewed as distorting intra-EC competition, subsidies continued to play a prominent role in member states' policies. In 1981–6 the average of total state aids accounted for 3 per cent of the EC GDP with peaks of 6 per cent in Luxembourg, 5.7 per cent in Italy and 5.3 per cent in Ireland.[3] However, the percentage incidence of aids on gross value added in manufacturing was much higher: 6.2 per cent on average in the member states with peaks of 18.7 per cent in Italy and 12.9 per cent in Ireland and Greece. Particularly high was the percentage in the steel sector, also because of the restructuring that was taking place in the industry. In Ireland the ratio even exceeded 100 per cent. In Italy,

France and the UK the ratio of subsidies over gross value added was respectively 71.4 per cent, 58.3 per cent and 56.6 per cent.

US and EC steel crises and their impact on trade relations between the two trading partners

Among the so-called basic industries steel was the one that showed the steepest and most prolonged decline on both sides of the Atlantic. As illustrated by Table 25 steel production in the United States fell by 40 per cent between 1979 and 1986, though the slump hit its high in 1982; production in West Germany fell by about 20 per cent, while in France and in the UK it fell by 24 per cent and 31 per cent respectively. The declining trend was not only the result of market forces but, as explained in detail below, it was influenced, that is, rendered more pronounced or less steep and rapid, by domestic measures and international arrangements. The decline in most OECD countries, including Japan, was offset by the rise in the developing countries, with the conspicuous exception of Brazil, and in the Communist countries.

In the European Community the steel industry was affected from the early summer of 1980 by a sharp decline of demand from the internal and world markets, leading to an overall drop in production, in turn resulting in an unprecedented fall in the rate of capacity utilization which by the autumn fell to around 50 per cent. The fall in demand entailed a lowering of prices which by early autumn declined by 13 per cent compared to the beginning of the year. Input prices, in particular ores, fuel, coke, electricity, labour and overheads, went up on average by about 5 per cent. Consequently, most firms were no longer able to cover depreciation costs as well as a part of variable costs. The decline in profitability led most EC steel firms, struggling for their survival, to dodge the straitjacket of the voluntary discipline agreed in 1977 to stabilize the market. The so-called 'Bresciani firms', which had tried to exceed the market share assigned by the 1977 agreement because they were able to increase production efficiently, that is to say securing a good profit margin, were followed by a growing number of firms that, in order to avoid going out of business, were willing to sell at prices that did not cover their total production costs. In this difficult context the Commission submitted a request to the Council for the compulsory establishment of a system of production quotas on the basis of Art. 58 of the European Coal and Steel Community (ECSC) Treaty.[4] The quotas were to be imposed for a maximum period until June 1981 on all undertakings with a steel production of over 1,000 tonnes per month, with the exception of companies producing only liquid steel for casting. The Commission's request was opposed by West Germany which had a particularly efficient number of producers and, therefore, felt it had little to gain from a compulsory curtailment of production. It was only at the end of October 1980, after the exception was extended to certain special steels, that the whole EC Council of Ministers, including the Federal Republic, gave its assent to the measures proposed by the Community's executive. The measures, the first of this kind to be applied since the coming into force of the ECSC Treaty, concerned crude steel and four groups of rolled products. Thus from October 1980 steel production in the EC member countries was officially regulated from the top.

The industry's plight did not show any sign of abatement and in June 1981 the Community adopted three sets of measures which were not significantly altered in the next four years. Firstly, the quota system, was kept in place for a second year and extended to new items, i.e. concrete reinforcing bars and merchant bars. It was later renewed till June 1983 and subsequently until the end of 1985, as the problems facing the industry, that is, overcapacity, no rally of demand in the Community market and imbalance between supply and demand on the world market, remained substantially the same. Three further items (reversing-mill plate, wide flats and heavy sections) were brought into the quota system. Secondly, in line with the objectives of the quota and minimum price regime, namely the curtailment of production capacity to balance the declining level of demand and the achievement of remunerative prices, new rules (known as aids code) were introduced on aids to the steel industry by the member states and their local authorities.[5] Aids by member countries should not entail further supply and should not therefore lower prices. They were not to result in distortion of competition and had to be gradually phased out. The aids had to be authorized by the Commission not later than 1 July 1983 and had not to lead to payments after 31 December 1985. Allowable aids were to be directed to investments, closures of undertakings and R&D. Emergency aids to cope with acute social problems in the form of rescue measures were also allowed for a maximum duration of six months. Aids to continue operations could be admitted too, but their duration was to be limited to a maximum of two years and they could not lead to payments after December 1984. The fact that the deadline of this latter form of aid was later extended to December 1985 is a sign that some member states were finding it difficult to comply with the timetable set by the aids code to phase out their subsidies. At any rate Art. 12 of the aids code prudently provided that all the deadlines could be amended by unanimous assent of the Council in the line of market trends and price levels of steel and iron products.

Given the foreseeable impact of such measures on employment in the industry the third plank envisaged that the Community budget would contribute to the allowances paid by member states for early retirement and short-term employment. Following the path opened in 1977, domestic measures were joined by external measures to prevent a surge of imports from jeopardizing the endeavour to control quantities on the market and OMAs were negotiated with 14 countries.

The return to free competition was gradual and not without hitches; nor was the quota experiment judged an unconditional success. In 1985 the Commission sent the Council two communications on the management of the steel industry after that year.[6] In the first one it argued that, since the restructuring process had restored supply and demand to a better balance, starting from the onset of 1986 the production quota system should be relaxed for a number of sectors accounting for about 30 per cent of the market where overcapacity had been absorbed and the undertakings were moving out of the crisis. Yet, the return to free market was agreed by the Council for a limited share of products, nominally reinforcing bars and coated sheet, as the data showed that in other sectors the crisis had not been overcome. In its second communication the Commission called for a ban on new aids for investments and to cover operating losses, while aids for R&D, environmental protection and plant closure were allowed under strict conditions. In September 1986 the Commission sent a further communication to the Council suggesting to liberalize the market for wire rod, merchant bars, galvanized sheet and products used for its manufacture in the following year, arguing that the quota system had introduced rigidities that were starting to create increasing difficulties for the sound management of undertakings in those sectors. According to the Commission, the volume of products still under the quota system would be reduced to about 45 per cent of total Community production.[7]

In the United States the decline in steel demand during 1980 was the outcome of the downturn in domestic automotive manufacture along with the impact of high interest rates on inventories and machinery and construction markets. Domestic shipments plunged by 18 per cent relative to 1979 and hit the lowest level since 1975. From June to August more than 40 per cent of the domestic industry's production capability was rendered idle and by August the industry employed only 264,000 workers, the lowest number since 1933. As 1980 was a recession year, steel imports declined too (–11.5%), but since they fell less sharply than domestic shipments, import penetration grew magnifying the effects of an already depressed market.[8]

In March 1980, a volley of antidumping petitions was fired against EC steel exports. The US Steel Corporation filed 28 petitions covering five categories of steel products for a trade value totalling $147 million from seven European Community member states. Soon after the United States suspended its Trigger Price Mechanism (TPM) applied on steel imports, arguing that it had to devote its limited resources to the investigations provoked by the petition. As noted in Chapter 3, the TPM was a somewhat biased means of ascertaining likelihood of dumping based on the presupposition, subject to contrary proof, that sales in the US at prices below the steelmaking cost of the most efficient producer, Japan, were evidence of dumping. However, European products usually stood up to this test. Apparently the Carter administration had tried to dissuade US Steel from filing the antidumping complaints, fearing that it would make cooperation with the Community more difficult, but antidumping investigations were based on quasi-judicial proceedings with no room for interference from the executive. The European Community complained that the threat posed by the antidumping investigations was not consistent with the 1977 OECD consensus on steel, obstructing EC exports when domestic and world demand was plummeting. Only in September did the petitioner withdraw its complaint, but the Department of Commerce (DOC), reinstating the Trigger Price Mechanism, had to introduce a series of amendments which portended new troubles for the EC steel industry in the near future. The most significant amendments were the monitoring of surges of unfairly priced imports and the extension of the TPM to subsidization. Under the modified mechanism, whenever imports captured more than 15.2 per cent of the US domestic market and when the US steel industry was operating at less than 87 per cent of its productive capacity, the DOC was to initiate a 90-day review to determine whether the surge in imports appeared to be the result of dumping or subsidization practices. In the affirmative case the DOC could either initiate an autonomous investigation or provide non-confidential material to interested parties in the US who might file complaints on their own behalf. Unfortunately for the EC steel industry, there was no denying that it benefited from a host of domestic subsidies.

After a brief rally the steel market rapidly deteriorated in the course of 1981.[9] The American steel industry started the year with major investment plans and high operating rates, but by the summer high interest rates sharply curtailed demand from the industry's major consumers. Steel operating rates fell from 84.5 per cent for the first six months to 53.7 per cent by the end of the year and fell below 50 per cent during the first ten months of 1982. At the same time import penetration climbed from 13.9 per cent in the first quarter of 1981 to 23.7 per cent in the last quarter of the year. In short, slackening domestic demand was compounded by the inflow of competing imports, which mostly came from the European Community and a number of developing countries. The US administration reacted by applying a strict enforcement of the Trigger Price Mechanism and took the step of self-initiating ten antidumping and countervailing duty investigations in November 1981.

Although the measures adopted by the US executive soon attracted strong criticism from the European Community, which claimed they were further proof of a drift to protectionism on the American side, they were soon overcome by the avalanche of antidumping and countervailing duty petitions filed by the private sector. In January 1982 seven domestic steelmakers filed 132 petitions against 41 suppliers in 11 countries, seven of which were EC members, covering approximately 20 per cent of carbon steel imports in the previous year. The DOC decided to initiate 109 investigations based on the private petitions, while discontinuing all duplicative self-initiated cases. The US International Trade Commission decided to terminate, for lack of reasonable evidence of injury, 54 cases which, however, involved only a small part of the products concerned. On the other hand, several other petitions were filed in the course of the year. In June the DOC imposed preliminary countervailing measures and in August announced that subsidy margins ranging from 0.5 per cent to 21 per cent had been definitely found on imports under investigation from France, Italy, the United Kingdom, the Federal Republic of Germany and Luxembourg, the lower margin of subsidies being found in the products of the latter two countries. Producers in the Netherlands were not found to subsidize. Preliminary dumping margins were announced on imports from six companies in five countries, including the Netherlands.

Even before the DOC's findings, the Council of the European Communities mandated the Commission to negotiate a settlement with the United States. The negotiations were made more difficult by disagreements within the opposite blocks. In the US the steel industry was initially reluctant to withdraw its petitions, but it finally accepted a negotiated settlement. In the Community the main difficulty arose from the fact that the subsidy margin, and thus the amount of countervailing duty, was high for exporters from Belgium, France, Italy and the United Kingdom, while overall it was much lower for the other EC producers. Germany in particular objected to paying twice for the proliferation of steel subsidies in other member countries, which already caused an artificial supply on the German market and cut off German exports in the Community. At the end, however, the Federal Republic grudgingly accepted the principle of Community solidarity invoked by the country most hard hit by the imposition of countervailing duties. The Netherlands and Luxembourg followed suit.

On 26 October the United States and the European Community reached agreement, through exchange of letters, on two 'Arrangements', that is OMAs, covering a large share of US imports.[10] The first arrangement provided that the EC would limit its exports to the United States of ten carbon steel products to specific percentages of the US projected market: altogether 5.5 per cent with subceilings for individual products. The arrangement did not provide for fixed tonnage quotas but established specific percentages of the US apparent consumption, meaning shipments minus exports plus imports, thus giving a greater margin of flexibility. The agreement covered the period 1 November 1982 to 31 December 1985 and was to be enforced through the establishment by the EC of a system of mandatory export licences. The entry into effect was conditional on the withdrawal of the various antidumping and countervailing duties and other petitions filed in respect of imports of the products covered by the agreement. The exchange of letters also provided that the Community reserved the right to terminate the arrangement if new antidumping or countervailing duties investigations or section 201 (escape clause) and section 301 (relief from unfair trade practices) of the Trade Act of 1974 investigations were initiated against the products in question. The exchange of letters also included a short-supply clause allowing the Community to increase its exports (up to 10 per cent of the allowed ceiling).

Under the unfavourable circumstances, the EC welcomed the arrangement stressing that it meant peace in the steel sector until the end of 1985. The relief turned out to be premature. The flexible quota system and the guarantees it provided to the Community concerned only a large but limited share of EC steel exports leaving aside other products and in particular higher value and more technology intensive products. The same arrangement provided that for products other than the ten items to which the licence system applied, consultation would be held between the US and the ECSC if imports in the United States showed a significant increase indicating the possibility of diversion of trade.

The second arrangement involved neither control nor licence system but only provided for consultation if imports of EC pipes and tubes exceeded the 1979–81 average share of US apparent consumption, estimated at 5–9 per cent. If no solution had been found within 60 days, the parties could take the measures they deemed necessary, having recourse to their respective legislations.

In July 1983 Reagan announced the application of an escape clause increasing tariffs and imposing quantitative restrictions on imports of speciality steel products from a number of sources including four EC member states. The EC Council of Ministers reacted claiming that US unilateral measures were not reconcilable with the commitments of the EC ministerial council and the Williamsburg Summit declaration regarding the halting of protectionism. The European Commission contended in the OECD Steel Committee that exports from the EC were not the cause of problems within the US steel industry and that the measures unilaterally adopted by the US would squeeze out Community exports of products subject to additional duties and severely reduce exports of products subject to quantitative restrictions. Concurrently, the Commission started negotiations in the GATT challenging the conformity of the measures with Art. XIX of the General Agreement and submitting claims for compensation under the aforesaid article. As the negotiations in the GATT broke down, in February 1984 the Community retaliated against US chemicals, plastic and other products by increasing EC duties by about $160 million a year.[11] The retaliatory measures were renewed the following February but with adjustments in the level of compensation to take account of the degressive nature of the import restrictions adopted by the transatlantic trading partner.

In January 1984, following receipt of a petition filed by the Bethlehem Steel Corporation and the United Steelworkers of America, the US International Trade Commission (USITC) started an escape clause investigation under section 201 of the Trade Act of 1974. In Congress a bill for fair trade in steel was introduced which would have limited imports of all grades of steel to 15 per cent of domestic consumption. In July the USITC found that imports of carbon and alloy steel products injured the US domestic industry and recommended the imposition of a mixture of tariffs, quotas and tariff-rate quotas. The president ruled that such relief would not be in the national economic interest as it would raise steel prices, cut jobs and undermine the competitiveness of the US steel consuming industry. Reagan announced, on the other hand, a programme designed to handle the growing volume of imports entering the United States by which imports should account for about 18.5 per cent of US consumption. The programme was a two-pronged one. The first plank was the vigorous enforcing of unfair trade statutes to counteract subsidization and dumping. The second was the negotiation of steel trade arrangements for products whose exports had surged. Such arrangements would serve as an alternative to the imposition of countervailing and antidumping duties. Shortly after the president's programme was announced, Congress passed the Trade and Tariff Act of 1984 giving the president authority to enforce these steel arrangements. A section of the Act manifested a sense of Congress that imports should take between 17 per cent and 20 per cent of the US market under conditions of fair, unsubsidized competition. On the other hand, it included a provision ensuring that generated profits would be ploughed back into the industry and committed the companies to retraining their employees. Agreements were soon signed with 14 countries. Each agreement had a similar structure. It was retroactive to 1 October 1984 and would remain in effect for a five-year period during which the exporting country was provided a percentage share of the US market rather than being subject to fixed quotas.

Soon after troubles arose in the pipes and tubes sector where the United States called for negotiations with the Community as imports had exceeded the 5.9 per cent ceiling stipulated by the 1982 agreement. The Community offered to limit exports to a market share of 7.6 per cent but the US rejected the offer and in November 1984 imposed an embargo.

The Community requested consultations under Article XXIII: 1 of the GATT (nullification or impairment of benefits accruing to a party to the General Agreement) and bilateral negotiations were opened. On 10 January 1985 a pipes and tubes arrangement was concluded through an exchange of letters which restrained EC exports of the mentioned products to a level of 7.6 per cent of US apparent consumption from January 1985 through December 1986.[12] Within this general limit a 10 per cent market share was established for oil country tubular goods. The arrangement, which was to be enforced through EC establishment of a system of mandatory export licences, also provided that the US would accept exports of pipes and tubes above the above-mentioned percentages where a shortage of supply was identified, i.e., where the US industry was unable to meet domestic demand for a particular product. Things did not go smoothly. Confrontation was sparked by the All-American Pipeline project for which EC enterprises, mainly French, German and Belgian, had signed contracts for some 320,000 tonnes even before the tube arrangement. The Americans argued that domestic manufacturers were in a position to supply the required tubes and even more. The Community rejoined that American producers were not able to supply all tubes of the required quality and hence the gap might be filled by EC firms. As a compromise the US negotiators offered to allow in 60,000 tonnes, which, however, fell far short of the European claim. At the same time the US called for negotiations on some of the products other than the ten items to which the licence system applied under the 1982 arrangement whose exports from the Community had soared in the last three years. While the EC argued that this was the natural effect of the unstoppable appreciation of the dollar, the US contended that these growing exports were a sign of trade diversion and that quantitative restrictions should therefore apply. Finally the United States put pressure on the Community for an extension of the 1982 arrangement beyond 1985.

The final compromise satisfied both parties, but overall it was the US that could claim to carry the day. EC manufacturers were allowed to export 100,000 tonnes of tubes under the short-supply clause. On 6 August a further exchange of letters modified the 1982 arrangement by subjecting to specific restraints 11 products that were previously included in the consultation products category.[13] The new agreement limited these products to 179,648 tonnes from 1 August to 31 December 1985 with a subceiling for each of the 11 items. In September of the same year the EC and the US started negotiations for the extension to September 1989 of both the arrangement on carbon steel products of 1982 as complemented in August 1985 and the pipes and tubes arrangement of 1985. Agreement was reached in December.[14] As regards the first arrangement, the number of items subject to a percentage of the projected US apparent consumption or to a specific number of tonnes ceiling rose to 31 items, including special steel, and in February 1986 the United States terminated the safeguard measures it had applied since 1983 on the mentioned product and concurrently the EC withdrew its retaliatory measures. In line with the previous agreements on steel products, the EC was allowed to revoke the agreement if antidumping, countervailing measures or safeguard and relief from unfair trade practices proceedings were applied against its exports. Semi-finished products were not subject to quantitative restrictions remaining 'consultation programs' as under the 1982 arrangement.

Thus the European Community could believe that, although with some constraints, peace was secured with the United States and with it a clearer picture of its export potential. Once again its hopes were disappointed. In December 1985 the US applied unilateral restriction on semi-finished products. The Community complained that such restrictions were not economically justified and contrary to the arrangement negotiated in October and, as the talks with its transatlantic trading partner failed to produce concrete results, the Community adopted retaliatory measures on imports of cattle, fertilizers and coated paper.[15]

The European Community repeatedly complained that its transatlantic trading partner's policy on steel was protectionist and it was right. On the other hand, the steel crisis in the United States was no less dramatic than across the Atlantic and certainly the Community was not in the best position for preaching. The EC too had export restraining agreements with many steel exporting countries. One of the main weapons in the US steel policy was the threat of countervailing measures as the EC industry, in contrast to the American industry, was heavily subsidized; this was an accusation that the Community could not deny as it was itself trying to hold in check and eventually phase out state aids in its member countries.

The decline of the US and EC car industry and the attempt to harness the Japanese onslaught

The difficulties experienced by the US automobile industry in the period under review were certainly aggravated by the second oil shock which highlighted the industry's failure to adapt production to growing demand for fuel-efficient cars, but were also the result of other long-standing factors. The first trade deficit dated back to 1968, becoming, however, thirteen times as high ten years later and over fourteen times in 1980 (Table 3). The higher price assurances given by foreign manufacturers from Europe, Canada and Japan, to obtain the discontinuance of a mega antidumping investigation opened in 1976 only entailed a weak and short respite.

The first firm to run into trouble was Chrysler, the smallest of the 'Big Three' US automakers, after Ford and General Motors. The company closed 1978 with a net loss of $204.6 million and its deficit grew by $53.8 million in just the first quarter of 1979, which made the corporation's bankruptcy and massive redundancies for its 130,000 workers in the US alone a likelihood, if not a certainty. Realizing that the company would go out of business if it did not receive a significant amount of money to continue and enhance its activities, Chrysler's president and CEO, Lee Iacocca, called for public aid. Iacocca received support from the powerful automobile workers union, UAW, which lobbied for the approval of a financial package in Congress and convinced the company's employees to accept financial sacrifices in order to save their jobs.[16] After a difficult process, Congress, with the backing of the executive, gave its approval to a $3.5 billion aid package. Public aid did not come directly as a loan but as a $1.5 billion loan guarantee, conditional on the company's coming up with a matching $2 billion in help from creditors, dealers and workers. In his memoirs Lee Iacocca expressed the unreserved view that Chrysler was lucky to have 'appealed to a Democratic administration that put people ahead of ideology' and that it was quite likely that a Republican administration would not have endorsed the rescue package for ideological reasons.[17] Indeed, the way Reagan coped with the widespread crisis in the US automotive industry partially differed from his predecessor's.

The Chrysler bailout did not put an end to the sector crisis, rather it was its herald. Things started to get worse for the whole industry in 1980 when a steadily rising oil price accelerated consumer demand for a switch to smaller cars. Production plummeted to a 19-year low while unemployment in the car industry and in its suppliers surged to 40 per cent of a work force of 2.5 million persons. The domestic production downturn was mirrored by a surge in imports, the Japanese share of which went on growing. Passenger car imports, excluding Canada, rose from 2,192 thousands of units in 1978 to 2,522 in 1980 (+15%), while exports declined from 164 thousands of units in 1978 to 105 thousands in 1980.[18]

The plight of the US industry and the rise in imports resulted in the introduction of several bills in Congress to raise trade barriers on automobiles. However, the response of the Carter administration was cautious and could not be classified as protectionist. In March 1980 an administration panel, composed of the US Trade Representative, the Council of Economic Advisers and the Departments of Commerce, Transportation and Energy, testified against new import barriers, arguing that the crisis was due to a cyclical depression in the market exacerbated by the slow response of the US industry to the change of demand to smaller and more fuel-efficient cars which was met by foreign, prevalently Japanese, models. However, the panel pointed out that the decline in overall demand far exceeded the number of purchases of imported cars. The administration also stressed that if the industry believed that imports were the cause of its worsening economic conditions, it should pursue the remedies provided by section 201 of the Trade Act of 1974, i.e. adoption of safeguard measures. However, when a petition for import relief was filed by the United Automobile Workers in June 1980 and by the Ford Motor Company in July, the US International Trade Commission determined that car imports had not increased in the medium term to such an extent as to constitute a cause of serious injury to the domestic industry in the United States. The executive, therefore, preferred to rely on special assistance programmes for the domestic auto industry and advances to the Japanese government to achieve further liberalization of the trade in automotive parts. In July 1980, Carter announced a set of support initiatives including a special $50 million Community Assistance programme, a special Small Business Administration loan programme for auto dealers and measures to reduce the economic impact of safety, fuel economy and emission standards to the automobile industry.[19] In May 1980, in response to the US requests, the Japanese government announced the elimination of duties on most automobile parts to facilitate American manufacturers' access to the Japanese replacement market.[20] In short, Carter, rather than adopting tariff and quota restrictions to solve the problems of the ailing motorcar industry, opted for domestic aid, quite akin to subsidization, and efforts to reduce the obstacles to American exports.

The Reagan administration did not want to appear to be wavering in its stated policy of opposing protectionism, nor did it want to make conspicuous exception to its stance against subsidization of industries in distress and interference with the market. On the other hand, Reagan could not disown his electoral pledge to help the American car industry get over, especially as in 1981 car imports reached 35.2 per cent of sales in the US market and legislation to restrict the inflow was gaining support in Congress. The solution was found in trade diplomacy and the obvious party in the prospective agreement was Japan. Between 1975 and 1980 Japanese car exports had more than doubled and their share of total production had grown from 38.6 per cent to 54 per cent.[21] Japanese cars, which in 1973 accounted for 40 per cent of total US car imports, amounted to 79 per cent of imports seven years later. In April 1981 a US delegation, headed by the new United States Trade Representative, William Brock, flew to Tokyo for talks with Japanese officials. A month later the MITI announced a voluntary restraint agreement with the US. The VER reduced exports of passenger cars to the US by 7.7 per cent from 1.82 million cars to 1.68 million units.[22] Japan also agreed to limit exports to Puerto Rico to 70,000 cars and to limit sport utility vehicle (SUV) exports to 82,500. Cars manufactured in the US would not count against these limits. The agreement was initially scheduled to expire after three years but in 1984 it was extended for a further year while the ceiling of 1.68 million cars was increased to 1.85 million. Also the ceiling on exports to Puerto Rico and of SUVs was raised.

In the first two years of the arrangement the American industry did not experience any significant improvement, but in 1983 it was back to the black and in 1984 it had its best profit year since 1977, while capacity utilization strongly improved. In January 1985 the MITI hinted that Japan's voluntary ceiling on automobile exports would not be renewed given the improving earnings of the big US automakers and the sharp reduction of unemployment in the US auto industry. In March Reagan decided not to ask Japan to continue its voluntary restraint, but soon a number of resolution were introduced in Congress calling for continued import limits, if necessary by the imposition of quotas. Thus Japan agreed to go on restraining its exports, which from 1985 to early 1992 were limited to 2.3 million passenger cars plus 206,000 SUVs and shipments to Puerto Rico.[23] At the same time the US administration implemented an 'auto program' to prop up the industry. In contrast with Carter's policy and in line with the philosophy of the Republican executive, the programme was prevalently based on fiscal benefits. It also provided for revision and elimination of 34 auto-related safety and environment regulations. It is, therefore, arguable that the Reagan administration, in spite of its general condemnation of such policies, was carrying out an industrial policy, this time with the active support of Japanese firms and of the MITI.

The prospect of trade barriers also meant a shift in the Japanese vehicle strategy. Up to 1981 the Japanese penetration in the US market had been based on exports. Japanese investments in the US had been growing rapidly since the mid-1970s, reaching $7.7 million in 1981, but they were a distant third relative to investments from Europe and Canada. Besides the largest sector of Japanese investments was trade while manufacturing constituted a lesser share. This was the result of the clear Japanese preference for manufacturing goods in Japan and exporting them to the United States with the support of an extensive trade network. However, by 1984 Japanese FDIs jumped to $16 million, overtaking Canadian investments and the share of manufacturing, among which automotive vehicles in particular, steadily grew. By 1983 Japanese car manufacturers with US operations included Toyota, which had signed a twelve-year joint venture agreement with General Motors to manufacture about 200,000 automobiles yearly; Nissan, which had a light truck plant in Smyrna, Tennessee; and Honda, which operated a plant in Marysville, Ohio.

On the other side of the Atlantic concerns over the declining weight of the Community member states' industry in the international market and over the inflow of Japanese cars in the domestic market had been growing since the late 1970s. Between 1980 and 1985 Japanese exports accounted for about 10 per cent of the British and German markets and for over 20 per cent of the Dutch market. However, the import penetration of Japanese cars in the French market remained constantly below the 5 per cent threshold and the Italian market remained almost impermeable.[24]

In 1981 a Commission report on the European automobile industry stressed the need for strengthening the EC internal market by greater harmonization of motor vehicle taxation and energy policies and by monitoring state aids to avoid trade distortions as well as for the adoption of a coherent commercial policy towards non-Community countries.[25] In January a Parliament resolution called for 'voluntary export restraint on the part of the Japanese'. The Commission made analogous requests during its meetings with the Japanese counterpart which, however, not without reason, cunningly replied that Japan did not intend to impose restrictions on exports to the Community as a whole in view of the restrictions already applied by France, Italy and the United Kingdom. West Germany followed suit and in 1981 negotiated an 'informal promise' from the Japanese automobile manufacturers to limit the rate of increase in the number of automobiles exported to the Federal Republic and keep the Japanese share of the West German market at about 10 per cent. The Belgian government announced that the Japanese had agreed to keep automobile exports to Belgium in 1981 approximately the same as that of the 1980 level and to review the restraint level at the end of March 1982 to see if it should continue for another year. Also in 1981, the Japanese announced that exports to the Netherlands would remain at the 1980 level.[26]

After the announcement of the Japanese authorities' decision to limit car exports to the United States the EC authorities asked for clarification from the Japanese and United States government and later called for an arrangement between the Community and Japan which should have resulted in Japanese car exports being submitted to a limitation analogous to the one decided by Japan vis-à-vis the United States.[27] In 1982 Japan pledged moderation in car exports and the engagement was renewed in the talks held in Tokyo in February 1983. However, car imports from Japan went on increasing and soon were joined by growing imports from state-trading and developing countries.

The acceleration of decline trend in the textile and clothing industry

The reports submitted by the Commission at the eve of the expiry of MFA II pointed out the absence of any improvement in the textile and clothing industry in the Community due to a slowdown in the growth of consumption, falling production, declining exports and a steep rise in imports.[28] Between 1973 and 1980 output had contracted by 3.6 per cent in textiles and 2 per cent in clothing; the number of workers employed in the sector had fallen by 25 per cent, from 3,124,000 in 1973 to about 2,330,000 in 1980, with no sign of the trend levelling off, while the number of firms had fallen by 15 per cent. The average growth rate of consumption had been steadily declining from the pre-1973 level of 3–4 per cent to 1.2 per cent for textiles and 1.1 per cent for clothing. Exports had risen by 16 per cent since 1973 but imports had increased much faster, accounting for 45 per cent of total consumption in the Community by 1980. The Commission, therefore, emphasized the need for a restructuring of the EC industry based on the establishment of economy of scale made possible by a really unified market, which in turn would foster continued renewal and improvement of equipment. As regards external policy the Commission and the Council looked favourably to the renewal of the Multifibre Arrangement, and to the continuation of the system of bilateral restraint agreements with supplying countries. They made it clear, however, that, given the decline in consumption growth in the Community and the obstacles raised to EC exports, it was not possible to accept an overall textile import growth rate of 6 per cent. They also stressed that provisions for cutting dominant suppliers' levels of market access and for preventing sudden surges of imports within underutilized quotas should be adopted.

The EC had traditionally posted a substantial surplus in textile and apparel with the US, but from 1977 the United States started to close the gap as its exports to the EC more than doubled while its imports started to level off. Yet, the US overall balance did show signs of rapid deterioration, worsening by 77 per cent between 1977 and 1981 (Table 4).

The protocol that provided for the extension of the MFA until 31 July 1986 took, although partially, account of the worries of the industrial countries.[29] In particular, as was the case for the 1977 protocol, the possibility of a growth rate lower than 6 per cent was envisaged, but only when there was a recurrence or exacerbation of market disruption. On the other hand, decline in per capita consumption in textiles and clothing was considered relevant in this regard. A clause for preventing import surges within underutilized quotas was introduced, also providing for negotiation of suitable compensation. Particular attention was also given to problems relating to the circumvention of the agreement by providing that where evidence was available regarding the country of true origin of the product there should be a corresponding adjustment of charges to existing quotas.

The attitude of the Community towards the rules incorporated in the MFA and towards the net of bilateral agreements within its framework changed in the years that followed its renewal in 1981. The directives given by the Council to the Commission in the run-up to the fourth arrangement envisaged some liberalization of the MFA and a greater degree of differentiation between exporting countries. Willy De Clercq, member of the Commission responsible for external relations and trade policy, expressed the hope, with clear reference to the US, that 'the courageous attitude of the Community would have a positive influence on certain industrialized countries which might be tempted by a more protectionist approach'.[30] On the other hand, the Community called for measures to ensure greater protection of intellectual property rights, such as trademarks and designs. It also requested that all members of the arrangement should commit themselves to take measures to open up markets commensurate to their level of development and economic capabilities. In other words, the Community was implicitly recognising that it was useless to try stemming the inflow of competing products and it was time to move up on the production ladder and secure its position.

In the United States conditions in the textiles and clothing industries rapidly deteriorated with the appreciation of the dollar. Between 1981 and 1985 the deficit in the two sectors almost tripled as imports almost doubled while exports remained stagnant. Almost 300,000 jobs were lost. As previously noted, in vetoing a bill that would have severely restricted imports, in particular from the main textile exporting countries, Hong Kong, Taiwan and South Korea, promised that a new arrangement would be at least as restrictive towards imports as MFA III.

The new protocol, which extended the MFA for a period of five years until 31 July 1991, stressed the importance of promoting liberalization of trade in textiles and clothing with the final objective of applying GATT rules. It provided that exporting countries might agree with importing participants to any mutually acceptable solution as regards growth and flexibility, stressing, however, that in no case should such growth and flexibility be negative. It also provided that significantly more favourable treatment was to be accorded to least developed countries.

The growing threat of Japan in high-tech industry and the US and EC responses

As expected, high-technology production and trade was concentrated in the OECD countries and high-tech exports as a share of total manufactures exports went on increasing during the 1970s and 1980s. On the other hand, the two decades witnessed significant changes in the competitive position of the main producers as well as a growing erosion of the OECD countries' absolute dominance by non members of the Paris organization, the Asian NICs in particular.[31] In the 1970–3 years US high-tech exports had a 29.5 per cent share of world exports; the European Community had a 46.4 per cent share, including intra-EC trade, while Japan accounted for a modest 7 per cent share. In the 1982–5 period the US share had fallen to 25.2 per cent and the EC countries' share had declined to 39.3 per cent, while that of Japan had stepped up to 12.9 per cent. During the same years the OECD's share had fallen from 95.6 per cent to 86.8 per cent and the share of the Asian NICs had grown from 1.3 per cent to 6 per cent. The erosion of American and European positions was especially pronounced in the electronics sector that comprised computers, telecommunication equipments, consumer electronics, electronic parts, including semiconductors and business electronics. By the early 1980s Japan had taken the export leadership and in 1986 it exported $45 billion in particular in consumer electronics and telecommunication equipment, boasting a surplus of $44 billion.[32] The United States was the second main exporter, maintaining a leadership in computers, but by 1986 its deficit in the whole sector reached $15 billion. The EC was the third largest exporter and the second largest importer. Its surplus of the previous decade had turned into a growing deficit that reached $14 billion by 1986.

Electronics was a highly concentrated industry where the top 200 electronics companies accounted for about 80 per cent of world output. It was also an industry that attracted, for a multiplicity of reasons, the greatest variety of trade policies based on a number of different instruments often marked by a level of complexity and sophistication higher than in other sectors. In turn, these policies were bound to affect each player's trading partners as well as their policies. A number of objectives, both domestic and external – though it is quite difficult and inappropriate to keep the two goals apart – were pursued, going from industrial growth and employment improvement, response to the claims of special-interest groups and reinforcement of political control over a key sector to protection of infant industries, increased competitiveness in international markets, reduced dependence on foreign sources of supply for strategic reasons and improved access to advanced foreign economic technology.[33] Focusing on industrial growth and competitiveness in international markets Bush puts forward two further factors ('independent variables', in the author's words) to explain actions and interactions in high-tech international competition: the potential for a state's economy to 'consume' and 'internalize' the externalities exhibited by national champions.[34] The consumption variable implies that upstream and downstream industries or the economy in general are able to profit from the spillover externalities generated by firms directly benefiting from public support. For instance, externalities in high-definition television industry can spread to wider sectors of the consumer electronic industry. The internalization variable implies that external benefits generated by an industry accrue in dominant measure within national boundaries.

Tariff went on being extensively used after the Tokyo Round to restrict imports both by developed and developing countries. As regards industrial countries tariff applied by the United States and Japan were lower than those applied by the EC, which maintained particularly high rates for semiconductors and a range of consumer electronics. Irrespective of their legitimacy under the provisions of the General Agreement some European countries, among which Spain, Portugal, Greece and Italy, still applied quantitative restrictions on imports of electronic products. Government-to-government export restraint agreements were signed in the period under review by the US, the EC and some of its member states, France in particular, on one side and Japan, Korea, Hong Kong and Taiwan on the other. Also antidumping proceedings were used to keep the growth of electronic imports from East Asia at bay, but their number was not particularly high relative to imports in other sectors. A frequently adopted proceeding to block the inflow of foreign electronic products was patent and copyright protection, which included the banning of imports of electronic products or software infringing domestic patents and the establishment of procedures for control and implementation of intellectual property rights that do not constitute a barrier to fair trade. A further obstacle to electronics imports was the establishment of a monopoly in a high-tech primary user sector which, in turn prevented foreign products from entering the market. Thus the US and the EC exercised considerable pressure on Japan that finally convinced the Japanese parliament to approve legislation in 1984 that privatized the Nippon Telegraph and Telephone Public Corporation and open up the world's second largest telecommunication market for foreign competition.[35] Likewise, public procurement were exploited to provide market opportunities to domestic firms, while excluding potential foreign bidders. Finally, the establishment of standards that were not shared by potential foreign competitors played an important role in isolating the domestic market and allowing the development of domestic firms, as shown by the policy adopted by the Community from 1986 not to lose the high-definition television market to Japanese competition. On the other side of the spectrum were export promoting measures, in particular subsidies. Their gamut included subsidies to military R&D, obviously with spillover in the civil sector, which were used by the US, the UK and France; subsidies to civil R&D, which were bestowed, among others, by both the US and the EC as well as by Japan; and general subsidies, which were granted by many countries, among which Japan and France.

Japan in particular was able through the mid-1980s to promote its electronics industry through a skilful combination of tariff and non-tariff protection from competing products and R&D and general subsidies. The Ministry of International Trade and Industry was also particularly active in fostering and directing the synergies of Japanese firms towards the export market, a policy that amazed and quite often incensed foreign government and scholars which accused the Japanese government of deviously interfering in the national and internal economy, although it could be argued that the MITI was only fulfilling – too effectively, perhaps – its task. To use a technical term, Japan was efficient and successful in 'targeting' various sectors of the electronics industry.

In the 1980s, the first attempt to keep the inflow of Japanese products in check was conducted by the European Community, on incitement in the first of France, and concerned videocassette recorders (VCRs). France was supporting the creation of European champions in VCRs through the merger of existing national champions, in particular Thomson, controlled by the French government with the German Grundig, although the former was importing and distributing Japanese products. The French government in late 1982 started to force all VCR imports to be cleared at the customs post at Poitier, 200 km from Paris, also requesting that all instruction books be in French. At the same time Grundig and the Dutch company Philips appealed to the European Commission to win temporary protection from the overflow of Japanese products on account of the unfair competition, the worsening of the unemployment problem in the Community and the potential loss of R&D capacity and the consequent dependence on imported technologies. The Community negotiated an agreement with Japan, which was announced in February 1983 along with export moderation pledges concerning a host of other products. The VER was the first negotiated by the Community with Japan outside the steel sector, although VERs between the governments of the member states and Japan were already in existence. The VER provided restraints on exports of completed products and export of unfinished products to be assembled in Europe till 1985 and a minimum price system, which, though its terms were not declared, seems to have been connected to the factory prices of Philips and Grundig.[36]

At the VER expiration in December 1985, the Community reached agreement with Japan on raising from 8 per cent to 14 per cent the duty on videocassette recorders while reducing or eliminating them on other electronic goods. The prospect of higher tariffs along with that of subsidies provided by EC member states, among which the UK was the most generous, to attract Japanese VCR investments, induced many Japanese firms to move their production facilities to Europe. It also stimulated Japanese companies to form joint ventures with their European competitors. As a result VCR production in the EC strongly increased but the market was dominated by Japanese firms and not by European champions. In short, the Community ended up accepting a second-best solution as local production was preferable to imports in a variety of ways stretching from the provision of jobs and skill acquisition for local workers to spillover benefits for regional development and an increased tax base.

Partial similarities can be found in the path to and the pattern of the agreement reached three years later by the United States with Japan in the more technically sophisticated semiconductor sector. Here the United States, which for a large part of the 1970s had the dominant share of the market, started to lose ground at the end of the decade and by 1985 was overtaken by Japan. In the Dynamic Random Access Memory (DRAM) sector the overtaking had already taken place in 1981. The EC member states remained a distant third. The overtaking was the result of an active policy of the Japanese government to boost its infant industry in this strategic high-tech market and subsequently of the highly organized and pent structure of the Japanese industry once it had achieved maturity. In 1985 the Semiconductor Industry Association (SIA) filed a section 301 petition against unfair trade practices by the Japanese companies. It was followed by a series of antidumping petitions against Japanese firms and, as expected, the DOC did not fail to assess very large dumping margins. The July 1986 Semiconductor Trade Agreement (STA) addressed in particular two areas of concern for the United States: access to the Japanese market and dumping by Japanese firms in the US market.[37] As regards market access the Japanese government pledged to encourage a long-term relationship between Japanese users and foreign firms and, more specifically, in a side letter declared it would make efforts to assist foreign companies in reaching a 20 per cent market within five years. Dumping from Japanese firms was to be prevented, in general terms, by establishing a cost-based price floor, monitored by the MITI, only above which Japanese companies could set export prices. It must be noted that the agreement did not expressly refer to American firms and the American market. It referred, instead, to access to the Japanese market by foreign companies, that is, not only foreign subsidiaries of US MNCs but also European firms. Likewise, the antidumping provisions concerned foreign markets as well. Indeed, the price monitoring was extended to Japanese exports to third countries as it was feared that an agreement simply halting dumping in the US market would leave American producers exposed to unfair Japanese competition elsewhere[38]

The STA put into effect for the first time the philosophy shared by Congress and executive that foreign markets had to be opened, forcefully if necessary, to American products and also represented a major step towards managed trade run by two countries that together dominated the world market. Things did not go smoothly. In April 1987 Reagan applied 100 per cent tariffs on Japanese computers and electropneumatic hammers – both of which competed with domestic production in the US – in retaliation for the non-fulfilment of the 1986 pledges. Only then did the US share of the Japanese market start to rise along with prices in the international market, which was an opportunity for the Japanese firms to strengthen their financial position. In the meantime, however, South Korea made its entry in the sector becoming a competitor for both American and Japanese firms. The European Community, for its part, accused the US and Japan of interfering with the legitimate interests of their trading partners without consulting them and requested the establishment of a GATT panel to examine whether the provision of the STA complied with GATT rules.

8

The Particular Case of Agriculture and its Impact on Trade Relations in the 1980s

The years following the second oil crisis witnessed dramatic changes in the fortunes of those competing in the farm trade arena. In 1986 the EC briefly overtook the United States as the largest agricultural exporter, totalling, with the entry of Spain and Portugal, $28.1 billion.[1] The data provided by the Food and Agriculture Organization show that, while world trade declined and the share of some traditional exporting countries, in particular the US, shrank, the exports of the EC member countries, including intra-EC trade, continued to grow overall and their share of the world market increased (Figure 14). Regarding the main trade commodity, cereals, while American exports fell both in quantity and value, France, the major EC producer, became the second largest exporter, having surpassed Canada in 1985. Yet, the Community's export success masked overproduction problems and budget pressures which sparked severe strains among member states and conflicts with trading partners.

The crisis of the farm industry in the US

To protest against the December 1979 Soviet invasion of Afghanistan, on 4 January 1980 Jimmy Carter announced a grain embargo on exports to the Soviet Union, suspending delivery of all US grain sales in excess of the eight million tons guaranteed by a 1975 bilateral agreement. The USSR had made plans to import a record 35 million tons, mostly from the United States, as its grain harvest had fallen short of production targets by over 20 per cent. Whatever the political and economic effectiveness of the embargo, it was bound to cause serious problems to US exporting companies and farmers. The Commodity Credit Corporation (CCC), the financial branch of the Department of Agriculture, covered the contractual obligations of the exporters for undelivered embargo grains, at a cost to the government of $2 billion, and subsequently managed to gradually retender the bulk of the grains it had acquired. To relieve farmers from the potential price depression caused by the recycling of grains, the loan rate – that is, the amount of credit for bushels of produce covered by government programmes – was increased with further costs to the taxpayer.[2] It is quite likely that the lavish amount of financial support provided to ease the pain of the 1980 grain embargo could have fallen under a subsidization ban had a code on agriculture been signed in the Tokyo Round. But this was not the case.

Despite the executive's financial efforts, farmers were highly critical of Carter's policy and the Republican platform for the November 1980 elections vowed to end the embargo immediately. Actually, the embargo did not entail any slowdown in farm exports as the fall in exports to the Soviet Union was offset by an upsurge in demand from other countries, prominent among which was China (Figure 15).[3] Likewise, farmers' gross income rose significantly thanks to governmental price support, growing demand from countries other than the USSR, along with the effect on prices of a severe drought. What fell was net income as farmers were hit by soaring input costs and growing interest rates. After improving in 1981, farmers' conditions deteriorated in the subsequent years.

The year 1982 saw a dramatic u-turn in the fortunes of American agriculture. The crisis, by some commentators equated to the crisis of the 1920s and 1930s, had many facets. The US share of world farm exports declined sharply (from 19.4 per cent in 1981 to 12.3 per cent in 1986) and the share of agricultural exports in farmers' revenue shrank.[4] Farmers' net income deteriorated along with the value of farm property. From 1982 severe financial strains affected both farmers and credit institutions. Several causes were advanced to explain the crisis: excessively high (real) interest rates and the strength of the dollar which made US exports uncompetitive; the distorting role played by the US farm regime itself; and the unfair competition of foreign producers.

The administration's proclaimed goals of reducing the growth of overall federal spending by eliminating those activities that overstepped the proper sphere of government responsibilities and reducing the federal regulatory burden in areas where the government interfered with the efficient conduct of private business were faithfully reflected in the executive's proposals for the 1981 farm bill, which was to replace the expiring 1977 Food and Agriculture Act, setting the stage for farm policy in the following four years. The executive pursued two objectives – to keep the annual budget cost for farm spending at around \$1.5–\$2 billion per year, principally targeting the dairy programme, and to get rid of certain programmes which were not consistent with the administration's free-market approach and allegedly hampered American competitiveness in the international market. Concerning wheat, feed grains, cotton, rice and soybeans, the secretary for Agriculture John Block proposed, rather baldly, to Congress to terminate target prices and deficiency payments, to terminate authority for set aside (a form of production control) and to grant the Department of Agriculture authority to set commodity loan levels, which were usually fixed by law.[5] The proposal boiled down to repeal the bulk of income support and government interference in the quantities that farmers were allowed to produce and market. Regarding price support, in the previous decade commodity loan rates had only played the role of safety nets in the apparently unlikely event of market prices falling below their level. However, as signs of price volatility were increasingly present, the administration wanted to obtain leeway in fixing the intervention price to prevent it from rising above the sinking market price lest the CCC be loaded with stocks to be disposed of at extremely low prices, causing extra burden to the budget compounded by storage costs. As expected, the lawmakers considered the administration's proposals too radical and dangerously susceptible to alienate the support of a large part of their constituencies. The administration was all in all successful in withstanding Congress's demands for substantial assistance to its commodity lobbies. On the other hand, it was far from achieving its aim of reshaping the farm support mechanism.

The bill that Reagan signed into law on 22 December 1981 significantly reduced the minimum support level for dairy products. Target prices were not abolished, but the law provided for annual increases in grains and cotton target prices that fell short of the expected inflation rate. Concurrently, loan rates for grains were frozen at the 1982 level, while those for rice and cotton were allowed to increase at a rate lower than the expected rate of inflation. In short, the Agriculture and Food Act of 1981 continued the declining trend in price support in real terms, without altering its mechanism. There was the rub, however. The prospective decrease rested on stable market prices. Agricultural conditions soon deteriorated. From the 1982 market year main US farm exports fell causing carry-over stocks to increase (except for 1984 thanks to a severe drought the previous year and the implementation of a new programme directed at reducing production and inventories, known as payment in kind – PIK). This was bound to cause growing strain on the Agriculture Department's budget.

Some commentators have argued that there was a direct, negative correlation between the appreciation of the dollar in the exchange market and the shrinking share of US produce exports.[6] McCalla, accepting in principle such a perspective, noted that the impact of the dollar rise was bound to change according to the relationship between the various foreign currencies and the dollar. Those countries whose currencies moved with the US dollar were to experience the same trend of contracting exports and declining prices. Those countries, like the EC member states, whose currencies were depreciating against the dollar were heading for an improvement in their export competitiveness. For those importers whose currencies were pegged to the US dollar, the exchange rate impact was neutralized vis-à-vis US exports, but their imports from countries with depreciating currencies would become cheaper relative to US exports. Finally, US farm produce would become more expensive for importing countries whose currencies were depreciating and for inconvertible currency countries which relied on primary product exports and gold sales to finance food imports.[7]

Batten and Belongia argued that foreign demand for US agricultural exports was about 75 per cent more sensitive to changes in foreign income than to those in the real exchange value of the dollar.[8] Regarding grains in particular, in the period under review production exceeded consumption as developing countries affected by the debt crisis had to reduce demand for foreign produce they could not afford to purchase while some of the main importers of US farm produce in the 1970s made great strides in productivity and, therefore, in self-sufficiency. The trend was not limited to the European Community but extended to China, India and South East Asia.

As to the relative position of the United States, some scholars as well as the US administration argued that a further factor played a more decisive role than the strength of the dollar: the impact of the federal farm policy.[9] As world market prices fell, loan rates, which at the outset of the decade were far below the market level, became high enough relative to world prices to encourage farmers to forfeit their produce to the CCC. The result was that while exports shrank government stocks swelled from 12.3 million metric tons in 1981 to 45.5 million two years later.[10] The message that the administration conveyed to the lawmakers was that the system preserved by the 1981 farm law was crowding out American farmers in the international market, as the safety net it provided had turned into a viable substitute for market prices making it easier to produce for the US government. It was also contended that, adding insult to injury, the increase in US stocks, which averaged 60 per cent of world stocks, by preventing the world market from being a viable outlet for American produce, buoyed up prices to the advantage of foreign competitors.[11] In short, the US regime was indirectly subsidizing its competitors, particularly the EC.

A further factor could have played a role in the relative decline of American farm exports. The role of government in farm trade competition went well beyond bestowing export subsidies or providing safety nets for farmers. State-to-state long-term agreements were a key factor in securing outlets for domestic produce. Guaranteed provision of credit, in particular facilitated loans (i.e. with interest rates lower than those prevailing in the market) were also an essential component as the decision to import by countries other than industrial ones was often linked to availability and credit terms. In turn, facilitated loans provided by public agencies depended on favourable political relations between the lender and the recipient.

The Reagan administration promptly lifted the embargo on the Soviet Union.[12] Once again, however, general foreign policy concerns stood in the way of a farm deal. To react against the declaration of martial law in Poland, the US government refused to start negotiations for a new long-term grain agreement, preferring to extend the expiring agreement on a year-to-year basis. The Soviet government formerly paid for food imports with its exports, principally oil and gold sales. In 1981, however, the Soviet Union, in spite of gold and diamond sales, was unable to cover all its grain imports and for the first time asked for supplier credit. The US executive refused official credit for Russian purchases, although it did not try to prevent private banks from offering loans at market rates. Finally, in July 1983 the secretary of agriculture announced a five-year grain sale agreement that committed the United States to sell and the Soviet Union to buy at least 9 million metric tons and up to 12 million metric tons of wheat and corn yearly.[13] Meanwhile other countries, like Australia, Canada and Argentina, had established a foothold in the Soviet market, offering the expectation of a grain supply less dependent on political factors and, therefore, less volatile and often on better credit terms than the US. In 1982 France, asserting its autonomy within the European Community in the conduct of farm trade agreements, entered into an agreement with the USSR for the provision of an 'unspecified' quantity of grain.[14]

In 1983, the administration tried to persuade Congress to block scheduled increases in target prices in an attempt to push through a new version of its cost-cutting proposal. It was not successful. The main problem with which the administration was, therefore, confronted was how to curb the mounting and increasingly costly stock of agricultural produce. The initial response was far from the free-market approach the executive had claimed to pursue. In short, in order to realize its wider objectives, the Reagan administration adopted the strategy of avoiding a clash with Congress on a particular item which in the end led to unwarranted increases in budget outlays.

In 1983, in the hope of winning Congressional approval for the freeze of target prices, agriculture secretary John Block gave his backing to the so-called 'paid diversion dairy plan', though he withdrew his support in the final part of the Congressional session. Reagan was not favourable to the programme, noting that paying farmers for not producing contradicted his free-market philosophy. His economic advisers were opposed to the bill as it increased pressure on the budget. The president, however, refrained from vetoing and the new law, which authorized payments to dairymen to 'produce less', was signed by Reagan on 28 November 1983.[15]

The same interventionist philosophy underpinned the PIK plan, though the programme did not need Congressional approval as it was based on existing statutory authority. The PIK, which covered wheat, corn, sorghum, rice and cotton, aimed at killing two birds with one stone by curbing production and reducing inventories. Under this regime farmers who agreed to retire an additional 10 per cent to 30 per cent of their land would receive a payment in kind equal to an established quantity of the commodity normally grown on the property (95 per cent of yield per acre for wheat and 80 per cent for other crops). The payment was taken either from government stocks or from crops used as collateral for CCC loans. Coupled with the severe drought of 1983, the PIK allowed a 50 per cent reduction in grain stocks in 1984, but inventories climbed again a year later.[16] However, the administration itself warned that the PIK had drawbacks in the international market, as production cuts at home were likely to stimulate extra production by competing countries. Once again the executive was emphasizing that government interference with the free play of the market had spillover effects beneficial to foreign competitors and, therefore, detrimental to American producers.[17]

The decline in exports contributed to worsen the American farmers' financial stress, whose main cause, however, was soaring real interest rates. During the 1970s farm debt had substantially increased as rising export sales and relatively favourable export prices stimulated investments in land and agricultural equipment while, as frequently occurs in time of inflation, the real cost of the loan was exceptionally low, sometimes negative. Things changed radically in the first half of the following decade with inflation slowing down and rising costs of debt. The burden of debt servicing increased while real estate value plunged as a result of several factors: the fall in market prices and export contraction resulted in lower gross and net income, depressing expected farm rent; the inflation slowdown deprived real estate of its appeal as a refuge against financial asset devaluation. Thus many farmers found it more and more difficult to repay their debts and to have them renewed as their prospective collateral had lost part of its market value. As of 1 January 1985, financially distressed farmers (i.e. those with debts amounting to more than 40 per cent of assets and negative cash flow) averaged 12.5 per cent of the farming population, the brunt being borne by predominantly family-sized commercial farms. The question for the government was, therefore, whether to bolster the American farmers in difficulty or to let market forces take their toll and subsequently create a better environment for the more efficient.

At the beginning of Reagan's second term in office, on 23 February 1985 the administration asked Congress to eliminate or radically curtail the network of income and price support plus production control that had marked the American farm policy since the Roosevelt reform. The executive gave the bill the provocative heading of Agricultural Adjustment Act, the same as that adopted in 1933. Block explained before the House of Representatives' Committee on Agriculture that the 'aim of the executive was to set a new course for agricultural policy'. He pointed out that the 1933 Act, which laid the groundwork for ongoing farm programmes, 'was the government's response to an unprecedented crisis, ... but it is apparent that the New Deal programs are not working for today's agriculture'.[18] According to Block, agriculture should not be a sector severed from the rest of the economy by market-distorting protection but must recognize its full integration and contribution to the general economic environment, as factors other than price and income support, like interest rates and inflation, had greater impact on farmers' welfare.[19] In other words, Block was suggesting that by causing pressure on the budget the ongoing farm programmes contributed to the ills affecting farmers' costs and, on the other hand, prevented them from aggressively competing in the world market.

In particular, the bill required that loan rates be cut to about 75 per cent of average market levels over the previous three years. It also required farmers to repay the loans, at least partially, within a set time instead of defaulting if they chose. This meant that farmers had to take into account only the market and its prices with no viable alternative. Secondly, target prices had to be phased down by 5 per cent a year until they reached the loan rate and deficiency payments would stop completely. Finally, payments for acreage reduction had to be phased out.

As expected, the executive's proposal for far-reaching dismantlement of the 50-year-old farm regime was not enthusiastically received by Congress. The president repeatedly threatened to veto any bill that would load the budget beyond a pre-established threshold. A compromise formula that would not run counter to the administration's basic goals, while not accepting its most radical provisions, was finally agreed. The law, which had the less ambitious title of Food Security Act, reauthorized the basic set of farm programmes which, however, were significantly reoriented towards market forces. Loan rates were set at 75 per cent of a moving average of market prices, excluding the higher and lower years, which meant that they would move up and down according to market trends. For the 1986 market year, loan rates were permitted to fall by 25 per cent. Target prices were frozen for one or two years according to the commodity and later allowed to decline. In the short-run this latter provision did not help reduce the budget deficit. Indeed, as loan rates fell below market prices the gap with the target price, and therefore the amount of deficiency payments, rose.[20]

The market-oriented reform of the domestic market was accompanied by a set of provisions designed to assist exports through subsidization. They included additional funding for traditional programmes such as credit assistance and food aid, as well as new programmes described in more detail below such as the Export Enhancement Program.

Problems in the Community: overproduction and pressure on the budget

The attainment of self-sufficiency in agricultural produce in the EC and its overrun accelerated in the early 1980s. The main temperate zone farm produce exceeded the 100 per cent threshold, though with great variance between member countries. The main overproduction problems lay in the dairy sector, closely followed by the grain sector where there was the highest chance of attrition with the dominant exporter, the United States. Since the beginning of the decade the European Commission had submitted several reports identifying causes of the perverse effects of the CAP and ways to secure a more balanced farm regime.[21] The Commission centred its criticisms on the absence of a regulatory mechanism to balance supply and demand and on the concentration of CAP benefits on the largest producers and most prosperous regions. It also noted that the continuous increase in farm production had engendered uncontrollable increases in budget expenditures without benefit to farmers. Thus, according to the Commission, 'in the present stage of agricultural technology it is neither economically sound nor financially feasible to guarantee price or aid levels for unlimited quantities.'[22]

The suggested remedy was based on two concurrent elements: 'guarantee thresholds' and 'producer co-responsibility'. Unrestricted price guarantee and income support could only be allowed for limited amounts of supply above which farmers shared in the cost of surplus disposal. Farmer co-responsibility then aimed at allowing the Community to better adjust to budgetary constraints. The guarantee threshold and co-responsibility mechanism could be implemented according to various formulas varying from one commodity to another.[23] The scheme was, however, to apply to a limited number of farm products and was not an absolute novelty. On the other hand, the Commission pointed out that since restraints were imposed on EC farmers, the principle of Community preference must be strengthened to reduce the inflow of competing foreign products wherever the Community was limiting its own production. The Commission also suggested a Community involvement in export promoting policies, like long-term contracts based on the US pattern which would secure the export of established amounts of EC produce for a given period at conditions attractive to importing countries. The Council's initial response was lukewarm. The CAP reform scheme was reproduced in the Commission's proposals for the farm year 1981–2 price review, but the relatively moderate 7.8 per cent average price increase proposed by the Commission was raised to 11 per cent in national currencies by the Council.[24] Only France endorsed the proposal for long-term export contracts. Germany and the UK criticized the scheme since it would entail further pressure on the budget. The other members remained indifferent. The Community signed voluntary export restraint (VER) agreements with Thailand, Indonesia and Brazil allowing the Community to impose a tariff quota to imports of manioc from developing countries.[25] The Commission also requested authorization from the Council to open consultation within the GATT to renegotiate tariff concessions on other cereal substitutes like corn gluten feed, citrus pellets and soybean, a move bound to meet American resistance.[26]

Why did the Commission choose to run a course that was bound to arouse fierce opposition from EC farmers whose declining income was to be further threatened? Actually, the Commission not only found it unmanageable to stock and dispose of growing farm surpluses – the part of the story that most attracted public attention – but, more importantly, the costs generated by this severely curbed Community leeway both regarding the management of agricultural programmes and with respect to the implementation of concurrent programmes financed by the Community's budget, like the Social Fund and the Regional Fund. The then General-Director of the Budget of the European Commission noted that the margin of available EC resources, totalling just 819.2 million ECU in 1982, had tailed off and could have disappeared if the growth rate of the European Agricultural Guidance and Guarantee Fund (EAGGF)-Guarantee expenditures had not slowed down from 1979 to 1981, bouncing back, however, by 20 per cent the following year.[27] Matters reached a head in 1983, when budget expenditures overran available resources, and the paralysis of the CAP mechanism and of the other funds of the EC budget could only be avoided by member states' decisions to cover the deficit. Though the crisis was eventually averted, the situation did not subsequently improve.

A single pattern did not emerge regarding the attitudes of member states towards the joint problems of overproduction in agriculture and exhaustion of available resources in the budget. One could infer that political interests prevailed over opposing financial preoccupations in both domestic and Community policy. On the other hand, during most of the 1980s member states' efforts to reform the Community budget went side by side with the attempt to solve the agricultural surplus problem. For instance, the need to curb farm expenditure was the war cry in the British campaign for a fair return to its contribution.

Nicols described the EC general budget as 'Lilliputian by comparison to the national states budgets'.[28] In 1980, the EC budget was just 0.8 per cent of the Community GDP. However, apart from financing certain new policies, essential to the development of the West European economy, the budget had a pivotal role in the management of the CAP because the largest share of the EAGGF, the Guarantee expenditures, underpinned the EC farm price/income support policy. In its absence the sector would be promptly renationalized, disrupting the principle of market unity around which the CAP revolved, though with the contradictions entailed by the Monetary Compensatory Amount mechanism. Two factors are relevant in understanding the attitude of the member states: net contribution, that is, the balance between payments and receipts; and return rate, that is, the member state's share in budget expenditures.

Generally, one would expect that everything else being equal, the greater the gap between expense and receipts, the greater the resistance to expense increase, as well as the interest in its curtailment. Conversely, the greater the positive balance in revenue and expenditure, the greater the interest in opposing budgetary constraints. As the guarantee expenditure of the EAGGF is the bulk of the Community budget, budgetary expense reductions would be immediately associated with containment of farm expenditures. The UK could, therefore, expect, if not the active support, at least the sympathy of Germany whose gap between contribution and receipts was greater than Great Britain's (Table 26). Yet, there was a snag. The picture was completely different regarding rates of return particularly in the EAGGF-Guarantee section (Table 27). The UK's rate of return in this section was extremely low and indeed could be viewed as the main cause of its negative balance. Germany, however, had quite a high rate of return, being often the second main beneficiary after France, though closely followed by Italy. Moreover, the weight of the EAGGF–Guarantee in the funds allocated to Germany was particularly high, and well above the EC average. The Federal Republic's share in the funds allocated to key farm products like cereals, milk products, sugar and meat was particularly satisfactory. Funds received by Germany for milk products even surpassed those destined for France. EC funds were a primary tool for the fulfilment of the traditional commitment of the German government to buoy up farmers' income relative to the industrial sector, which, otherwise, would have required direct outlays from the Federal budget. This could explain Germany's apparently schizoid attitude which on many occasions emphasized the need for strict budgetary discipline, but at the crucial point pressed for options bound to increase farm expenditure. As expected, France secured the greatest share by far of the EAGGF funds, both in the Guarantee and the Guidance section. It was, therefore, likely that the French Republic would be a staunch supporter of the EC farm policy. The odds, therefore, favoured an 'entente cordiale' between France and Germany, although their goals and their policies did not always coincide.

At the May 1982 meeting when the Council fixed farm prices for the market year 1982–3, the United Kingdom claimed that there was a 'fundamental link' between the budget problem and the level of farm prices, which was bound to generate surpluses. Britain argued that the 'proposed measures would probably push up the costs to be supported by approximately 200 million ECU and would therefore represent an additional burden on the United Kingdom and the Federal Republic of Germany'. The British delegation thus claimed that any majority decision taken by the Council was likely to damage its interests and, therefore, required the enforcement of the 'Luxembourg Compromise' of January 1966.[29] It must be recalled that in January 1966, France having withdrawn for six months from Community institutions (the so-called 'empty chair'), the Council agreed on the application of a unanimity rule whenever vital interests of a member state might be considered at stake. This meant that in the absence of a general consensus, no majority vote could be taken on issues considered fundamental by a member. It is arguable that the UK expected the Federal Republic's backing.

The British manoeuvre backfired.[30] The Italian and French delegates promptly counterattacked, claiming that the 'Luxembourg Compromise' did not allow a member state to paralyse the normal functioning of the Council in a sector of negotiation, in this instance, agriculture, to obtain satisfaction in other negotiating areas: that is, regarding a change in the United Kingdom's contribution to the EC budget. Only Greece and Denmark backed the British request not to put to the vote the regulation on the 1982–3 farm prices, noting, nevertheless, that this was just 'for political reasons and that any delay in price fixing could seriously disturb the EC agricultural system'. The other participants, among whom the Germans, proceeded to vote and the price fixing for the 1982–3 market year was adopted by majority vote. Great Britain, however, continued to try to restrain farm expenditure and to pursue a revision of its contribution to the EC budget.

The Stuttgart European Council of June 1983 adopted a declaration engaging the member states to negotiations on the improvement of Community policies, the focus of which was the question of how to increase the Community's financial resources, especially in view of its imminent enlargement. The Declaration of the heads of state and government concurrently stressed the need for budgetary discipline and, regarding the CAP, provided that the review of the Common Agricultural Policy should result in steps 'compatible with market conditions' to ensure 'effective control of agricultural expenditure'[31] The Commission was requested to submit its proposals by 1 August, which it dutifully did, tightening the reins further.[32] Whereas previous communications had excluded nominal price cuts, though admitting them in real terms, now the European executive suggested a restrictive price policy which implied a freeze or even a reduction of the common prices expressed in ECU. No mention was made, however, of prices in national currencies, affected by the MCA mechanism, which determined farmers' revenue in member states. The European Commission called for the adoption of a quota system for the milk sector where the disequilibrium between supply and demand was stronger and which accounted for over 26 per cent of the EAGGF-Guarantee expenditure, arguing that the only alternative way to avoid a growth in supply above the guarantee threshold was a price cut of at least 12 per cent in nominal terms. The latter alternative was bound to impact heavily on milk producers' income and above all would have been politically impracticable. Finally, the Commission recommended that monetary compensatory amounts (MCAs) be phased out in three stages by altering the green rate. This was welcomed by the French farmers but not by their counterparts across the Rhine, who had already borne severe reductions in income.

After the failure of the Athens European Council in December 1983, and in the absence of a framework agreement worked out by the heads of government, the CAP was temporarily rescued by their ministers of agriculture who accepted the proposals tabled by the Commission in July 1983, though reshaping them in a carefully balanced compromise. In January 1984 the Commission submitted its proposals for market year 1983–4 price fixing, which almost amounted to a price freeze. The price freeze request was joined by a call for a quota system for milk. However, it had the political defect of presenting the member states with a marked variance in the price in national currencies if coupled with the dismantlement of MCAs. In particular, farmers in countries with positive MCAs like West Germany, the UK and the Netherlands were bound to suffer severe cuts in nominal prices, and even more in real prices, while farmers in countries with negative MCAs like France, Ireland and Italy would enjoy a nominal rise. The worst hit would be farmers in the Federal Republic.

In France the introduction of dairy quotas met with the opposition of the powerful Fédération Nationale des Syndicats d'Exploitants Agricoles (FNSEA) which wanted to catch up with its more advanced competitors in Northern Europe and believed that the introduction of quotas, by limiting any supply increase to an additional percentage of a benchmark established with reference to previous years would have blocked that process. On the other hand, all French farm unions favoured the abolition of MCAs to boost French farmers' income and competitiveness. In Germany the Agriculture Minister, Kiechle, a member of the Bavarian-based Christian Social Union (CSU), and the German Farmers Union (DBV) favoured the quota system, deeming it the best way to prevent a fall of milk producers' income, the only alternative put forward by the Commission being a drastic support price cut. However, the DBV and its staunch ally in the government were opposed to the MCAs dismantlement, as this would have brought about a steep decline in support prices in Deutschmarks.[33] The Germans thus tabled a proposal aimed at smoothing over the controversy on MCAs with France, without affecting their farmers' income. The proposal centred on the establishment of a direct link between the ECU used to fix farm prices and the strongest currency in the ECU basket, the Deutschmark. It had the advantage of eliminating or reducing positive MCAs in Germany and in other strong currency countries, while raising prices paid to farmers in weaker currencies. However, as the Agriculture Commissioner Poul Dalsager pointed out, defending the Commission's proposal, 'such solution would also have consequences for the Community budget'.[34]

The package the agriculture ministers agreed on 31 March 1984 largely accepted the Commission's proposals first embodied in its communication of July 1983. The quota allocated among member states was secured by a super levy on overshoots equal to 75 per cent of the target price for milk in the case of producers' surplus and 100 per cent in dairy overruns.[35] However, despite the fact that the quota was below the level of deliveries in 1983, which totalled 104 million tonnes, the agreed ceiling of 99.5 million tonnes a year fell far short of the 97.2 million tonnes target proposed by the Commission and was much higher than the Community's consumption of about 85 million tonnes, thus allowing exports and other forms of disposal that had to be financed by the Community budget.[36]

The MCA reform that emerged from the 'compromise' incorporated most German requests. The so-called Green ECU used for CAP purposes was worth 3.4 per cent more than the ECU otherwise used by the Community. This would reduce the German MCA which was to be dismantled by five percentage points by 1985 and completely phased out, along with the Netherlands MCA, by the 1987/8 market year. The resulting price reduction for German farmers was to be compensated by a VAT rebate equal to 3 per cent of the price paid on farm products, with effect from January 1985, to be financed partly by the Germans and partly by the Community.[37]

The Council also accepted the Commission's price freeze proposal. The result, however, was not as negative for farmers' income as initially expected, since while prices in ECU declined on average by 0.5 per cent, prices in national currencies increased by 3.3 per cent. However, the nominal increase was more than offset by the rate of inflation.[38]

As regards extra-EC trade the Agriculture Council gave its green light to GATT negotiations 'to stabilise cereal substitutes' as suggested by the Commission. Hence the EC notified the GATT of its intention to partially suspend tariff concessions previously granted on corn gluten feed and other non-grain feed ingredients. The US, though recognizing that the withdrawal of tariff concessions granted under GATT is legal, soon threatened retaliation, pointing out that, given the political and economic significance of the proposed action, it was unlikely that compensation of equivalent value could be offered.

The adoption of the package was not welcomed by EC farmers, particularly the French, and violent demonstrations marked the spring of 1984. However, the farm agreement made it possible for the French president to end France's semester with striking political success at Fontainebleau in June. The agreement to hold farm expenditure in check, without relinquishing principles and mechanisms of the CAP, allowed Mitterrand to strike a deal on the thorny question of the budgetary refund to Great Britain and on the medium-term increase in resources available, which, in turn, facilitated the entry of Portugal and Spain to the European Community by January 1986.

The European Council agreed that the level of expenditure would be fixed as a function of available resources and that expenditure related to the agricultural market, on a three-yearly basis, would increase at a lower rate than available resources.[39]

The Federal Republic's aim was the defence of its farmers' income, whatever the cost, and all in all it succeeded. At Fontainebleau, the German chancellor, Helmut Kohl, accepted the VAT contribution increase from 1 per cent to 1.4 per cent and the abatement of the British contribution. Thus Germany, which already provided approximately 30 per cent of available resources, would foot the largest share of the new bill.[40] In exchange Kohl got the date of VAT compensation to German farmers brought forward from January 1985 to July 1984, raising it from 3 to 5 percentage points.

As a nonmarket-oriented solution was found to stem the tide of farm expenditure in the milk sector, cereals, particularly wheat, became the fastest growing component of the EAGGF-Guarantee section. The market-oriented remedy envisaged by the Commission centred on the gradual alignment of EC prices with world market prices, a course previously established and helped by the strength of the EC currencies vis-à-vis the dollar. However, soon after the Fontainebleau summit, the German Minister of Agriculture, Ignaz Kiechle, started complaining of the deteriorating situation of his farm constituency under the double weight of the MCA removal and the implementation of dairy quotas. The German minister's protest clearly aimed at preventing further income-reducing measures. In February 1985, the Commission's proposals for the 1985–6 price fixing called for a limited reduction (–3.6 per cent) of cereal prices in nominal terms. The United Kingdom called for a more severe 5 per cent price cut. France sided with the Commission. The Republic as the main EC exporter saw this cut as a precondition of continuous expansion in cereal exports, based on the alignment of EC prices with its main competitors, and of the prevention of a dangerous exhaustion of agricultural guarantee funds.

Conversely, Kiechle insisted that the main goal of EC farm policy be the defence of small family farmers by buoying up their income and argued that the price cut suggested by the Commission was counterproductive as it stimulated greater supply to compensate the loss of revenue on the price side.[41] Kiechle was not isolated in the German government. According to press reports, Chancellor Kohl sent a message to the president of the European Commission, Jacques Delors, requesting his assistance to Germany on the cereal issue.[42] In other words, Germany, which had already committed itself to meeting the increase in budget available resources did not need to be constrained by collective financial prudence, especially when the Christian Democrats had recently performed badly in the elections in some Länder with strong farming constituencies. Besides, further domestic support to farmers would prove more costly and its implementation dicier since authorization from Brussels was required.

In a series of compromise proposals made by the Italian presidency and by the Commission, the price cut was reduced to a modest 1.8 per cent. Yet, in May the German minister replied that he could only accept a price reduction not exceeding a symbolic 0.9 per cent, accompanied by a shorter deadline for intervention payments to farmers, and declared that 'in the matter of cereals ... major national interests were at stake for the Federal Republic of Germany'.[43] In the following session the German delegation invoked the 'Luxembourg Compromise' and this time it was not overruled. Belgium, Italy and the Netherlands voted for the last draft regulation put forward by the Presidency, but without securing the qualified majority. The other delegations did not participate in the vote.[44]

However, the Commission pressed ahead with the implementation of its compromise proposal, using its executive powers to ensure that the market functioned smoothly even without a Council decision. Prices were nominally cut by 1.8 per cent, though the actual reduction was less than 1 per cent, as the Commission concurrently adopted some of the German requests, specifically a two-month reduction in intervention payment delay.[45] Only in April 1986, during price fixing for the 1986–7 market year, did Kiechle unofficially drop his veto.

US–EC clashes on export policies

The United States attacked the EC farm policy on two fronts: a spate of legal cases aimed at demonstrating the inconsistency of the Common Agricultural Policy with the GATT provisions on export subsidies, as modified and, in US opinion, strengthened by the Tokyo Round Agreement; and a fierce, subsidized competition in foreign markets.

Between 1981 and 1982 the US lodged four complaints to the GATT concerning EC subsidizing practices that affected trade in wheat flour, pasta, poultry and sugar. The disputes over poultry and sugar were promptly settled by agreement. The US prevailed over the European Community in the pasta case, as pasta was not considered a primary product and therefore fell within the scope of paragraph 4 of GATT Art. XVI, which laid down stricter rules for industrial products. Thus the US victory was a blow for EC exporters of processed agricultural produce but did not legally endanger the Community's farm export subsidy mechanism.[46] The wheat flour complaint, on the other hand, was directed at the heart of the Common Agricultural Policy, because the United States classified wheat flour as agricultural produce and the claim concerned the export refund which, along with intervention costs, was the main item of EAGGF-Guarantee expenditure. The Millers' National Federation filed a section 301 petition in 1981, two years after the Tokyo Round Subsidies Agreement had recognized the right of third-country suppliers against displacing subsidization practices by competing countries in regional markets. The US complained to the GATT which in December 1981 set up a panel to adjudicate. However, though recognizing that EC exports had strongly increased in the period with the help of the export refund mechanism, the panel report held that the information provided by the US was not enough to prove market displacement caused by EC practices and, therefore, the acquisition by the latter of a 'non equitable share of the market'.[47] The report, however, was never adopted because of US opposition.

It is likely that since the beginning of the long legal match with the European Community, the US became convinced that reliance on the Tokyo Round rules would bear a poor, uncertain outcome, and to obtain concrete results in the trade dialogue with its European counterpart, whether bilaterally or multilaterally, economic rather than legal pressure was required. On 11 January 1983, speaking at the annual meeting of the conservative, and still powerful, American Farm Bureau Federation, but probably also addressing the Europeans, waving the spectre of an upsurge in agricultural protectionism in the US Congress, Reagan stated: 'we will not give in to protectionist measures, but at the same time, we aren't going to let ourselves be plowed under'.[48] In mid-February 1983 Block announced that over 700,000 tonnes of wheat would be released from the CCC's stocks to provide over 1 million tonnes of wheat flour to Egypt, for long a secure French market, at a price around $15 per tonne below the world price and the EC offered price. The president of the European Commission, Gaston Thorn, expressed 'the considerable surprise of the Commission on the US action to take over for 12 to 14 months the total Egyptian flour market at subsidized prices well below the world market', adding that such action was hardly compatible with the spirit in which official talks on agriculture had started in December 1982. Soon after the Commission took the matter to the GATT.[49] In February the US negotiated a trade agreement with Iraq for the sale of wheat, rice, barley and other commodities. In August the US carried a second attack to the Egyptian market, this time for the provision of dairy products. The contract provided for the sale of 18,000 tonnes of butter and 10,000 tonnes of cheese on special terms including a three-year interest free loan and repayment in Egyptian currency financed by a blended credit of up to $250 million. The Community promptly complained to the International Dairy Products Council, arguing that the price offered to Egypt was below both the world price and the minimum price set by the Council. The United States, however, vetoed the resolution urged by the Community, which called on the US not to repeat such action.[50]

The Community promptly counterattacked. In October 1983 the Commission introduced a special refund, 7 ECUs over the general one, for up to 400,000 tonnes of wheat flour shipped to Egypt.[51] The special refund was specifically directed to help French exporters recover a share of the Egyptian market. However, France, the main EC competitor of the US agricultural colossus, withstood the US assault not only because of the flexible export refund policy adopted by the Community but also because of its ability to provide agrifood soft loans to its clients. In 1984 and 1985, France renewed its farm credit agreement with Egypt and concluded two agreements with Morocco and Tunisia. It also strengthened its presence in the Soviet and Chinese markets.

In May 1985 the US administration, pressed by Congress, raised the stakes and launched the Export Enhancement Program – EEP (also known as BICEP for 'Bonus Export Incentive Commodity Export Program'). The executive initially resisted the idea of a new subsidized export programme. However, the administration agreed to implement this plan in exchange for the support of several farm-belt congressmen to the deficit reduction package for the fiscal year 1986 backed by the president. The programme institutionalized, on a larger scale, the method used in 1983 to oust EC competitors from North African markets. The programme provided for the release of CCC stocks of wheat, corn and dairy products to reduce the overall cost of US commodities abroad. Under the EEP, if a foreign purchaser agreed to buy additional quantities, some portions of the additional purchase were provided at no cost by the CCC, thus cutting the unit price. By late May the first BICEP sales of dried milk, butter oil and wheat flour were made to Spain, Jamaica and Egypt respectively. The Community reacted by threatening action in the GATT against the US export subsidy and, more practically, by raising the minimum export subsidy to EC traders to outbid American offers to Algeria, Egypt, Yemen and Morocco.

BICEP subsequently became one of the main items of the export support provisions of the 1985 Food Security Act. The Act required that at least $2 billion of CCC-owned commodities be used to enhance export sales during the fiscal years from 1986 through 1988. The $2 billion funding level was amended by the Food Security Improvement Act of 1986 requiring that not less than $1 billion and not more than $1.5 billion in CCC-owned commodities be used as EEP bonuses in the mentioned period. The programme was later extended to 1991. Other sections of the Food Security Act provided for short-term (6 months to 3 years) credit guarantees for at least $5 billion a year and broadened the existing programme of loan guarantees for intermediate term (3 to 10 years) export credits.

It is likely that those in Congress who first negotiated the EEP with a lukewarm administration and then pressed for its incorporation in the Food Security Act, expected a prompt recapture of foreign markets. It is, however, doubtful that this was the dominant goal of the executive. Two weeks after the announcement of BICEP, Block, during a speech at the Midwest Conference on business planning, declared that retaliation was needed to encourage future trade talks.[52] Thus, Libby argued that the real aim of the executive was not the quick recovery of world market shares, as the funds actually allocated to the task were rather modest and, though the US managed to increase its exports, it did not significantly succeed in taking markets away from the EC.[53] In particular, the EEP targeted the Middle East and North Africa, by then a French preserve, but ignored for the first two years of implementation the Soviet Union and China where French exporters were making successful inroads. It was argued too that as far as US trade in grains was concerned the Export Enhancement Programme was even counterproductive as, although it prevented further falls in exported quantity, it also depressed average world prices and, thus, further slackened the total US export value. Libby, also relying on statements of top US Department of Agriculture officials in Congressional hearings, concluded that the real EEP target rather than the EC markets was the EC budget, as the programme forced the European Community to provide higher export refunds for its exporters to outbid American offers, thus raising a fundamental component of the EAGGF-Guarantee expenditure. The correlation between the US Export Enhancement Programme and the export refund expenditure hike in the Community is borne out by the analysis conducted by the Organisation for Economic Cooperation and Development which stated that after 1985 export restitutions for major commodities and some processed products increased both at individual and aggregate levels.[54]

However, the available aggregate data do not provide an answer to the question of the impact of American programmes on the EEC budget relative to concurrent factors, notably the dollar fall in the years that followed the announcement of the September

1985 Plaza Agreement. This happened just when EC farm produce exporters, especially French exporters, were hoping that the upward trend of the dollar would make export refunds unnecessary, and with the end of subsidization free them from the 'equitable share' limit provided by the GATT rules on primary export subsidies. To understand the kind of pressure put by the above-mentioned factors on the EAGGF-Guarantee fund we must take into account that the appreciation of the dollar, that is, the currency in which most farm prices were quoted, would entail a reduction of export restitution to EC producers whereas the depreciation of the US currency would bring about export refund increase.[55] Thus from the end of 1985 the EC budget had to bear the brunt of both BICEP and dollar decline, but while the former affected the price of particular products in specific markets, the latter had an across-the-board impact.

If the EEP main goal was the reform, that is, the dismantlement of the CAP, the export refunds in particular, its success was only partial and above all slow. Actually, by the end of 1985 the Community was already prepared to include agriculture among the items of the prospective multilateral negotiating round. However, it took over six years for the adoption of a significant reform of the CAP which paved the way for a multilateral trade agreement. The US, like Great Britain previously, rightly saw the weight of agriculture expense on the Community budget but did not foresee that the EC member states were more prepared to work out makeshift amendments to budget financing than to sacrifice the planks of the Common Agricultural Policy.

As illustrated by the data provided by the OECD, significant changes occurred in the relative level of subsidization and budget costs in those years. If subsidization is an economic sin, as it interferes with the optimal allocation of resources and trade, as the US repeatedly contended, then the United States, though not the greatest sinner, was certainly among the speediest on the road to perdition. The average US Producer Subsidy Equivalent (PSE) in the 1984–6 period soared by 80 per cent relative to the 1979–81 average, while the growth rate in the EC was a modest 8 per cent.[56] The US PSE growth skyrocketed in those sectors in which the United States struggled to defend its role as main world supplier: 212 per cent for wheat and 223 per cent for coarse grains, compared with 30 per cent and 12 per cent respectively for the EC. Thus, the United States' share of worldwide PSE increased from 20 per cent to 29 per cent approximately, while the EC share declined from 49 per cent to 37 per cent.[57] Likewise, the cost of agricultural policy growth, both for taxpayers and consumers, was slower in the European Community. In particular, though the cost for the EC taxpayer rose by a robust 44 per cent in five years, it was dwarfed by the increase of its American counterpart, which soared by over 200 per cent.[58] All this was in stark contrast with the asserted goals of the Reagan administration, while a market-oriented reform of the CAP remained an unlikely prospect. A solution was, therefore, to be found, as soon as possible, through multilateral negotiations.

9

The Long Road to Punta del Este and the Launch of the Uruguay Round

The 1982 GATT ministerial meeting

As in most areas of international negotiations, intervals between two GATT rounds are not blank. Not only mechanisms to verify the implementation of the agreements reached in previous stages are in place, but talks go on in which topics of particular interest for the parties or for some of them emerge and in which prevailing attitudes among the participants take shape. This was the case of the period that followed the close of the Tokyo Round. Each of the codes signed during the round had its own committee to vet its fulfilment and to solve dispute. In the Public Procurement code case the committee might also extend the sectors covered by the agreement and modify it. The Consultative Group of Eighteen, established in June 1975 with the task, among others, of 'following international trade developments with a view to the pursuit and maintenance of trade policies consistent with the objectives and principles of the General Agreement' went on meeting after 1979. The US and the Community had a constantly active role in the working of the group. The GATT work programme adopted in November 1979 stressed the need for further cooperative action in several sectors including agriculture. Thus, if the summoning of a ministerial meeting for 1982 was the result of diplomatic pressure from the United States and if many of the topics proposed for discussion corresponded to US economic interests and to its new Republican administration's perspective, such an upshot did not come out of the blue. Setting the stage for a ministerial meeting might not have been a very easy task for the US delegation in Geneva, but slowing the pace that the US wanted to give to the GATT discussions was probably more difficult for those parties that did not agree with their agenda or some of the items.

In June 1981 the fifteenth meeting of the Consultative Group of the Eighteen reached the conclusion that 'it would be useful to consider at the political level the overall condition of the trading system' and that 'to this end it would be appropriate for the GATT Contracting Parties to envisage convening a ministerial meeting during 1982'.[1] The ministerial meeting, whose date was subsequently fixed for November 1982, was the first in over nine years after the meeting that launched the Tokyo Round. According to the majority of the group the declared objective was to give the GATT parties an opportunity to confirm their will to continue to support the multilateral trade system and to affirm their determination to maintain a forward-looking attitude in the face of current economic difficulties. The declared goal was rather open-ended and several members, though not all of them, stated that it was clear that the meeting would not be called to launch a new round of negotiations.[2] The participants also agreed that purposes and expected results of the prospective meeting should be clarified before it was called. In December 1981 a preparatory committee was set up with the task of making proposals on the agenda and documentation for the thirty-eighth session of the GATT parties to be held at ministerial level.

The agenda gradually included a growing number of subjects but the attention of those who took part in the preparatory works focused on safeguards, trade in agriculture, textiles, subsidies, and the trade problems of developing countries. No consensus emerged on the content of the statements to be made by the ministers on the mentioned topics. The agenda also included new subjects, such as services, intellectual property rights and trade and investments, that were of special interest for the United States, but many parties, the developing countries in particular, argued that they lay outside the scope of GATT talks.

The attitude of the European Community towards the ministerial conference was rather cautious even bordering on reluctance. Indeed, the EC member states, some of them in particular, were quite wary of reopening discussions on hard-won achievements in the Tokyo Round, while not seeing reasonable prospect of progress on issues of interest for which no deal had been struck just three years before. It also considered that the present economic environment was far from favourable to a process of further liberalization as appeared to be the United States' hope. The guidelines worked out by the Council in the run-up to the GATT meeting envisaged several main points which dwelt upon a negotiation scheme submitted by the Commission in July.[3] In the first place the EC argued that the task of the November meeting ought to be the reaffirmation of the willingness of the GATT contracting parties to oppose protectionist tendencies and to respect the spirit and the provisions of the General Agreement as well as the agreements reached during previous negotiations, and in particular in the Tokyo Round. Consequently, there was no question of organizing new global negotiations on customs reduction or trade regulation, although there might be the possibility of specific and limited accords covering particular sectors like public markets and civil aviation. As regards agriculture, new negotiations on the rules to be applied to the sector were excluded as the conclusions of the Tokyo Round held and had to be respected. The developing countries had to be brought more tightly into the frame of international trade, with ensuing advantages but also with further responsibilities. More specifically, on the one hand, it was difficult to envisage new market opening commitments beyond the obligations entered into in the Tokyo Round; on the other hand, the principle of non-reciprocal tariff negotiations could not in future form the general basis of talks with all the less developed countries, being replaced by the so-called graduation principle with regard to the more developed among them. The Community hoped to repropose the question of selectivity in applying the safeguard clause, but was sceptical of the prospect of success given the continuous opposition of the developing countries. On the other hand, the Community was interested in taking part in a long-period study programme that might lead to a decision on the possibility of introducing international regulations in the service sectors. The EC, therefore, was open to the US proposal, as many of its countries were among the main exporters of services along with the United States (Figure 12). Likewise, the Community was interested in a study suggested by the United States with the aim of drawing up a list of rules on investments capable of affecting international trade. It was also open to discuss guidelines to be applied in the conflict between the need to maintain protection of new industries and free competition for all trading parties in the sectors concerned. As regards the settlement of disputes, the Community favoured an approach based on the idea of conciliation and which refrained from giving legal nature to GATT procedures as suggested by the United States.

Among the member states France was the one that showed the most critical view of the ministerial conference and advocated the toughest line in the discussions. In particular France remarked that the economic crisis at the base of trade difficulties had its roots in monetary disarray. Therefore, the stabilization of exchange rates and a drop in interest rates should be among the objectives addressed by the November meeting. Agriculture and farm export subsidies in particular were not to be discussed. As France believed that there was no chance of a selective safeguard clause being accepted in the Geneva conference, it was opposed to any notification system or other disciplines for 'grey area' measures, a term that indicated measures like VERs and OMAs for which developing countries were calling for GATT scrutiny and possibly for a final ban. In short, as so-called 'grey area' measures were a substitute for the lack of selectivity, no progress in the latter would prevent any progress in the former.

The EC position was bound to conflict with the positions of other delegations. The United States along with Australia, Canada and New Zealand were asking for greater freedom of competition in the agricultural sector and were attacking export subsidies for farm products. The US was also demanding liberalization of services. In general terms the US made it clear that it expected the November meeting to set the direction of international trade policy in the decade, making a firm commitment to improve the issues negotiated under GATT in the past, and to start working in sectors where GATT had not yet played a very active role, such as agriculture and, prospectively, services and investment.

The depth of the rift in perspectives and goals emerged during the drafting of the ministerial declaration. Just a few days before the start of the ministerial meeting the Commission sent a communication to the GATT Council suggesting a series of amendments to key points of the document drawn up by the preparatory committee, the main one of which aimed at avoiding too strict commitments in the prospective reform of the agricultural sector.[4] The amendments were partially accepted in the final text.

The Ministerial Declaration issued on 29 November 1982 consisted of three parts.[5] In the first it focused on the difficulties encountered by the multilateral trading system brought about by the economic crisis to which the lack of convergence in national economic policies had contributed and which had aroused protectionist policies and disregard of GATT discipline. As regards the results of the Tokyo Round, the Declaration, though acknowledging that they had provided some impetus to the functioning of the trading system, pointed out that 'the stresses on the system, which are reflected by the growing number and intensity of disputes between contracting parties, many of which remained unresolved, have made more pronounced certain shortcomings in its functioning'. In less diplomatic words, it meant that the Tokyo Round deal had not been sufficient to solve the problems that besieged the world trading system. Secondly, in a policy declaration the parties made a reaffirmation of their commitment to GATT obligations and to the preservation of the unity and consistency of the GATT system.

The third part contained a set of undertakings, which, however, were not specific enough to determine the future course of international trade. Thus the participants to the meeting made a political commitment to refrain from taking and maintaining any measures inconsistent with GATT and secondly undertook to make determined efforts to ensure that trade policies and measures should be consistent with GATT principles, resist protectionist pressures and avoid measures limiting or distorting international trade. Yet, the chairman of the meeting announced his understanding that some governments would need time to fulfil the undertaking.[6] Secondly, as the chairman of the GATT Council in 1982, Bhagirath Das, remarked, no parties to the GATT would deliberately or, even less, admittedly take or maintain measures inconsistent with the General Agreement. The Declaration also contained a strong recommendation to the parties to the General Agreement to effectively implement the previous decisions on differential and more favourable treatment for developing countries and to this effect instructed the Trade and Development committee to start consultations with contracting parties to examine the ways they had responded to the requirement of Part IV of the GATT on 'Trade and Development'.

At any rate, the Declaration undertook to review, entrusting an ad hoc group, existing quantitative restrictions, the grounds on which they were maintained and their conformity to the GATT provisions in view of their elimination or their being brought into conformity with the General Agreement. The report of the group with its findings and conclusions had to be made available to the GATT parties in their 1984 session. It also undertook to carry out a study on the importance of textile and clothing for the world trade and for the trade prospects of developing countries, on the consequences of the phasing out of the MFA, and on the modalities of further trade liberalization in these sectors and on the possibilities of bringing about the full application of GATT rules. A deadline of 1984 was set for the presentation of the result of these studies too.

On agriculture there was an undertaking to improve the effectiveness of GATT rules, provisions and disciplines and a commitment to work for improving the terms of access to markets and to bring export competition under greater discipline. The wording of the Declaration differed slightly from that of the EC amendment as the latter provided for the 'full operation of relevant GATT rules'. The difference was not marginal. As Das noted, 'the undertaking to improve the "effectiveness" of GATT rules is wider than improving the "operation" of such rules'. This was because the latter concerned the manner of application of existing rules whereas the former could include the adoption of more effective rules.[7] A committee was established to examine a series of agricultural policies, including tariff and non-tariff measures affecting market access and supplies, subsidies, export subsidies in particular, and special exceptions and derogations enjoyed by some contracting parties. The committee had to report periodically on the results achieved and make recommendations to the GATT Council no later than the 1984 session.

No undertaking was made on the substance of the safeguard issue. The ministers only adopted a procedural decision to work for a comprehensive understanding by the 1983 meeting of the GATT parties which was to be based on the principles of the General Agreement. As regards services the Declaration did not envisage an examination of the subject in the GATT, at least in a first stage, but only invited the parties to the General Agreement to undertake national examination of the topic and exchange information among themselves. The results of these individual examinations were to be reviewed at the 1984 session of the GATT also in order to consider whether any multilateral action was appropriate.

Bland as they were, the pledges of the Ministerial Declaration were not enough to assuage the worries of the European Community which made a number of qualifying statements.[8] In particular, it underlined that its acceptance of the work programme on agriculture was on the understanding that this was not a commitment to any new negotiation or obligation concerning agricultural products. As regards the undertaking to refrain from taking or maintaining any measures inconsistent with GATT, the EC made it clear that it considered such an undertaking as only an engagement to deploy the best efforts to avoid taking or maintaining such measures. Later, however, the Community changed its attitude when the pressure of American measures deemed not in line with GATT principles became more threatening. Reservations were also made by several developing countries on a range of issues including safeguards, settlement of disputes and agriculture. Some of these countries reaffirmed their opposition to the inclusion of services in the work programme.

The outcome of the ministerial meeting signalled growing tensions between the US and the Community, or at least the prevailing part of its member states, which were not prepared to accept the pressing from their transatlantic counterpart. However, in spite of all the threats of reprisal by members of both American Congress and the executive and the prophecies of looming protectionism by some free-market oriented periodicals, it was not a defeat for the US; perhaps, not even a stumbling block. Certainly, if, as is likely, the Reagan administration hoped for rapid progress towards engagements in sectors of urgent interest like agriculture, or even in the launching of a new round, the outcome of the November GATT conference proved a disappointment. Yet, the agenda set in the meeting included most of the subjects to which the US executive gave particular attention like subsidies, dispute settlement procedures, services and trade in counterfeit goods, not to mention agriculture. The Community was among the dissenting voices, but its disagreement focused on specific areas. For most of the subjects the agreement reached by the ministers referred only to studies and consultations but their direction was already established and they had to result in reports to be presented to the GATT contracting parties. And as noted by *The Economist*, studies and reports had provided the background for the launching of the Kennedy and Tokyo Rounds.[9] In short, the door to a new GATT round was not closed but ajar.

Studies and parties' attitudes before the Punta del Este ministerial meeting

The fora where dialogue on international trade regulation and thus pressure for a new round of GATT negotiations could be held were substantially three: G7 summits, the Organisation for Economic Cooperation and Development, on whose works the United States had traditionally a strong influence, and the GATT itself.

In the May 1983 Williamsburg summit the heads of state and government stated that they 'should work to achieve further trade liberalization negotiations in the GATT, with particular emphasis on expanding trade with and among developing countries' and agreed to continue consultations on proposals for a new negotiating round in the GATT.

A year later, during the OECD meeting in May 1984, the participants agreed that a new round of multilateral trade negotiations would be 'of the utmost importance to a strengthening of the liberal trade system and the growth of trade opportunities'.[10] The ministerial communiqué expressed concern for the strains in a large number of farm products 'due to a large extent to domestic support policies'. However, conscious that the industrialized countries, which were members of the Paris organization, were dominant from an economic perspective but numerically were far from being the majority in Geneva, the participants of the meeting were careful to stress that thorough preparation for the prospective negotiations were necessary and extensive consultations with all GATT partners had to take place 'so as to ensure a broad consensus on objectives, participation and timing'. The guidelines worked out in the OECD ministerial meeting were in large part reproduced in the declaration of the G7 summit that took place in London a month later.

The US bid for a prompt beginning of a new round with a wide set of subjects was helped by the discreet but adroit support of the GATT Secretariat. In December 1983, an independent group of seven experts, chaired by the Swiss economist and central banker, Fritz Leutwiler, president of the Bank for International Settlements, was set up on the initiative of the Director-General of GATT, Arthur Dunkel, with the task of identifying the main causes of the problems afflicting international trade.[11] After two years the group issued a report, known as the 'Leutwiler Report', which pointed out the erosion of GATT rules and the urgent need for action, proposing a programme based on fifteen recommendations.[12] Overall the report was music to the ears of the Reagan administration, although some of its suggestions went beyond American wishes. Many of its recommendations were far less agreeable to the Community's ears.

As regards agriculture, the report argued that the then ongoing GATT rules governing the use of export subsidies had failed to prevent major distortions in world markets and, therefore, in the long run, export subsidization should be eliminated altogether. Chiefly, the provisions of the GATT and SCM code, allowing export subsidies for primary products only on condition that they should not lead to acquisition of more than an 'equitable share' of world export trade, boiled down to an economic misconception as those provisions implicitly endorsed market sharing. The report also contended that other exceptions from the GATT provisions should be subject to strengthened rules. The exceptions to which the Leutwiler Report referred included restrictions maintained under past waivers, which were a clear reference to the quotas imposed by the United States under the waiver obtained in 1955 to the GATT ban on quotas. They also comprised variable levies which were one of the tenets of the CAP.

With regard to subsidies, the report argued that they had become the main source of unfair competition and that 'GATT is not, to the extent it should be, a forum where subsidy actions affecting trade can be discussed, and differences over them resolved'. On the other hand, clearer and more strictly defined rules were to be applied to actions against subsidies and dumping as they could be applied unfairly and result in harassment of importers. What was primarily needed was a definition of the term 'subsidy' and the strengthening of complaint procedures in the GATT.

The recommendations were also opposed to the idea of selectivity in safeguard measures put forward by the Community. To the argument that restricting imports from all sources while only one or two may be causing injury would be unnecessarily disruptive, the authors of the report rejoined that concentrating import restrictions on the most disruptive competitors boiled down to discriminate by definition the most competitive and might be followed by a proliferation of bilateral deals with efficient suppliers. In contrast non-discrimination would discourage governments from applying the safeguard provision unless the industry concerned really needed help as all suppliers, actual and potential, that were affected by the measure would have a common interest in the early removal of the restriction. They also recommended that safeguards should preferably take the form of tariffs rather than quantitative restrictions and should be progressively phased out over a predetermined period.

The seven experts also addressed their criticisms to abuses in the establishment of customs unions and free-trade areas, notably by the EC, which, in their opinion had been allowed by ambiguities in GATT Art. XXIV. According to the group of experts, although the European Community and the European Free Trade Association met the conditions envisaged by the General Agreement, many other agreements, including some agreements between the European Community and its associates, did not comply with GATT requirements. Therefore, GATT rules had to be redefined and applied more strictly to avoid ambiguities.

The report suggested that GATT's dispute settlement procedures should be reinforced by establishing a permanent roster of non-governmental experts to examine disputes and by giving more attention to the implementation of panel reports. In short, the experts suggested that dispute settlement should be carried out in a more judicial way, which was in line with the American viewpoint.

In agreement with the American perspective, the experts contended that the prospective GATT negotiations should avoid a North–South dialogue approach. They argued that preferential tariff schemes in favour of developing countries were of little value, often distracting them from the fact that tariff escalation on semi-finished and finished products handicapped their exports, while tariff protection against imports from industrial countries could help their infant industries in the short term, but might turn counterproductive in the long run. What was needed was their integration into the trading system, 'with all the appropriate rights and responsibilities'. Discarding the developing countries' fears, the report suggested that particular attention should be given to the integration of services into the GATT system because of their growing importance in the world economy and because, in the absence of a multilateral discipline, bilateral and regional rules would be developed to segment the market.

The recommendations were extremely critical of trade restrictions outside the GATT, the so-called 'grey area'. Here the Leutwiler Report, in keeping with its philosophy of protection of competitive advantage as well as of bidirectional integration of developing countries in the multilateral trade system, argued that there should be prompt identification of all such measures and their elimination over an agreed, credible, timescale. Likewise, trade in textiles and clothing had to be brought back within the normal GATT rules over a clearly defined time period. In this case, it is open to dispute whether the advice of the report was really music to American ears as the US, though supporting an effective GATT discipline over such measures, had often resorted and would continue to resort to market-sharing deals.

Finally, the report expressed strong support for the launching of a new round of negotiations as soon as possible, provided, as was to be expected from the foregoing, that 'they were directed toward further opening world markets'.

The United States reaffirmed its position, arguing that there was urgent need to improve and strengthen the international trade system and that the work programme initiated in 1982 had reached a stage where further progress depended on multilateral negotiations.[13]

As regards negotiations on trade in goods, the US focused on five points. Firstly, an expeditious and effective dispute settlement mechanism was essential. Secondly, the preparatory work carried out since 1982 constituted a solid basis for negotiations directed at providing an effective discipline on import restrictions and export subsidies in agriculture. Thirdly, an effective GATT discipline over all import restraints had to be introduced, the first step being an agreement on the application of transparency, surveillance, limited duration and degressivity. Fourthly, NTBs codes negotiated during the Tokyo Round, notably those on subsidies and public procurement, needed improvement. Finally, international protection for intellectual property rights was to have its place in GATT negotiations as a primary element in securing a sound environment for world trade.

With respect to international investments, the US advocated multilateral discipline over practices that distorted or restricted international investment flows. Within services, the US proposals called for an agreement on a set of rules and principles to conduct trade in the sector which had to be complemented by negotiations for the removal of barriers in individual service industries.

On 19 March 1985 the trade ministers of the EC met to discuss the Community's position on the prospective new round of GATT negotiations on the basis of a communication from the Commission which was conditionally favourable to the participation of the Community.[14] There were differences of opinion among the ten ministers, which, in spite of the final agreement set out in the communiqué, tended to reappear in the subsequent phases of the multilateral dialogue that preceded the launching of the Uruguay Round. The majority of the member states, notably the UK and Germany, supported the prompt launching of a new multilateral negotiating round with the objective of further expansion of trade and the strengthening of GATT structures and disciplines. The countries of the southern area headed by France argued that the launching of the round should be conditional on previous international consensus on objectives, participation and schedule. Even if this was not necessarily a delaying tactic, it actually boiled down to a delay of the start of the multilateral negotiations as, if we take into account the developing countries, the GATT members in 1985 were not near to an agreement as to the subjects to be dealt with in the talks. It also offered the Community, and some of its members in particular, greater leeway in establishing a negotiating agenda that did not simply meet the goals of the United States. To reach a consensus among all the potential participants in the round, certain subjects had to be dropped from the agenda or, at least, modified. France in particular pressed for the defence of the 'Community preference', the preservation of the Community's agricultural export capacity and the strengthening of the CAP mechanism. Dismantling of 'grey area' measures might be negotiated in exchange for a more flexible attitude on selectivity.

If we take the declaration issued at the end of the meeting at face value, it seems that in March 1985 the EC trade minister ironed out their differences expressing willingness to participate in the prospective GATT round, but with a series of caveats that greatly conceded to the worries of France and its Mediterranean allies. The EC ministers in the first place pointed out that the new round, important as it might be in strengthening the multilateral trading system, was not of itself sufficient and thus three separate but related desiderata had to receive parallel consideration. The term 'desiderata' clearly indicated that they were not preconditions. On the other hand, their fulfilment was deemed to influence the Community's stance before and during the prospective GATT round. Specifically, the Council requested a standstill, that is, the halting of protectionist measures, and their rollback, that is, their gradual dismantling. The call for standstill and rollback reflected the member states' anxiety towards both the growing pressure for protectionist measures in the US Congress and the measures that the US administration had already adopted or was about to take in several sectors, notably steel. In the third place, concerted action was urged to improve the functioning of the international monetary system and the flow of financial resources to overcome imbalances whose solution could not be found in trade talks.

As regards the general frame of the prospective GATT negotiations and their topics, the Council affirmed the need for reciprocity and a better balance of rights and obligations and the avoidance of too selective an approach to specific negotiating points. On agriculture, the ministers adopted a less rigid attitude than that suggested by France, declaring that the Community was ready to work towards improvements of the GATT discipline on all aspects of trade in agricultural products, but within the existing framework of rules and 'taking full account of the specific characteristics and problems' of the sector. Besides, the fundamental objectives and mechanisms of the CAP, both internal and external, were not to be placed in question. The ministers considered that trade in services and problems of counterfeit goods were suitable for inclusion in the GATT talks. Unsurprisingly, the declaration called on Japan to bring its import propensity in line with that of its partners as, despite previous trade rounds, the country's growth of imports of manufactured goods had fallen far behind its export growth.

The declaration ended by affirming the Community's readiness to participate in the launching of a new round, hopefully in Brussels, but 'subject to the establishment of an adequate prior international consensus on objectives, participation and timing', which had also to include the developing countries. Therefore, a precise date for the formal launching of a new round could not be fixed as solid progress was dependent on a step-by-step approach.

In an effort to accelerate progress towards the prompt start of a GATT round, the United States Trade Representative, William Brock, tried to get at least the agreement of the developed countries on the launch of multilateral negotiations in early 1986 during the OECD ministerial Council of May 1985. His proposal, however, was opposed by the representatives of the European Commission and of France who stuck to the guidelines hammered out by the Council of Ministers two months earlier. On the other hand, during the same OECD meeting, the US Secretary for the Treasury, James Baker, signalled the US availability to discussions in a suitable forum on monetary issues, which, however, had to be kept separate from GATT negotiations.

The declaration issued at the end of the May 1985 G7 summit in Bonn endorsed 'the agreement that a new GATT round should begin as soon as possible', adding that 'most of us think that this should be in 1986'. The declaration concealed a clash of opinions in which the dissenting voice was that of the French president, François Mitterrand.[15]

The French delegation submitted an amendment to the declaration according to which a group of senior officials would examine the content of multilateral trade talks and determine whether a broad consensus existed between all the contracting parties, including the developing countries, to begin negotiations as soon as possible. The amendment also provided that a balanced package of subjects to be negotiated had to be agreed upon. As regards agriculture, the French proposal contended that the special nature of the sector had to be taken into account while the basic internal and external mechanisms of national and Community farm policy were not to be called into account. Once the aforementioned conditions had been fulfilled, the round could begin immediately. The French amendment was rejected. On the other hand, the declaration adopted by the heads of state and government, though avoiding making it a precondition to the talks, provided that 'it would be useful that a preparatory meeting of senior officials should take place in the GATT before the end of the summer to reach a broad consensus on subject matter and modalities for such negotiations'.

Yet, it is arguable that the French were starting to fight a rearguard action and that most industrialized countries were getting impatient with the lack of rapid progress, among which Germany, whose chancellor was not happy that the summit he had hosted had been overshadowed by the impossibility of announcing a date for the opening of multilateral negotiations.

The June 1985 meeting of the GATT Council did not signal significant progress to the launch of a new round. Many developing countries, led by India, made their participation conditional on several prior confidence-building actions ranging from a commitment from the industrial countries not to introduce new restrictive trade measures and rollback those already in place to the dismantlement of the MFA and to a concurrent reform of the international monetary and financial system. The United States found, however, important allies among several developing countries like South Korea, Chile and the members of the Association of South East Asia Nations (ASEAN). Thus it decided to call a special session of the GATT to discuss the start of a new negotiating round without waiting for an unlikely consensus to emerge but exploiting Art. XXV of the GATT, according to which 'except as otherwise provided . . . decisions of the Contracting Parties shall be taken by a majority of the votes cast'.[16] Actually, the decision to convene the session was taken by consensus since the countries that had opposed the meeting abstained from calling for a vote. The special session, which concluded its work on 2 October, held that 'a preparatory process on the proposed new round of multilateral trade negotiations has now been initiated'. On 28 November the GATT parties agreed to establish a preparatory committee to determine objectives, subject matters, modalities for and participation in the multilateral trade negotiations and to make recommendations by mid-July 1986 for adoption at a ministerial meeting to be held in September. The venue chosen for the ministerial conference was Punta del Este, in Uruguay, largely because of the feeling that the new round had to have the endorsement of the developing countries.

In June 1986 the EC Council of Ministers agreed the Community's 'overall position' for the Uruguay Round.[17] In reaffirming the decision of March 1985 the Council stressed the need for a standstill as new protectionist measures might jeopardize the negotiations and for an approach to the negotiations resulting in a coherent package of measures between the GATT parties. As regards the subjects of the negotiations, the EC ministers reiterated that the Community would not agree to discuss certain CAP mechanisms like export subsidies in isolation without bringing in the protectionist and trade-distorting practices of other countries. They also underscored that a single GATT body had to be responsible for the entire farm trade sector. The overall position also advocated a twofold approach on services: the assessment of the viability of a framework of rules applying to all trade in services; and the drawing up of specific rules for each sector according to its differing characteristics.

In the run-up to the conference three draft declarations were presented. The first, sponsored by a group of ten hard-line developing countries led by Brazil and India, made no concession to the discussion of the new subjects of services, intellectual property and trade and investment. A second draft text, drawn up by the Colombian ambassador, Felipe Jaramillo, and by the Swiss ambassador, Pierre-Louis Girard, the so-called 'café-au-lait' proposal, was the product of the cooperation between a group of industrialized countries, joined in the last stages by the big three, the EC, the US and Japan, and some developing countries that opposed the stance of the hardliners headed by Brazil and India. A third text, submitted by Argentina, was a modification of the Colombian-Swiss proposal. The Jaramillo-Girard draft became the basis for negotiations at the opening of the Punta del Este meeting on 14 September 1986, although some amendments had to be made to accommodate divergences in sectors like agriculture and services.

The Punta del Este Declaration and its consequences

In the words of Winston Smith in George Orwell's *Nineteen Eighty-Four*, 'the end is contained in the beginning'. The Punta del Este Declaration does not allow so deterministic a conclusion, if only because the close of the round had to wait for eight years that were particularly rich in events that modified the economic and political scene and could, therefore, be deemed concurrent causal factors. Yet, the Declaration set the agenda of the round, that is, it fixed the items that were to be negotiated, although the newly established Group of Negotiations on Goods was allowed to 'decide upon inclusion of additional subject-matters in the negotiations'. Besides, in many cases it also determined the tone of the negotiation and with it, if not the final results, the direction of the discussions. It is, therefore, apposite to examine briefly the major or at least the most contentious subjects of the agenda, focusing in particular on the convergences and divergences of the two transatlantic partners. The analysis must be conducted according to the rules of history, that is, leaving aside any comparison with the results of the round and considering instead the stance of the participants in the phase that preceded the Punta del Este meeting, especially during the work of the preparatory committee.

The Declaration was divided into two parts, the first of which concerned trade in goods while the second one referred to trade in services.[18] The first part consisted of a preamble, which stated the basic decision to negotiate and reverse protectionism, and seven sections. In particular, the second section adopted the idea upheld by the Community that the negotiations had to be treated from start to finish as parts of a single undertaking. The same section, reproducing what had been decided at the end of the Tokyo Round, laid out the principle of differential and more favourable treatment for developing countries, which, however, was to be applied in inverse relation to their economic development. The third section set out the 'standstill' and 'rollback' commitments. The first commitment required that no trade restrictions inconsistent with the GATT be introduced and that even GATT-consistent measures should not go beyond what was strictly necessary to remedy specific situations. This could be read as a clear reminder to some developed countries, notably the United States, not to overexploit for protectionist ends GATT remedies, such as antidumping and countervailing measures. The rollback commitment called for the progressive phasing out of restrictive or distorting measures inconsistent with the General Agreement or for their being brought back within GATT rules not later than by the date of the formal completion of the round.

Although tariff cuts and harmonization no longer had the same significance as in previous rounds, they were still an important issue after the Tokyo Round. A committee on tariff concessions had been established to supervise the implementation of previously agreed upon tariff reductions and to provide a forum to discuss tariff issues, both recurrent in tariff negotiations and new ones. Prominent among the new issues, in line with the new round's stated goal of creating a more favourable trade environment for developing countries, was tariff escalation. Tariff escalation occurs when importing countries impose higher duties on partially and fully-processed products than on their underlying primary products as well as higher tariffs on finished goods than on semimanufactured products. The result, which was more severe than a simple difference in tariff rate, was to provide domestic producers low-cost access to primary inputs while protecting them from competition on further processed goods.[19] The preparatory committee, along with tariff escalation, was concerned with the following issues: the persistence of tariff peaks of over 40 per cent; the presence of numerous tariffs that had no longer any relevant impact on imports, which, however, were not yet duty-free (so-called nuisance tariffs); the difference in levels of bindings between industrialized and developing countries; and the credit to give to those countries, that had unilaterally cut tariff levels when they bounded such reductions.[20]

The Punta del Este Declaration rather succinctly called for the improvement, clarification and expansion, as appropriate, of the codes on non-tariff barriers negotiated in the Tokyo Round. A group on Multilateral Trade Negotiation (MTN) agreements and arrangements dealt with five of them (technical barriers to trade, government procurement, customs valuation, import licensing and antidumping) while the subsidy and countervailing duty code was entrusted to another group. Although the debate on the MTN codes started in earnest immediately after the Punta del Este meeting, especially as regards those on technical barriers (standards) and public procurement, differences in outlook between the US and the Community can be detected in the works of both the Tokyo Round committees and the preparatory committee for the 1986 ministerial meeting. On public purchasing, the US sought to extend the coverage to sectors like telecommunications, heavy electrical and transportation equipment and to include service contracts, at a moment in which progress towards a really unified market in the Community was still patchy and the 1992 deadline was distant. In turn, the EC argued for coverage of state and local government and the effective removal of the Buy America legislation.

Prospective difficulties for the standards code derived from the different approach to standard establishment and certification in the two areas. In the US the role of public policy was traditionally limited to technical regulations in fields like safety and environment whereas standard-making was left to industry and private bodies. Also, in the sectors where public policy had a role this was not always at the federal level but responsibility was often left to states and other local authorities. The process in the European Community was much more institutionalized with bodies entrusted with standard-making at EC level, and as a result its influence on the work of international standard bodies was much stronger than that of the United States. Hence, the proposals made by the United States, lamenting the obstacles to the acceptance by foreign governments of US test data, related to transparency of bilateral and regional standard activities.[21] The Community focused, instead, on two issues.[22] The first concerned the effective extension of major code obligations, particularly those of notification of proposed technical regulation, to local government bodies. The second called for the establishment of a code of good practice for non-governmental standardizing bodies.

Antidumping, which turned out to be one of the thorniest issues of the Uruguay Round, did not attract much controversy in the phase preceding its launching. Things went quite differently for agriculture and subsidies. The two subjects, which were connected as one of the main lines of attack to the EC Common Agricultural Policy by its trading partners, or more exactly its competitors, were directed to its export refunds which were viewed as a form of export subsidy.

As mentioned in a previous chapter, the SCM code had failed to solve many problems concerning subsidies and countervailing measures and to prevent disputes which were growing in number and acrimony under the trade difficulties that were experienced by the signatories of the code in sectors ranging from steel to agriculture. The issues under scrutiny included in particular export subsidies, especially with reference to primary products, domestic subsidies that could distort trade, as well as the definition and calculation of countervailable subsidies.[23] A further issue concerned the measures that could be labelled as subsidies and, therefore, subject to the discipline of the GATT and SCM codes. Another one referred to the assessment of the subsidy amount. According to the European Community, the assessment had to be based on the financial contribution made by a public authority. For the United States what was to be assessed was the competitive benefit received by the firms concerned.

In the preparatory committee the United States repeatedly stressed that 'it was not possible to talk about strengthening and improving the system without dealing with subsidies', as they were one of its fundamental weaknesses 'which had to be dealt with on as wide a front as possible'. It, therefore, 'strongly supported negotiations which could restore discipline over the use of trade-distorting subsidies'.[24] The US opinion was shared by other OECD countries, the most assertive of which was Australia which contended that a radical reform of the subsidy discipline that specifically addressed the issue of primary products' subsidization was needed. Also the chairman of the preparatory committee remarked that, in spite of the efforts made in different fora of the GATT to overcome the difficulties marking the regulation of subsidies and countervailing measures, it appeared that such problems 'could only be solved in a negotiating context and with due attention to all their aspects'.[25] The EC delegation, in contrast, stated that it was not convinced of the utility of treating subsidies as a separate item and argued that a wrong approach to subsidies seemed to prevail as they were accused of exhausting budgetary resources while unduly expanding the part played by the State in the economy, neglecting the fact that governments had to have recourse to subsidies to protect national interests in times of economic difficulties.[26] The EC delegation also contended that since subsidies could take many forms and the complexity of the issues made it necessary to take account of the context in which subsidization occurred, subsidies applied to agricultural products had to be discussed in the context of trade in agriculture along with other trade-distorting practices affecting that sector.[27]

On balance the Declaration did not meet the hopes of the Community. Subsidies and countervailing measures were listed as a separate subject, with the objective of improving GATT discipline relating to measures that affect international trade. And, with a logical shift from the Tokyo Round's middle ground, it was implicit that domestic subsidies also had to be eliminated or reformed inasmuch as they might have trade-distorting effects. On the other hand, countervailing measures also were not immune from scrutiny.

Rewarding the Community's efforts, agriculture was treated as a separate subject and export subsidies were not the only item on the agenda, but were mentioned along with all other measures that might affect import access – terms that appeared to refer particularly to import quotas as well as to variable levies – and export competition. Besides, the aim of the negotiations included greater liberalization of trade, but also the reduction of uncertainty, imbalances and instabilities in the world agricultural market, which did not exclude a concerted approach favoured by the Community. Yet, subsidies, and not only export subsidies, were put under the spotlight as the Declaration focused on the improvement of the competitive environment in farm trade by increasing discipline on the use of all direct and indirect subsidies, including the phased reduction of their negative effects. Moreover, the prospective negotiating environment did not bode well for the EC. Just a month before the opening of the round, in Cairns (Australia) the representatives of fourteen agricultural exporting states, both OECD members and developing countries, which dubbed themselves 'key fair trading countries in agriculture', but are better known as the Cairns Group, formed an alliance pledging to work together on agricultural trade issues. The Americans, thus, found an organized ally in their fight for freer and fairer trade in farm products, while the EC was bound to become a defendant in the battle at the centre of which was its CAP's mechanism and ideology.

On the issue of safeguards, the Declaration was a compromise which did not take sides on the various stances. The text only stated that the result of the Uruguay Round negotiations should clarify and reinforce the discipline of the General Agreement, should apply to all parties and should contain, *inter alia*, elements like transparency, objective criteria, degressivity, structural adjustment and compensation. No reference was made to the 'selectivity' option sponsored by the EC. On the other hand, the Brazilian proposal that safeguards be treated on a priority basis in the negotiations and safeguard actions be based on the MFN principle did not find a place in the Declaration.

On dispute settlement, the Declaration was a step towards acceptance of the requests of the United States as it envisaged that the negotiations should aim at strengthening the rules and procedures of the dispute settlement process and should include adequate arrangements for overseeing compliance with adopted recommendations by dispute settlement bodies.

The Declaration addressed three issues that had not been previously dealt with in the GATT forum: trade-related investment measures (TRIMS), trade-related aspects of intellectual property rights (TRIPS) and services. Their inclusion resulted from US initiatives. A fourth new subject concerned the possibility of reintegrating the textile and clothing sector into GATT.

TRIMS were part of a wider set of issues of concern for the United States. The objectives pursued by the US included the reduction of barriers to foreign direct investments, the expansion of the principle of national treatment, the development of internationally agreed rules on dispute settlement for foreign investments, and the reduction or elimination of trade distortive effects of certain TRIMS, that is, in other words, investment performance requirements.[28] In a paper circulated by the US in the Consultative Group of Eighteen in 1981, investment performance requirements were defined as any requirements placed by a host nation government upon a foreign controlled enterprise, either as conditions under which various investment incentives are provided or as conditions for foreign investors to attain entry to a country. The measures in question included export requirements, import substitution requirements, requirements concerning the amount of capital invested or employment levels, requirements concerning the location of industries, limits to foreign ownership, restrictions on the remittance of earnings, technology transfer, and so on.[29] The US, however, proposed that in the initial stage the GATT should only handle the measures having the greatest impact on trade, i.e. export requirements and import substitution.

The trade-related investment issue was not mentioned in the 1982 Ministerial Declaration but the US managed to reintroduce the subject in a later stage, arguing that encouragement of unhampered foreign investment would add significantly to GATT's contribution to promoting structural adjustment and more efficient economic development, which was to be a main goal underpinning the prospective negotiations. In the preparatory committee for the Punta del Este ministerial conference, the US proposed negotiating stricter discipline on trade-distorting investment measures and argued that such negotiations should also address other factors which had an impact on investment flows. More specifically, the US proposed that GATT contracting parties should consider the application to foreign investment of the core GATT principles of national treatment (which would entail equality between domestic and foreign firms as regards the right to invest and run local operations) and the MFN treatment (which would place all foreign investors on an equal footing).[30]

The US position was opposed by most developing countries, Argentina, Brazil and India in particular, which not only disputed the permissibility of investment negotiations under the GATT, but also insisted that negotiations, if any, would have to address issues relating to transnational corporations, including transfer price and restrictive business practices.[31]

In a first stage the Community was rather cautious and, although it acknowledged that something had to be done in the investment area, it argued that 'nobody could keep GATT from studying the consequences on trade, but to study was not to negotiate' and that there were other institutions outside the GATT that were better equipped to address the issue.[32] Subsequently, however, the EC delegate stated that issues such as right of establishment, transfer of resources and practices of private companies in conducting their cross-frontier investment policies were not a suitable subject for inclusion in the new round, but that 'in the more specific case of trade-related investment measures, he would question the claim that there was no room for GATT to be concerned'.[33] In the end, the different positions resulted in a negotiating mandate narrowly focused in scope, that is, addressing only investment measures considered to be trade-distorting under existing specific GATT rules.

Since the beginning of the 1970s most industrial countries had been insisting that international treaties on intellectual property rights be strengthened to provide effective enforcement of their rules. However, efforts to amend the Paris Convention on industrial property were not successful and no significant progress was made in reforming the Berne Convention covering copyright. The US was not even a party to the Berne Convention, preferring to rely on its domestic copyright law and on bilateral treaties. In the course of the 1980s the developed countries became more and more concerned about the lack of protection of their domestic intellectual property interests in foreign countries as their industries that produced intellectual property were significantly affected by piracy and counterfeiting. The need for a response to this problem was particularly felt in the United States where the 1984 Trade Act made intellectual property protection actionable under the amended section 301 and made it a condition for eligibility under the Generalized System of Preferences to developing countries.

The United States tabled a proposal in the preparatory committee for the Punta del Este conference contending that GATT was the appropriate forum to seek enforcement of international protection of intellectual property rights, and that its mandate should not be limited to the protection of trademarked goods but should also include other property rights like trademarks, copyright and trade secrets.[34] Numerous developing countries, led by Brazil, retorted that not only were counterfeit trademarked goods beyond the GATT authority, but also that GATT could not extend itself to issues like copyrights and patents, as they covered intangible objects.[35] The EC, along with other industrialized countries, supported the US proposal, arguing that protection of intellectual property had a bearing on international trade and that there were a number of GATT articles that were of direct relevance to the subject. On the other hand, the Community pointed out that the intellectual property issue would require a balancing of the roles which should be played by GATT and specialized bodies such as the World Intellectual Property Organization (WIPO) which administered both the Paris and the Berne conventions.[36]

The perspective of the United States, supported by its industrialized partners, prevailed. The Punta del Este Declaration mentioned, among the subjects of negotiations in the new round, the trade-related aspects of intellectual property rights, including (among others) trade in counterfeit goods. It stressed, however, that the negotiations should be without prejudice to other complementary initiatives taken in the WIPO or elsewhere.

The European Community, along with most developed countries, was a supporter of the US proposal for the immediate inclusion of services in the new negotiating round. This does not mean that the EC and its member states saw eye to eye with the US on the whole gamut of services. In some of them, like those based on information technology, they felt that time and ability were required to be on a par with the US. In other sectors, like financial services, the Community felt, initially, that the elimination of barriers between its member countries by 1992 was not mirrored by the highly segmented American market. Many developing countries, among which Brazil and India in particular, argued that GATT lacked legal competence on this issue.

The industrial countries overall carried the day. Services were included in the Declaration which, however, was divided into two parts: one for trade in goods and the other set apart for services, which might let developing countries interested in protecting their infant service industries hope that services were left outside the overall package to be negotiated for goods. In other words, concessions on services might not be exchanged for concessions on trade in goods.

The stance of the two transatlantic trading partners with regard to trade in textiles and clothing was similar. It was a question of degree rather than substance in their respective positions. Many developing countries called for the prompt dismantlement of the MFA, possibly even before the renewal of the Multifibre Arrangement. The

MFA was extended for the fourth time, for a further five years to 1991, less than three months before the Punta del Este meeting. For the developing countries the rescission of the arrangement was a logical result of the rollback principle. The US delegation opposed the idea that improvements in GATT discipline resulting from the new round should be fully applicable to textiles, arguing that it was impossible to envisage the immediate termination of the MFA. Referring to the existence of strong textile lobbies in the United States and elsewhere, it said that improved access to overseas markets and the reduction or removal of subsidies in various sectors would make it easier for the US administration to press for trade liberalization in the textiles sector.[37] Subsequently, it argued that 'any standstill and rollback agreement would apply only to actions taken on textiles that were inconsistent with a new MFA'.[38] The Community showed major flexibility and a better command of dialectic. Substantially in line with the Community's position on the extension of the Multifibre Arrangement till 1991, the EC delegation on the one hand stressed that 'the Community agreed with the aim of liberalizing trade in textiles by applying the rules of the General Agreement'. On the other hand, it made it clear that the Community 'was not in favour of proceeding in a hasty manner, or of unilateral reductions or elimination of trade measures because this would only be sowing the seeds of disorder for tomorrow' and that 'to insist that the rollback commitment should require all measures in textiles and clothing to be eliminated in a very short period of time, was tantamount to rejecting the need for a new round'.[39]

The result was a commitment in the Declaration to start negotiations aimed at formulating modalities that would permit the eventual integration of the sector into GATT.

There is no denying that Punta del Este marked a success for the United States. The ministerial meeting crowned five years of US diplomatic pressure whereas the attitude of other major GATT parties varied from partially and cautiously favourable to reluctant. The agenda set by the Declaration included all the subjects that the United States wanted to negotiate and their content mostly gave it ample room for manoeuvre in pursuing its objectives in the subsequent talks. The United States was able to introduce, with the support of the industrialized countries, the new items of 'trade related investment measures', 'trade related property rights' and 'services'. It was also able to reopen negotiations on subsidies and agriculture putting in jeopardy the advantages that the ambiguities of the Tokyo Round agreements seemed to have offered to the EC.

The European Community had a major supporting role in the inclusion of the three mentioned new subjects in the round and in some cases it helped smooth over the differences between the US and developing countries. On the other hand, it was the recalcitrant party with regard to the reform of agricultural trade. As regards subsidization, the Declaration reopened the question of domestic subsidies giving new emphasis to their potentially trade-distorting effects. No detectable favour was given by the Declaration to the idea of 'selectivity' put forward by the EC for the amendment of the safeguards discipline.

Conclusion

The attempt to individuate a single dominant thread in the events examined in the foregoing chapters would be far-fetched. What the analysis of the 1967–86 period shows is that each of the areas listed for consideration in the Introduction (cause and impact of the trade movements; response of each of the two main transatlantic trading partners to trade difficulties and rise of protectionist and interventionist tendencies; their role in reshaping of the international trading system) had its own main thread and each of the three areas influenced the others.

The backdrop – dominated by the performance of the industrial countries – for a large part of the period under review was less bright than in the previous decade. Certainly the volume of merchandise trade continued to show an upward trend and went on outpacing that of merchandise production. Yet, the positive trend was becoming flat and the gap with production growth was closing: In 1963–73 world exports in volume grew on average by 8.5 per cent, while world commodity output grew 6 per cent; in 1973–9 they grew by 4.5 per cent and 3.5 per cent respectively; in 1980–6 they grew by 3 per cent and 2 per cent.[1] What is also relevant is that from 1975 onwards the rate of growth was no longer constantly positive (Table 20).

As regards the two transatlantic partners the trend conceals different phases, which, however, have a common feature: the erosion of the transatlantic predominance by the steady advance, both in absolute and relative terms, of another OECD country, Japan, followed by the NICs, while the unhindered rise in production of all the industrial countries is threatened by the sway of the OPEC members. A further factor to take into account is that in the period under review the United States had lost its status of hegemon within the Western world. Yet, if by the close of the 1960s the US could no longer claim to be the hegemonic power, it kept a dominant position in key sectors of the world economy. Despite the end of the Bretton Woods regime, because of pressure from the United States, the US dollar remained the primary medium for commercial and financial transactions. The simple fact that the US market was the favourite export outlet for both industrialized countries, with the partial exception of the EC member states, and developing countries gave it leverage to impose its viewpoint on international trade. The majority of multinational corporations had their parent company in the US. As the US was the main provider of security for a Western world threatened by external and internal forces, the threat of shifting the burden of military expenses made its allies pay greater attention to its suggestions. The EC surpassed the US in both merchandise and service exports, even if about 50 per cent of the amount was constituted by intra-EC trade (Figures 9 to 12). In manufacturing exports West Germany alone outshone the US. Yet, there was no EC balance of payments. The prosperous German balance of payments was distinct from that of France and Italy. There was no common EC fiscal policy and the attempt to establish a monetary system involving the member states was limited in scope and stability. In spite of the establishment of a Common Commercial Policy many measures affecting international trade, such as subsidies, remained in the domain of member states. If the Commission was the statutory negotiator for the Community, its decisions had to receive the endorsement of the member states, whose viewpoint was far from homogeneous. The establishment of a real common market was a work in process for the whole period under review.

Yet, relatively greater strength does not secure hegemony. Hegemony (ἡγεμονία) means supreme direction, that is the capacity, deriving from the predominance within a coalition, of dictating the rules, with the (sometimes grudging) acceptance on the part of other members. By the 1960s American hegemony was over along with America's absolute economic and political predominance. In his seminal 'After Hegemony' Keohane argued that after the end of the American hegemony cooperation among states, that is, states of the Western Bloc, might continue relying on the institutions that the former hegemonic power had helped establish.[2] The question is how smoothly and to what extent the cooperation worked.

Against this historical background, what evidence is provided by the various chapters?

The first chapter demonstrates that the achievements of the Kennedy Round were remarkable if viewed in the light of the liberalization drive that marked the years following the Second World War. Yet, the success story had its limits, with regard to both what was agreed and to what was left out. Concessions in those sectors in which the transatlantic partners were losing ground were modest, while key agricultural sectors did not find their place or a long-lasting place in the agreements. Venturing in new areas such as non-tariff barriers proved limited in scope and success.

From the beginning of the 1970s, tensions in world trade became pronounced and frequent. A thread that emerges in most chapters is the interaction between trade and monetary issues. The period 1971–3 witnessed firstly the readjustment of the parity grill based on the Bretton Woods agreements and soon after the repeal of the fixed but adjustable parity regime itself. Economists and historians prevalently look back at the reform of the monetary system from the currency angle. However, profound changes in the currency regime should also be considered from the perspective of trade, as trade worries in the US were among the main factors that triggered the process and, in a first stage, the threat of tariff barriers was prominent among the strategies employed by the Americans. The US drive for a radical reform of the exchange rate system met with the opposition of France which pointed out the dangers caused to trade stability. Giscard d'Estaing, for instance, made it clear, even during the cosy talks beside 'la cheminée' that lowering of tariffs was rendered insignificant by fluctuation in currencies that did not reflect the real economic situation, adding that such fluctuations were a source of disorder in the world economy.[3] Eventually the disagreement was papered over during the economic summit. The Rambouillet Declaration stated, rather candidly, that 'We welcome the rapprochement, reached at the request of many other countries, between the views of the U.S. and France on the need for stability that the reform of the international monetary system must promote'. But the differences in attitude over this topic were destined to re-emerge when in the Carter years the US was accused of benign neglect over the depreciation of the dollar and, even more so, in the years of ups and downs of the dollar during the Reagan presidency.

The evidence drawn from the chapters dealing with the first and second oil shocks indicates that they had a negative impact on the domestic economies of the industrialized countries, both directly and through the effect of fiscal and monetary policies that were not most apt to cope with inflationary pressures from exogenous factors. The first oil crisis also showed unequivocally that the years of American hegemony were over. As the US was unable to promptly provide a replacement for the oil imported from OPEC, the Community, following the lead of France, rejected the proposal put forward by the US for an industrial countries coalition, under American leadership, to withstand the threat posed by the oil producing countries, and called instead for a dialogue with them.[4]

It has been also argued that the shocks strengthened the long-term factors that would weigh down the economies across the Atlantic. An American scholar argues that when, in about 1973, growth became primarily based on technological and organizational innovation, in Western Europe the institutional conditions that until then had proved ideal were no longer able to adapt to the new deteriorating economic environment.[5] Productivity declined on the other side of the Atlantic during the Carter years and their recovery during the Reagan administration was far from outstanding.[6] With a more specific perspective, the research illustrates that the recovery, which on the European side was rather slow to materialize, both in the 1970s and 1980s, concealed the decline of several basic industries and the deceleration in the competitiveness of some more technologically advanced industries. The crises and their aftermath also created a political environment in which the voice of the lobbies calling for protection and support was bound to gain attention also because the calls could point to a jump in unemployment. With regard to unilateral policies, as the traditional trade barrier, tariff, tended to become irrelevant, it had to be replaced or supplemented by other measures, whose number and sophistication was on the rise during the years under consideration. It cannot, however, be said that such measures were in open denial of the free-trade oriented regime that had taken shape after the Second World War. Rather, these measures tended to dodge or bend the established rules, as was respectively the case for OMAs and antidumping and countervailing proceedings. In the case of subsidies they exploited the sheer absence of international provisions or their loopholes. Both the US and the EC stepped up the adoption of such measures against third countries and also employed them against each other. Similarities between the instruments used by the two trading blocs were, however, accompanied by remarkable differences. For instance, countervailing measures were widely adopted in the US along with antidumping duties, but much less so in the EC where, especially at member states level, subsidization was commonly used to prop up industries in decline or to boost emerging ones. The differences in policies were particularly marked in specific sectors like agriculture. For most of the 1970s the rising fortunes of American exports helped keep the financial assistance provided by the Department of Agriculture at a low level, whereas the same did not happen in the EC, where many farm products were starting to exceed the self-sufficiency threshold. Things started to change during the Carter administration as the potential for subsidized intervention, inherent in previous legislation, was put into practice. The Reagan administration, in spite of its rhetoric and its efforts, at home as well as in multilateral fora, faced with the need to buoy up a sector that was going through a period of unprecedented strain since the 1930s, ended up surpassing its transatlantic competitor in level of support and in burden for the budget. Meanwhile the Community was finding it more and more difficult to cope with the pressure on its budget as production was exceeding domestic consumption in all the sectors of temperate zone farming.

Which was the stance of the two transatlantic commercial powers in the multilateral negotiations during the years of recurrent crises and trade strains in the 1970s and 1980s? Did cooperation between them prevail over confrontation?

Winham argued that the Tokyo Round replaced the long-gone American hegemony with a harmonious bipolar structure centred on the US and the EC, which opened the way to changing GATT rules from statement of broad principle to more detailed regulations relating to domestic and international procedures.[7] Yet the fleshing out of GATT rules was marked by diplomatic ambiguities and limitations in scope, which resulted in a large margin for manoeuvre for the parties to the round. At any rate the facts reported in this research demonstrate that the new, more ideologically committed, American administration gainsaid the idea that the arrangements worked out in the Tokyo Round had established lasting and stable rules for international trade. Actually, the Reagan administration viewed them as unsatisfactory and insufficient, soon calling for a new round of multilateral negotiations, which were to address both the issues dealt with in the previous round and a set of new issues that the developments of the world economy made it necessary to address. The European Community in contrast, though not rejecting the idea of a new liberalization cycle, thought it unwise to launch it so quickly as the recovery was uncertain and it appeared unlikely that the developing countries would accept new multilateral talks. In any case it was not happy to discuss again in a multilateral forum issues such as agriculture when the process of CAP reform was still at the tentative stage within the domestic arena. Thus, at least in a first stage, the cooperation through compromise, that had characterized the final years of the Tokyo Round, appeared to have been replaced by a US attempt to reaffirm its lost hegemony by imposing its trade philosophy and interests in the GATT. A similar judgement of uncooperative unilateralism was reached with regard to the US refusal to intervene in the market to stop the dollar appreciation. Only in 1985 did the deterioration of the trade balance and its impact on a growing number of industries convince the new head of the US Treasury to cooperate with the main trading partners to bring the value of the dollar down. In the years that preceded the opening of the Uruguay Round the Community was, instead, preparing to launch a process of reform of its own market, based on the elimination of the still remaining host of obstacles hampering the flow of goods, services and capital. This research, however, does not show that the process of reform, which was to be completed by 1992, was also meant to entail the opening of the EC market to foreign producers. In other words, till the final months covered by this research the issue as to whether the reform of the internal market would result or not in a 'Fortress Europe' was still in the balance. It took a long time before a sufficiently wide and stable common ground was established and a deal also covering agriculture was struck.

Notes

Introduction

1 The analysis will be limited to the countries with greater economic weight, i.e. the G7 members: France, the Federal Republic of Germany, Italy and the UK.

Chapter 1

1 John W. Evans, *The Kennedy Round in American Trade Policy: the twilight of the GATT?* (Cambridge, MA: The Harvard University Press, 1971), 281.
2 General Agreement on Tariffs and Trade (hereinafter GATT). *Meeting of Ministers, 16–21 May 1963. Resolution Adopted on 21 May 1963.* MIN (63)9, 22 May 1963.
3 GATT. Trade Negotiations Committee, *Meeting of the Committee at Ministerial Level.* TN.64/25, 2 May 1964.
4 The data in the following paragraphs are taken from Ernest H. Preeg, *Traders and Diplomats. An analysis of the Kennedy Round negotiations under the General Agreement on Tariffs and Trade* (Washington, DC: The Brookings Institution, 1970), 208, Table 13-1 and 209, Table 13-2; also European Communities Commission, *General Report 1967,* sect. 487.
5 Thomas B. Curtis et al., *The Kennedy Round and the Future of American Trade* (New York and London: Praeger, 1971), 117 et seq.
6 See Twelfth Annual Report of the President of the United States on the Trade Agreements Program (hereinafter ARPTAP) 1967, 17.
7 Ibid., 18.
8 Thomas B. Curtis et al., *The Kennedy Round and the future*, 127.
9 See Peter H. Lindert, 'U.S. Foreign Trade and Trade Policy in the Twentieth Century', in Stanley L. Engerman and Robert E. Gallman (eds), *The Cambridge Economic History of the United States, Volume III: The Twentieth Century* (Cambridge: Cambridge University Press, 2000), 429.
10 Ibid., 426.
11 European Communities Commission, *General Report 1967*, sect. 487.
12 Thomas B. Curtis et al., *The Kennedy Round and the Future*, 127.
13 Benyamin Bardan, 'The Cotton Textile Agreement 1962–1972', *Journal of World Trade Law*, 7 (1973), 9.
14 Ibid., 17.
15 Hans-Helmut Taake et al., 'The World Textile Arrangement. The Exporters' Viewpoint', *Journal of World Trade Law*, 8 (1974), 626 et seq.; Joseph Pelzman, 'The Multifiber Arrangement and Its Effect on the Profit Performance of the U.S. Textile Industry', in Robert Baldwin and Anne O. Krueger (eds), *The Structure and Evolution of Recent U.S. Trade Policy* (Chicago, London: University of Chicago Press, 1984), 114.
16 Ernest H. Preeg, *Traders and Diplomats*, 214.

17 Ibid., 214, Table 13-5.
18 Ibid.
19 Public Papers of the Presidents of the United States (hereinafter PPPUS) – John F. Kennedy, 1965. *Special Message to the Congress on Foreign Trade Policy*, January 25, 1962.
20 John W. Evans, *The Kennedy Round in American Trade Policy*, 203.
21 Communautées Européennes, Secrétariat Général du Conseil. *Aperçu des Activités du Conseil, 8–10 1963–64*; *Memorandum from the Special Representative for Trade Negotiations (Herter) to President Johnson, Washington November 27, 1963*, Foreign Relations of the United States (hereinafter FRUS) 1961–1963, Vol. IX Trade and Commercial Policies, Doc. 291.
22 GATT. Committee on Agriculture – *Statement by the Representative of the European Economic Community before the GATT Committee on Agriculture regarding the Negotiating Plan of the EEC for the Agricultural Part of the Kennedy Round*, TN.64/AGR/1, 19 February 1964; also GATT. Committee on Agriculture – *Contribution of the EEC Relating to the Negotiations on Agricultural Products in the GATT Trade Negotiations*, TN.64/AGR/5, 3 August 1964.
23 TN.64/AGR/1, para 25.
24 It was the OECD that towards the middle of the 1970s and in the 1980s produced basic studies on overall support level in agriculture.
25 GATT. Committee on Agriculture. *Statement of the United States Delegation on its Position Concerning the Proposal of the European Economic Community for Agricultural Negotiation in the Kennedy Round* TN.64/AGR/4, 17 June 1964.
26 Ernest H. Preeg, *Traders and Diplomats*, 147.
27 GATT, Group on Cereals. *Proposals for General Arrangements*, INT (65)160, 3 June 1965.
28 Gian Paolo Casadio, *Transatlantic Trade. USA-EEC Confrontations in the GATT Negotiations* (Westmead Farnborough: Saxon House-Lexington Books, 1973), 124.
29 INT (65)160, 3 June 1965.
30 Gian Paolo Casadio, *Transatlantic Trade*, 124.
31 Draft minutes of the 188th meeting of the Council of Ministers, 13–14 June 1966.
32 Gian Paolo Casadio, *Transatlantic Trade*, 132; A detailed historical analysis of the various phases of the agricultural negotiations is provided by Lucia Coppolaro, *The Making of a World Trading Power. The European Economic Community (EEC) in the GATT Kennedy Round Negotiations (1963–67)* (Farnham: Ashgate, 2013), Chapter 6.
33 Ernest H. Preeg, *Traders and Diplomats*, 251.
34 GATT. Basic Instruments and Selected Documents (hereinafter BISD), 15th Suppl. *Trade Conference Final Act – Memorandum of Agreement on Basic Elements for the Negotiation of World Grain Arrangements*, 18 et seq.
35 *Memorandum from the President's Special Assistant (Rostow) to President Johnson, November 3, 1967*, FRUS 1964–1968, Vol. IX Commodities and Strategic Materials, Doc. 354; Thomas B. Curtis et al., *The Kennedy Round and the Future*, 60.
36 GATT. BISD 15th Suppl. *Trade Conference Final Act – Memorandum of Agreement*, 22.
37 Michael Tracy, *Agriculture in Western Europe: Challenge and Response 1880–1980* (London: Granada, 1982), 279. Some contradictory aspects of the German attitude towards agriculture are also evidenced in N. Piers Ludlow, 'The Making of the CAP. Towards a Historical Analysis of the EU's First Major Policy', *Contemporary European History*, 14 (2005), 362–3.

38 EUROSTAT, Agriculture Yearbook, various issues.
39 See Christopher Ritson and Alan Swinbank, 'Europe's Green Money', in C. Ritson and R. Harvey (eds), *The Common Agricultural Policy* (Wallingford: CAB International, 1997), 127.
40 Denis Bergmann et al., *Politique d'Avenir pour l'Europe Agricole* (Paris: Economica, 1989), 61.
41 Willard W. Cochrane, *The Development of American Agriculture. A Historical Analysis* (Minneapolis: University of Minnesota Press, 1979), 147.
42 GATT. TN.64/AGR/4, 17 June 1964.
43 GATT. MIN (63)9, 22 May 1963.
44 PPPUS – Lyndon B. Johnson, 1968. *Special Message to the Congress: 'Greater Prosperity Through Expanded World Trade'*. 28 May 1968.
45 GATT. Contracting Parties – Twenty-Fourth Session. *Summary Record of the Nineteenth Meeting, Held on Friday 24 November 1967*. SR. 24/19, 12 December 1967.
46 GATT. Contracting Parties – Twenty-Fourth Session. *Programme for the Expansion of International Trade. Statement by the Representative of the United States on 14 November 1967*. W.24/10, 16 November 1967.
47 GATT. Contracting Parties – Twenty-Fourth Session. *Programme for the Expansion of International Trade. Statement by the Spokesman for the Communities on 10 November 1967*. W.24/2, 13 November 1967.
48 The CET was actually completed in 1968.
49 Jacques Pelkmans, 'Is Convergence Prompting Fragmentation? The EMS and national protection in Germany, France and Italy', in Paolo Guerrieri and Pier Carlo Padoan (eds), *The Political Economy of European Integration. States, Markets and Institutions* (New York and London: Harvester Wheatsheaf, 1989), 108.
50 *Memorandum from the Special Representative for Trade Negotiations (Roth) to President Johnson, Washington June 26, 1967*. FRUS 1964–1968, Vol. VIII Trade and Commercial Policy, Doc. 367.
51 Ibid.
52 PPPUS – Lyndon B. Johnson, 1967. *Special Message to the Congress Transmitting Multilateral Trade Agreement Concluding the Kennedy Round of Trade Negotiations*. 27 November 1967.
53 Thomas W. Zeiler, *American Trade and Power in the 1960s* (New York: Columbia University Press, 1992), 240.
54 Ibid.
55 *Memorandum from Secretary of State Rusk to President Johnson, October 10, 1967*. FRUS, 1964–1968, Vol. VIII Trade and Commercial Policy, Doc. 372.
56 J. Warley, 'Western Trade in Agricultural Products', in Andrew Shonfield (ed.), *International and Economic Relations of the Western World 1959–1971, Vol. I, Politics and Trade* (London: Oxford University Press for the Royal Institute of International Affairs, 1976), 387.
57 Jacob Viner, *The Customs Union Issue* (London: Stevens & Sons Limited, 1950), Chap. IV.
58 Twelfth ARPTAP 1967, 31.
59 GATT. *Generalized System of Preferences. Decision of 25 June 1971*. L/3545, 28 June 1971.
60 Ibid., p. 32.
61 Economic and Social Committee of the European Communities. *Avis du Comité économique et sociale sur la 'communication de la Commission au Conseil relative à*

l'élaboration d'une conception globale en vue des prochaines négociations multilatérales', 24 May 1973.

62 Giuseppe La Barca, *International Trade in the 1970s. The US, the EC and the Growing Pressure of Protectionism* (London: Bloomsbury, 2013), Table 5.

63 Robert Brenner, *The Economics of Global Turbulence. The Advanced Capitalist Economies from Long Boom to Long Downturn, 1945–2005* (London, New York: Verso, 2006), 112.

64 John H. Dunning, 'United States Foreign Investments and the Technological Gap', in Charles P. Kindleberger and Andrew Shonfield (eds), *North America and Western European Economic Policies. Proceedings of a Conference Held By the International Economic Association* (London: Macmillan and Co. Ltd, 1971), 398.

65 John Dunning, *International Production and the Multinational Enterprise* (London: George Allen and Unwin, 1981), Chap. 2.

66 PPPUS – John F. Kennedy, 1962. *Message to the Congress Presenting the President's First Economic Report*, 22 January 1962.

67 Bela Balassa, *Trade Liberalization among Industrial Countries. Objectives and Alternatives* (New York: McGraw-Hill Book Company, 1967), 125.

68 Ibid., 128.

69 Jean-Jacques Servan-Schreiber, *The American Challenge* (London: Hamish Hamilton, 1968), Chapter I–VI.

70 Robert Gilpin, *U.S. Power and the Multinational Corporation* (New York: Basic Books Publisher, 1971), 176 et seq.

Chapter 2

1 Jeffrey A. Frankel et al., 'International Capital Flows and Domestic Economic Policies' in Martin Feldstein (ed.), *The United States in the World Economy* (Chicago, London: The University of Chicago Press, 1988), 566.

2 Barry Eichengreen, 'U.S. Foreign Financial Relations in the Twentieth Century', in Stanley L. Engerman and Robert E. Gallman (eds), *The Cambridge Economic History of the United States,* 494.

3 Jeffrey A. Frankel et al., 'International Capital', 566.

4 See Giuseppe La Barca, *International Trade in the 1970s. The US, the EC and the Growing Pressure of Protectionism* (London, New York: Bloomsbury, 2013), 180, Table 2.

5 Robert Brenner, *The Economics of Global Turbulence,* 112.

6 PPPUS – Lyndon B. Johnson, 1968. *Statement by the President Outlining a Program of Action to Deal With the Balance of Payments Problem,* 1 January 1968.

7 Robert Solomon, *The International Monetary System, 1945–1981* (New York: Harper & Row Publishers, 1982), 105.

8 As regards Germany the trend is illustrated in Herbert Giersch et al., *The Fading Miracle. Four decades of market economy in Germany* (Cambridge: Cambridge University Press, 1990), 237, Table 28.

9 Eric Owen Smith, *The German Economy* (London, New York: Routledge, 1994), 503; Hans-Joachim Braun, *The German Economy in the Twentieth Century. The German Reich and the Federal Republic* (London/New York: Routledge, 1990), 238.

10 Klaus Hinrich Hennings, 'West Germany', in Andrea Boltho (ed.), *The European Economy: Growth and Crisis* (Oxford: Oxford University Press, 1982), 487.

11 Ibid., 489.
12 Samuel Rosenberg, *American Economic Development since 1945: Growth, Decline and Rejuvenation* (Houndmills: Palgrave Macmillan, 2003), 170.
13 Charles A. Coombs, *The Arena of International Finance* (New York: John Wiley & Sons, 1976), 189.
14 PPPUS – Richard Nixon, 1971. *Address to the Nation Outlining a New Economic Policy: 'The Challenge of Peace'*, 15 August 1971.
15 Economic Report of the President (hereinafter ERP). Transmitted to the Congress January 1972, 67.
16 PPPUS – Richard Nixon, 1971. *Address to the Nation.*
17 Charles A. Coombs, *The Arena,* 196.
18 Supplement 6/71 Annex to Bull. EC 9/10-1971. *Consequence for the Community of the present situation in the monetary and commercial field* (15 September 1971).
19 BISD, 18th Suppl. *Report of the Working Party on the United States Temporary Import Surcharge* (L3573).
20 *Paper Agreed by President Nixon and President Pompidou, in Angra (Azores)*, Undated. FRUS 1969–1976 Vol. III, International Monetary Policy, 1968–1972, Doc. 220; Henry Kissinger, *White House Years* (Boston: Little Brown and Company, 1979), 961.
21 Ibid.
22 West Germany 13.6 per cent, Japan 16.8 per cent, Belgium and the Netherlands 11.6 per cent, France and the UK 8.6 per cent, Italy and Sweden 7.5 per cent, Switzerland 13.9 per cent, Austria 11.6 per cent, while Canada went on floating.
23 See Federico Caffè, *Lezioni di Politica Economica* (Torino: Boringhieri, 1981), 332.
24 Brian Tew, The *Evolution of the International Monetary System 1945–77,* second edition *(*London: Hutchinson, 1986*)*, 160.
25 John Williamson, *The Failure of the World Monetary Reform* (Sunbury on Thames: Thomas Nelson and Son Ltd., 1977), 77.
26 Ibid., 88.
27 J.H.B. Tew, 'Policies aimed at improving the Balance of Payments', in F.T. Blackaby (ed.), *British Economic Policy 1960–74* (Cambridge: Cambridge University Press, 1978), 315.
28 John Llewellyn et al., 'Competitiveness', in Andrea Boltho (ed.), *The European,* 145.
29 U.S. Code Congressional and Administrative News. 93rd Congress – First Session 1973. Legislative History. *Agriculture and Consumer Protection Act of 1973 (P.L. 93–86). Statement of the Honorable Earl L. Butz, Secretary of Agriculture,* 1801.
30 François Duchêne et al., *New Limits on European Agriculture. Politics and the New Agricultural Policy* (London: Croom Helm Ltd., 1985), 61.
31 See John Charles Nagle, *Agricultural Trade Policies* (Westhead: Saxon House, 1976), 53.
32 U.S. Code Congressional and Administrative News. *Agriculture and Consumer*, 1750–1800.
33 D. Gale Johnson, *World Agriculture in Disarray* (London: Fontana/Collins for The Trade Policy Research Centre, 1973), 40.
34 U.S. Code Congressional and Administrative News. *Agriculture and Consumer*, 1806.
35 ERP Transmitted to the Congress February 1974, 133.
36 See *Memorandum from the President's Deputy Assistant for National Security Affairs (Snowcroft) to Secretary of the Treasury Shultz*. FRUS 1969–1976 Vol. 31, Trade Policy 1973–1976, Doc. 173.
37 See Catherine R. Schenk, 'Foreign Trade and Payments in Western Europe', in Max-Stephan Schulze (ed.), *Western Europe Economic and Social Change since 1945* (London/New York: Longman, 1999), 111.

38 A.D. Morgan, 'Commercial Policy', in I. F.T. Blackaby (ed.), *British Economic Policy*, 555, Table 12.2.
39 Ernest Mandel, *Europe versus America?: Contradiction of Imperialism* (London: N.L.B., 1970), 63.
40 See W.G.C.M. Haack, 'The Economic effects of Britain's entry into the Common Market', *Journal Of Common Market Studies*, 11 (1973), 147 et seq.
41 Stephen George, *An Awkward Partner. Britain in the European Community*, third edition (Oxford: Oxford University Press, 1998), Chapter 2.
42 Bull. EC 3-1974, point 1104.
43 PPPUS – Richard Nixon, 1970. *Letter to Chairman of the House Committee on Ways and Means on United States Trade Policy*, 11 May 1970.
44 Nineteenth ARPTAP 1974, 14.
45 Ibid.
46 *Telegram from Secretary of the Treasury Connally to the White House, Rome November 30, 1971*. FRUS 1969–1976. Vol. III, International Monetary Policy 1969–1972, Doc. 211.
47 See Bull. EC, 1-1972, *Preparation of trade negotiations between the Community and the United States*, 15 et seq.
48 Bull. EC 3-1972, *Commission Memorandum to the Council on the results of the commercial negotiations with the United States*, 4 February 1972.
49 GATT. *Joint European Community-United States Declaration – 11 February 1972*. L/3670, 11 February 1972.
50 Ibid.
51 GATT. *Joint Japan-United States Statement on International Economic Relations – 8 February 1972*. L/3669, 10 February 1972.
52 GATT. *Council 7 March 1972. Minutes of the Meeting*. C/M/76, 22 March 1972.
53 PPPUS – Richard Nixon, 1973. *Special Message to the Congress Proposing Trade Reform Legislation*, 10 April 1973.
54 See Robert A. Pastor, *Congress and The Politics OF U.S. Foreign Economic Policy 1929–1976* (Berkeley: University of California Press, 1980), 142.
55 'House Passes Trade Act; USSR Denied Tariff Concessions', *1973 Congressional Quarterly Almanac*, 833 et seq.
56 Commission of the European Communities. *Development of an overall approach to trade in view of the coming multilateral negotiations in GATT. Memorandum from the Commission to the Council, forwarded on 9 April and amended on 22 May 1973*. COM (73) 556; COM (73) 556/2.
57 Economic and Social Committee of the European Communities, Brussels 21 March 1973. *Exposé de M. Wallenstein, représentant de la Commission*.
58 GATT. Multilateral Trade Negotiations. *Statement by the European Economic Community*. L/3879, 4 July 1973.
59 Council of the European Communities. *Note de Transmission. Projet de rapport du Comité de préparation des négociations commerciales du GATT*. Brussels, 10 August 1973.
60 *Briefing Paper*. FRUS, 1969–1976 Vol.31, Trade Policy, 1973–1976, Doc. 185.
61 Economic and Social Committee of the European Communities. *Annexe au Procès Verbal de la 6ème réunion – Exposé de M. Phan Van Phi, 6 novembre 1973*.
62 GATT. Ministerial Meeting – *Tokyo. Declaration of Ministers approved at Tokyo on 14 September 1973*. Min (73)1, 14 September 1973.

63 Economic and Social Committee of the European Communities. *Annexe au Procès Verbal de la 6ème réunion.*

Chapter 3

1 An outline of the political developments that preceded and accompanied the onset of the oil crisis is provided by Giuseppe La Barca, *International Trade in the 1970s*, Chapter 3. For the reader looking for a more in-depth analysis of events, the bibliography in the book could be of use.
2 Allen J. Matusow, *Nixon's Economy. Booms, Busts, Dollars and Votes* (University Press of Kansas, 1998), Chapter 10; Anthony S. Campagna, *U.S. National Economic Policy, 1917–1985* (New York, London: Praeger, 1987), Chapter 11.
3 Ernest Mandel, *The Second Slump: A Marxist Analysis of Recession in the Seventies* (London: N.L.B., 1978), 22.
4 Derek H. Aldcroft, *The European Economy 1914–2000*, fourth edition (London and New York: Routledge, 2001), 197.
5 W.W. Rostow, *Getting from Here to There* (London: The Macmillan Press Ltd, 1979), 45.
6 Philip Armstrong et al., *Capitalism since World War II. The making and breakup of the great boom* (London: Fontana Paperbacks, 1984), 311.
7 Banca d'Italia, *Abridged Version of the Report for the Year 1974*, 15.
8 ERP Transmitted to Congress February 1975, Chapter 4.
9 Ibid.
10 Twenty-fourth ARPTAP 1979, 159, Table 15 and Table 16.
11 Fiona Venn, *The Oil Crisis* (London, New York: Longman, 2002).123
12 Nineteenth ARPTAP 1974, 4.
13 Albert L. Danielsen, 'Oil Price Regulations and the United States', *Journal of World Trade Law*, 13 (1979), 383.
14 Twenty-fourth ARPTAP 1979, 159, Table 15 and Table 16.
15 Philip Armstrong et al., *Capitalism since World War II*, 319.
16 W.M. Corden et al., 'Economic Issues for the Oil Importing Countries', in T.M. Rybczynski (ed.), *The Economics of the Oil Crisis* (London: The Macmillan Press Ltd, 1976), 26.
17 A.P. Thirlwall, 'The Balance of Payments Constraint as an Explanation of International Growth Rate Differences', *Banca Nazionale del Lavoro Quarterly Review*, 32 (1979), 46.
18 Simon Bromley, *American Hegemony and World Oil: The Industry, the State System and the World Economy* (Cambridge: Polity Press, 1991), 146, Table 4.1.
19 Allen J. Matusow, *Nixon's Economy*, 284.
20 ERP, Transmitted to Congress February 1974, 49.
21 Allen J. Matusow, *Nixon's Economy*, 239.
22 Anthony S. Campagna, *U.S. National Economic Policy*, 400.
23 N. Piers Ludlow, 'U.S.-West European Relations during the Ford Administration', *Journal of Cold War Studies*, 15 (2013), 154 et seq.
24 Herbert Giersch et al., *The Fading Miracle. Four decades of market economy in Germany* (Cambridge: Cambridge University Press, 1990), 187.
25 See Carluccio Bianchi, 'The Balance of Payments Constraint and the Growth of the Italian Economy', in Carluccio Bianchi and Carlo Casanova (eds), *The Recent Performance of the Italian Economy. Market Outcomes and State Policy* (Milan: Franco Angeli, 1991), 28 et seq.

26 Alec Cairncross, The *British Economy since 1945: Economic Policy and Performance, 1945–1995*, second edition (Oxford: Blackwell Publishers, 1995), 222.
27 See Pierre Secret, 'L'Activité Économique Française en 1974', *Révue d'Économie Politique*, 85 (1975), 1037 et seq.
28 Jean-François Eck, *Histoire de l'économie française depuis 1945* (Paris: Armand Colin Éditeur, 1990), 45.
29 Ibid., 46; Alain Gélédan, 'Crise et politique de sortie de crise', in *L'Économie Française. Mutation 1975–1990* (Paris: Le Monde - Sirey, 1989), 118 et seq.
30 Bull. EC 4-1978, point 1.3.2.
31 Peter H. Lindert, 'U.S. Foreign Trade and Trade Policy', 444.
32 Bull. EC, Supplement 7/1977, 5
33 Ibid., 6.
34 Bull. EC, Supplement 7/1979, 9.
35 Ibid., 11.
36 Walter Adams et al., 'The Steel Industry', in Walter Adams (ed.), *The Structure of American Industry*, sixth edition (New York: Macmillan Publishing Co. Inc., 1982), 74 - Table 1.
37 Ibid.
38 David G. Tarr, 'The Steel Crisis in the United States and the European Community: Causes and Adjustments', in Robert Baldwin, Carl B. Hamilton and André Sapir (eds), *Issues in US-EC Relations* (Chicago, London: The University of Chicago Press, 1988), 174, Table 7.1.
39 Twenty-second ARPTAP 1977, 74.
40 Bull. EC 11-1977, point 1.3.2.
41 Bull. EC 12-1977, point 1.1.2.
42 Commission of the European Communities, État d'Avancement des Travaux Concernant les Objectifs Généraux Acier et la Restructuration de la Sidérurgie Communautaire. Eléments d'Information pour la Préparation du Conseil du 27 Juin 1978. Com. (78) 290 final, 21 June 1978.
43 Bull. EC 12-1977, point 2.2.46.
44 Twenty-third ARPTAP 1978, 103.
45 Joseph Pelzman, 'The Multifiber Arrangement', 115.
46 Bull. EC 7/8-1977, points 1.5.1. et seq.
47 Ibid.
48 Bull. EC, Supplement 11/75, 15
49 Ibid, 20, Table 9.
50 D. Gale Johnson, 'The Food and Agriculture Act of 1977: Implications for Farmers, Consumers, and Taxpayers', in William Fellner (Project Director), *Contemporary Economic Problems, 1978* (Washington, DC: American Enterprise Institute for Public Policy Research, 1978), 206.
51 François Houllier, 'L'Agriculture et son Évolution depuis 1960 (La Situation en 1977)', *Revue d'Économie Politique*, 88 (1978), 894 et seq.
52 See John Jackson et al., *Legal Problems of International Economic Relations. Cases Material and Text* (St. Paul, MN: West Group, 1995), Chapter 13.
53 Twenty-third ARPTAP, 68 et seq.
54 See Enzo Grilli, *Italian Commercial Policies in the 1970* (World Bank Staff Working Paper, n. 428, October 1980), 28, Table IV.1.
55 Ibid.

56 Patrick A. Messerlin, 'Trade Policies in France' in Dominick Salvatore (ed.), *National Trade Policies. Handbook of Comparative Economic Policies, Vol. 2* (New York, London: Greenwood Press, 1992), 161.
57 J.M. Finger et al., 'The Political Economy of Administered Protection', *The American Economic Review*, 72 (1982), 455.
58 Takatoshi Ito, *The Japanese Economy* (Cambridge, MA: The MIT Press, 1992), 236.
59 Ivo Van Bael, 'Ten Years of EEC Anti-Dumping Enforcement', *Journal of World Trade Law*, 13 (1979), 408.
60 Twenty-second ARPTAP, 30.
61 Data provided by Joseph M. Grieco, *Cooperation among Nations. Europe, America, and Non-Tariff Barriers to Trade* (Ithaca/London: Cornell University Press), 178, Table 7.5.
62 Ibid.
63 Herbert Giersch et al., *The Fading Miracle*, 217; also Eric Owen Smith, *The West German Economy* (London, Canberra: Croom Helm, 1983), 93 et seq.
64 H.H. Glismann et al., *The Political Economy of Protection in Germany* (World Bank Staff Working Paper n. 427, 1980), 22.
65 Bela Balassa, 'The New Protectionism and the International Economy', *Journal of World Trade Law*, 12 (1978), 419.

Chapter 4

1 Gilbert Winham, *International Trade and the Tokyo Round Negotiations* (Princeton: Princeton University Press, 1986), 133.
2 See I.M. Destler, *American Trade Policy* (Washington, DC, New York: Institute of International Economics and the Twentieth Century Fund, 1995), 142–5.
3 U.S. Code Congressional and Administrative News. 93rd Congress-Second Session, 1974. Legislative History. *Trade Act of 1974 (P.L. 93-618). Senate Report n. 93-1298*, 7197.
4 Ibid., 7228.
5 Ibid., 7227.
6 The International Trade Commission (formerly Tariff Commission) is the US agency especially charged with establishing the impact of imports on the domestic industry.
7 U.S. Code Congressional and Administrative News. *Trade Act*, 7306 et seq.
8 U.S. Code Congressional and Administrative News. *Trade Act*, 7318 et seq.
9 Gilbert Winham, *International Trade*, 101.
10 Council of the European Communities. *Directives for the GATT multilateral trade negotiations (final version)*. Brussels, 24 April 1975, I/40/1/75 (Cos 4) rev. 1.
11 GATT. Multilateral Trade Negotiations – Group 'Tarif'- *Statement made by the United States Delegation at the Group 'Tariffs' Meeting, March 1976*. MTN/TAR/W/15, 23 March 1976.
12 GATT. Multilateral Trade Negotiations – Group 'Tariff' – *Statement made by the Delegation of the Commission of the European Communities at the Group 'Tariffs' Meeting, March 1976*. MTN/TAR/W/20, 26 March 1976.
13 Ibid., 4.
14 GATT. Multilateral Trade Negotiations – Group 'Tariff' – *Tariff Cutting Formula, Proposal by Switzerland*. MTN/TAR/W/34, 12 October 1976.
15 Saul L. Sherman, 'Reflections on the New Customs Valuation Code', *Law and Policy in International Business*, 12 (1980), 121

16 GATT. *United States Statement at Meeting of Group 3 (e), 2 April 1974.* MTN 3E/W/12, 2 April 1974.
17 Commission of the European Communities, EC Directorate General For External Relations. Brussels 3 January 1974. *Note for Information: Meeting of Special Committee (Art. 113) on Friday 21 December 1973.*
18 Twentieth ARPTAP 1975, 18.
19 See T.E Josling, *Agriculture in the Tokyo Round Negotiations* (London: Trade Policy and Research Centre, 1977), 17.
20 Bob Bergland, 'Preface – Agriculture', *Law and Policy in International Business*, 12 (1980), 257.
21 FAO Trade Yearbook Vol. 30, 1976: Table 5; FAO Trade Yearbook Vol. 35, 1981: Table 6.
22 James P. Houck, 'U.S. Agricultural Trade and the Tokyo Round', *Law and Policy in International Business*, 12 (1980), 266, 268.
23 GATT. Multilateral Trade Negotiations – Group 'Agriculture' – *Meeting of July 1977. Chairman's Summing up and Record of Decisions.* MTN/AG/7, 28 July 1977.
24 Timothy E. Josling et al., *Agriculture in the GATT* (Basingstoke: Macmillan, 1996), 90.
25 Ibid.; also Theodore Cohn, 'The 1978–9 negotiations for an international wheat agreement: an opportunity lost?', *International Journal*, 35 (1979–80), 136; Twenty-third ARPTAP 1978, 57.
26 Theodore Cohn, 'The 1978–79 Negotiations', 136.
27 GATT. Multilateral Trade Negotiations – Group 'Non-Tariff Measures' – Sub-Group 'Customs Matters' – *Value of Goods for the Purposes of Levying ad Valorem Duties on Customs GATT – MTN – Draft Valuation Code.* MTN/NTM/W/122, 8 November 1977; GATT. Multilateral Trade Negotiations – Group 'Non-Tariff Measures' – Sub-Group 'Customs Matters' – *Statement Made by the Commission of the European Communities at the Meeting of the Sub-Group of 15 November 1977.* MTN/NTM/W/126, 21 November 1977.
28 GATT. Multilateral Trade Negotiations Group 'Non-Tariff Measures' – Sub-Group 'Customs Matters'. *Meeting of November 1977. Summing-up by the Chairman.* MTN/NTM/38, 18 November 1977.
29 Gilbert R. Winham, *International Trade,* 189.
30 Ibid.
31 Morton Pomeranz, 'Toward a New International Order in Government Procurement', *Law and Policy in International Business,* 11 (1979), 1278.
32 Ibid., 1277.
33 Ibid.
34 GATT. Multilateral Trade Negotiations – Group 'Non-Tariff Measures' – Subgroup 'Government Procurement'. – *Government Procurement Draft Integrated Text.* MTN/NTM/W/174, 17 July 1978.
35 GATT. Multilateral Trade Negotiations – *Subsidies/Countervailing Duties – Outline of an Approach.* MTN/INF/13, 23 December 1977.
36 Richard R. Rivers et al., 'The Negotiation of a Code on Subsidies and Countervailing Measures: Bridging Fundamental Policy Differences', *Law and Policy in International Business,* 11 (1979), 1471 et seq.
37 GATT. Multilateral Trade Negotiations – Group 'Non-Tariff Measures' – Subgroup 'Subsidies and Countervailing Duties' – *Subsidies/Countervailing Duties Outline of an Arrangement.* MTN/NTM/W/168, 10 July 1978.

38 GATT. Multilateral Trade Negotiations – *Statement by several delegations on Current Status of Tokyo Round Negotiations – Geneva 13 July 1978*. MTN/INF/33, 14 July 1978.
39 Bull. EC 9-1978, point 2.2.11.
40 Bull. EC 10-1978, point 2.2.10.
41 Commission of the European Communities. *Multilateral Trade Negotiations. Communication from the Commission to the Council.* COM (78) 750 final, 17 December 1978.
42 Commission of the European Communities. *Multilateral Trade Negotiations*. Com (79) 99, 23 February 1979.
43 General Agreement on Tariffs and Trade, *Activities in 1979 and Conclusion of the Tokyo Round of Multilateral Trade Negotiations (1973–79): Tariffs* (Geneva: GATT, 1980).
44 Twenty-fourth ARPTAP 1979, 52.
45 See Angel Viñas et al., 'Trade policy and external relations: new dynamics', in *The European Commission 1973–86. History and Memories of an Institution* (Luxembourg: Publication Office of the European Union, 2014), 417 et seq.
46 Bull. EC 4-1979, point 1.2.7.
47 House of Lords – Select Committee on the European Communities. Session 1979–80, 41st report. *Final Report on the GATT Multilateral Trade Negotiations (The Tokyo Round). Minutes of Evidence Taken Before the European Communities Commission,* 23 May 1979. Submission by the Department of Trade, 12.
48 Bull. EC 11-1979, point 1.3.7.
49 House of Lords – Select Committee, p. X.
50 Twenty-fourth ARPTAP, 42; Bull. EC 4-1979, point 1.2.6.
51 Hugh Corbet, 'Importance of Being Earnest about Further GATT Negotiations', *The World Economy*, 2 (1979), 324.
52 Twenty-fourth ARPTAP, 46.
53 Ibid.
54 For an in-depth analysis of the wine gallon method issue see Gilbert R. Winham, *International Trade*, 280 et seq.
55 General Agreement on Tariffs and Trade, *The Tokyo Round, Report by the Director-General of GATT* (Geneva: GATT, 1979), 129.
56 Bull. EC 4-1979, point 1.2.4.
57 Victoria Curzon Price, 'Surplus Capacity and What the Tokyo Round Failed to Settle', *The World Economy*, 2 (1979), 306.
58 Bull. EC 11-1979, point 1.3.5.
59 Twenty-fourth ARPTAP, 76.
60 Robert S. Strauss, 'Forward', *Law and Policy in International Business,* 11 (1979), 1258.
61 Twenty-fifth ARPTAP 1980–1981. Statement on U.S. Trade Policy, 8.
62 BISD 29th – 32nd Suppl., *Report of the Committee on Anti-Dumping Practices presented to the Contracting Parties.*
63 BISD 29th – 32nd Suppl., *Report of the Committee on Subsidies and Countervailing Measures presented to the Contracting Parties.*
64 Gilbert R. Winham, 'Robert Strauss, the MTN, and the Control of Factions', *Journal of World Trade Law*, 14 (1980), 386.
65 This brief critical outline of the main points of the Trade Agreements Act is based on U.S. Code Congressional and Administrative News. 96th Congress First Session 1979. Legislative History. *Trade Agreements Act of 1979 (P.L. 96-39).*
66 Ibid., 418.

67 Ibid., 471.
68 Hans Mueller et al., 'Perils in the Brussels-Washington Steel Pact of 1982', *The World Economy*, 5 (1982), 264.
69 'Massive Trade Bill Sails Through Congress', *Congressional Quarterly Almanac*, 1979, 287.
70 See, in particular, Steven K. Vogel, *Freer Markets, More Rules: Regulatory Reform in Advanced Industrial Countries* (Ithaca and London: Cornell University Press, 1998), Chapter 10; also Arthe Van Laer, 'The European Community and the Paradoxes of U.S. Economic Diplomacy: The Case of IT and Telecommunication Sectors', in Kiran Klaus Patel et al. (eds), *European Integration and the Atlantic Community in the 1980s* (New York: Cambridge University Press, 2013), 124 et seq.
71 Joseph M. Grieco, *Cooperation among Nations*, 177.

Chapter 5

1 Michel Pébereau, *La Politique Économique de la France. Les Objectifs* (Paris: Armand Colin, 1987), 302 – Table VIII.
2 Anthony S. Campagna, *U.S. National Economic Policy*, 435.
3 Stephen H. Axilrod, *Inside the Fed: Monetary Policy and its Management, Martin through Greenspan to Bernanke* (Cambridge, MA: MIT Press, 2011), 92 et seq.
4 ERP Transmitted to the Congress January 1980, 54; *Federal Reserve Bulletin*, 66 (1980), 40.
5 PPPUS – Jimmy Carter, 1980. *Remarks and a Question-and-Answer Session with Local Residents.* Lansdowne, PA, 2 October 1980.
6 Commission of the European Communities, *European Economy*, *Annual Economic Report, 1980–81* (Luxembourg: Office for Official Publication of the European Communities, 1981), 35.
7 Ibid., 36.
8 Luigi Spaventa, 'The Political Economy of European Monetary Integration', *PSL Quarterly Review*, 66 (2013), 326.
9 Ibid.; Daniel Gros et al., *European Monetary Integration: from the European Monetary System to Economic and Monetary Union,* second edition (London: Longman Ltd, 1998), Chapter 2; Peter Ludlow, *The Making of the European Monetary System: A case study of the politics of the European Community* (London/Boston: Butterworth Scientific, 1982).
10 Éric Brussière et al., 'Economic and monetary affairs: new challenges and ambitions', in *The European Commission 1973–86. History and Memories of an Institution* (Luxembourg: Publication Office of the European Union, 2014), 308.
11 Barry Eichengreen, *The European Economy since 1945: coordinated capitalism and beyond* (Princeton: Princeton University Press, 2007), 284.
12 A description of the mechanism regulating the system is provided by Daniel Gros et al., *European Monetary Integration*, 65 et seq.
13 See Emmanuel Mourlon-Druol, *A Europe Made of Money: The Emergence of the European Monetary System* (Ithaca, London: Cornell University Press, 2012), 258 et seq.
14 Régis Platel, 'L'Environnement International en 1980', *Révue d'Économie Politique*, 91 (1981), 852.
15 Michel Volle, 'Synthèse de l'Évolution de l'Économie Française en 1980 et 1981', *Révue d'Économie Politique*, 91 (1981), 813.

16 N.W.C. Woodward, 'Inflation', in N.F.R. Crafts and N.W.C. Woodward (eds), *The British Economy since 1945* (Oxford: Clarendon Press, 1990), 191 et seq.
17 Margaret Thatcher, *The Downing Street Years 1979–1990* (New York: Harper Perennial, 1995), 33.
18 See J. Foreman-Peck, 'Trade and the Balance of Payments', in N.F.R. Crafts and N.W.C. Woodward (eds), *The British Economy*, 148, Fig. 5.5.
19 Twenty-fifth ARPTAP 1980–1981, 52.
20 Bull. EC, 11-1980, point 1.2.1.
21 Twenty-fifth ARPTAP, Table 5.1.
22 Ibid., Table 5.2.
23 ERP Transmitted to the Congress February 1982, 172.
24 See ARPTAP 1984–85 Twenty-eight issue, 11 et seq.; ERP Transmitted to the Congress January 1987, 99 et seq.
25 ERP Transmitted to the Congress January 1987, 117.
26 See U.S. International Transactions in 1982, *Federal Reserve Bulletin*, April 1983, p. 252 et seq.; U.S. International Transactions in 1985, *Federal Reserve Bulletin*, May 1986, 288 et seq.; Sven W. Arndt, 'The External Effects of U.S. Disinflation', in William Fellner (project dir.), *Essays in Contemporary Economic Problems. Disinflation 1983–1984* (Washington D.C.: American Enterprise Institute for Public Policy Research, 1984), 141 et seq.; Phillip Cagan, 'Financing the Deficit, Interest Rates, and Monetary Policy', in Phillip Cagan (ed.), *Essays in Contemporary Economic Problems, 1985. The Economy in Deficit* (Washington D.C.: American Enterprise Institute for Public Policy Research, 1985), 217 et seq.
27 Herbert Giersch et al., *The Fading Miracle*, 247, Figure 17.
28 Alec Cairncross, *The British Economy*, 265.
29 Pierre-Alain Muet, 'Economic management and the international environment, 1981–1983', in Howard Machin and Vincent Wright (eds), *Economic Policy and Policy Making Under the Mitterrand Presidency* (London: Frances Pinter Publishers, 1985), 71.
30 Catherine Huguel, 'La Balance des Paiements Française. Des comptes extérieurs en net redressement', *Révue d'Économie Politique*, 95 (1985), 655 – Table 9.
31 Derek Aldcroft, *The European Economy*, 216 – Figure 8.1.
32 Catherine Huguel, 'La Balance des Paiements Française. Une contrainte extérieure qui demeure', *Revue d'Économie Politique*, 94 (1984), 674.
33 Barry Eichengreen, *Globalizing Capital. A History of the International Monetary System* (Princeton: Princeton University Press, 1996), 147.
34 See Steven K. Vogel, *Freer Markets, More Rules*, 175.
35 ARPTAP 1984–85 Twenty-eighth issue – Appendix C.
36 See Yōichi Funabashi, *Managing the dollar: from the Plaza to the Louvre* (Washington D.C.: Institute for International Economics, 1988), 238 et seq.
37 Treasury and Federal Reserve Foreign Exchange Operations, *Federal Reserve Bulletin*, July 1987, 553.
38 A long-term comparative analysis of the US fiscal deficit and its causes is provided by Iwan Morgan, *The Age of Deficits: Presidents and Unbalanced Budgets from Jimmy Carter to George W. Bush* (Lawrence: University Press of Kansas, 2009).
39 Peter Dicken, *Global Shift. The Internationalization of Economic Activity*, second edition (London: Paul Chapman Publishing Ltd, 1992), 41 – Table 2.12.
40 ARPTAP 1984–85, Twenty-eighth issue, 44.
41 Houpt Stefan et al., 'Sectoral Developments, 1944–2000', in Stephen Broadberry and Kevin H. O'Rourke (eds), *The Cambridge Economic History of Modern Europe*,

Volume 2: 1870 to the Present (Cambridge and New York: Cambridge University Press, 2010), 343 – Table 13-3, 354

42 ARPTAP 1984–85, 44.

43 Joan Edelman Spero, *The Politics of International Economic Relations,* fourth edition (London: Routledge, 1990), 107.

44 It must be noted that currency movements, with regard in particular to the US dollar, not only might have influenced investment decisions, but might also have affected the consistency of the statistics concerning FDIs, both as flows and stocks.

45 Peter Dicken, *Global Shift*, 396.

46 Twenty-sixth ARPTAP 1981–1982, 40.

47 United Nations Centre on Transnational Corporations, *Transnational Corporations in World Development. Third Survey* (New York: United Nations, 1983), 118.

48 United Nations Centre on Transnational Corporations, *Transnational Corporations in World Development: Trends and Prospects* (New York: United Nations, 1988), 327.

49 Ibid., Table V.1.

50 Ibid.; for the contraction of US investments in the developing countries of the Western Hemisphere see Table 6.

51 Twenty-sixth ARPTAP, 40.

Chapter 6

1 ERP Transmitted to the Congress February 1984, 58.

2 Twenty-sixth ARPTAP 1981–82, Statement of U.S. Trade Policy, 32 et seq.

3 Paul Dymock et al., 'Protectionist Pressure in the U.S. Congress?', *Journal of World Trade Law*, 17 (1983) 506.

4 Thomas O. Bayard et al., *Reciprocity and Retaliation in U.S. Trade Policy* (Washington D.C.: Institute for International Economics, 1994), 19.

5 A.J. Hay et al., 'U.S. Trade Policy and "Reciprocity"', *Journal of World Trade Law*, 16 (1982), 475.

6 PPPUS – Ronald Reagan, 1985, *Remarks at a White House Meeting With Business and Trade Leaders*, 23 November 1985.

7 Bull. EC 4-1985, point 2.3.7.

8 I.M. Destler, *American Trade Policy*, 84 et seq.

9 Bull. EC 2-1982, point 3.4.1. *Memorandum on Strengthening the Instruments of a Common Commercial Policy.*

10 Com (83) 87 final, 28 February 1983.

11 Council Regulation 2641/84 EEC, 17 September 1984, Official Journal of the European Communities (hereinafter OJ), L.252.

12 Bull. EC 11-1981, point 3.5.1.; Europe Documents n. 1274, 16 September 1983; See Joan Pearce and John Sutton, *Protection and Industrial Policy in Europe* (London, Boston: Routledge and Kegan Paul, 1985), chapters 6 and 11.

13 A political scientist has made a comparative assessment of the role played by various actors (big business lobbies; the head of the Commission; and the member states' governments). He convincingly argues that the primary role was played by the member governments which, especially after 1983, shared the idea that the steady recovery of the EC economy should not depend on interventionist initiatives, either at Community or national level, but on its being set free from the host of administrative

and fiscal obstacles that were hindering the potential that the European institution had been created to achieve. Andrew Moravcsik, 'Negotiating the Single European Act: national interest and conventional statecraft in the European Community', *International Organization,* 45 (1991), 19–56. Also N. Piers Ludlow, 'From Deadlock to Dynamism. The European Community in the 1980s', in Desmond Dinan (ed.), *Origins and Evolution of the European Union,* second edition (Oxford: Oxford University Press, 2014), 221 et seq.

14 White Paper from the Commission to the European Council, *Completing the Internal Market,* Com (85) 310, 14 June 1985.

15 An in-depth analysis of the White Paper is provided by Jacques Pelkmans and Peter Robson, 'The Aspiration of the White Paper', *Journal of Common Market Studies,* XXV (1987); also Loukas Tsoukalis, *The New European Economy. The Politics and Economics of Integration* (Oxford: Oxford University Press, 1993), Chapter 5.

16 Ibid., 299.

17 Ksenia Demidova, 'The Deal of the Century: The Reagan Administration and the Soviet Pipeline' in Kiran Klaus Patel and Kenneth Weisbrode (eds), *European Integration,* 62 et seq.

18 Margaret Thatcher, *The Downing Street Years,* 256.

19 GATT. *European Community – Tariff Treatment on Imports of Citrus Products from Certain Countries in the Mediterranean Region. Report of the Panel.* L/5776, 7 February 1985.

20 GATT. *European Community-Subsidies on Export of Pasta Products.* SCM/43, 19 May 1983.

21 Bull. EC 9-1986, point 2.4.8.

22 See Takashi Shiraishi, *Japan's Trade Policies 1945 to the Present Day* (London and Atlantic Highlands, NJ: The Athlone Press, 1989), 203, Table 52.

23 Communication from the Commission to the Council. *Analysis of the Relations between the Community and Japan.* Com (85) 574 final, 15 October 1985.

24 See Robert Brenner, *The Economics of Global Turbulence,* 217.

25 See Robert Solomon, *The Transformation of the World Economy, 1980–93* (New York: St Martin's Press, 1994), 69.

26 Takatoshi Ito, *The Japanese Economy,* 298, Table 10.3.

27 Bull. EC 4-1985, point 2.3.7.

28 Bull. EC 3-1982, point 2.2.35.

Chapter 7

1 ERP Transmitted to the Congress February 1985, 114.

2 J. Michael Finger, 'Trade Policies in the United States', in Dominik Salvatore (ed.), *National Trade Policies. Handbook of Comparative Economic Policies* – Volume 2 (New York, London: Greenwood Press, 1992), 98.

3 Commission of the European Communities, *First Survey on State Aids in the European Community* (Luxembourg: OOPEC, 1989).

4 Commission of the European Communities. *Steel. Request for the Council's assent to the establishment of a system of production quotas for the steel industry.* Com (80) 586 Final, 6 October 1980.

5 OJL 228/14, *Commission Decision n. 2320/81/ECSC of 7 August 1981 establishing Community rules for aids to the steel industry.*

6 *Rules on aid and financial transfer to the Community Steel Industry After 1985*, Com (85) 515 final; Com (85) 509 final.
7 Communication from the Commission to the Council. *Organization of the Steel Market in 1987*. Com (86) 503.
8 Twenty-fifth ARPTAP 1981–82, 67 et seq.
9 Twenty-sixth ARPTAP 1981–82, 114.
10 OJL 307, 1.11.1982.
11 OJL 40, 11.2.1984.
12 Bull. EC 1-1985, point 2.2.13; OJL 9, 10.1.1985.
13 OJL 215, 12.8.1986.
14 OJL 355, 31.12.1985.
15 Bull. EC 12-1985, point 2.1.36.
16 Steve Jefferys, *Management and Managed. Fifty Years of Crisis at Chrysler* (Cambridge: Cambridge University Press, 1986), 206 et seq.
17 Lee Iacocca, *An Autobiography* (New York: Bantam Books, 1984), 239.
18 Twenty-fifth ARPTAP, Table 4.1.
19 Ibid., 50.
20 Ibid.
21 Michael Cusumano, *The Japanese Automobile Industry. Technology and Management at Nissan and Toyota* (Cambridge, MA: Council on East Asian Studies, Harvard University, 1985), Appendix E: Japanese Automobile Exports, 1957–1984.
22 United States International Trade Commission, *A Review of Recent Developments in the U.S. Automobile Industry Including An Assessment of the Japanese Voluntary Restraint Agreements*, USITC Publication 1648, 1985.
23 Steven Berry et al., 'Voluntary Exports Restraints on Automobiles: Evaluating a Trade Policy', *The American Economic Review*, 89 (1999), 41.
24 Peter Dicken, *Global Shift*, 275, Figure 9.5.
25 Bull. EC Supplement 2/1981, *The European automobile industry. Commission statement.*
26 United States International Trade Commission, *A Review of Recent Developments.*
27 Bull. EC 5-1981, point 1.3.5.
28 Bull. EC 4-1981, points 1.2.1 et seq.; Bull. EC 7/8, 1981, points 1.4.1 et seq.
29 GATT, *Protocol Extending the Arrangement Regarding International Trade in Textiles*, L/5276, 23 December 1981.
30 Bull. EC 3-1986 points 2.2.1 et seq.
31 See Laura D'andrea Tyson, *Who's Bashing Whom? Trade Conflict in High Technology Industries* (Washington, DC: Institute for International Economics, 1992), Table 2.3.
32 Data from Michel M. Kostecki, 'Electronics Trade Policies in the 1980s', *Journal of World Trade* (1989), 17–18 – Table 1.
33 Ibid., 19.
34 Marc L. Bush, *Trade Warriors. States, Firms and Strategies in High-Technology Competition* (Cambridge: Cambridge University Press, 1999), 16 et seq.
35 Michel M. Kostecki, 'Electronics Trade Policies', 30.
36 Major detail on the VCRs VER are provided by Brian Hindley, 'EC Imports of VCRs from Japan. A Costly Precedent', *Journal of World Trade Law*, 20 (1986), 171 et seq.
37 See in particular Laura D'andrea Tyson, *Who's Bashing Whom?*, 109 et seq.
38 Masaru Kitamura, 'U.S.-Japan Semiconductor Agreement Revisited', http://kitamuralaw.com/publications/high_tech_trade_policy_1991.pdf

Chapter 8

1 Mark Newman et al., A *Comparison of Agriculture in The United States and the European Community* (New York: United States Department of Agriculture, Economic Research Service, 1987), Table 7.
2 'Agriculture'. *Congressional Quarterly Almanac*, 1980, 270.
3 Robert L. Paarlberg, 'Lesson of the Grain Embargo', *Foreign Affairs*, 59 (1980–1), 161; Twenty-Fifth Annual Report 1980–1981, 15, 116.
4 FAO Trade Yearbook 1982, Vol. 36: Table 6; FAO Trade Yearbook 1987, Vol. 41: Table 6.
5 *Congressional Quarterly Almanac 1981*, 540.
6 Barbara Insel, 'A World Awash in Grain', *Foreign Affairs*, 63 (1985), 898.
7 Alex F. McCalla, 'Impact of Macroeconomic Policies upon Agricultural Trade and International Agricultural Development', *American Journal of Agricultural Economics*, 64 (1982), 866.
8 Dallas S. Batten et al., 'The Recent Decline in Agricultural Exports: Is the Exchange Rate the Culprit?', *Federal Reserve Bank of Saint Louis Review*, 66 (1984) n. 8, 13.
9 See in particular, Bruce L. Gardner, 'International Competition in Agriculture and U.S. Farm Policy – Introduction', in Martin Feldstein (ed.), *The United States in the World Economy*, 443.
10 ERP Transmitted to the Congress, February 1986, 135 et seq.
11 See Gordon C. Rauser, 'The Political Economy of Agriculture in the United States', in Hans J. Michelmann, Jack S. Stabler and Gary Stoney (eds), *The Political Economy of Agricultural Trade and Policy* (Boalden: Westview Press, 1990), 72; Robert Paarlberg, 'The Political Economy of the American Agricultural Policy: Three Approaches', *American Journal of Agricultural Economics*, 71 (1989), 1162.
12 *Congressional Quarterly Almanac*, 1981, 548.
13 *Congressional Quarterly Almanac*, 1983, 387.
14 See on this issue *EuropeAgence Internationale d'Information pour la Presse*, 28 October, 1982, n. 3475.
15 *Congressional Quarterly Almanac*, 1983, 375.
16 Ibid., 381
17 Robert Paarlberg, 'The Political Economy', 1162.
18 U.S. Code Congressional and Administrative Service, 88th Congress – Legislative History. *Food Security Act (P.L. 99–198) Statement by John R. Block Secretary of Agriculture Before the Committee on Agriculture U.S. House of Representatives.*
19 Ibid.
20 See Bruce L. Gardner, 'Farm Policy and the Farm Problem', in Philip Cagan (ed.), *Essays in Contemporary*, 245.
21 Communication from the Commission to the Council. *Reflections on the Common Agricultural Policy*, Com. (80) 800 final, 5 December 1980; *Commission Report on the Mandate of 30 May 1980*. Com. (81) 300, 24 June 1981; *Guidelines for European Agriculture. Memorandum to complement the Commission's Report on the Mandate on 30 March 1980*, Com (81) 608 final, 23 October 1981.
22 Com. (80) 800 final, para 26.
23 Nominally: a) limiting the increase in the target or intervention price if production exceeded a certain amount; b) reducing the amount of aid available under the CAP if production exceeded the threshold; c) imposing an overall limit on the amount of aid payable in connection with the market organisation; d) imposing a contribution, by

means of a levy, to the cost of disposing of any additional production; e) setting a production ceiling, i.e. a quota, on each member state or undertaking.

24 Draft minutes of the 701st meeting of the Council of Ministers, 30 March–1 April 1981.

25 The Agricultural Situation in the Community, 1982 Report, 68; Bull. EC 7-1982, point. 2.1.91.

26 Bull. EC, 4-1982, point 2.1.51.

27 Daniel Strasser, 'Le Financement de la Politique de Guarantie des Marchés Agricoles', in Jean Raux (ed.), *Politique Agricole Commune et Construction Communautaire* (Paris: Economica, 1984), 36, table 8; The decision of 21 April 1970 on the establishment of the European Community's own resources replaced financial contribution from member states with autonomous EC fiscal revenues, i.e. agricultural levies, customs duties and the equivalent of 1 per cent of the VAT calculated by member states on a uniform basis in accordance with the Sixth VAT Directive.

28 W. Nicols, 'EEC budgetary strains and constraints', *International Affairs*, 64 (1987/88), 27.

29 Draft minutes of the 771st meeting of the Council of Ministers, 17–18 May 1982. See Martin Vasey, 'Decision Making in the Agriculture Council and the Luxembourg Compromise', *Common Market Law Review*, 25 (1988), 725.

30 Draft Minutes of the 771st meeting of the Council.

31 Bull. EC 6-1983, points. 1.5.1 et seq.

32 Communication from the Commission to the Council; *Common Agricultural Policy – Proposals of the Commission*. Com (83) 500 final. 28 July 1983.

33 See Gisella Hendriks, 'Germany and the CAP: national interests in the European Community', *International Affairs*, 65 (1989), 70.

34 Bull. EC 2-1984, point. 21.96.

35 Draft minutes of the 921st meeting of the Council of Ministers, 26–31 March 1984; The Agricultural Situation in the Community. 1984 Report, 22 et seq.

36 Graham Avery, 'The Common Agricultural Policy: a Turning Point', *Common Market Law Review*, 21 (1984), 493.

37 Draft minutes of the 921st meeting of the Council.

38 The Agricultural Situation in the Community. 1984 Report, 25.

39 Bull. EC 6-1994, points 1.1.1 et seq.

40 See Geoffrey Denton, 'Restructuring of the EEC Budget: Implication of the Fontainebleau Agreement', *Journal of Common Market Studies*, XXIII no. 2 (1984), 132 et seq.

41 Martin Vasey, 'The 1985 Farm Price Negotiations and the Reform of the Common Agricultural Policy' *Common Market Law Review*, 22 (1985), 659; *Europe Agence Internationale d'Information pour la Presse*, 28–29 May 1985, n. 4097.

42 *Europe Agence Internationale d'Information pour la Presse*, n. 4085.

43 Draft minutes of the 1002nd meeting of the Council of Ministers, 13–15 May 1985.

44 Draft minutes of the 1014th meeting of the Council of Ministers, 11–12 June 1985; Gisella Hendriks, 'Germany', 84 et seq.

45 Draft minutes of the 1022nd meeting of the Council of Ministers, 15–16 July 1985.

46 A synthesis of the unpublished panel decision is provided by Robert E. Hudec, *Enforcing International Trade Law. The Evolution of the Modern GATT Legal System* (Salem: Butterworth, 1993), 151 et seq.

47 Ibid., 490.

48 PPPUS – Ronald Reagan, 1983. *Remarks at the Annual Meeting of the American Farm Bureau Federation in Dallas.*
49 Bull. EC 9-1983, point 2.2.19.
50 Bull. EC 9-1983, point. 2.2.19.
51 Bull. EC 10-1983, point 2.2.21.
52 Congressional Quarterly Weekly, 8 June 1985, p. 1103.
53 Ronald T. Libby, *Protecting Markets: U.S. Policy and the World Grain Trade* (Ithaca: Cornell University Press, 1987), 81.
54 Organization for Economic Cooperation and Development, *Agricultural Policies, Markets and Trade. Monitoring and Outlook 1988* (Paris: OECD, 1988), 88.
55 See Nicolas-Jean Brehon, *Le Budget de l'Europe* (Paris: L.G.D.J., 1997), 128.
56 The producer subsidy equivalent (PSE) measures the loss of farm income that would result from the removal of a given set of policies (Organisation for Economic Cooperation and Development, *National Policies and Agricultural Trade* (Paris: OECD, 1987), 102). The formula adopted by the OECD to assess PSE is as follows: $PSE = Q(Pd - Pw) + D - L + B$, where Q is the level of production, PD is the domestic price, PW is the world price, D are direct payments, L are levies collected from producers and D summarizes all other forms of support and % PSE =100(PSE/QPd) + D – L.
57 Organisation for Economic Cooperation and Development, *Agricultural Policies, Markets and Trade. Monitoring and Outlook 1988* (Paris: OECD, 1988), 48, Table III.2.
58 Ibid., Table III.3.

Chapter 9

1 GATT. *Fifteenth Meeting of the Consultative Group of Eighteen*. 1291, 26 June 1981.
2 GATT. *Consultative Group of Eighteen – Fifteenth Meeting 25–26 June 1981*. CG 18/15, 30 July 1981.
3 Minutes of the 789th Council of Ministers 19–20 July 1982; Minutes of the 807th Council of Ministers 22–23 November 1982; *Europe Agence Internationale d'Information pour la Presse*, n. 3477, n. 3484, n. 3486, n. 3491; *The Economist*, 13 November 1982, 83.
4 GATT. *Preparation for the Ministerial Meeting – Communication from the European Communities (Suggestions for amendments to document C/W/403)*. C/W/404, 19 November 1982.
5 GATT, Contracting Parties – Thirty-Eighth Session – *Ministerial Declaration – Adopted on 29 November 1982*, L 5424, 29 November 1982.
6 Bhagirath L. Das, 'The GATT Ministerial Meeting 1982. An Interpretative Note', *Journal of World Trade Law*, 18 (1984), 6.
7 Ibid., 8
8 Bull. EC 11-1982, point 1.1.1.
9 *The Economist*, 4 December 1982.
10 OECD Ministerial Communiqué (1984). Text reproduced in Appendix G of the Annual Report of the President of the United States on the Trade Agreements Program 1984–85.
11 *GATT Focus*, December 1983, 1.
12 *Trade Policies for a better future: proposals for action/Chairman: Fritz Leutwiler* (Geneva: GATT, 1985).
13 ARPTAP 1984–85, 59 et seq.

14 Bull. EC 3-1985, point 2.2.12; Minutes of the 994th meeting of the Council of Ministers, 17–21 and 28–30 March 1985; *Europe Agence Internationale d'Information pour la Presse,* n. 4052, n. 4053.
15 *Europe Agence Internationale d'Information pour la Presse,* n. 4084.
16 See John Croome, *Reshaping the World Trading System. A History of the Uruguay Round* (Geneva: World Trade Organization, 1995), p. 25.
17 Bull. EC 5-1986, points 2.2.1 et seq.; Bull. EC 6-1986, point 2.22; *Europe Agence Internationale d'Information pour la Presse,* n. 4341.
18 GATT. *Ministerial Declaration on the Uruguay Round.* GATT/1396, 25 September 1986.
19 Charles A. St. Charles, 'Tariff', in Terence P. Stuart (ed.), *The GATT Uruguay Round: A Negotiating History (1986–1992)* (Deventer: Kluwer Law and Taxation, 1993), 399.
20 GATT. Preparatory Committee – Record of Discussions – *Discussions of 4–5 February.* PREP.COM (86)SR/2, 18 March 1986.
21 GATT. Committee on Technical Barriers to Trade. *Proposal by the United States.* TBT/21, 23 September 1985.
22 GATT. Committee on Technical Barriers to Trade – *Statement by the Delegation of the European Economic Community.* TBT/23, 13 November 1985.
23 PREP.COM (86)SR/2, 18 March 1986.
24 Ibid.
25 Ibid.
26 GATT. Preparatory Committee – Record of Discussions – *Discussions of 5–7 May.* PREP.COM (86)SR/6, 16 July 1986.
27 PREP.COM (86)SR/2, 18 March 1986.
28 William A. Fennell, Joseph W. Tyler, 'Trade Related Investment Measures', in Terence P. Stewart (ed.), *The GATT Uruguay Round,* 2036.
29 GATT. Consultative Group of Eighteen. Fourteenth Meeting 25–27 March 1981, *Investment Performance Requirements and Incentives.* CG.18/W/51, 17 March 1981.
30 In particular, GATT. Preparatory Committee. Record of Discussions – *Discussions of 16–17 March.* PREP.COM (86)SR/4, 23 May 1986.
31 Ibid.
32 GATT. Senior Officials' Group. Record of Discussions – *Discussions on 31 October.* SR.SOG/10, 22 November 1985.
33 PREP.COM (86)SR/4, 23 May 1986.
34 GATT. Preparatory Committee. Record of Discussions – *Discussions of 17–20 March.* PREP.COM (86)SR/3, 11 April 1986.
35 GATT. Preparatory Committee. Record of Discussions – *Discussions of 8–31 July.* PREP.COM (86)SR/9, 26 August 1986.
36 Ibid.
37 PREP.COM (86)SR/3, 11 April 1986.
38 GATT. Preparatory Committee. Record of Discussions – *Discussions of 5–7 May.* PREP.COM (86)SR/6 July 1986.
39 Ibid.

Conclusion

1 General Agreement on Tariffs and Trade 1979–80 (Geneva GATT, 1980), 2 –Table 1; General Agreement on Tariffs and Trade 1986–1987 (Geneva: GATT 1987), Table 1.1.

2 Robert O. Keohane, *After Hegemony. Cooperation and Discord in the World Political Economy* (Princeton: Princeton University Press, 1984), Chapters 9 and 11.
3 *Memorandum from Secretary of the Treasury Simon to President Ford, Washington July 26, 1975.* FRUS, 1969–1976, V. XXXI, Economic Summit at Rambouillet, June 1975–January 1976, Doc. 93; *Memorandum of Conversation. Rambouillet, France, November 16, 1975.* FRUS, 1969–1976, V. XXXI, Economic Summit at Rambouillet, June 1975–January 1976, Doc. 123
4 Bull. EC 12-1973, points 1101 et seq., The Copenhagen Summit Conference - Annex to the Summit Conference. Final Communiqué - Energy; Bull. EC 2-1974, points 1204 et seq., The Washington Energy Conference.
5 Barry Eichengreen, *The European Economy*, Chapter 9.
6 ERP Transmitted to the Congress February 1990: Table C-47, Changes in productivity and related data, business sector, 1948–89; Iwan Morgan, *The Age of Deficits*, 119.
7 Gilbert R. Winham, *International Trade*, 386.

Statistical Appendix

Tables

Table 1 US gross national product, with its components, and gross domestic product, 1951–86 (billions of 1982 US dollars)

1	2	2[a]	3	3[a]	4	5	5[a]	5[a]β	6	7	7[a]	8	8[a]	9	10
Year	**GNP**	**% Year change**	**GDP**	**% Year change**	**Personal consump.**	**Gross Private Domestic Invests.**	***Fixed invests. Total***	***Fixed invests. Non residential***	**Govern. Purchases**	**Exports**	**I.N. 1951=100**	**Imports**	**I.N. 1951=100**	**7/2%**	**8/2%**
1951	1328.2		1320.3		748.7	235.2	*204.3*	*131.7*	329.7	72	100	57.4	100	5.4	4.3
1952	1380	3.9	1371.7	3.9	771.4	211.8	*201.8*	*130.6*	389.9	70.1	97.4	63.3	110.3	5.1	4.6
1953	1435.3	4	1427.4	4.1	802.5	216.6	*213.8*	*140.1*	419	66.9	92.9	69.7	121.4	4.7	4.9
1954	1416.2	−1.3	1407.8	−1.4	822.7	212.6	*217.3*	*137.5*	378.4	70	97.2	67.5	117.6	4.9	4.8
1955	1494.9	5.6	1485.5	5.5	873.8	259.8	*243.5*	*151*	361.3	76.9	106.8	76.9	134	5.1	5.1
1956	1525.6	2.1	1515	2	899.8	257.8	*244.9*	*160.4*	363.7	87.9	122.1	83.6	145.6	5.8	5.5
1957	1551.1	1.7	1539.7	1.6	919.7	243.4	*240.4*	*161.1*	381.1	94.9	131.8	87.9	153.1	6.1	5.7
1958	1539.2	−0.8	1529.7	−0.6	932.9	221.4	*224.8*	*143.9*	395.3	82.4	114.4	92.8	161.7	5.4	6
1959	1629.1	5.8	1619.1	5.8	979.4	270.3	*253.8*	*153.6*	397.7	83.7	116.3	101.9	177.5	5.1	6.3
1960	1665.3	2.2	1654.1	2.2	1005.1	260.5	*252.7*	*159.4*	403.7	98.4	136.7	102.4	178.4	5.9	6.1
1961	1708.7	2.6	1696.6	2.6	1025.2	259.1	*251.8*	*158.2*	427.1	100.7	139.9	103.3	180	5.9	6
1962	1799.4	5.3	1785.6	5.2	1069	288.6	*272.4*	*170.2*	449.4	106.9	148.5	114.4	199.3	5.9	6.4
1963	1873.3	4.1	1858.5	4.1	1108.4	307.1	*290.5*	*176.6*	459.8	114.7	159.3	116.6	203.1	6.1	6.2
1964	1973.3	5.3	1957.1	5.3	1170.6	325.9	*310.2*	*194.9*	470.8	128.8	178.9	122.8	213.9	6.5	6.2
1965	2087.6	5.8	2070.6	5.8	1236.4	367	*341.8*	*227.6*	487	132	183.3	134.7	234.7	6.3	6.5
1966	2208.3	5.8	2192.5	5.9	1298.9	380.5	*353.7*	*250.4*	532.6	138.4	192.2	152.1	265	6.3	6.9
1967	2271.4	2.9	2255	2.9	1337.7	374.4	*345.6*	*245*	576.2	143.6	199.4	160.5	279.6	6.3	7.1
1968	2365.6	4.1	2347.9	4.1	1405.9	391.8	*370.7*	*254.5*	597.6	155.7	216.3	185.3	322.8	6.6	7.8
1969	2423.3	2.4	2406.2	2.5	1456.7	410.3	*385.1*	*269.7*	591.2	165	229.2	199.9	348.3	6.8	8.2
1970	2416.2	−0.3	2399.1	−0.3	1492	381.5	*373.3*	*264*	572.6	178.3	247.6	208.3	362.9	7.4	8.6
1971	2484.8	2.8	2464.1	2.7	1538.8	419.3	*399.7*	*258.4*	566.5	179.2	248.9	218.9	381.4	7.2	8.8
1972	2608.5	5	2584.9	4.9	1621.9	465.4	*443.7*	*277*	570.7	195.2	271.1	244.6	426.1	7.5	9.4
1973	2744.1	5.2	2711.8	4.9	1689.6	520.8	*480.8*	*317.3*	565.3	242.3	336.5	273.8	477	8.8	10
1974	2729.3	−0.5	2693.5	−0.7	1674	481.3	*448*	*317.8*	573.2	269.1	373.8	268.4	467.6	9.9	9.8

1975	2695	−1.3	2665.7	−1	1711.9	383.3	*396.1*	*281.2*	580.9	259.7	360.7	240.8	419.5	9.6	8.9
1976	2826.7	4.9	2793.7	4.8	1803.9	453.5	*431.4*	*290.6*	580.3	274.4	381.1	285.4	497.2	9.7	10.1
1977	2958.6	4.7	2921.2	4.6	1883.8	521.3	*492.2*	*324*	589.1	281.6	391.1	317.1	552.4	9.5	10.7
1978	3115.2	5.3	3073	5.2	1961	576.9	*540.2*	*362.1*	604.1	312.6	434.2	339.4	591.3	10	10.9
1979	3192.4	2.5	3136.6	2.1	2004.4	575.2	*560.2*	*389.4*	609.1	356.8	495.6	353.2	615.3	11.2	11.1
1980	3187.1	−0.2	3131.7	−0.2	2000.4	509.3	*516.2*	*379.2*	620.5	388.9	540.1	332	578.4	12.2	10.4
1981	3248.8	1.9	3193.6	2	2024.2	545.5	*521.7*	*395.2*	629.7	392.7	545.4	343.4	598.3	12.1	10.6
1982	3166	−2.5	3114.8	−2.5	2050.7	447.3	*471.8*	*366.7*	641.7	361.9	502.6	335.6	584.7	11.4	10.6
1983	3279.1	3.6	3231.2	3.7	2146	504	*510.4*	*361.2*	649	348.1	483.5	368.1	641.3	10.6	11.2
1984	3501.4	6.8	3457.5	7	2249.3	658.4	*596.1*	*425.2*	677.7	371.8	516.4	455.8	794.1	10.6	13
1985	3607.5	3	3571.5	3.3	2352.6	636.1	*628.7*	*454.1*	726.9	365.3	507.4	473.6	825.1	10.1	13.1
1986	3713.3	2.9	3683.5	3.1	2450.5	654	*640.2*	*443.8*	754.5	377.4	524.2	523.2	911.5	10.2	14.1

Source: Economic Report of the President, February 1988: Table B-2, Table B-9; own calculations.

Table 2 US trade balance, current account balance and capital movements, 1960–86 (millions of US dollars)

Year	Merchandise Trade Balance*			Balance on Goods and Services	Balance on Current Account	Balance on Current Account as % of GDP	US Assets Abroad,net [increase/capital outflow (–)]	Foreign Assets in the US,net [increase/capital inflow (+)]
	Exports	Imports	Net					
1960	19,650	14,758	4,892	5,191	2,824	0.17	–4,099	2,294
1961	20,108	14,537	5,571	6,484	3,822	0.23	–5,538	2,705
1962	20,781	16,260	4,521	6,127	3,387	0.19	–4,174	1,911
1963	22,272	17,048	5,224	7,244	4,414	0.24	–7,270	3,217
1964	25,501	18,700	6,801	9,724	6,823	0.35	–9,560	3,643
1965	26,461	21,510	4,951	8,378	5,432	0.26	–5,716	742
1966	29,310	25,493	3,817	6,095	3,031	0.14	–7,321	3,661
1967	30,666	26,866	3,800	5,838	2,583	0.11	–9,757	7,379
1968	33,626	32,991	635	3,693	611	0.03	–10,977	9,928
1969	36,414	35,807	607	3,524	399	0.02	–11,585	12,702
1970	42,469	39,866	2,603	5,773	2,331	0.10	–9,337	6,359
1971	43,319	45,579	–2,260	2,423	–1,433	–0.06	–12,475	22,970
1972	49,381	55,797	–6,416	1,742	–5,795	–0.22	–14,497	21,461
1973	71,410	70,499	911	11,244	7,140	0.26	–22,874	18,388
1974	98,306	103,811	–5,505	9,392	1,962	0.07	–34,745	34,241
1975	107,088	98,185	8,903	22,984	18,116	0.68	–39,703	15,670
1976	114,745	124,228	–9,483	9,521	4,207	0.15	–51,269	36,518
1977	120,816	151,907	–31,091	–9,488	–14,511	–0.50	–34,785	51,319
1978	142,054	176,001	–33,947	–9,875	–15,427	–0.50	–61,130	64,036
1979	184,473	212,009	–27,536	5,138	–991	–0.03	–64,331	38,752
1980	224,269	249,749	–25,480	9,466	1,873	0.06	–86,118	58,112
1981	237,085	265,063	–27,978	14,344	6,884	0.22	–110,951	83,032
1982	211,198	247,642	–36,444	278	–8,679	–0.28	–121,153	93,746
1983	201,820	268,900	–67,080	–36,766	–46,246	–1.43	–49,777	84,869
1984	219.900	332.422	–85910	–94835	–107013	–3.10	–22.291	102,467
1985	215,935	338,083	–122,148	–101,093	–116,393	–3.26	–31,399	129,872
1986	224,361	368,700	–144,339	–125,694	–141,352	–3.84	–95,982	213,386

* Excluding military.

Source: Economic Report of the President, February 1988: Table B-102; own calculations.

Table 3 US exports and imports by broad end-use class, 1951–86 (millions of US dollars)

Year	Foods, Feeds and Beverages			Industrial Supplies and Materials			Capital Goods, except Automotives			Automotive Vehicles, Parts and Engines			Consumer Goods (nonfood), except Automotives		
	Exports	Imports	Balance	Exports	Imports	Balance	Exports	Imports	Balance	Exports	Imports	Balance	Exports	Imports	Balance
1951	2,433	3,087	−654	6,190	6,952	−762	2,526	170	2,356	1,218	38	1,180	1,111	666	445
1952	2,201	3,156	−955	5,553	6,537	−984	2,812	227	2,585	1,024	56	968	1,015	663	352
1953	1,838	3,282	−1,444	4,826	6,456	−1,630	2,929	224	2,705	998	53	945	1,086	757	329
1954	1,713	3,317	−1,604	5,479	5,764	−285	2,919	220	2,699	1,072	53	1,019	1,097	787	310
1955	2,119	3,108	−989	6,065	6,843	−778	3,071	254	2,817	1,276	85	1,191	1,134	991	143
1956	2,807	3,190	−383	7,383	7,674	−291	3,834	364	3,470	1,395	145	1,250	1,246	1,133	113
1957	2,781	3,306	−525	8,669	7,595	1,074	4,487	400	4,087	1,349	339	1,010	1,336	1,210	126
1958	2,590	3,472	−882	6,436	5,944	492	4,752	460	4,292	1,123	555	568	1,314	1,195	119
1959	2,871	3,445	−574	6,146	8,343	−2,197	4,617	591	4,026	1,187	844	343	1,371	1,632	−261
1960	3,170	3,286	−116	7,924	7,887	37	5,511	562	4,949	1,266	633	633	1,396	1,901	−505
1961	3,418	3,331	87	7,705	7,714	−9	5,910	693	5,217	1,188	383	805	1,441	1,889	−448
1962	3,829	3,573	256	7,132	8,573	−1,441	6,443	758	5,685	1,301	521	780	1,455	2,276	−821
1963	4,282	3,753	529	7,822	8,874	−1,052	6,604	823	5,781	1,468	586	882	1,558	2,389	−831
1964	4,849	3,915	934	9,185	9,563	−378	7,463	1,039	6,424	1,729	767	962	1,751	2,694	−943
1965	4,928	3,946	982	8,917	11,024	−2,107	8,039	1,458	6,581	1,929	939	990	1,799	3,305	−1,506
1966	5,489	4,499	990	9,613	12,162	−2,549	8,892	2,136	6,756	2,354	1,910	444	2,035	3,912	−1,877
1967	4,998	4,586	412	9,971	11,856	−1,885	9,913	2,382	7,531	2,784	2,634	150	2,111	4,213	−2,102
1968	4,813	5,271	−458	11,006	14,159	−3,153	11,072	2,825	8,247	3,453	4,295	−842	2,334	5,330	−2,996
1969	4,687	5,239	−552	11,758	14,163	−2,405	12,322	3,331	8,991	3,888	5,346	−1,458	2,596	6,503	−3,907
1970	5,874	6,147	−273	13,795	15,343	−1,548	14,659	3,978	10,681	3,870	5,515	−1,645	2,798	7,403	−4,605
1971	6,110	6,364	−254	12,703	17,444	−4,741	15,372	4,334	11,038	4,698	7,358	−2,660	2,913	8,388	−5,475
1972	7,504	7,258	246	13,966	20,958	−6,992	16,914	5,919	10,995	5,484	8,685	−3,201	3,583	11,104	−7,521
1973	15,199	9,119	6,080	19,862	28,049	−8,187	21,999	8,263	13,736	6,878	10,257	−3,379	4,800	12,892	−8,092
1974	18,638	10,568	8,070	30,129	54,428	−24,299	30,878	9,819	21,059	8,678	12,028	−3,350	6,399	14,380	−7,981
1975	19,234	9,642	9,592	29,945	51,030	−21,085	36,639	10,166	26,473	8,625	11,693	−3,068	6,560	13,211	−6,651
1976	19,800	11,500	8,300	32,000	63,700	−31,700	39,100	12,300	26,800	12,200	16,800	−4,600	8,000	17,200	−9,200
1977	19,724	13,981	5,700	34,312	79,933	−45,600	39,766	13,985	25,800	13,536	19,359	−5,900	8,931	21,796	−12,900
1978	25,155	15,397	9,800	39,044	83,613	−44,600	46,471	19,705	26,800	15,742	24,993	−9,300	10,466	28,943	−18,500

(Continued)

Table 3 (Continued)

Year	Foods, Feeds and Beverages			Industrial Supplies and Materials			Capital Goods, except Automotives			Automotive Vehicles, Parts and Engines			Consumer Goods (nonfood), except Automotives		
	Exports	Imports	Balance	Exports	Imports	Balance	Exports	Imports	Balance	Exports	Imports	Balance	Exports	Imports	Balance
1979	30,005	17,366	12,600	58,139	108,976	−50,900	58,843	25,029	33,800	18,402	26,433	−8,000	12,845	30,566	−17,800
1980	35,721	18,127	35,600	71,947	133,290	−61,400	74,210	31,161	43,000	17,540	27,903	−10,400	16,633	34,445	−17,800
1981	38,163	18,113	20,050	69,949	135,222	−65,273	81,613	36,679	44,934	19,791	30,895	−11,104	16,386	38,664	−22,278
1982	31,629	17,108	14,521	63,620	113,311	−49,691	73,675	38,338	35,337	17,393	34,083	−16,690	14,723	39,660	−24,937
1983	31,598	18,485	13,113	58,446	109,706	−51,260	68,887	43,064	25,623	18,657	43,501	−24,844	14,039	46,969	−32,930
1984	31,625	21,303	10,322	63,362	123,885	−60,523	74,115	61,061	13,054	22,508	56,577	−34,069	13,751	61,262	−47,511
1985	23,989	21,308	2,681	60,430	112,958	−52,528	76,411	63,962	12,449	25,026	65,022	−39,996	12,979	65,148	−52,169
1986	22,580	23,987	−1,407	64,021	102,776	−38,755	79,824	75,446	4,378	25,431	78,084	−52,653	14,490	77,802	−63,312

Source: Historical Statistics of the United States Colonial Times to 1970 – Part 2: Series U 249–263; Statistical Abstract of the United States: Exports and Imports – Value, by Broad End-Use Class, various issues; own calculations.

Table 4 US domestic exports and imports of selected commodity groups, 1956–86. Trade balance in millions of US dollars and index numbers (1956 base)

	Mineral Fuels and Related Materials			Textile and Clothing			Iron and Steelmill products			Chemicals and Related Products			Transport Equipment including Aircraft			Telecommunication Apparatus			Other Machinery and Apparatus		
Year	Bal.	Ex. I.N.	Im. I.N.	Bal.	Ex. I.N.	Im. I.N.	Bal.	Ex. I.N.	Im. I.N.	Bal.	Ex. I.N.	Im. I.N.	Bal.	Ex. I.N.	Im. I.N.	Bal.	Ex. I.N.	Im. I.N.	Bal.	Ex. I.N.	Im. I.N.
1956–60	−318	81.7	118	−101	102	116.2	410	86.9	165.9	758	113.4	136.8	1069.6	94.9	225.3	84	88.4	305	3171	107.5	132.1
1961	−927	51.7	130.9	−217	107.6	142.2	120	58.7	204.1	1055	135.4	135.3	1078	93	209.9	−7	92.7	795	3709	127.8	173.7
1962	−1026	54.1	141.4	−436	107.6	181.3	0	57.4	268.8	1078	139.6	141.4	1000	96.8	263.4	−38	106.1	1060	3960	138.4	204.2
1963	−947	64	146.6	−490	108	191.1	−88	64.4	353.5	1273	149.9	130.5	1028	100.5	276.9	−23	114.6	1055	4100	145.1	228
1964	−1085	61.7	154.6	−449	126.8	202	−64	81.7	420	1651	178.6	130.7	1121	114	330.4	8	141.4	1120	4685	169.9	299.2
1965	−1274	64.1	172	−670	124	238.6	−533	76.3	670.6	1635	182	142	2056	180.5	420.5	31	210.4	1570	5104	194.2	411.6
1966	−1286	66.1	175.2	−799	132.7	269.9	−646	67.5	695.9	1720	202.6	176.5	1343	195.9	782	−105	232.3	2430	5094	215	610
1967	−1144	74.7	174.1	−762	128.5	259.3	−750	67.7	758.2	1844	212.3	177.1	1599	236.8	954.2	−59	290.9	2680	5240	230	710
1968	−1477	71.1	195.7	−1119	129	323	−1379	73.2	1154.1	2158	249	208.7	1388	315.7	1544	−202	326.2	3685	5274	244.9	840.7
1969	−1664	76.5	216.4	−1339	145.1	377.9	−783	118.2	1014.1	2155	256.3	227	1074	353	1901.8	−388	376.8	5030	5954	280.6	987.5
1970	−1480	108	238.2	−1603	148.1	427.8	−764	149.2	1148.2	2376	289.8	268	399	349.1	2123.8	−442	402.4	5510	6753	324.9	1183.4
1971	−2218	101.4	287.8	−2580	154	518.3	−1855	95.5	1538.2	2225	290.7	298	−227	429.2	2873.6	−640	414	6595	6428	329.1	1313
1972	−3247	105.1	371.7	−2391	188.3	606.8	−1943	100.5	1613.5	2118	313.1	372.5	−1553	447.9	3481.3	−836	509.8	8360	6482	375.1	1729.6
1973	−6503	113.1	633.2	−2245	277.8	666.9	−1517	158	1632.3	3286	435.5	455.3	−645	579.2	4002.2	−1030	634.1	10350	8468	487.7	2238.2
1974	−22010	233.2	1971.7	−1751	405.7	702.1	−2256	314.1	2797.6	4801	668.1	742.7	1620	781.5	4487.6	−920	829.9	11405	13429	676.6	2639.3
1975	−22006	302.6	2050.8	−1754	374.7	672.8	−1655	299.2	2374.7	4995	658.4	683.2	4965	926.9	4207.7	−503	959.8	10385	17569	814.7	2740.4
1976	−29770	299.7	2633.3	−2788	458.6	937.5	−1976	230.3	2240.6	5187	754.5	882.1	3010	979.6	5266.7	−1658	1217.8	18275	18325	887.6	3266.2
1977	−40353	283.3	3449.8	−3258	476.5	1038.4	−3694	202	3118.8	5842	819.1	918.7	48	992.6	6436.3	−2594	1439	24770	16387	892.1	3845.4
1978	−38215	262.8	3260.7	−4955	536.4	1398	−5035	206.8	3930	6193	956.3	1188.5	−1675	1192.3	8364.8	−3447	1639.6	30680	16800	1043.8	5156.8
1979	−54445	380.2	4652.3	−3972	761.6	1439.9	−4537	279.8	3978.8	9821	1311.1	1383.6	−571	1384.6	9211.7	−3218	1803	30875	23302	1345.6	6192.5
1980	−74942	540.4	6423.2	−4114	890	1588.8	−3694	376.6	3936.5	12147	1571.2	1588.3	−894	1541.7	10351.6	−3262	2106	33580	28226	1585.9	7086.4
1981	−71138	695.9	6306.5	−5756	892.2	1883.1	−7546	351.9	6086.5	11741	1605.1	1746	−105	1763.9	11507.3	−5054	2351.2	44550	31268	1785.1	8116.9
1982	−78138	861.8	5066.5	−7257	686.7	1952.3	−7083	263.9	5402.4	10397	1506.8	1754.7	−7195	1502.4	12404	−5187	2356.1	45255	26210	1668.6	8422.7
1983	−48452	643.2	4488.9	−9644	584.8	2279	−4923	177.8	3728.3	8972	1496.3	1992.4	−30654	1537.9	14340.7	−7474	2319.5	56390	15773	1517.1	9890
1984	−51669	630.4	4723,5	−14870	583.7	3207.8	−8960	156.8	6004.7	8639	1692.1	2531.8	−22293	1712.3	18609	−11991	2404.3	79670	5065	1695.3	14530.7
1985	−43946	675.1	4176.4	−16729	576.7	3531.8	−9114	144.7	6038.8	7226	1648.4	2686.3	−28259	2024.4	22697.8	−14492	2540.9	93295	−235	1662.3	15689.7
1986	−29196	549.4	2890	−19607	637.5	4261.9	−7148	128.1	4804.7	7765	1724.7	2772.8	−39987	2043.6	27111	−16313	2687.2	103600	−9972	1662.3	18512.2

Source: Statistical Abstract of the United States: Domestic Exports, By Selected Commodity Groups, various issues; General Imports, By Selected Commodity Groups, various issues; own calculations.

Table 5 US exports and imports of merchandise by areas of destinations and origins, 1960–85. Balance (millions of US dollars); percentage share of exports (% E); percentage share of imports (% I)

Year	Americas						Europe									Asia									Austr. and Oc.			Africa		
	Canada			Other Western Emisph. Countries			EC			Other Western Europe Countries including EFTA			Communist Areas in Europe			Japan			Middle East Countries			Other Asian Countries including NICS								
	Balance	% E	% I	Balance	% E	% I	Balance	% E	% I	Balance	% E	% I	Balance	% E	% I	Balance	% E	% I	Balance	% E	% I	Balance	% E	% I	Balance	% E	% I	Balance	% E	% I
1960	909	17	20	−89	19	27	1711	19	15	1306	16	13	113	1	1	298	7	8	220	3	2	947	11	9	248	2	2	259	4	4
1961	373	19	22	−4	19	25	1328	19	15	914	14	12	53	1	1	704	9	7	191	3	2	624	10	8	101	2	2	160	4	5
1962	173	20	22	−349	18	24	1263	19	14	591	14	13	47	1	0	71	7	8	271	3	2	822	11	8	38	2	3	228	5	5
1963	289	20	22	−566	16	24	1432	19	15	741	14	13	86	1	0	227	8	9	244	3	2	1113	12	8	21	2	3	211	5	5
1964	506	19	25	15	17	22	1733	19	15	1028	14	12	234	1	1	178	8	9	294	3	2	1136	11	8	298	3	2	302	5	5
1965	811	21	23	−97	16	21	1930	19	16	1139	14	13	3	1	1	−334	8	11	455	3	2	1363	11	8	506	3	2	351	4	4
1966	536	22	24	748	14	19	1379	18	16	748	14	14	11	1	1	−599	8	12	537	3	2	1519	11	8	212	3	2	370	5	4
1967	58	23	27	84	15	17	1190	18	17	862	14	13	18	1	1	−304	9	11	601	3	1	1501	11	8	436	3	2	276	4	4
1968	−867	23	27	210	15	15	190	18	18	612	14	13	19	1	1	−1107	9	12	691	3	1	1083	10	8	332	3	2	148	4	3
1969	−1247	24	28	413	15	14	1207	18	16	1047	14	12	54	1	1	−1398	9	14	931	3	1	453	9	8	170	3	2	346	4	3
1970	−2013	21	28	697	15	15	1814	19	17	1480	14	10	125	1	1	−1223	11	15	998	3	1	631	9	9	318	3	2	467	4	3
1971	−2426	23	28	454	15	13	865	19	16	702	13	11	161	1	0	−3206	9	16	1173	4	1	100	9	9	274	3	2	457	4	3
1972	−2492	25	27	271	15	13	−123	18	16	61	13	12	498	2	1	−4101	10	16	1142	4	1	−861	9	10	−111	2	2	−18	3	3
1973	−2611	21	25	322	14	14	1140	23	22	934	6	5	1275	3	1	−1363	12	14	1444	4	2	181	10	10	182	3	2	−277	3	4
1974	−2350	20	22	−2615	16	18	2863	22	19	2040	7	4	542	1	1	−1777	11	12	431	5	5	−391	10	10	1192	3	1	−2962	4	7
1975	−407	20	23	1041	16	17	6472	22	17	2581	6	4	2056	3	1	−1862	9	12	2862	8	6	−24	10	10	669	2	2	−3350	5	9
1976	−2131	21	22	2579	17	14	8010	23	15	1597	5	4	2773	3	1	−5359	9	13	223	8	7	−4502	9	12	1019	2	1	−7438	4	10
1977	−3811	21	20	−3135	15	14	5248	23	15	1843	6	4	1412	2	1	−8021	9	13	−2811	8	9	−7044	9	12	1149	2	1	−11575	5	12
1978	−5151	20	19	−928	15	13	3574	23	17	−128	5	4	2177	3	1	−11573	9	14	999	9	7	−7660	10	13	1114	2	1	−11011	4	10
1979	−4950	18	18	−2004	16	15	9926	24	16	2735	6	4	3818	3	1	−8667	10	13	−3959	6	7	−5342	11	12	1247	2	1	−18083	3	12
1980	−6064	16	17	1491	18	15	18217	25	15	2693	6	4	2423	2	1	−9924	9	13	−6772	5	8	−3434	12	13	1484	2	1	−25350	4	14
1981	−6850	17	18	3081	18	15	10739	22	16	2783	6	4	2784	2	1	−15789	9	14	−3579	6	7	−8816	12	14	3083	3	1	−15974	5	10
1982	−12757	16	19	−4398	16	16	5423	23	17	2285	6	4	2543	2	1	−12757	8	15	4138	8	5	−7648	13	15	2569	3	1	−7499	5	7
1983	−13886	19	20	−15747	13	16	419	22	17	1677	6	4	1532	1	1	−19289	11	16	6661	7	3	−15023	14	17	1783	2	1	−5657	4	6
1984	−19954	21	20	−18210	14	15	−10384	22	18	−2750	5	4	2034	2	1	−33560	11	18	3071	5	2	−25110	14	17	2187	3	1	−5528	4	4
1985	−21755	22	20	−15440	15	14	−18985	21	19	−4008	5	4	1279	1	1	−46152	11	20	3442	5	2	−28428	13	16	2580	3	1	−4576	3	3

Source: Statistical Abstract of the United States: Exports, Imports and Merchandise Trade Balance, By Continent, Area and Country, various issues; own calculations.

Table 6 US direct investments in foreign countries by areas, 1958–86 (millions of US dollars; index numbers and percentage of total investments)

Year	All Areas		Canada			Latin America and Carib.			Europe			*Eropean Comm.*		Australia, N. Z., S. Africa			Other Africa and Mid. East			Other Asia including Japan.		
	$ Mill	I.N	$ Mill	I.N.	%	$ Mill.	I.N.	%	$ Mill.	I.N.	%	*$ Mill.*	%	$ Mill.	I.N.	%	$ Mill.	I.N.	%	$ Mill.	I.N.	%
1958	27387	100	9470	100	34.6	8447	100	30.8	4573	100	16.7	*1908*	*7*	1107	100	4	1649	100	6	954	100	3.5
1959	29805	108.8	10310	108.9	34.6	8866	105	29.7	5323	116.4	17.9	*2208*	*7.4*	1202	108.6	4	1723	104.5	5.8	1024	107.4	3.4
1960	32778	119.7	11198	118.2	34.2	9271	109.8	28.3	6681	146.1	20.4	*2644*	*8.1*	1280	115.6	3.9	1778	107.8	5.4	1152	120.8	3.5
1961	34664	126.6	11614	122.6	33.5	9209	109	26.6	7713	168.7	22.3	*3087*	*8.9*	1416	127.9	4.1	1856	112.6	5.4	1234	129.3	3.6
1962	37226	135.9	12133	128.1	32.6	9474	112.2	25.4	8930	195.3	24	*3722*	*10*	1628	147.1	4.4	2114	128.2	5.7	1300	136.3	3.5
1963	40686	148.6	13044	137.7	32.1	9891	117.1	24.3	10340	226.1	25.4	*4400*	*10.8*	1871	169	4.6	2292	139	5.7	1515	158.8	3.7
1964	44386	162	13796	145.7	31.1	10205	120.8	23	12109	264.5	27.3	*5426*	*12.2*	2060	186.1	4.6	2550	154.6	5.7	1780	186.6	4
1965	49328	180.1	15223	160.7	30.9	10836	128.3	22	13985	305.8	28.3	*6304*	*12.8*	2342	211.6	4.7	2925	177.4	5.9	2219	232.6	4.5
1966	54777	200	17017	179.7	31.1	11498	136.1	21	16212	354.5	29.6	*7587*	*13.9*	2666	240.8	4.9	3141	190.5	5.7	2228	233.5	4.1
1967	59486	217.2	18097	191.1	30.4	12044	142.6	20.2	17926	392	30.2	*8444*	*14.2*	3186	287.8	5.4	3356	203.5	5.6	2540	266.3	4.3
1968	64983	237.3	19535	206.3	30.1	13101	155.1	20.2	19407	424.4	29.9	*9012*	*13.9*	3508	316.9	5.4	3783	229.4	5.8	2919	306	4.5
1969	71016	259.3	21127	223.1	29.7	13841	163.9	19.4	21650	473.4	30.5	*10255*	*14.4*	3865	349.1	5.4	4032	244.5	5.7	3416	358.1	4.8
1970	75480	275.6	21015	221.9	27.8	12962	153.5	17.2	25255	522.3	33.5	*11516*	*15.3*	4067	367.4	5.4	3948	239.4	5.2	3742	392.2	5
1971	82760	302.2	21818	230.4	26.4	14013	165.9	16.9	28654	626.6	34.6	*13070*	*15.8*	4457	402.6	5.4	4288	260	5.2	4101	429.9	5
1972	89878	328.2	22985	242.7	25.6	14896	176.3	16.6	31696	693.1	35.3	*15339*	*17.1*	5056	456.7	5.6	4161	252.3	4.6	5539	580.6	6.2
1973	101313	369.9	25541	269.7	25.2	16484	195.1	16.3	38255	836.5	37.8	*30919*	*30.5*	5746	519.1	5.7	2602	157.8	2.6	6489	680.2	6.4
1974	110172	402.3	28404	299.9	25.8	19492	230.8	17.7	44782	979.3	40.6	*35453*	*32.2*	6520	589	5.9	−4139	−251	–	7858	823.7	7.1
1975	124050	453	31038	327.8	25	22167	262.4	17.9	49305	1078.2	39.7	*38773*	*31.3*	7013	633.5	5.7	−1626	−98.6	–	9086	952.4	7.3
1976	136809	499.5	33838	357.3	24.7	23934	283.3	17.5	55139	1205.7	40.3	*43215*	*31.6*	7530	680.2	5.5	−526	−31.9	–	9701	1016.9	7.1
1977	145990	533.1	35052	370.1	24	27515	325.7	18.8	62552	1367.8	42.8	*49150*	*33.7*	7923	715.7	5.4	−1216	−3	–	10096	1058.3	6.9
1978	162727	594.2	36396	384.3	22.4	31771	376.1	19.5	70647	1544.9	43.4	*55991*	*34.4*	8781	793.2	5.4	−400	−24.3	–	11620	1216	7.1
1979	186760	681.9	40243	425	21.5	35056	415	19.8	82622	1806.7	44.2	*65681*	*35.2*	9595	866.8	5.1	2029	123	1.1	13648	1430.6	7.3
1980	215375	786.4	45119	476.4	20.9	38761	458.9	18	96287	2105.6	44.7	*77152*	*35.8*	10583	956	4.9	5941	360.3	2.8	14730	1544	6.8
1981	228348	833.8	47073	497.1	20.6	38838	459.8	17	101601	2221.8	44.5	*80743*	*35.4*	12003	1084.2	5.3	2205	133.7	1	17879	1874.1	7.8
1982	207752	758.6	43511	459.5	20.9	26314	311.5	12.7	92449	2021.6	44.5	*71712*	*34.5*	12014	1085.3	5.8	7755	470.3	3.7	18549	1944.3	8.9
1983	207203	756.6	44339	468.2	21.4	24133	285.7	11.6	92176	2015.7	44.5	*70210*	*33.9*	11558	1044.1	5.6	8574	520	4.1	20700	2169.8	10
1984	211480	772.2	46730	493.5	22.1	24626	291.5	11.6	91589	2002.8	43.3	*69501*	*32.9*	10868	981.8	5.1	9481	575	4.5	22981	2408.9	10.9
1985	230250	840.7	46909	495.3	20.4	28261	334.6	12.3	105171	2299.8	45.7	*81378*	*35.3*	10743	970.5	4.7	9103	552	4	24635	2582.3	10.7
1986	259562	947.8	49994	527.2	19.3	34790	411.9	13.4	122165	2671.4	47.1	*98473*	*37.9*	11200	1011.7	4.3	8903	539.9	3.4	27909	2925.5	10.8

Source: Statistical Abstract of the United States: U.S. Investments Abroad – Value and Income Receipts, by Country and by Industry, various issues; U.S. Direct Investment Position Abroad, by Country and by Selected Industries, variousissues; U.S. Investment Position Abroad, by Country, 1980 to 1987; own calculations.

Table 7 Foreign direct investments in the United States by main areas and industries, 1951–86 (millions of US dollars)

Year	All Areas				Canada				Europe				Japan
	Total	Petroleum	Manufact.	Finace and Insurance	Total	Petroleum	Manufact.	Finance and Insurance	Total	Petroleum	Manufact.	Finance and Insurance	Total
1951	3658	466	1274	1105	1109	62	525	150	2410	404	747	912	
1952	3945	552	1377	1170	1218	90	592	149	2575	462	782	977	
1953	4251	706	1451	1219	1350	168	611	162	2751	538	836	1014	
1954	4633	776	1582	1371	1427	192	651	168	3049	584	925	1158	
1955	5076	853	1759	1499	1542	196	711	179	3369	657	1040	1272	
1956	5459	937	1940	1534	1690	200	775	196	3598	737	1155	1289	
1957	5710	1043	2083	1496	1773	211	816	208	3753	832	1248	1238	
1958	6115	1099	2232	1660	1835	214	863	222	4070	885	1332	1384	
1959	6604	1184	2471	1734	1896	207	907	227	4452	972	1501	1451	
1960	6910	1238	2611	1810	1934	203	932	246	4707	1028	1611	1504	
1961	7392	1325	2754	2025	1989	194	975	274	5129	1125	1708	1690	
1962	7612	1419	2885	1943	2064	212	1015	269	5245	1203	1797	1611	
1963	7944	1513	3018	2045	2183	213	1063	337	5491	1306	1881	1640	
1964	8363	1612	3213	2181	2284	205	1129	382	5819	1404	2005	1723	
1965	8797	1710	3478	2169	2388	208	1219	370	6076	1481	2167	1724	
1966	9054	1740	3789	2072	2439	98	1342	386	6273	1620	2335	1611	
1967	9923	1885	4181	2193	2575	99	1397	354	7005	1772	2669	1758	
1968	10815	2261	4475	2305	2659	100	1413	376	7750	2146	2941	1855	
1969	11818	2493	5344	2189	2834	132	1644	325	8510	2322	3530	1766	
1970	13270	2992	6140	2256	3117	190	1836	324	9554	2777	4091	1805	
1971	13914	3139	6722	2553	3335	207	2013	330	10336	2893	4455	2048	
1972	14868	3272	7262	2911	3466	243	2201	353	11087	3012	4836	2336	
1973	20556	4792	8231	3415	4203	426	2319	376	13937	4079	4790	2174	
1974	25144	5614	10387	3530	5136	547	2905	425	16756	4714	6109	1954	
1975	27662	6213	11386	3928	5352	596	3061	451	18584	5478	6673	2218	591
1976	30770	5921	12620	4741	5907	676	3386	541	20162	4999	7426	2815	1178

1977	34595	6573	14030	5398	5650	710	3077	464	23754	5523	9267	3273	1755
1978	42471	7762	17202	6392	6180	734	3213	540	29180	6569	11717	3905	2749
1979	54462	9906	20876	9395	7154	943	3615	839	37403	8010	13952	6080	3493
1980	83046	12200	33993	12027	12162	1817	5227	1612	54688	10137	21953	8673	4723
1981	108714	15246	40533	14748	12116	1801	3376	1806	72377	12854	30897	10084	7697
1982	124677	17660	44065	17933	11708	1550	3500	1801	83193	15071	33032	12601	9677
1983	137061	18209	47665	10934	11434	1391	3313	1061	92936	16326	36866	8450	11336
1984	164583	25400	51802	24881	15286	1544	4115	3245	108211	23142	39083	15945	16044
1985	184615	28270	59584	27429	17131	1589	4607	4008	121413	25636	45841	17022	19313
1986	220414	29094	71963	34978	20318	1432	6108	4283	144181	26139	56016	21787	26824

Source: Historical Statistics of the United States Colonial Times to 1970 – Part 2: Series U 47–74; Statistical Abstract of the United States: Foreign Direct Investment in the U.S. – Value, by Area and Industry, various issues.

Table 8 US federal and total government receipts and expenditures, 1950–86 (billions of US dollars)

Year	Receipts	Expenditures	Surplus or Deficit	Surplus-Deficit as % of GDP	Receipts	Expenditures	Surplus or Deficit	Surplus-Deficit as % of GDP
1950	50.4	41.2	9.2	3.6	69.4	61.4	8	3.1
1951	64.6	58.1	6.5	2.2	85.6	79.5	6.1	2.1
1952	67.7	71.4	−3.7	−1.2	90.5	94.3	−3.8	−1.2
1953	70.4	77.6	−7.1	−2.2	95	102	−7	−2.1
1954	64.2	70.3	−6	−1.8	90.4	97.5	−7.1	−2.2
1955	73.1	68.6	4.4	1.2	101.6	98.5	3.1	0.9
1956	78.5	72.5	6.1	1.6	110.2	105	5.2	1.4
1957	82.5	80.2	2.3	0.6	116.7	115.8	0.9	0.2
1958	79.3	89.6	−10.3	−2.6	115.7	128.3	−12.6	−3.2
1959	90.6	91.7	−1.1	−0.3	130.3	131.9	−1.6	−0.4
1960	96.9	93.9	3	0.7	140.4	137.3	3.1	0.7
1961	99	102.9	−3.9	−0.8	145.9	150.1	−4.3	−0.9
1962	107.2	111.4	−4.2	−0.8	157.9	161.6	−3.8	−0.8
1963	115.6	115.3	0.3	0.1	169.8	169.1	0.7	0.1
1964	116.2	119.5	−3.3	−0.6	175.6	177.8	−2.3	−0.4
1965	125.8	125.3	0.5	0.1	190.2	189.6	0.5	0.1
1966	143.5	145.3	−1.8	−0.3	214.4	215.6	−1.3	−0.2
1967	152.6	165.8	−13.2	−1.9	230.8	245	−14.2	−2
1968	176.9	182.9	−6	−0.8	266.2	272.2	−6	−0.8
1969	199.7	191.3	8.4	1	300.1	290.2	9.3	0.5
1970	195.4	207.8	−12.4	−1.4	306.8	317.4	−10.6	−1.2
1971	202.7	224.8	−22	−2.4	327.3	346.8	−19.5	−2.1
1972	232.2	249	−16.8	−1.6	374	377.3	−3.4	−0.3
1973	263.7	269.3	−5.6	−0.5	419.6	411.7	7.9	0.7
1974	293.9	305.5	−11.6	−0.9	463.1	467.4	−4.3	−0.3
1975	294.9	364.2	−69.4	−5.2	480	544.9	−64.9	−4.8
1976	340.1	393.7	−53.5	−3.6	549.1	587.5	−38.4	−2.6
1977	384.1	430.1	−46	−2.7	616.6	635.7	−19.1	−1.1
1978	441.4	470.7	−29.3	−1.5	694.4	694.8	−0.4	0
1979	505	521.1	−16.1	−0.8	779.8	768.3	11.5	0.5
1980	553.8	615.1	−61.3	−2.7	855.1	889.6	−34.5	−1.5
1981	639.5	703.3	−63.8	−2.5	977.2	1006.9	−29.7	−1.1
1982	635.3	781.2	−145.9	−5.5	1000.8	1111.6	−110.8	−4.2
1983	659.9	835.9	−176	−6.1	1061.3	1189.9	−128.6	−4.5
1984	726	895.6	−169.6	−5.3	1172.9	1277.9	−105	−3.3
1985	788.6	984.6	−196	−5.7	1268.5	1401.4	−132.9	−3.9
1986	827.4	1032	−204.7	−5.7	1339.3	1487.1	−147.8	−4.1

Source: Economic Report of the President, February 1988: Table B-79;Table B-8; own calculations.

Table 9 GDP growth rate in the EC member states, 1961–86

Year	Belgium	Denmark	France	Germany	Greece	Ireland	Italy	Luxem.	Netherl.	Portugal	Spain	UK
1961	5	*6.4*	5.5	4.6	*11.1*	*4.7*	8.2	3.8	3.1	*5.5*	*11.8*	*3.3*
1962	5.2	*5.7*	6.7	4.7	*1.5*	*3.7*	6.2	1.4	4	*6.7*	*9.3*	*1.1*
1963	4.4	*0.6*	5.3	2.8	*10.1*	*4.8*	5.6	3.4	3.6	*5.9*	*8.8*	*4.2*
1964	7	*9.3*	6.5	6.7	*8.3*	*4.2*	2.8	7.9	8.3	*6.6*	*6.2*	*5.1*
1965	3.6	*4.6*	4.8	5.5	*9.4*	*2*	3.3	1.9	5.2	*7.5*	*6.3*	*2.3*
1966	3.2	*2.7*	5.2	2.9	*6.1*	*1*	6	1.1	2.7	*4.1*	*7.1*	*1.9*
1967	3.9	*3.4*	4.7	−0.1	*5.5*	*5.1*	7.2	0.2	5.3	*7.5*	*4.3*	*2.7*
1968	4.2	*4*	4.3	5.6	*6.7*	*8.1*	6.5	4.2	6.4	*8.9*	*6.8*	*4.1*
1969	6.6	*6.3*	7	7.5	*9.9*	*6.1*	6.1	10	6.4	*2.1*	*8.9*	*1.3*
1970	6.4	*2*	5.7	5.1	*8*	*3.5*	5.3	1.7	6.7	*9.1*	*4.1*	*2.3*
1971	3.7	*2.7*	5.4	2.9	*7.1*	*3.4*	1.6	2.9	4.3	*6.6*	*5*	*2.7*
1972	5.3	*5.3*	5.9	4.2	*8.9*	*6.4*	3.2	6.6	3.4	*8*	*8.1*	*2.3*
1973	5.9	3.6	5.4	4.7	*7.3*	4.7	7	8.8	5.7	*11.2*	*7.9*	7.7
1974	4.1	−0.9	3.2	0.3	*−3.6*	4.3	4.1	3.9	3.5	*1.1*	*5.7*	−1
1975	−1.5	−0.7	0.2	−1.6	*6.1*	3.7	−3.6	−5.6	−1	*−4.3*	*1.1*	−0.6
1976	5.2	6.5	5.2	5.4	*6.4*	1.4	5.9	2.3	5.3	*6.9*	*3*	3.8
1977	0.4	1.6	3.1	3	*3.4*	8.2	1.9	1.8	2.4	*5.6*	*3.3*	1.1
1978	3	1.5	3.8	2.9	*6.7*	7.2	2.7	3.8	2.5	*3.4*	*1.8*	3.5
1979	2.1	3.5	3.3	4.2	*3.7*	3.1	4.9	3	2.4	*6.1*	*0.2*	2.2
1980	4.1	−0.4	1.1	1.4	*1.8*	3.1	3.9	1.4	0.9	*4.8*	*1.5*	−2.3
1981	−1.5	−0.9	0.5	0.2	−0.3	3.4	1.1	−1	−0.7	*0.5*	*−0.2*	−1.2
1982	1.9	3	1.8	−0.6	−0.2	1.4	0.2	1.5	−1.4	*3.2*	*1.2*	1
1983	−0.3	2.5	0.7	1.5	0.4	−1.9	0.5	3.2	1.4	*−0.3*	*1.8*	3.8
1984	1.7	3.5	1.5	2.7	2.8	4.2	3.5	5.5	2.4	*−1.6*	*1.9*	2.2
1985	1.5	3.9	1.1	2.6	2.1	2	2.7	2.9	1.7	*3.3*	*2.2*	3.7
1986	2.3	3.4	2	2.6	1.3	−0.3	2.7	2.5	2	4.3	3.5	2.9

Source: Commission of the European Communities. European Economy, Number 34 November 1987: Statistical Annex, Table 8.

Table 10 Current account balance of EC member states as per cent of GDP, 1961–86

Year	Belgium	Denmark	France	Germany	Greece	Ireland	Italy	Luxem.	Netherl.	Portugal	Spain	UK
1961	−0.1	−1.7	1.1	1	−2.2	0.2	1.2	6.5	1.4	−10	1.9	0
1962	0.6	−3.2	1	−0.3	−1.6	−1.8	0.6	0.6	1	−3.4	−0.1	0.4
1963	−0.5	0.1	0.3	0.3	−2.2	−2.8	−1.4	0.2	0.7	−3.3	−1.5	0.3
1964	0.2	−2.2	−0.3	0.1	−4.3	−3.5	1.1	−0.1	−1.1	0	0.1	−1.3
1965	0.6	−1.8	0.8	−1.4	−5.8	−4.4	3.6	0.7	0.1	−0.4	−2.1	−0.4
1966	−0.3	−1.9	0.1	0.1	−2	−1.6	3.2	1.7	−1	0.8	−2.1	0.1
1967	0.8	−2.4	0	2.1	−2.2	1.4	2.2	7.4	−0.3	3.7	−1.5	−0.9
1968	0.9	−1.7	−0.5	2.4	−3.6	−1.3	3.3	9.7	0.3	1.5	−0.8	−0.8
1969	1.2	−2.8	−1.1	1.5	−4	−4.8	2.7	14	0.2	3.6	−1.1	0.6
1970	2.8	−3.9	0.1	0.7	−3.1	−4	1.2	14.4	−1.4	1.9	0.2	1.2
1971	2.1	−2.4	0.6	0.5	−1.5	−3.8	1.8	5.5	−0.3	2.5	2.2	1.7
1972	3.6	−0.4	0.5	0.6	−1.2	−2.2	1.6	9.6	2.8	5.5	1,2	0.1
1973	2	−1.7	−0.2	1.5	−3.8	−3.5	−1.7	15.6	3.8	3	0.6	−2
1974	0.4	−3.1	−2.3	3.2	−2.8	−9.9	−4.6	25.3	3.1	−6.2	−3.5	−4.6
1975	−0.1	−1.5	0	1.4	−3.7	−1.5	−0.2	16.1	2.5	−5.5	−3	−2.1
1976	0.1	−4.9	−1.5	1.5	−1.9	−5.3	1.5	20.7	2.9	−8	−3.5	−1.7
1977	−1.3	−4	−0.7	1	−1.9	−5.4	1.2	21	0.8	−9.4	−1.8	−0.1
1978	−1.4	−2.7	0.6	1.9	−1.3	−6.8	2.4	19.6	−0.9	−5.7	0.9	0.4
1979	−2.7	−4.7	0	−0.5	−1.9	−13.4	1.7	22.4	−1.2	−1.7	0.3	0
1980	−4.5	−3.7	−1.4	−1.3	0.5	−11.8	−2.2	19.9	−1.5	−5.9	−2.4	1.5
1981	−4.6	−3	−1.4	−0.5	−0.7	−14.7	−2.2	23	2.2	−11.8	−2.7	2.3
1982	−3.3	−4.2	−3	0.5	−4.4	−10.6	−1.6	35.2	3.2	−12.7	−2.5	1.2
1983	−0.5	−2.6	−1.7	0.6	−5.1	−7	0.3	38.5	3.1	−6.3	−1.5	0.7
1984	−0.4	−3.5	−0.8	1.1	−4.1	−6.1	−0.6	38.9	4.1	−1.9	1.3	−0.3
1985	0.5	−4.6	−0.8	2.2	−8.3	−3.8	−0.9	42.4	4.3	3	1.7	1
1986	2.4	−5.1	0.6	4.1	−5.4	−1.8	0.8	40.4	2.8	3.9	2	−0.3

Source: Commission of the European Communities: European Economy, Number 34, November 1987: Statistical Annex, Table 34.

Table 11 EC member states' total exports, 1960–86 (million ECU)

	1960	1965	1968	1969	1970	1971	1972	1973	1974	1975	1976	1977	1978	1979	1980	1981	1982	1983	1984	1985	1986
Belgium – Lux.	3775	6382	8164	10065	11609	12184	14404	18203	23703	23193	29340	32892	35203	41033	46459	49881	53551	58460	65956	70649	70168
France	6863	10048	12672	14880	17739	19576	23042	28902	38469	41981	49915	55667	60120	71510	80151	91122	94379	102651	118433	128180	121377
Germany F.R.	11415	17892	24842	29052	34189	39141	41633	54397	74753	72666	91155	103316	111332	125243	138787	157881	180026	190388	218141	241369	247517
Italy	3468	7200	10186	11729	13206	14465	16583	18102	25557	28246	33507	39698	43978	52614	56116	68170	74935	81908	93407	103443	99401
Netherlands	4028	6393	8341	9965	11767	13468	15045	19511	27745	28593	36149	38283	39290	46434	53184	61559	67658	73583	85995	94156	85851
EC - 6	**29549**	**47915**	**64205**	**75691**	**88510**	**98834**	**110707**														
Denmark	*1471*	*2273*	*2584*	*2960*	*3290*	*3412*	*3869*	5063	6464	7024	8139	8816	9224	10767	12195	14526	15843	18278	20651	22811	22126
Ireland	*428*	*618*	*873*	*970*	*1120*	*1257*	*1441*	1727	2226	2585	2992	3852	4460	5222	6101	7006	8238	9701	12254	13621	12803
UK	*10349*	*13722*	*15365*	*17519*	*19258*	*21423*	*21708*	24795	32373	35288	41458	50276	56093	66038	82060	95081	102698	104503	120511	131621	107665
EC - 9								**170700**	**231290**	**239576**	**292655**	**332800**	**359700**	**418861**	**475053**						
Greece	*203*	*328*	*468*	*554*	*643*	*632*	*776*	*1159*	*1702*	*1855*	*2295*	*2411*	*2645*	*2841*	*3728*	3860	4381	5028	6138	5950	5749
EC - 10																**549086**	**601709**	**644500**	**741486**	**811800**	
Portugal	*327*	*576*	*762*	*853*	*950*	*1021*	*1157*	*1500*	*1904*	*1566*	*1639*	*1782*	*1906*	*2626*	*3330*	*3751*	*4253*	*5153*	*6563*	*7460*	7319
Spain	*726*	*966*	*1589*	*1900*	*2387*	*2804*	*3390*	*4190*	*5918*	*6186*	*7792*	*8954*	*10282*	*13276*	*14958*	*18215*	*20691*	*22231*	*28724*	*30675*	26982
EC - 12																					**806958**

Source: Eurostat, EXTERNAL TRADE Statistical Yearbook 1986: Table 8 – World; Eurostat, EXTERNAL TRADE Statistical Yearbook 1988: Table 4 - World.

Table 12 EC member states' total imports, 1960–86 (million ECU)

	1960	1965	1968	1969	1970	1971	1972	1973	1974	1975	1976	1977	1978	1979	1980	1981	1982	1983	1984	1985	1986
Belgium – Lux.	3957	6374	8333	9989	11362	12357	13812	17910	25015	24818	31714	35418	38093	44053	51632	55613	59095	62475	70750	74347	70401
France	6279	10336	13927	17222	18922	20262	23818	30042	44293	43682	57646	61784	64217	77705	97102	108421	117882	118154	131572	141642	130551
Germany F.R.	10103	17472	20150	24926	29184	34431	35827	44106	58046	60442	78912	88803	95398	116310	135243	146855	158445	171851	194029	208334	194368
Italy	4725	7378	10286	12467	14970	15298	17217	22645	34438	31128	39489	42143	44313	56763	71813	82108	87740	90403	107281	119416	101947
Netherlands	4531	7464	9293	10991	13393	14624	15466	19799	27847	28389	35832	39970	41530	49053	55368	59272	63934	69077	81669	90217	81297
EC - 6	**29595**	**49024**	**61989**	**75595**	**87831**	**96972**	**106140**														
Denmark	*1799*	*2811*	*3226*	*3799*	*4388*	*4343*	*4513*	6333	8331	8383	11093	11616	11422	13670	14106	15899	17452	18501	21327	24265	23639
Ireland	*633*	*1041*	*1239*	*1473*	*1624*	*1761*	*1877*	2263	3193	3046	3764	4728	5592	7176	7998	9488	9870	10306	12291	13167	11821
UK	*12714*	*16103*	*18936*	*19936*	*21643*	*22915*	*24848*	31562	45347	42905	50122	55522	61642	74745	85652	95571	105986	114168	134688	143486	127524
EC - 9								**174660**	**246510**	**242793**	**308572**	**339984**	**362207**	**439475**	**518914**						
Greece	*702*	*1134*	*1394*	*1594*	*1958*	*2002*	*2091*	*2787*	*3694*	*4301*	*5426*	*5999*	*6150*	*7028*	*7634*	8017	10189	10863	12259	13361	11550
EC - 10																**581244**	**630593**	**665798**	**765866**	**828235**	
Portugal	*546*	*924*	*1178*	*1296*	*1582*	*1768*	*1991*	*2471*	*3877*	*3158*	*3892*	*4374*	*4120*	*4951*	*6837*	*8892*	*9666*	*9113*	*10030*	*10184*	9608
Spain	*722*	*3003*	*3502*	*4202*	*4714*	*4711*	*6021*	*7742*	*12821*	*12976*	*15462*	*15466*	*14619*	*18510*	*24348*	*28735*	*31929*	*32784*	*33431*	*36257*	33299
EC - 12																					**796005**

Source: Eurostat, EXTERNAL TRADE Statistical Yearbook 1986: Table 8 - World; Eurostat, EXTERNAL TRADE Statistical Yearbook 1988: Table 4 - World.

Table 13 EC member states' exports to the US, 1960–86 (million ECU)

	1960	1965	1968	1969	1970	1971	1972	1973	1974	1975	1976	1977	1978	1979	1980	1981	1982	1983	1984	1985	1986
Belgium – Lux.	366	532	770	695	697	812	879	1021	1328	946	1044	1384	1454	1535	1556	2108	2357	3001	3992	4465	3714
France	396	594	765	815	954	1057	1232	1371	1879	1647	2260	2862	3353	3496	3544	5029	5339	6474	9597	11090	8985
Germany F.R.	897	1436	2707	2727	3124	3780	3857	4605	5614	4311	5110	6872	7857	8268	8509	10333	11835	14467	20926	24957	25943
Italy	385	619	1090	1273	1354	1419	1623	1552	1938	1840	2161	2648	3134	3402	2981	4628	5285	6318	10172	12679	10673
Netherlands	198	244	436	448	506	535	561	693	1096	778	1019	1312	1300	1302	1335	1980	2197	3112	4310	4765	3914
EC – 6	**2242**	**3425**	**5768**	**5958**	**6635**	**7603**	**8152**														
Denmark	*103*	*159*	*216*	*255*	*263*	*270*	*316*	364	378	370	475	511	527	526	569	797	974	1362	2012	2326	1901
Ireland	*31*	*25*	*117*	*136*	*144*	*140*	*136*	169	215	517	208	239	275	255	321	439	588	784	1193	1333	1117
UK	*968*	*1458*	*2185*	*2174*	*2264*	*2556*	*2711*	3026	3464	3152	3961	4671	5244	6262	7750	11519	13946	14442	17578	19602	15463
EC – 9								**12801**	**15912**	**13561**	**16238**	**20499**	**23144**	**25046**	**26565**						
Greece	*27*	*31*	*48*	*54*	*48*	*57*	*76*	*75*	*103*	*94*	*131*	*112*	*116*	*158*	*211*	336	389	316	510	485	408
EC-10																**37169**	**42910**	**50276**	**70290**	**81702**	
Portugal	*37*	*61*	*80*	*80*	*83*	*99*	*124*	*146*	*189*	*113*	*110*	*120*	*134*	*161*	*190*	*196*	*262*	*313*	*579*	*688*	514
Spain	*72*	*116*	*279*	*285*	*337*	*430*	*553*	*580*	*694*	*650*	*796*	*880*	*953*	*925*	*795*	*1226*	*1320*	*1614*	*2832*	*3133*	2519
EC-12																					**75151**

Source: Eurostat, EXTERNAL TRADE Statistical Yearbook 1986: – Table 10 – United States; Eurostat, EXTERNAL TRADE Statistical Yearbook 1988: Table 6- United States.

Table 14 EC member states' imports from the US, 1960–86 (million ECU)

	1960	1965	1968	1969	1970	1971	1972	1973	1974	1975	1976	1977	1978	1979	1980	1981	1982	1983	1984	1985	1986
Belgium – Lux.	392	550	689	767	995	790	778	1012	1627	1575	1939	2133	2200	2972	3982	4066	4261	4300	4529	4483	3712
France	745	1088	1319	1466	1896	1730	1948	2516	3438	3290	4222	4289	4683	5254	7729	7876	8202	7907	8587	9066	7958
Germany F.R.	1423	2296	2173	2618	3293	3553	3007	3725	4524	4665	6235	6080	6432	7611	9724	10798	11290	11356	12845	13517	11747
Italy	670	993	1197	1418	1547	1379	1423	1875	2626	2710	3111	2930	2998	3850	4995	5563	5936	5369	6546	7114	5796
Netherlands	600	765	1014	1067	1308	1397	1256	1732	2481	2800	3244	3409	3575	4130	4867	5610	5982	6413	7490	7568	6509
EC – 6	**3830**	**5692**	**6392**	**7336**	**9039**	**8849**	**7156**														
Denmark	*177*	*240*	*274*	*293*	*326*	*364*	*321*	425	504	508	571	665	604	705	914	1381	1226	1015	1004	1333	1150
Ireland	*52*	*83*	*92*	*131*	*117*	*153*	*144*	156	207	219	322	421	471	526	627	976	1116	1327	1741	1892	1526
UK	*1586*	*1882*	*2554*	*2714*	*2817*	*2555*	*2628*	3229	4935	4833	5698	5810	7315	8725	11437	12905	15384	15398	18830	18627	13961
EC – 9								**14670**	**20342**	**20600**	**25342**	**25737**	**28278**	**33773**	**44275**						
Greece	*95*	*113*	*107*	*152*	*116*	*133*	*130*	*233*	*338*	*317*	*369*	*306*	*318*	*344*	*351*	410	431	397	359	420	349
EC-10																**49585**	**53828**	**53482**	**61931**	**64020**	
Portugal	*40*	*75*	*86*	*63*	*113*	*122*	*177*	*202*	*364*	*392*	*382*	*446*	*486*	*581*	*752*	*1064*	*1045*	*1283*	*1356*	*990*	657
Spain	*140*	*527*	*590*	*728*	*896*	*736*	*959*	*1256*	*1993*	*2083*	*2214*	*1872*	*1942*	*2286*	*3164*	*4008*	*4468*	*3889*	*3824*	*3933*	3278
EC-12																					**56643**

Source: Eurostat, EXTERNAL TRADE Statistical Yearbook 1986: – Table 10 – United States; Eurostat, EXTERNAL TRADE Statistical Yearbook 1988: Table 6- United States.

Table 15 Percentage of intra-EC imports over member states' total exports, 1960–86

	1960	1965	1968	1969	1970	1971	1972	1973	1974	1975	1976	1977	1978	1979	1980	1981	1982	1983	1984	1985	1986
Belgium – Lux.	50.3	60.8	63	66.5	67.3	70	67.2	72.3	69.2	68.6	70.8	67.9	67.1	71.1	68.4	68.2	69.4	68.6	70.2	72.6	72.9
France	30	41.1	43.3	48.6	49.2	51.3	50.8	56.8	53.8	50.5	52.2	52.9	53.9	54.1	53.6	51	53.9	53.5	52	52.8	57.8
Germany F.R.	29	33.7	36.2	39.4	39.4	37.5	39.3	46.8	44	43.3	44.2	42.8	43.7	46.1	45	44.3	44.5	45.2	44.4	45.1	50.8
Italy	30.8	40.5	40.5	43.2	43.4	46.9	45.6	53	46	46.6	49.1	48.9	50.4	49.9	49.5	43.8	45.5	45.5	44.2	43.7	53.5
Netherlands	45	54.4	56	59.2	60.1	63.6	62.7	73.3	65.8	69.4	69.8	73.4	73.3	75.6	73.6	74,,4	74.8	75.6	76.8	78.7	75.7
Denmark								44.8	42.5	41.3	42	44.1	48.8	49.1	50.5	47	50.1	48.1	43.3	43.8	46.8
Ireland								80.1	70	74.2	73.2	78.3	77.8	77.1	77.8	75.1	72.3	69.5	65.6	66.2	71.9
UK								31.3	32	30.9	35.1	35.4	36	38.2	39.5	38	38.1	41.7	41.2	43.2	47.9
Greece																68.2	62	64.2	62.9	66.7	63.5
Portugal																					68
Spain																					60.9
Total EC	**34.4**	**42.7**	**44.5**	**48**	**48.4**	**49.2**	**49.5**	**52.9**	**50**	**49**	**44.5**	**50.5**	**51.1**	**52.9**	**52.1**	**50.4**	**51.3**	**52.1**	**51.6**	**52.6**	**57.2**

Source: Calculations based on Eurostat, EXTERNAL TRADE Statistical Yearbook 1986: Table 9 – Intra- EC Trade (EUR 10), Eurostat, EXTERNAL TRADE Statistical Yearbook 1988: Table 4 – Intra-EC Trade (EUR 12).

Table 16 Percentage of intra-EC imports over member states' total imports, 1960–86

	1960	1965	1968	1969	1970	1971	1972	1973	1974	1975	1976	1977	1978	1979	1980	1981	1982	1983	1984	1985	1986
Belgium – Lux.	47.9	54.5	54.9	57.4	58.7	63.2	63.2	70.7	66.1	67.2	67.6	67.5	69.1	67.2	63	59.3	61	64.3	63.5	67	69.9
France	29.4	38.8	47.5	50.5	48.9	50	50	55.4	47.6	48.8	49.6	49.4	51.4	50.3	46	48.2	50.7	53	53.7	54.9	64.4
Germany F.R.	29.9	38.1	41.5	43.6	45.3	46.9	46.8	52.2	48.1	49.5	48.2	49	50.1	49.3	47	48.2	49.1	50.3	50	50.9	54.2
Italy	27.7	31.2	36.2	42	41.2	42.5	42.5	48.9	42.4	43	43.5	43.1	44.7	44.2	43.8	40.7	41.9	42.8	43.3	44.9	55.4
Netherlands	45.8	53.4	55.4	56.7	55.9	54.8	54.8	61	57.4	56.9	55.2	54.8	57.4	56.4	53.2	52.4	54	53.4	56.8	54	48.6
Denmark								45.8	45.5	45.8	47.2	47.7	49.7	49.3	49	47.9	48.8	48.7	47.3	49.1	53.2
Ireland								71.7	68.3	69.2	69.4	68.1	70.2	75.4	74.6	74.7	73.8	72.1	69.8	70.5	73
UK								32.8	30	32.4	32.2	38.5	37.9	40.8	38.4	39.6	40.8	43.1	42.3	44.3	50.4
Greece																50	46.2	48	47	46.7	58.3
Portugal																					58.8
Spain																					51.3
Total EC	**34.3**	**41.7**	**45.8**	**48.2**	**48.7**	**50.1**	**50.7**	**51.7**	**46.9**	**48.3**	**48.3**	**49.5**	**50.7**	**50.4**	**47.7**	**47.6**	**48.9**	**50.4**	**50**	**51.6**	**57.8**

Source: Calculations based on Eurostat, EXTERNAL TRADE Statistical Yearbook 1986: Table 9 – Intra- EC Trade (EUR 10), Eurostat, EXTERNAL TRADE Statistical Yearbook 1988: Table 4 – Intra EC Trade (EUR 12).

Table 17 EC trends in trade by commodity groups: exports, 1971–86 (million ECU) (1971–2: EC-6; 1973–80: EC-9; 1981–5: EC-10; 1986: EC-12)

Commodity/Year	1971		1972		1973		1974		1975		1976		1977		1978		1979		1980		1981		1982		1983		1984		1985		1986	
	M.ECU	%	M.ECU	%	M.ECU	%	M.ECU	%	M. ECU	%	M.ECU	%	M.ECU	%	M.ECU	%	M.ECU	%	M.ECU	%	M.ECU	%	M.ECU	%	M.ECU	%	M.ECU	%	M.ECU	%	M.ECU	%
Food, Beverages and Tobacco	9576	10	11556	11	19225	11	22999	10	25808	11	30312	10	33961	10	37585	11	42349	10	48421	10	59541	11	63812	11	67151	11	75939	11	80660	10	83347	11
Fuel Products	4249	4	4631	4	6761	4	12503	6	12706	5	16076	6	18786	6	19511	6	28918	7	38594	8	47497	9	52190	9	55978	9	63564	9	69421	9	40356	5
Raw Materials	3646	4	4242	4	7080	4	9962	4	8454	4	10556	4	11532	3	12041	3	14644	4	16071	4	16934	3	17728	3	20210	4	23818	3	27497	4	25343	3
Chemicals	9776	10	11397	10	18046	11	29711	13	26044	11	33352	12	37548	12	40734	12	49719	12	54976	12	54795	11	60764	11	68400	11	81057	12	90252	12	87355	12
Machinery and Transport Equip.	34413	37	39950	37	59665	35	74227	33	86643	37	106456	37	120415	37	127442	36	141712	35	157899	34	173490	34	194510	35	204073	34	231157	34	259860	34	276887	36
Other Manufactured Goods	32721	35	37580	34	57777	34	77713	34	75513	32	90771	32	104161	32	116137	33	133438	33	149441	32	162955	32	175344	31	186986	31	216887	31	237765	31	248479	33
Total EC	94381	100	109356	100	168554	100	227115	100	235168	100	287523	100	326403	100	353450	100	410780	100	465402	100	515212	100	554348	100	602798	100	692422	100	765455	100	761767	100

Source: Eurostat, EXTERNAL TRADE Statistical Yearbook 1986: Table 12; Eurostat, EXTERNAL TRADE Statistical Yearbook 1988: Table 7; own calculations.

Table 18 EC trends in trade by commodity groups: imports, 1971–86 (million ECU) (1971–2: EC-6; 1973–80: EC-9; 1981–5: EC-10; 1986: EC-12)

Commodity/Year	1971		1972		1973		1974		1975		1976		1977		1978		1979		1980		1981		1982		1983		1984		1985		1986	
	M.ECU	%	M.ECU	%	M.ECU	%	M.ECU	%	M. ECU	%	M.ECU	%	M.ECU	%	M.ECU	%	M.ECU	%	M.ECU	%	M.ECU	%	M.ECU	%	M.ECU	%	M.ECU	%	M.ECU	%		
Food, Beverages and Tobacco	13807	15	16188	15	27664	16	30897	13	34253	14	41362	14	47390	14	49203	14	53124	12	57057	11	64338	12	72016	12	76329	12	84356	11	91177	12	94115	12
Fuel Products	11580	13	12459	12	20275	12	49797	20	46886	20	59654	20	61597	19	59128	17	81273	19	113767	22	134377	24	139216	23	134928	21	151523	21	156368	20	86495	12
Raw Materials	10790	12	11652	11	20194	12	27972	12	22892	10	29341	10	30846	9	30092	8	37236	9	40703	8	41577	8	42608	7	46461	7	56804	8	58489	7	52470	7
Chemicals	6930	7	7910	7	12797	7	20181	8	17850	7	23839	7	26439	8	28747	8	36848	9	40458	8	45049	8	49824	9	55980	9	67533	9	75053	9	77924	10
Machinery and Transport Equip.	21567	23	24306	23	38581	22	44957	19	49718	21	64440	21	73742	22	83874	24	97133	22	109883	22	121012	22	135799	23	150742	24	173775	24	197548	25	222618	29
Other Manufactured Goods	27834	30	32425	31	53352	31	68823	28	65678	28	84388	28	94052	28	104540	29	125352	29	145121	29	143311	26	155325	26	167204	27	194075	27	210399	27	226239	30
Total EC	92508	100	104940	100	172863	100	242627	100	237277	100	303024	100	334066	100	355584	100	430966	100	506989	100	549664	100	594788	100	631644	100	728066	100	789034	100	759861	100

Source: Eurostat, EXTERNAL TRADE Statistical Yearbook 1986: Table 12; Eurostat, EXTERNAL TRADE Statistical Yearbook 1988: Table 7; own calculations.

Table 19 General government surplus and deficit and its components in EC member states as percentage of GDP, 1960–86

Year	Belgium			Denmark			France			Germany			Greece			Ireland			Italy			Luxembourg			Netherlands			UK		
	C.R.	T.Ex.	NL/B	C.R.	T.Ex.	NL/B	C.R.	T.Ex.	NL/B	C.R.	T.Ex.	NL/B	C.R.	T.Ex.	NL/B	C.R.	T.Ex.	NL/B	C.R.	T.Ex.	NL/B	C.R.	T.Ex.	NL/B	C.R.	T.Ex.	NL/B	C.R.	T.Ex.	NL/B
1960	27.5	30.3	−2.8	27.3	24.8	3.1	34.9	34.6	0.9	35.1	32.5	3				24.8	28	−2.4	28.8	30.1	−0.9	32.5	30.5	3.1	33.9	33.7	0.8	30.1	32.4	−1
1961	28.4	29.8	−1.4	26.6	27.1	0.1	36.2	35.7	1	36.3	33.8	2.8				25.7	29.7	−3.2	28.2	29.4	−0.8	34.1	30.3	4.8	34.9	35.4	0.1	31.3	33.1	−0.7
1962	29.2	30.5	−1.3	28.2	28.1	0.6	36.3	37	−0.1	36.6	35.6	1.4				25.2	29.5	−3.6	29.1	30.5	−1	33.5	32.2	2.3	34.4	35.6	−0.6	32.9	34	0
1963	29.4	31.5	−2.1	29.9	28.6	1.9	37.1	37.8	−0.1	36.9	36.4	0.9				26.1	30.5	−3.6	29.5	31.1	−1.2	33.6	32.1	2.6	35.6	37.6	−1.3	31.5	35.4	−2.8
1964	30	30.8	−0.8	29.7	28.4	1.8	38	38	0.7	36.4	36.1	0.7				26.9	31.8	−4.1	30.6	31.8	−0.8	33.5	32,3	2.2	35.7	37.8	−1.5	31.5	33.7	−1.1
1965	30.7	32.3	−1.6	31.2	29.9	1.8	38.4	38.4	0.7	35.7	36.7	−0.6				27.9	33.1	−4.3	30.1	34.3	−3.8	35.2	33.3	2.9	37.3	38.7	−0.8	33.2	36.2	−2
1966	32.4	33.5	−1.1	33.5	31.7	2.3	38.4	38.5	0.6	36.2	36.9	−0.2				30	33.6	−2.8	30.1	34.3	−3.8	35.8	35	1.9	39.2	40.7	−0.9	34.4	35.4	0
1967	33.2	34.5	−1.3	34.1	34.3	0.4	38.2	39	0	36.9	38.8	−1.4				30.6	34.8	−3.3	31	33.7	−2.2	35.7	37.5	−0.7	40.6	42.5	−1.3	36.3	38.3	−1
1968	33.8	36.3	−2.5	36.9	36.3	1.1	38.8	40.3	−0.8	38	39.2	−0.8				31	35.2	−3.3	31.6	34.7	−2.8	34.5	37.3	−1.7	42.4	43.9	−0.9	37.7	39.3	−0.5
1969	34.3	36.1	−1.8	37.2	36.3	1.4	39.8	39.6	0.9	39.4	38.8	1.1				31.6	36.6	−4.2	30.7	34.2	−3.1	34.3	34.1	1.2	43.2	44.4	−0.5	39.6	41.3	−0.6
1970	35.2	36.5	−1.3	41.7	40.2	2.1	39	38.9	0.9	38.3	38.6	0.2				35.3	39.6	−3.7	30.4	34.2	−3.5	35	33.1	2.8	44.5	46	−0.8	40.5	39.2	2.5
1971	37.1	40.3	−3.2	46.9	43	3.9	39.1	38.3	0.7	40	40.2	−0.2							27.3	31.7	−4.5	39.2	36.9	2.3	43.5	44.5	−1	37.9	36.5	1.4
1972	37.6	41.3	−3.7	46.5	42.6	3.9	39	38.3	0.8	40.4	40.9	−0.5							27.1	33.5	−6.5	39.3	37.3	2	44.6	45	−0.4	36.2	37.5	−1.3
1973	38.2	41.5	−3.3	47.3	42.1	5.2	39.4	38.5	0.9	42.9	41.7	1.2							26.7	32.8	−6.1	39.4	36.1	3.3	46.4	45.4	1	35.6	38.3	−2.7
1974	39.2	41.8	−2.6	49.1	45.9	3.1	40.3	39.7	0.6	43.4	44.7	−1.3				34.3	42.5	−8.2	26.8	32.9	−6.1	40.5	35.8	4.8	47.1	47.3	−0.2	39.2	43	−3.8
1975	42	46.7	−4.7	46.8	48.2	−1.4	41.2	43.5	−2.2	43.4	49	−5.6				33.7	46.3	−12.5	27.4	37.5	−10.1	49.3	48.4	0.9	49.4	51.8	−2.4	39.7	44.2	−4.5
1976	41.8	47.2	−5.4	47.6	47.8	−0.2	43.5	44	−0.5	44.6	48	−3.4				36.9	45.5	−8.6	28.8	36.6	−7.8	50.5	49.1	1.4	49.8	52.7	−2.9	38.8	43.7	−4.9
1977	43.4	48.9	−5.5	48.3	48.8	−0.5	42.8	43.6	−0.8	45.7	48.1	−2.4				35.5	43.1	−7.6	30	36.9	−6.9	54.8	51.9	2.9	50.6	52.4	−1.8	38.4	41.6	−3.2
1978	44	50	−6	50.3	50.6	−0.3	42.5	44.6	−2.1	45.4	47.8	−2.4				34.3	44	−9.7	31.5	40	−8.5	56	51.5	4.4	51.1	53.8	−2.8	37	41.3	−4.3
1979	44.7	51.8	−7.1	51.5	53.2	−1.7	44.1	45	−0.8	45.1	47.7	−2.6				35	46.4	−11.4	31.2	39.4	−8.3	53.4	52.7	0.8	52.1	55.8	−3.7	37.9	41.1	−3.2
1980	44.3	53.3	−9	52.9	56.2	−3.3	46.1	46.1	0	45.4	48.3	−2.9				37.7	50.4	−12.7	33.1	41.6	−8.5	54	54.8	−0.8	53.5	57.5	−4	39.7	43.1	−3.4
1981	45.2	58	−12.8	52.9	59.8	−6.9	46.7	48.6	−1.9	45.6	49.2	−3.7	28.9	39.9	−11	38.4	51.8	−13.4	34.1	45.5	−11.5	54.7	57.9	−3.2	53.8	59.2	−5.5	41.8	44.4	−2.5
1982	46.8	57.8	−11	52	61.2	−9.1	47.6	50.3	−2.8	46.1	49.4	−3.3	32	39.7	−7.7	40.5	54.3	−13.7	36.2	47.6	−11.3	54.1	55.7	−1.6	54.2	61.3	−7.1	42.5	45	−2.4
1983	46.1	57.5	−11.4	54.4	61.6	−7.2	48.2	51.4	−3.2	45.8	48.4	−2.5	33.2	41.5	−8.3	42.7	54.5	−11.8	38.1	48.8	−10.7	56.4	56.2	0.2	55.6	62	−6.4	41.8	45.2	−3.4
1984	47.3	56.7	−9.4	56.7	60.7	−4.1	49.1	51.8	−2.7	46.1	48	−1.9	34.2	44.3	−10	43	52.9	−9.9	38	49.5	−11.5	54.5	52.5	2	54.4	60.7	−6.3	42	45.9	−3.9
1985	47.8	56.2	−8.4	57.4	59.5	−2.1	49.2	52.1	−2.9	46.4	47.5	−1.2	34.5	48.1	−13.6	43.1	54.7	−11.6	38.5	50.8	−12.3	56.9	52.5	4.4	55.1	59.9	−4.7	41.8	44.6	−2.9
1986	46.1	54.9	−8.8	58.7	55.4	3.3	48.8	51.8	−3	45.5	46.7	−1.2	36	46.7	−10.7	43.3	54	−10.7	39.2	50.5	−11.3	55.2	51.4	3.9	53.4	58	−4.6	41	43.6	−2.7

C.R. = Current Receipts; T.Ex. = Total Expenditure; NL/B = Net Lending-Net Borrowing.

Source: Commission of the European Communities. European Economy, Number 34. Nov. 1987: Statistical Annex, Tables 45–47.

Table 20 Growth of world merchandise trade in volume, 1965–86 (average annual percentage change)

1965	1966	1967	1968	1969	1970	1971	1972	1973	1974	1975	1976	1977	1978	1979	1980	1981	1982	1983	1984	1985	1986
Total Merchandise																					
6.8	7.1	5.3	13.2	11.8	8	6.5	8.7	10.8	3.5	−3	11	4.5	5.5	6	1.5	1	−3	3	9.5	3.5	4
Manufactures																					
8.4	10.3	5.8	14.4	15.1	10.2	5	9.9	17	8.5	−4.5	13	5	5	5	5	4	−2	5	12	5	4
Agricultural Products																					
3.4	5.7	0	4.6	2.2	7.9	3.3	5.8	−3.7	−3.5	5	9.5	2	9	7	7	4	−1	1	4	0	−1
Minerals (including fuels and non-ferrous metals)																					
3.1	5.3	9.3	12.4	5.2	7.7	3.6	5.9	12.1	8.5	−4.5	13	2	1.5	5	−6.5	−10	−6	−1	2	−2	7.5
Total Merchandise (production)																					
5.7	6.9	4.3	6.9	5.8	3.7	4.1	5.1	8.6	2.5	−1	7	4.5	4	4	1	1	−2	2	5.5	3	3

Source: Gatt, International Trade, various issues.

Table 21 Industrial production in major industrial countries, 1962–86 (1977 = 100)

Year	United States	Canada	Japan	European Community	France	West Germany	Italy	United Kingdom
1962	53.2	46.6	29.2	55.7	50	56.6	49.6	68.4
1963	56.3	49.6	32.5	58.1	56	58.2	54	70.7
1964	60.1	54.1	37.7	62.3	60	63.3	56.1	76.4
1965	66.1	58.7	39.2	64.9	61	66.9	58.7	78.6
1966	72	63	44.2	67.4	64	67.5	65.6	79.8
1967	73.5	65.5	52.8	68.5	66	65.5	70.7	80.4
1968	77.6	69.7	60.8	73.6	68	71.5	74.8	86.5
1969	81.2	74.5	70.4	80.5	75	80.6	77.6	89.5
1970	78.5	75.5	80.1	84.5	79	85.8	82.6	89.9
1971	79.6	79.6	82.3	86.4	84	87.5	82.2	89.5
1972	87.3	85.6	86.8	90.2	88	90.8	86.2	91.1
1973	94.4	94.7	99	96.8	95	96.7	94.5	99.2
1974	93	97.7	96.7	97.5	98	96.4	98.3	97.3
1975	84.8	91.9	86.5	91	91	90.5	89.6	92.1
1976	92.6	97.5	96.1	97.7	98	98.7	100	95.1
1977	100	100	100	100	100	100	100	100
1978	106.5	103.3	106.4	102.3	102	102.7	101.9	103
1979	110.7	109.7	113.9	107.4	107	107.7	108.8	106.9
1980	108.6	108.1	119.2	106.7	106	108	114.4	99.8
1981	111	108.6	120.4	104.2	106	106.2	112.6	96.4
1982	103.1	97.9	120.9	102.9	104	103.1	108.5	98.2
1983	109.2	104.3	125.1	104.3	104	104.1	105.8	101.7
1984	121.4	119	138.9	106.7	105	107.6	109.4	103.1
1985	123.7	125.2	145.1	110.2	106	112.9	110.9	107.9
1986	125.1	126.8	144.5	112.5	106	115.1	114.4	109.5

Source: Economic Report of the President, February 1988: Table B-109.

Table 22 Civilian unemployment rate in major industrial countries, 1960–86 (%)

Year	United States	Canada	Japan	France	West Germany	Italy	United Kingdom	EC-9
1960	5.5	6.5	1.7	0.7	1	7.2	1.6	2.5
1961	6.7	6.7	1.5	0.6	0.7	6.6	1.4	2.2
1962	5.5	5.5	1.3	0.7	0.6	5.5	1.9	2
1963	5.7	5.2	1.3	0.7	0.7	5.1	2.3	2.1
1964	5.2	4.4	1.2	0.6	0.6	5.2	1.6	1.9
1965	4.5	3.6	1.2	0.7	0.6	5.7	1.4	1.9
1966	3.8	3.4	1.4	0.7	0.6	5.5	1.4	1.9
1967	3.8	3.8	1.3	1	1.8	5	2.2	2.4
1968	3.6	4.5	1.2	1.3	1.2	4.7	2.3	2.3
1969	3.5	4.4	1.1	1.1	0.7	4.4	2.3	2
1970	4.9	5.7	1.2	1.3	0.6	4.4	2.5	2
1971	5.9	6.2	1.3	1.6	0.7	5.1	2.9	2.4
1972	5.6	6.2	1.4	1.8	0.9	5.2	3.2	2.7
1973	4.9	5.5	1.3	1.8	1.1	4.9	2.2	2.4
1974	5.6	5.3	1.4	2.3	2.3	4.9	2.2	2.9
1975	8.5	6.9	1.9	3.9	4.1	5.3	3.6	4.3
1976	7.7	7.1	2	4.2	4	5.6	4.9	4.8
1977	7.1	8.1	2	4.8	4	5.4	5.3	5
1978	6.1	8.3	2.3	5.2	3.8	6.1	5.1	5.2
1979	5.8	7.4	2.1	5.9	3.3	6.7	4.7	5.2
1980	7.1	7.5	2	6.4	3.4	7.2	6	5.8
1981	7.6	7.5	2.2	7.7	4.8	8.1	9.1	7.7
1982	9.7	11	2.4	8.7	6.9	9.7	10.6	9.3
1983	9.6	11.9	2.7	8.3	8.4	10.9	11.6	10.4
1984	7.5	11.3	2.8	10	8.4	11.9	11.8	10.9
1985	7.2	10.5	2.6	10.5	8.4	12.9	12	11.1
1986	7	9.6	2.8	10.7	8.1	13.7	12	11.1

Source: Economic Report of the President, February 1988: Table B-110; Commission of the European Community. European Economy -number 34, November 1987: Table 3.

Table 23 Annual growth rate in consumer prices in major industrial countries (%)

Year	United States	Japan	France	West Gerrmany	Italy	United Kingdom
1961	0.9	5.3	3.3	2.3	2.2	3.4
1962	1.2	6.9	4.9	3.1	4.6	4.3
1963	1.2	8.5	4.8	2.9	7.4	2
1964	1.3	3.9	3.4	2.3	5.9	3.2
1965	1.7	6.8	2.5	3.3	4.5	4.8
1966	2.8	5.1	2.7	3.6	2.3	3.9
1967	2.9	3.8	2.7	1.6	3.7	2.5
1968	4.2	5.3	4.5	1.6	1.4	4.8
1969	5.4	5.3	6.5	1.9	2.7	5.2
1970	5.9	7.6	5.2	3.5	4.9	6.4
1971	4.3	6	5.5	5.2	4.8	9.5
1972	3.3	4.6	6.1	5.6	5.8	7.2
1973	6.2	11.8	7.3	6.9	10.8	9.1
1974	11	24.4	13.7	7	19.2	16
1975	9.1	11.8	11.8	5.9	17	24.2
1976	5.8	9.3	9.6	4.4	16.8	16.6
1977	6.5	8	9.4	3.7	17	15.8
1978	7.7	3.8	9	2.7	12.1	8.3
1979	11.3	3.7	10.8	4.2	14.8	13.4
1980	13.5	8	13.5	5.3	21.1	18
1981	10.4	4.9	13.1	6.3	18.8	11.9
1982	6.1	2.7	12.1	5.3	16.3	8.6
1983	3.2	1.8	9.3	3.3	15	4.6
1984	4.3	2.2	7.7	2.4	10.6	5
1985	3.6	2.1	5.8	2.2	8.6	6.1
1986	1.9	0.6	2.7	−0.3	6.1	3.4

Source: Calculations based on Economic Report of the President, January 1975: Table C-97; Economic Report of the President, February 1988: Table B-109.

Table 24 Annual change in price deflator of imports of goods and services in national currencies in some major industrial countries (%)

Year	United States	Japan	France	West Gerrmany	Italy	United Kingdom
1961	−1	0.6	0.1	−2.4	−2.2	0
1962	−1.8	−2.6	2.7	−0.1	0.4	−0.2
1963	1.7	3.1	1.1	2.4	1.5	2.7
1964	1.9	1.3	0.9	1.7	3.4	2.5
1965	1	−2.1	1.4	2.9	0.6	1.6
1966	2	2.1	3.2	2	1.9	1.6
1967	0.6	−1.5	−1.3	−1.4	0.7	1.3
1968	1.1	2	−1.1	0.4	0.7	11.1
1969	2.4	3.8	4.9	2.4	1.4	2.8
1970	6.4	3	9.7	−0.2	3.7	7.2
1971	5.2	−1.9	3.7	1	5.3	3.8
1972	7.2	−4.4	−1.8	2.1	3.9	3
1973	17.5	18.5	6.8	8.1	26.1	23.1
1974	43.4	63.5	42	22.9	56.2	41.9
1975	9.5	9.1	−0.2	3.2	6.4	13.7
1976	2.5	5.9	8.6	5	24.1	21.8
1977	11	−3.7	10.7	2.2	17.1	14.1
1978	4.7	−14.7	1.2	−2.1	4.7	3
1979	17.3	28.7	10.3	8	17.4	8.7
1980	19.9	38.8	16.8	12.3	21.9	9.6
1981	1.6	0.8	16.2	11.6	27.8	7.5
1982	−6.4	3.5	9.2	2.9	12.4	6.3
1983	−2.5	−5.7	6.5	0.6	4.8	7.9
1984	−1.4	−3	8.8	4.7	10.8	9.1
1985	−1.1	−4	0.6	2.1	6.7	3.5
1986	−4	−38.7	−12.8	−11.6	−16.3	−3.5

Source: Commission of the European Communities. European Economy, Number 34. Nov. 1987: Statistical Annex, Table 20.

Table 25 Crude steel production in leading steel-producing countries, 1979–86 (million tonnes)

	1986	1985	1984	1983	1982	1981	1980	1979
USSR	160	155.2	154.2	152.5	147.2	148.5	147.9	149.1
Japan	98.3	105.2	105.6	97.2	99.5	101.7	111.4	111.7
USA	73.8	80.4	83.9	76.8	67.7	109.6	101.5	123.7
China	51.9	46.5	43.4	40	37.2	35.6	37.1	34.5
Germany F.R.	37.1	40.5	39.4	35.7	35.9	41.6	43.8	46
Italy	22.9	23.9	24.1	21.8	24	24.8	26.5	24.3
Brazil	21.2	20.5	18.4	14.7	13	13.2	15.3	13.9
France	17.9	18.8	19	17.6	18.4	21.3	23.2	23.4
Poland	17.4	15.8	16.5	16.2	14.8	15.7	19.5	19.2
United Kingdom	14.8	15.7	15.1	15	13.7	15.6	11.3	21.5
Czechoslovakia	15.3	15	14.8	15	15	15.3	14.9	14.8
Canada	14.1	14.6	14.7	12.8	11.9	14.8	15.9	16.1
Romania	13.8	13.8	14.4	12.6	13.1	13	13.2	12.9
North Korea	14.6	13.5	13	11.9	11.8	10.8	8.6	7.6
Spain	12	14.2	13.5	13	13.2	12.9	12.6	12.2
India	11.9	11.1	10.5	10.2	11	10.8	9.5	10.1
Belgium	9.7	10.7	11.3	10.2	10	12.4	12.4	13.5
South Africa	9.1	8.5	7.7	7.2	8.3	9	9.1	8.9
South Korea	9	8.4	6.5	6.1	5.8	5.5	5.8	5.4
German D.Rep.	7.9	7.9	7.6	7.2	7.2	7.5	7.3	7
Mexico	7.1	7.3	7.5	6.9	7.1	7.6	7.2	7.1
Australia	6.7	6.4	6.3	5.7	6.4	7.6	7.6	8.1
Turkey	6	5	4.3	3.8	3.2	2.4	2.5	2.4
Netherlands	5.3	5.5	5.7	4.5	4.4	5.5	5.3	5.8
Taiwan	5.2	5.1	5	5	4.2	3.2	3.4	3.2
Yugoslavia	5.3	4.5	4.2	4.1	3.8	4	3.6	3.5
Sweden	4.7	4.8	4.7	4.2	3.9	3.8	4.2	4.7
Hungary	3.8	3.6	3.8	3.6	3.7	3.6	3.8	3.9
Luxembourg	3.7	3.9	4	3.3	3.5	3.8	4.6	4.9

Source: Bull.EC 2-1985:Table 2; Bull.EC 2-1987:Table 4.

Table 26 Balance between annual receipts and contributions to EC resources (million ECU) by member states

	Belgium	Denmark	France	Germany	Greece	Ireland	Italy	Luxemb.	Netherlands	UK
					1981					
Receipts	597.9	575.3	3484.5	2502.3	394.7	717	2813.3	8.3	1284.8	3124.7
Contributions	990.5	354.4	3491.1	5057.1	254.5	158.9	2526	27.2	1287.1	3877.2
Balance	–329.6	220.9	-6.6	–2554.8	140.2	–558.1	287.3	–18.9	–2.3	–752.5
					1983					
Receipts	735.5	756.5	4254.8	3825.3	1351.4	1026.2	3775	5.6	1860.5	4083.6
Contributions	1215.9	479.9	4506.5	6472.1	377.7	269.6	2998.7	43.9	1564.9	5084.4
Balance	–480.4	276.6	-251.7	–2646.8	993.7	756.6	776.3	–38.3	295.6	–1000.8
					1985					
Receipts	1070	912.5	5416.4	4185	1702.8	1702.8	4480.3	8.5	2231.1	3107.4
Contributions	1292.6	620.4	5319.2	7504.3	388	388	3629.5	50.7	1889.4	5090.3
Balance	–222.6	292.1	97.2	–3319.3	1315	1315	850.8	–42.2	341.7	–1982.9

Source: Calculations based on Official Journal of the European Community, Information and Notices. Annual Report of the Court of Auditors, Years, 1981, 1982, 1983.

Table 27 Annual payments to the member states (million ECU)

	Average 1981–1983										
	Belgium	**Denmark**	**France**	**Germany**	**Greece**	**Ireland**	**Italy**	**Luxemb.**	**Netherlands**	**UK**	**EC-10**
EAGGF - Guarantee	545.4	581.7	3149	2378	612.7	517.9	2472	3.6	1427	1350	13038
Share of total (%)	92.5	89	84.7	80.6	67.3	59.2	74.3	55	91.1	36.3	70.8
EAGGF - Guidance	19.2	20.7	156.7	116.3	12.1	75.3	102	1.5	28.8	109	641.5
Share of total (%)	2.9	3.2	4.2	3.9	1.3	8.6	3.1	23	1.8	2.9	3.5
Fisheries	0.5	2.7	3.9	3.1		11.6	6.9		7.7	8.8	53.3
Share of total (%)	0.1	0.4	0.1	0.1		1.3	0.2		0.5	0.2	0.3
Social Fund	17.6	16.6	138.4	81.3	16.8	103.2	221	0.7	12.1	240	847.4
Share of total (%)	2.6	2.5	3.7	2.8	1.8	11.8	6.6	11	0.8	6.4	4.6
Regional Fund	9	14	138.7	47.6	163.9	89.5	279	0.3	9	259	1009
Share of total (%)	1.4	2.1	3.7	1.6	17.9	10.3	8.4	4.6	0.6	7	5.5
TOTAL	661	653.8	3720	2952	910.6	874.5	3329	6.5	1566	3723	1840.7

	Average 1984–1986												
	Belgium	**Denmark**	**France**	**Germany**	**Greece**	**Ireland**	**Italy**	**Luxemb.**	**Netherlands**	**UK**	**Portugal**	**Spain**	**EC-12**
EAGGF - Guarantee	860.4	924	4555	3783	1180	1088	3463	3.5	2096	2000	10.1	91	20054
Share of total (%)	84	88.2	85	86	71.2	75.3	74.4	40	92.4	56.7	6.1	11	76
EAGGF - Guidance	13.6	13.6	147.6	91.8	74.2	67.2	157	2.7	20	101			688
Share of total (%)	1.3	1.3	2.8	2.1	4.5	4.6	3.4	31	0.9	2.8			2.6
Fisheries	2.8	6	13.8	4.9	1.9	5.4	5.7		2.9	14.6	0.1		84.9
Share of total (%)	0.3	0.6	0.2	0.1	0.1	0.4	0.1		0.1	0.4	0.1		0.3
Social Fund	58.1	61	270	102.7	85.8	168.7	405	0.8	36.9	497	36.4	58	1780.4
Share of total (%)	5.7	5.8	5	2.3	5.2	11.7	8.7	9.2	1.6	14.1	21.9	7.3	6.7
Regional Fund	15.9	18.2	218	66	278.3	100.5	509	1.1	14.8	429	63	105	1818.8
Share of total (%)	1.5	1.7	4.1	1.5	16.8	7	10.9	13	0.7	12.2	38	13	6.9
TOTAL	1025	1048	5361	4398	1657	1444	4655	8.7	2268	3529	165.8	805	26397

Source: Calculations based on Official Journal of the European Community, Information and Notices. Annual Report of the Court of Auditors, Years 1981–1986.

Figures

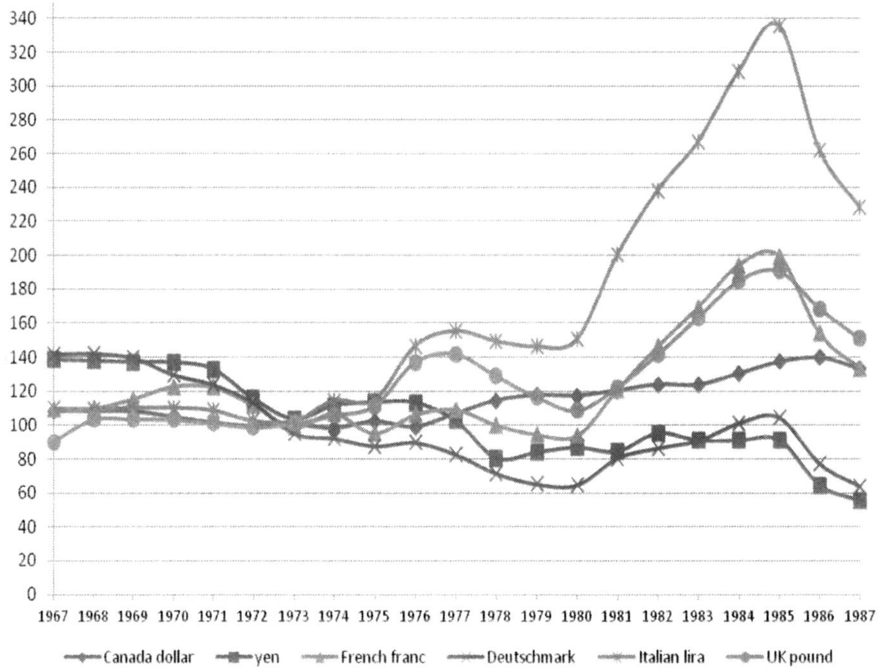

Figure 1 Currency unit per US dollar, 1967–87 (index: March 1973 = 100).

Source: Economic Report of the President, February 1988: Table B-108.

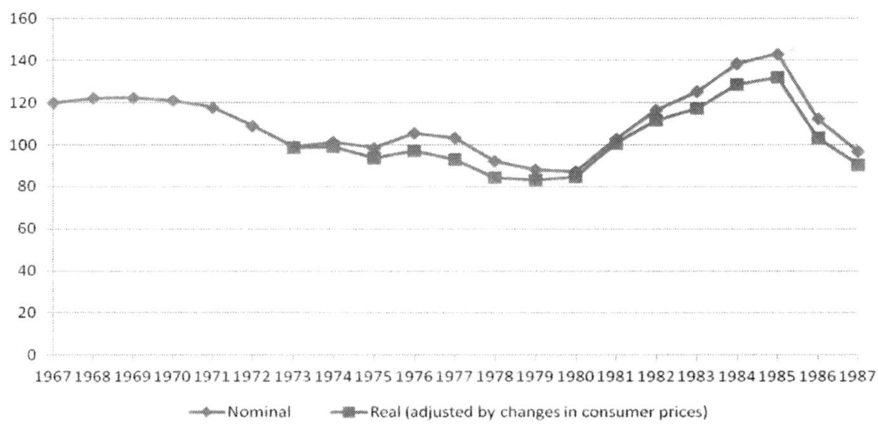

Figure 2 Multilateral trade-weighted value of the US dollar, 1967–87 (index: March 1973 = 100).

Source: Economic Report of the President, February 1988: Table B-108.

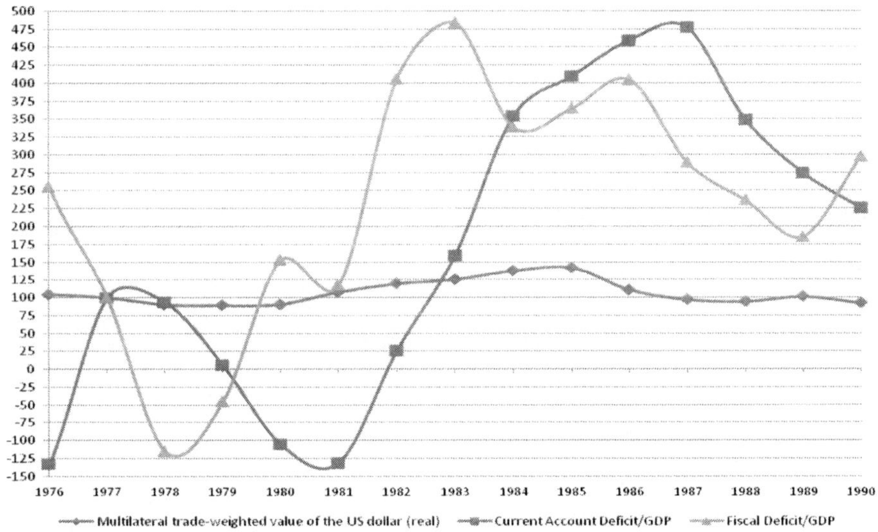

Figure 3 Multilateral trade-weighted value of the dollar and US current account and fiscal deficit over gross domestic product, 1976–90 (index: 1977 = 100).

Source: Calculations based on Economic Report of the President, February 1992: Table B-1; Table B-77; Table B-100; Table B-107.

Figure 4 Unit labour costs in manufacturing, 1967–86 (national currency base and US dollar base).

(Continued)

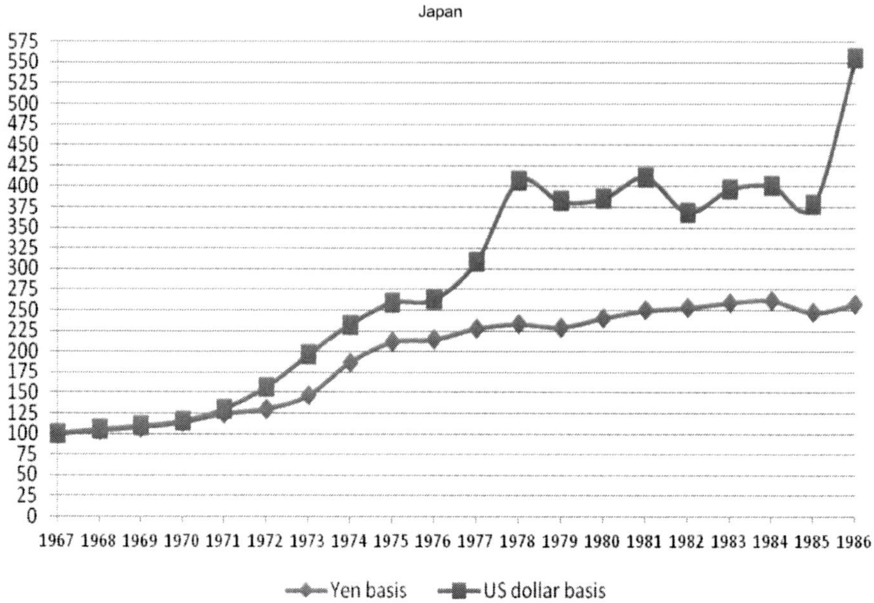

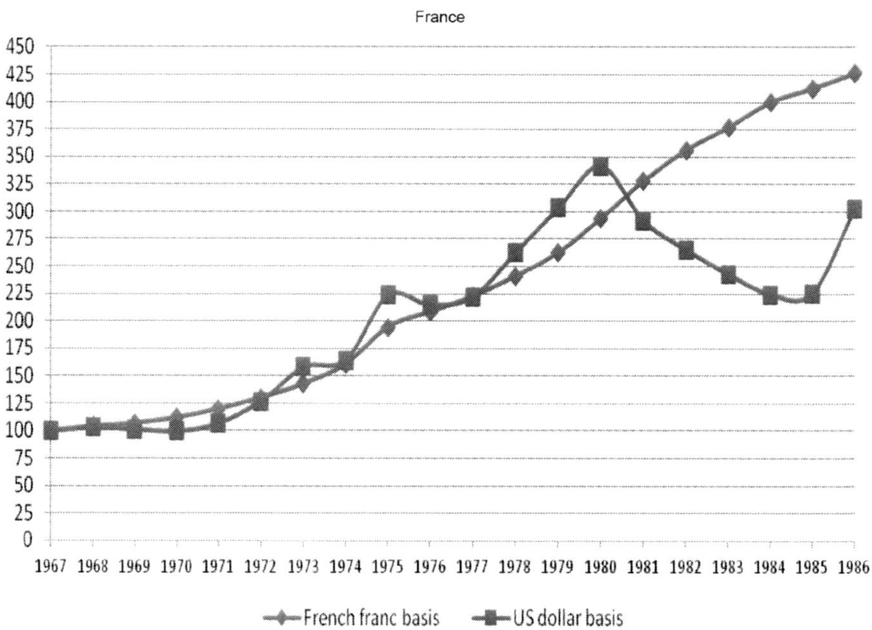

Figure 4 Continued

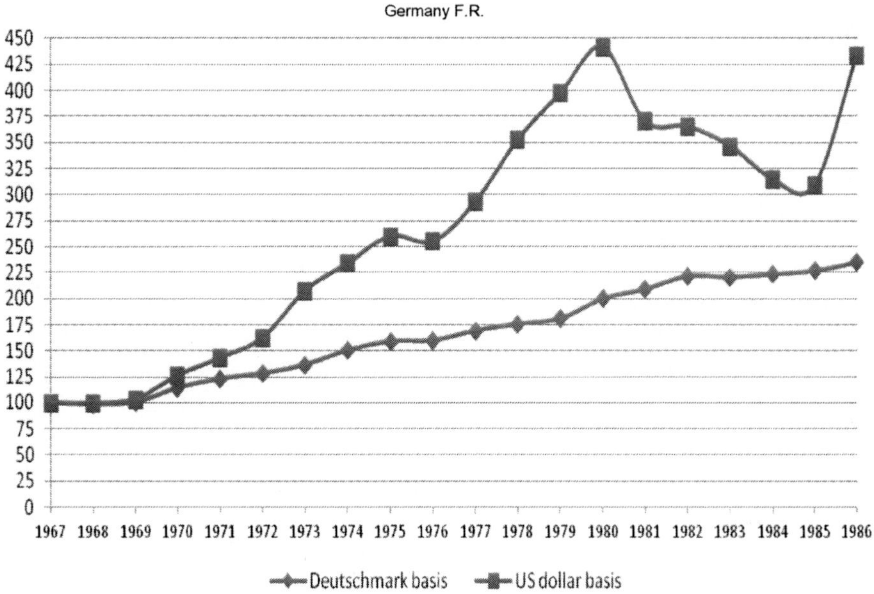

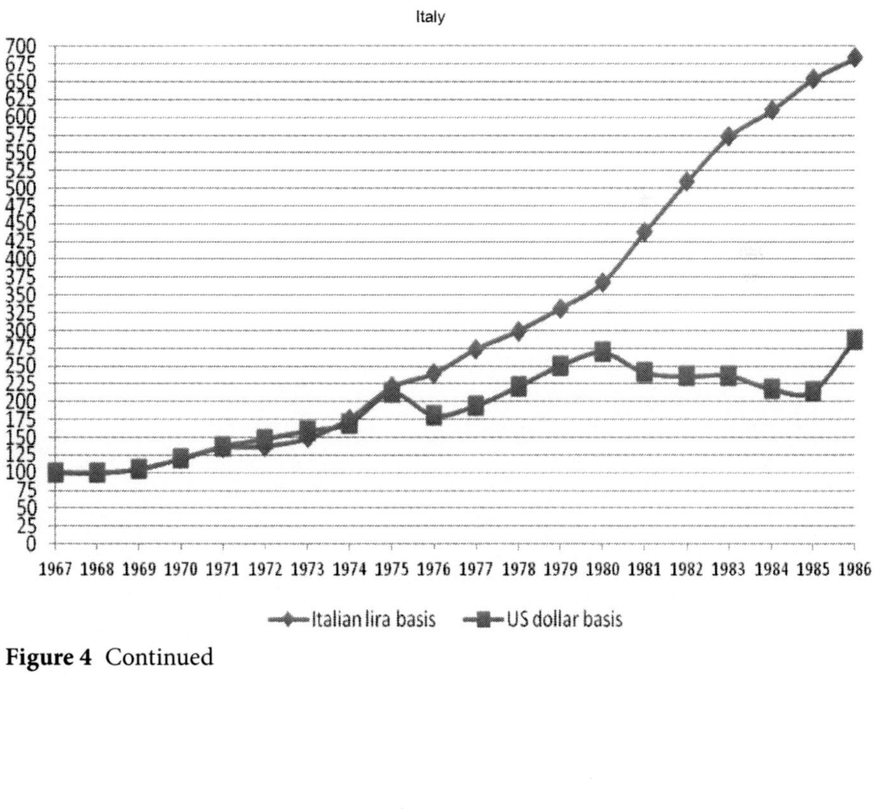

Figure 4 Continued

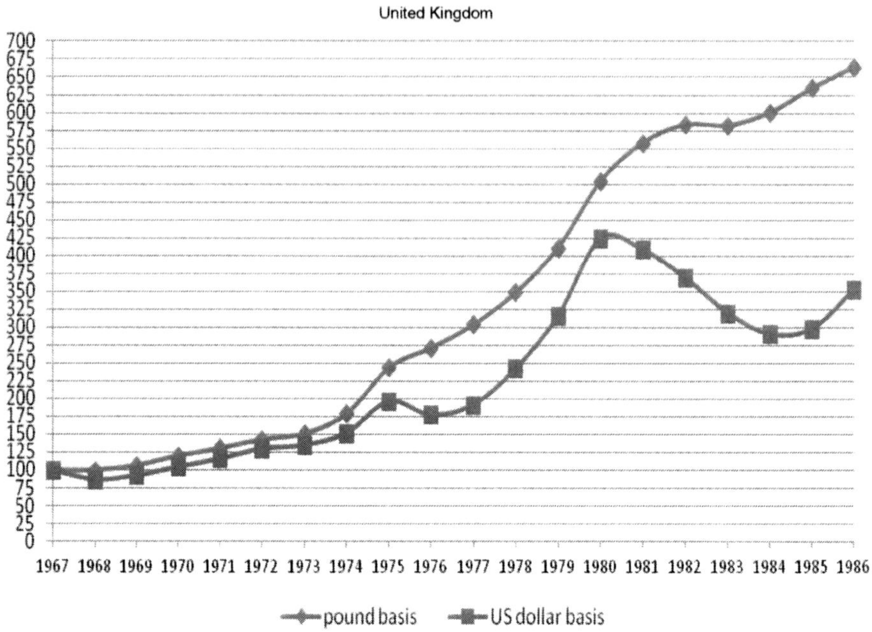

Figure 4 Continued

Source: US Department of Labor. Bureau of Labor Statistics. International Labor Comparisons. Supplementary Tables 1950–2008. Table 9.1 and Table 10.1.

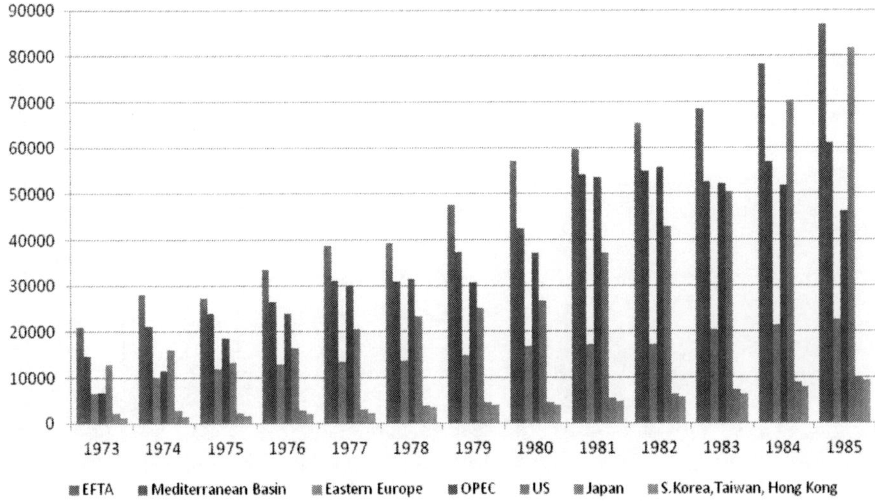

Figure 5 EC exports by main importing countries and areas, 1973–85 (million ECU)

Source: Eurostat, EXTERNAL TRADE Statistical Yearbook 1986: Table 10; Eurostat, EXTERNAL TRADE. Statistical Yearbook 1987: Table 6.

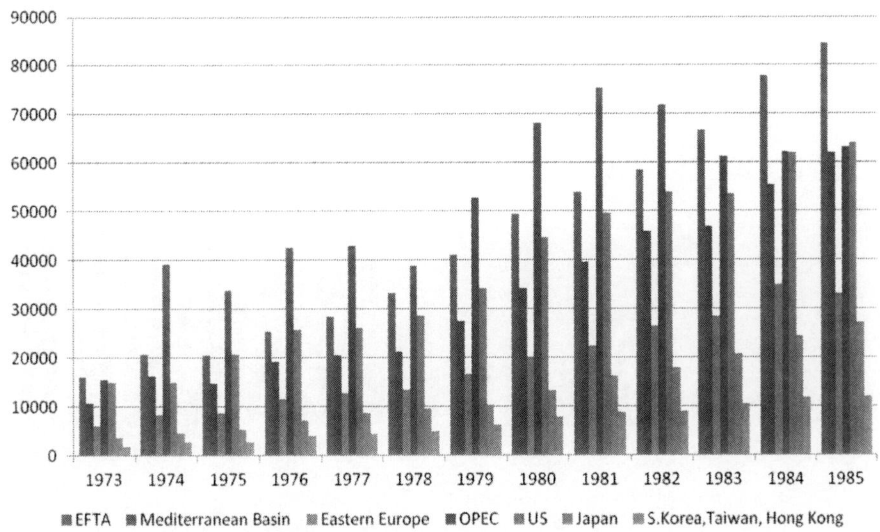

Figure 6 EC imports by main exporting countries and areas, 1973–85 (million ECU)

Source: Eurostat, EXTERNAL TRADE Statistical Yearbook 1986: Table 10; Eurostat, EXTERNAL TRADE. Statistical Yearbook 1987: Table 6.

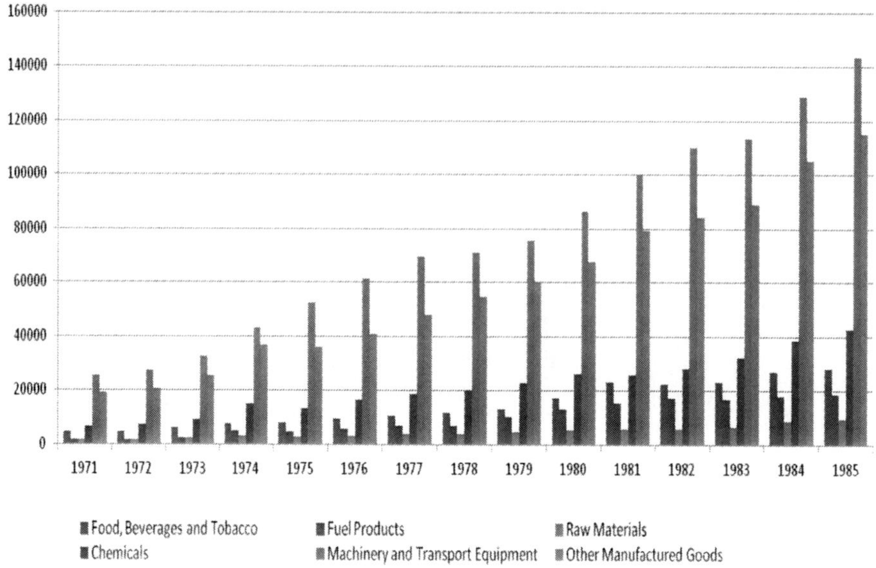

Figure 7 Extra-EC exports by products, 1973–85 (million ECU)*

Source: Eurostat, EXTERNAL TRADE Statistical Yearbook 1986: Table 12.

* For homogeneity the figure includes data for Denmark, Ireland, Greece and the UK for all years in review.

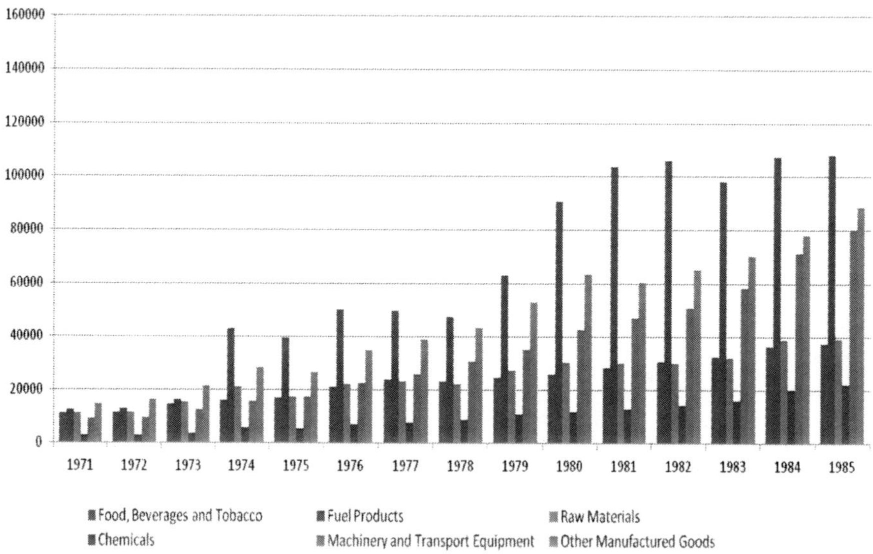

Figure 8 Extra-EC imports by products, 1973–85 (million ECU)*

Source: Eurostat, EXTERNAL TRADE Statistical Yearbook 1986: Table 12.

* For homogeneity the figure includes data for Denmark, Ireland, Greece and the UK for all years in review.

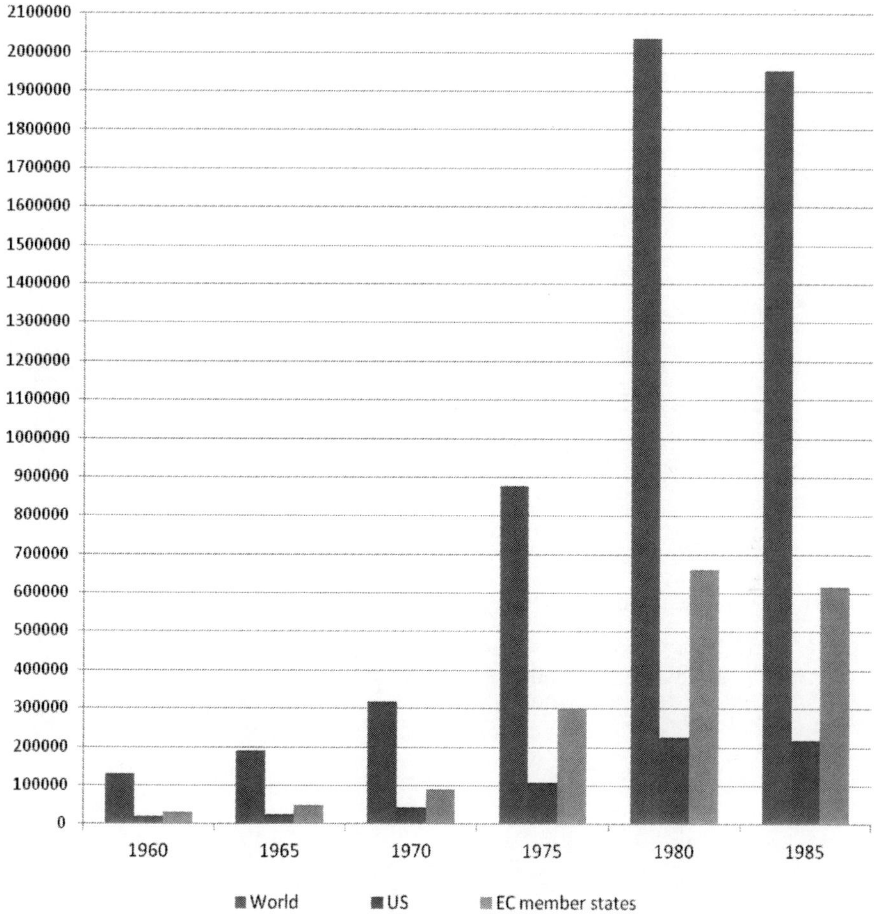

Figure 9 Total merchandise trade by main economic areas, 1960–85 (millions of US dollars)

Source: World Trade Organization-Time Series on International Trade-Total Merchandise Trade: http://stat.wto.org/StatisticalProgram/WSDBViewData.

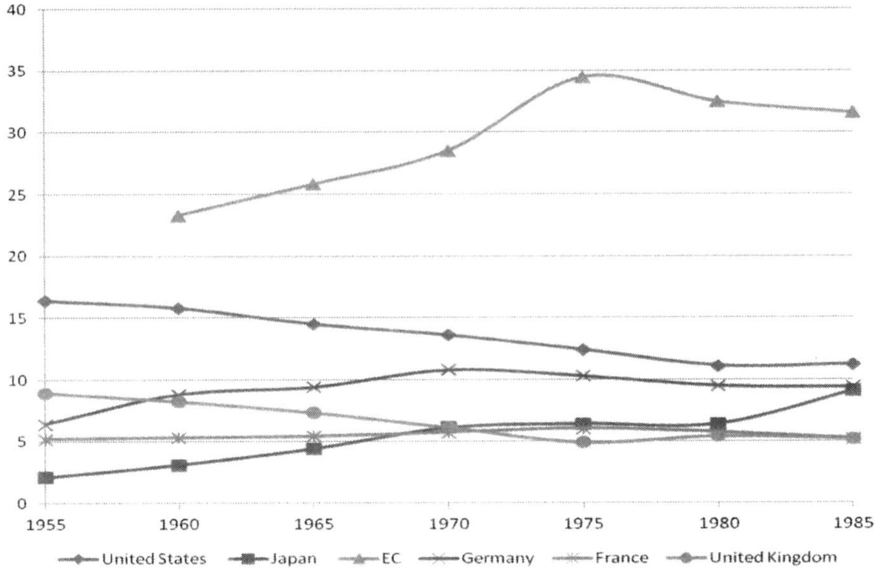

Figure 10 Share of main exporters in US$ total merchandise trade, 1955–85

Source: World Trade Organization-Time Series on International Trade-Total Merchandise Trade: http://stat.wto.org/StatisticalProgram/WSDBViewData.

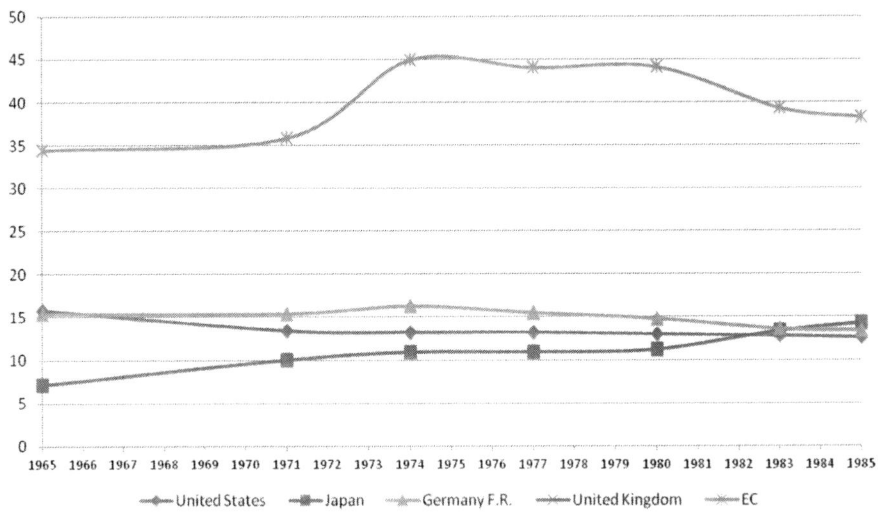

Figure 11 Share of main exporters in US$ manufacture trade, 1965–85

Source: Calculations based on US Department of Commerce Time Series Trade by Commodities and World Trade Organization-Time Series on International Trade-Merchandise Trade by Commodity-Manufactures, 1980–85: http://stat.wto.org/StatisticalProgram/WSDBViewData.

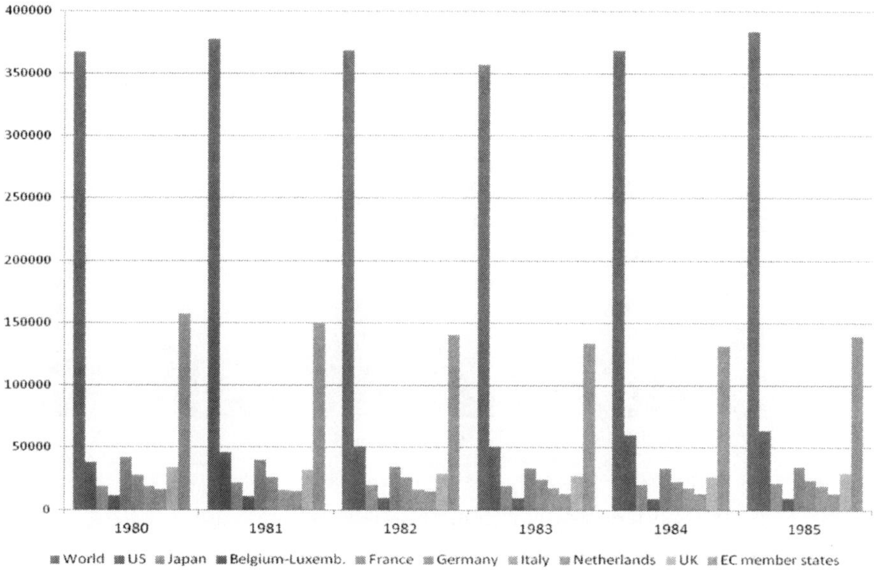

Figure 12 Trade in commercial services by main exporters 1980–5 (millions of US dollars)

Source: World Trade Organization-Time Series on International Trade-Trade in Commercial Services: http://stat.wto.org/StatisticalProgram/WSDBViewData.

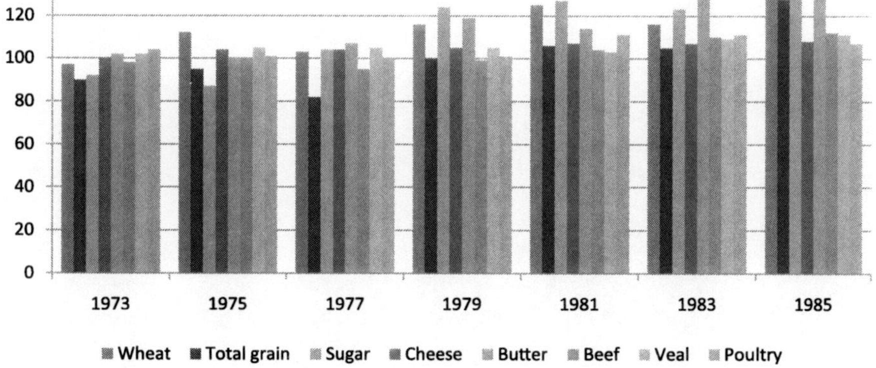

Figure 13 Degree of farm product self-sufficiency in the EC, 1973–85

Source: EUROSTAT Basic Statistics of the Community: Agriculture, Forest, Fishery, various issues.

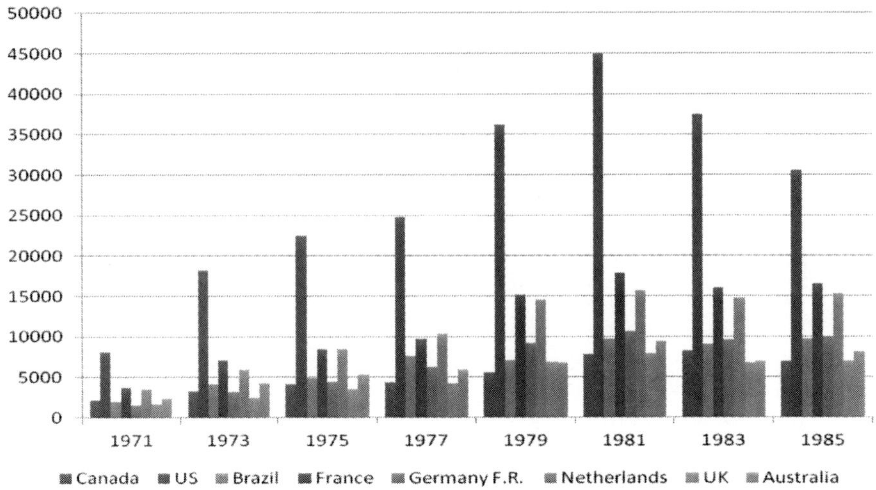

Figure 14 Main exporters of farm products, 1971–85 (millions of US dollars)

Source: FAO Trade Yearbook Vol. 30, 1976: Table 5: FAO Trade Yearbook Vol. 36, 1982: Table 5; FAO Trade Yearbook Vol. 40, 1986: Table 5.

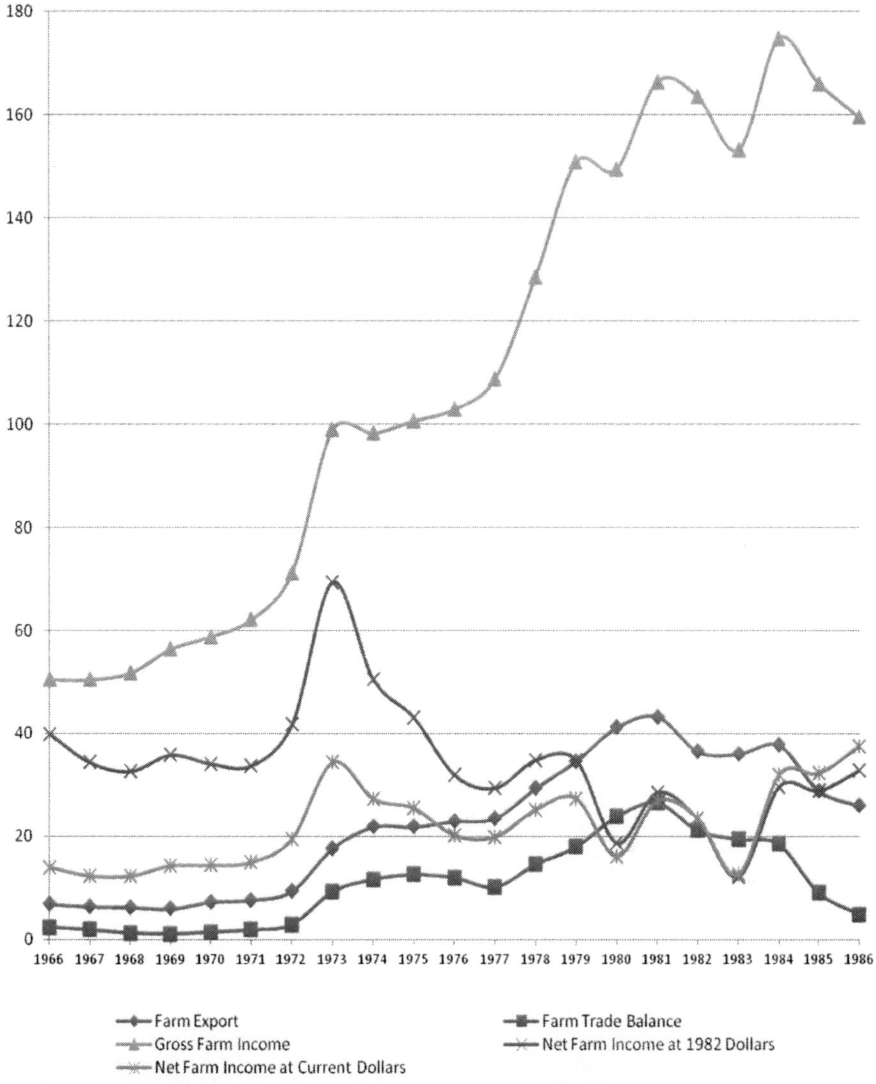

Figure 15 US farm trade and income, 1966–86 (US$ Bill)

Source: Economic Report of the President, February 1988: Table B-96, Table B-100.

Bibliography

Books

Aldcroft, Derek H. *The European Economy 1914–2000*, 4th Edition. London and New York: Routledge, 2001.

Axilrod, Stephen H. *Inside the Fed: Monetary Policy and Its Management, Martin through Greenspan to Bernanke*. Cambridge, MA: MIT Press, 2011.

Balassa, Bela. *Trade Liberalization among Industrial Countries. Objectives and Alternatives*. New York: McGraw-Hill Book Company, 1967.

Bayard, Thomas and Ann Elliott Kimberly. *Reciprocity and Retaliation in U.S. Trade Policy*. Washington, DC: Institute for International Economics, 1994.

Bergmann, Denis and Pierre Baudin. *Politique d'Avenir pour l'Europe Agricole*. Paris: Economica, 1989.

Biven, W. Carl. *Jimmy Carter's Economy: Policy in an Age of Limits*. Chapel Hill and London: University of North Carolina Press, 2002.

Brehon, Nicolas-Jean. *Le Budget de l'Europe* Paris: L.G.D.J., 1997.

Brenner, Robert. *The Economics of Global Turbulence. The Advanced Capitalist Economies from Long Boom to Long Downturn, 1945–2005*. New York: Verso, 2006.

Bromley, Simon. *American Hegemony and World Oil: The Industry, the State System and the World Economy*. Cambridge: Polity Press, 1991.

Bush, Marc L. *Trade Warriors. States, Firms and Strategic-Trade Policy in High Technology Competition*. Cambridge: Cambridge University Press, 1999.

Campagna, Anthony S. *U.S. National Economic Policy, 1917–1985*. New York and London: Praeger, 1987.

Casadio, Gian Paolo. *Transatlantic Trade: USA-EEC Confrontation in the GATT Negotiations*. Farnborough, Lexington: Saxon House-Lexington Books, 1973.

Cochrane, Willard W. *The Development of American Agriculture. A Historical Analysis*. Minneapolis: University of Minnesota Press, 1979.

Coombs, Charles A. *The Arena of International Finance*. New York: John Wiley & Sons, 1976.

Croome, John. *Reshaping the World Trading System. A History of the Uruguay Round*. Geneva: World Trade Organization, 1995.

Curtis, Thomas B. and John Robert Vastine Jr. *The Kennedy Round and the Future of American Trade*. New York and London: Praeger, 1971.

Cusumano, Michael, *The Japanese Automobile Industry. Technology and Management at Nissan and Toyota*. Cambridge, MA: Council on East Asian Studies, Harvard University, 1985.

D'andrea Tyson, Laura. *Who's Bashing Whom? Trade Conflict in High Technology Industries*. Washington, DC: Institute for International Economics, 1992.

Destler, I.M. *Making Foreign Economic Policy*. Washington, DC: The Brooking Institution, 1980.

Destler, I.M. *American Trade Policy*, 3rd Edition. Washington, DC: Institute for International Economics with The Twentieth Century Fund, 1995.

Dicken, Peter. *Global Shift. The Internationalization of Economic Activity*, 2nd Edition. London: Paul Chapman Publishing Ltd, 1992.

Duchêne, François, Edward Szczepanik and Wilffied Legg. *New Limits on European Agriculture. Politics and the New Agricultural Policy*. London: Croon Helm Ltd, 1985.

Dunning, John, *International Production and the Multinational Enterprise*. London: George Allen and Unwin, 1981.

Eck, Jean-François. *Histoire de l'économie française dépuis 1945*. Paris: Armand Colin Éditeur, 1990.

Edelman Spero, Joan. *The Politics of International Economic Relations*, 4th Edition. London: Routledge, 1990.

Eichengreen, Barry. *Globalizing Capital. A History of the International Monetary System*. Princeton: Princeton University Press, 1996.

Eichengreen, Barry, *The European Economy since 1945: Coordinated Capitalism and Beyond*. Princeton: Princeton University Press, 2007.

Evans, John W. *The Kennedy Round in American Trade Policy: The Twilight of the GATT?* Cambridge, MA: Harvard University Press, 1971.

George, Stephen. *An Awkward Partner. Britain in the European Community*, 3rd Edition. Oxford: Oxford University Press, 1998.

Giersch, Herbert, Karl-Heinz Paqué and Holger Schneding. *The Fading Miracle. Four Decades of Market Economy in Germany*. Cambridge: Cambridge University Press, 1990.

Gilpin, Robert. *U.S. Power and the Multinational Corporation. The Political Economy of Foreign Direct Investment*. New York: Basic Books Inc. Publisher, 1975.

Glismann, H.H. and F.D. Weiss. *The Political Economy of Protection in Germany*. World Bank Staff Working Paper n. 427, 1980.

Grieco, Joseph M. *Cooperation among Nations: Europe, America, and Non-Tariff Barriers to Trade*. Ithaca and London: Cornell University Press, 1990.

Grilli, Enzo. *Italian Commercial Policies in the 1970s*. World Bank Staff Working Paper n. 428, 1980.

Gros, Daniel and Niel Thygesen. *European Monetary Integration: from the European Monetary System to Economic and Monetary Union*, 2nd Edition. London: Longman Ltd, 1998.

Hau, Michel. *Histoire Économique de l'Allemagne XIXe-XXe siècles*. Paris: Economica, 1994.

Hudec, Robert E. *Enforcing International Trade Law. The Evolution of the Modern GATT Legal System*. Salem, NH: Butterworth Legal Publishers, 1993.

Iacocca, Lee. *An Autobiography*. New York: Bantam Books, 1984.

Ito, Takatoshi. *The Japanese Economy*. Cambridge, MA: The MIT Press, 1992.

Johnson, D. Gale. *World Agriculture in Disarray*. London: Fontana, 1973.

Josling, Timothy E. *Agriculture in the Tokyo Round Negotiations*. London: Trade Policy Research Centre, 1977.

Josling, Timothy E., Stefan Tangermann and T.K. Warley. *Agriculture in the GATT*. Basingstoke: Macmillan, 1996.

Keohane, Robert O. *After Hegemony. Cooperation and Discord in the World Political Economy*. Princeton: Princeton University Press, 1984.

Kindleberger, Charles. *American Business Abroad. Six Lectures on Direct Investment*. New Haven: Yale University Press, 1969.

Kissinger, Henry A. *White House Years*. Boston: Little, Brown and Company, 1979.

Kitamura, Masaru. *U.S.-Japan Semiconductor Agreement Revisited*, kitamuralaw.com/publications/high_tech_trade_policy

La Barca, Giuseppe. *International Trade in the 1970s. The US, the EC and the Growing Pressure of Protectionism*. London and New York: Bloomsbury, 2013.

Libby, Ronald T. *Protecting Markets: U.S. Policy and the World Grain Trade*. Ithaca: Cornell University Press, 1987.

Ludlow, Peter. *The Making of the European Monetary System. A Case Study of the Politics of the European Community*. London/Boston: Butterworth Scientific, 1982.

Mandel, Ernest. *Europe versus America?: Contradiction of Imperialism*. London: N.L.B., 1970.

Mandel, Ernest. *The Second Slump: A Marxist Analysis of Recession in the Seventies*. London: N.L.B, 1978.

Matusow, Allen J. *Nixon's Economy: Booms, Busts, Dollar and Votes*. Lawrence: University Press of Kansas, 1998.

Morgan, Iwan. *The Age of Deficits: Presidents and Unbalanced Budgets from Jimmy Carter to George W. Bush*. Lawrence: University Press of Kansas, 2009.

Mourlon-Druol, Emmanuel. *A Europe Made of Money: The Emergence of the European Monetary System*. Ithaca and London: Cornell University Press, 2012.

Nagle, J.C. *Agricultural Trade Policies*. Westhead: Saxon House, 1976.

Newman, Mark, Tom Fulton and Lewrene Glaser. *A Comparison of Agriculture in the United States and the European Community*. Washington, DC: United States Department of Agriculture-Economic Research Service, 1987.

Newton, Scott. *The Global Economy, 1944–2000. The Limits of Ideology*. London: Arnold, 2004.

Owen Smith, Eric. *The German Economy*. London and New York: Routledge, 1994.

Owen Smith, Eric. *The West German Economy*. London and Canberra: Croom Helm, 1983.

Pastor, Robert A. *Congress and the Politics of U.S. Foreign Economic Policy 1929–1976*. Berkeley: University of California Press, 1980.

Pearce, Joan and John Sutton. *Protection and Industrial Policy in Europe*. London, Boston: Routledge and Kegan Paul, 1985.

Péberau, Michel. *La Politique Économique de la France. Les Objectifs*. Paris: Armand Colin, 1987.

Preeg, Ernest H. *Traders and Diplomats. An Analysis of the Kennedy Round of Negotiations under the General Agreement on Tariffs and Trade*. Washington, DC: The Brooking Institution, 1970.

Rosenberg, Samuel. *American Economic Development since 1945: Growth, Decline and Rejuvenation*. Houndmills: Palgrave Macmillan, 2003.

Rostow, W.W. *Getting from Here to There*. London: The Macmillan Press Ltd, 1979.

Schenk, Catherine R. *International Economic Relations since 1945*. London: Routledge, 2011.

Servan-Schreiber, J.J. *The American Challenge*. London: Hamish Hamilton, 1968.

Shiraishi, Takashi. *Japan's Trade Policies 1945 to the Present Day*. London: The Athlone Press, 1989.

Skeet, Ian. *Opec: Twenty-Five Years of Rice and Politics*. Cambridge: Cambridge University Press, 1988.

Solomon, Robert. *The International Monetary System 1945–1981*. New York: Harper & Row Publishers, 1982.

Solomon, Robert. *The Transformation of the World Economy, 1980–93*. New York: St Martin's Press, 1994.

Tew, Brian. *The Evolution of the International Monetary System 1945–1981*, 2nd Edition. London: Hutchinson, 1986.

Thatcher, Margaret. *The Downing Street Years 1979–1990*. New York: Harper Perennial, 1993.

Tracy, Michael. *Agriculture in Western Europe. Challenges and Responses 1880–1980*. London: Granada, 1982.

Tsoukalis, Loukas. *The New European Economy. The Politics and Economics of Integration*. Oxford: Oxford University Press, 1993.

Vatter, Harold G. *The U.S. Economy in the 1950s. An Economic History*. New York: W. Norton & Company Inc., 1963.

Venn, Fiona. *The Oil Crisis*. London and New York: Longman, 2002.

Viner, Jacob. *The Customs Union Issue*. London: Stevens & Sons Limited, 1950.

Vogel, Steven K. *Freer Markets, More Rules, Regulatory Reform in Advanced Industrial Countries*. Ithaca and London: Cornell University Press, 1998.

Williamson, John. *The Failure of the World Monetary Reform*. Sunbury on Thames: Thomas Nelson and Son Ltd., 1977.

Winham, Gilbert R. *International Trade and the Tokyo Round Negotiation*. Princeton: Princeton University Press, 1986.

Wyant, Frank R. *The United States, OPEC and Multinational Oil*. Lexington: Lexington Books, 1977.

Zeiler, Thomas W. *American Trade and Power in the 1960s*. New York: Columbia University Press, 1992.

Chapters in edited books

Adams, Walter and Hans Mueller. 'The Steel Industry'. In Walter Adams (ed.) *The Structure of American Industry*, 6th Edition, pp. 73–135. New York: Macmillan Publishing Co. Inc., 1982.

Arndt, Sven W. 'The External Effects of U.S. Disinflation'. In William Fellner (project dir.) *Essays in Contemporary Economic Problems. Disinflation 1983–1984*, pp. 131–53, Washington D.C. and London: American Enterprise Institute for Public Policy Research, 1984.

Basosi, Duccio. 'The European Community and International Reaganomics, 1981–1985'. In Kiran Klaus Patel and Kenneth Weisbrode (eds) *European Integration and the Atlantic Community in the 1980s*, pp. 133–53. New York: Cambridge University Press, 2013.

Bianchi, Carluccio. 'The Balance of Payments Constraint and the Growth of the Italian Economy'. In Carluccio Bianchi and Carlo Casanova (eds) *The Recent Performance of the Italian Economy. Market Outcomes and State Policy*, pp. 27–45. Milan: Franco Angeli, 1991.

Branson, William H. 'Trends in United States International Trade and Investment since World War II'. In Martin Feldstein (ed.) *The American Economy in Transition*, pp. 182–257. Chicago/London: University of Chicago Press, 1980.

Brussière, Éric and Ivo Maes. 'Economic and Monetary Affairs: new challenges and ambitions'. In *The European Commission 1973–86. Histories and Memories of an Institution*, pp. 301–11. Luxembourg: Publication Office of the European Union, 2014.

Cagan, Phillip. 'Financing the Deficit, Interest Rates, and Monetary Policy'. In Phillip Cagan (ed.) *Essays in Contemporary Eonomic Problems, 1985. The Economy in Deficit*, pp. 195–221. Washington, DC and London: American Enterprise Institute for Public Policy Research, 1985.

Charles, Charles A. St. 'Tariff'. In Terence P. Stuart (ed.) *The GATT Uruguay Round: A Negotiating History (1986–1992)*, pp. 385–458. Deventer: Kluwer Law and Taxation, 1993.

D'Adda, C. and B. Salituro. 'The Recent Performance of the Italian Economy. Market Outcomes and State Policy'. In Carluccio Bianchi and Carlo Casanova (eds) *The Recent Performance of the Italian Economy. Market Outcomes and State Policy*, pp. 46–66. Milan: Franco Angeli, 1991.

Demidova, Ksenia. 'The Deal of the Century: The Reagan Administration and the Soviet Pipeline'. In Kiran Klaus Patel and Kenneth Weisbrode (eds) *European Integration and the Atlantic Community in the 1980s*, pp. 59–82. New York: Cambridge University Press, 2013.

Eichengreen, Barry. 'U.S. Foreign Financial Relations in the Twenty-Century'. In Stanley Engerman and Robert E. Galman (eds) *The Cambridge Economic History of the United States*, pp. 463–504. Cambridge and New York: Cambridge University Press, 1996.

Fennell, William A., Joseph W. Tyler, 'Trade-Related Investment Measures'. In Terence P. Stewart (ed.) *The* GATT *Uruguay Round: A Negotiating History (1986–1992)*, pp. 2001–240. Deventer: Kluwer Law and Taxation, 1993.

Foreman-Peck, James. 'Trade and the Balance of Payments'. In N.F.R. Crafts and N.W.C. Woodward (eds) *The British Economy since 1945*, pp. 140–79. Oxford: Clarendon Press, 1991.

Frankel, Jeffrey A., Saburo Okita, Peter G. Peterson and James R. Schlesinger. 'International Capital Flows and Domestic Economic Policies'. In Martin Feldstein (ed.) *The United States in the World Economy*, pp. 559–658. Chicago and London: The University of Chicago Press, 1988.

Gardner, Bruce L. 'Farm Policy and Farm Problem'. In Phillip Cagan (ed.) *Contemporary Economic Problems. The Impact of the Reagan Program 1986*, pp. 223–46. Washington D.C. and London: American Enterprise Institute for Public Policy Research, 1986.

Gardner, Bruce L., H.B. Atwater and John R. Block. 'International Competition in Agriculture and U.S. Farm Policy'. In Martin Feldstein (ed.) *The United States in the World Economy*, pp. 423–74. Chicago: National Bureau of Economic Research, 1988.

Gélédan, Alain. 'Crise et politiques de sortie de crise'. In *L'économie française. Mutations 1975–1990*, pp. 108–61. Paris: Le Monde – Sirey, 1989.

Hennings, Klaus Hinrich. 'West Germany'. In Andrea Boltho (ed.) *The European Economy: Growth and Crisis*, pp. 472–501. Oxford: Oxford University Press, 1982.

Houpt, Stefan, Pedro Lains and Schön Lennart. 'Sectoral Developments, 1944–2000'. In Stephen Broadberry and Kevin H. O'Rourke (eds) *The Cambridge Economic History of Modern Europe, Volume 2: 1870 to the Present*, pp. 340–64. Cambridge and New York: Cambridge University Press, 2010.

Johnson, Gale D. 'The Food and Agriculture Act of 1977. Implications for Farmers, Consumers and Taxpayers'. In William Felner (project director) *Contemporary Economic Problems 1978*, pp. 167–209. Washington D.C.: American Enterprise Institute for Public Policy Research, 1979.

Lindert, Peter H. 'U.S. Foreign Trade and Trade Policy in the Twentieth Century'. In Stanley Engerman and Robert E. Galman (eds) *The Cambridge Economic History of the United States*, pp. 407–62. Cambridge and New York: Cambridge University Press, 1996.

Lipsey, Robert E., Mario Schimberni and Robert V. Lindsay, 'Changing Patterns of International Investment in and by the United States'. In Martin Feldstein (ed.) *The United States in the World Economy*, pp. 475–558. Chicago: National Bureau of Economic Research, 1988.

Llewellin, John, Stephen Polter. 'Competitiveness and the Current Account'. In Andrea Boltho (ed.) *The European Economy: Growth and Crisis*, pp. 132–58. Oxford: Oxford University Press, 1982.

Ludlow, N. Piers. 'From Deadlock to Dynamism. The European Community in the 1980s'. In Desmond Dinan (ed.) *Origins and Evolution of the European Union*, 2nd Edition, pp. 217–32. Oxford: Oxford University Press, 2014.

Maunder, Peter. 'International Trade'. In W.P.J. Maunder (ed.) *The British Economy in the 1970s*, pp. 247–78. London: Heinemann Educational Books, 1980.

Messerlin, Patrick A. 'Trade Policies in France'. In Dominick Salvatore (ed.) *National Trade Policies. Handbook of Comparative Economic Policies – Vol. 2*. New York and London: Greenwood Press, 1992.

Morgan, A.D. 'Commercial Policy'. In F.T. Blackaby (ed.) *British Economic Policy 1960–74*, pp. 515–63. Cambridge: Cambridge University Press, 1978.

Pelkmans, Jacques. 'Is Convergence Prompting Fragmentation? The EMS and National Protection in Germany, France and Italy'. In Paolo Guerrieri and Pier Carlo Padoan (eds) *The Political Economy of European Integration. States, Markets and Institutions*, pp. 100–44. New York and London: Harvester Wheatsheaf, 1989.

Pelzman, Joseph, 'The Multifiber Arrangement and Its Effect on the Profit Performance of the U.S. Textile Industry'. In Robert E. Baldwin and Anne O. Kruger (eds) *The Structure and Evolution of Recent U.S. Trade Policy*, pp. 111–40. Chicago and London: The University of Chicago Press, 1984.

Rauser, Gordon G. 'The Political Economy of Agriculture in the United States'. In Hans J. Michelmann, Jack S. Stabler and Gary Stoney (eds) *The Political Economy of Agricultural Trade and Policy*, pp. 66–79. Boulder, CO: Westview Press, 1990.

Ritson, Christopher and Alan Swinbank. 'Europe Green Money'. In C. Ritson and R. Harvey (eds) *The Common Agricultural Policy*, pp. 115–37. Wallingford: CAB International, 1997.

Schenk, Catherine R. 'Foreign Trade and Payments in Western Union'. In Max-Stephan Schulze (ed.) *Western Europe Economic and Social Change since 1945*, pp. 105–21. London and New York: Longman, 1999.

Strasser, Daniel, 'Le Financement de la Politique de Garantie des Marchés Agricoles'. In Jean Raux (ed.) *Politique Agricole Commune et Construction Communautaire*, pp. 21–54. Paris: Economica, 1984.

Tarr, David G. 'The Steel Crisis in the United States and the European Communities: Causes and Adjustments'. In Robert E. Baldwin, Carl B. Hamilton and André Sapir (eds) *Issues in US–EC Relations*, pp. 173–98. Chicago and London: The University of Chicago Press, 1988.

Tew, J.H.B. 'Policies Aimed at Improving the Balance of Payments'. In F.T. Blackaby (ed.) *British Economic Policy 1960–74*, pp. 304–53. Cambridge: Cambridge University Press, 1978.

Van Laer, Arthe. 'The European Community and the Paradox of U.S. Economic Diplomacy'. In Kiran Klaus Patel and Kenneth Weisbrode (eds) *European Integration and the Atlantic Community in the 1980s*, pp. 105–32. New York: Cambridge University Press, 2013.

Viñas, Angel, Sigfrido Ramirez Perez and Éric Brussière. 'Trade policy and external relations'. In *The European Commission 1973–86. Histories and Memories of an Institution*, pp. 413–28. Luxembourg: Publication Office of the European Union, 2014.

Woodward, N.W.C. 'Inflation'. In N.F.R. Crafts and N.W.C. Woodward (eds) *The British Economy since 1945*, pp. 180–211. Oxford: Clarendon Press, 1991.

Articles

Avery, Graham. 'The Common Agricultural Policy: A Turning Point'. *Common Market Law Review*, 21 (1984), pp. 481–504.

Balassa, Bela. 'The New Protectionism and the International Economy'. *Journal of World Trade Law*, 12 (1978), pp. 409–36.

Bardan, Benyamin. 'The Cotton Textile Agreement 1962–1972'. *Journal of World Trade Law*, 7 (1973), pp. 8–35.

Batten, Dallas S. and Michael T. Belongia. 'The Recent Decline in Agricultural Exports: Is the Exchange Rate the Culprit?'. *Federal Reserve Bank of Saint Louis Review*, 66 (1984), pp. 5–14.

Bergland, Bob, 'Agriculture'. *Law and Policy in International Business*. 12 (1980), pp. 257–65.

Berry, Steven, James Levinson and Ariel Pakes. 'Voluntary Export Restraints on Automobiles: Evaluating a Trade Policy'. *The American Economic Review*, 89 (1999), pp. 400–30.

Cohn, Theodore. 'The 1978–9 Negotiations for an International Wheat Agreement: An Opportunity Lost?'. *International Journal*, 35 (1979–80), pp. 132–49.

Corbet, Hugh. 'Importance of Being Earnest about Further GATT Negotiations'. *The World Economy*, 2 (1979), pp. 319–41.

Curzon Price, Victoria. 'Surplus Capacity and What the Tokyo Round Failed to Settle'. *The World Economy*, 2 (1979), pp. 305–18.

Danielsen, Albert L. 'Oil Price Regulations and the United States'. *Journal of World Trade Law*, 13 (1979), pp. 383–94.

Das, Bhagirath L. 'The GATT Ministerial Meeting 1982. An Interpretative Note'. *Journal of World Trade Law*, 18 (1984), pp. 3–15.

Denton, Geoffrey. 'Restructuring the EEC Budget: Implication of the Fontainebleau Agreement'. *Journal of Common Market Studies*, XXIII (1984), pp. 117–40.

Dymock, Paul and Donna Vogt. 'Protectionist Pressure in the U.S. Congress?'. *Journal of World Trade Law*, 17 (1983), pp. 496–512.

Finger, J.M., H.K. Halland and D.R. Nelson. 'The Political Economy of Administered Protection'. *The American Economic Review*, 72 (1982), pp. 452–6.

Haack, W.G.C.M. 'The Economic Effects of Britain's Entry into the Common Market'. *Journal of Common Market Studies*, 11 (1973), pp.136–51.

Hay, Keith A.J. and B. Andrei Sulzenko. 'U.S. Trade Policy and Reciprocity'. *Journal of World Trade Law*, 16 (1982), pp. 470–9.

Hendriks, Gisella. 'Germany and the CAP: National Interests in the European Community'. *International Affairs*, 65 (1989), pp. 75–87.

Houch, James P. 'U.S. Agricultural Trade and the Tokyo Round Agriculture'. *Law and Policy in International Business*, 12 (1980), pp. 265–96.

Houillier, François. 'Agriculture et son Évolution Depuis 1960 (La situation en 1977)'. *Revue d'Économie Politique*, 88 (1978), pp. 894–918.

Huguel, Catherine. 'La Balance des Paiments Française. Une contrainte extérieure qui demeure'. *Revue d'Économie Politique*, 94 (1984), pp. 662–75.

Huguel, Catherine. 'La Balance des Paiments Française. Des comptes extérieurs en nette redressement'. *Revue d'Économie Politique*, 95 (1985), pp. 640–57.

Insel, Barbara. 'A World Awash in Grain'. *Foreign Affairs*, 63 (1985), pp. 892–911.

Kitamura, Masaru. 'U.S.-Japan Semiconductor Agreement Revisited'. Available from kitamuralaw.com/publications/high_tech_trade_policy_1991.pdf

Kostecki, Michel M. 'Electronics Trade Policies in the 1980s'. *Journal of World Trade*, 23 (1989), pp. 16–35.

Ludlow, N. Piers. 'The Making of the CAP: Towards a Historical Analysis of the EU's First Major Common Policy'. *Contemporary European History*, 14 (2005), pp. 347–71.

Ludlow N. Piers. 'The Real Years of Europe? U.S. West European Relations during the Ford Administration'. *Journal of Cold War Studies*, 15 (2013), pp. 136–61.

McCalla, Alex F. 'Impact of Macroeconomic Policies upon Agricultural Trade and International Agricultural Development'. *American Journal of Agricultural Economics*, 64 (1982), pp. 861–8.

Moravcsik, Andrew. 'Negotiating the Single European Act: National Interests and Conventional Statecraft in the European Community'. *International Organization*, 45 (1991), pp. 19–56.

Mueller, Hans and Hans Van der Ven. 'Perils in the Brussels-Washington Steel Pact of 1982'. *The World Economy*, 5 (1982), pp. 123–42.

Paarlberg, Robert. 'The Political Economy of the American Agricultural Policy: Three Approaches'. *American Journal of Agricultural Economics*, 71 (1989), pp. 1157–64.

Paarlberg, Robert. 'Lesson of the Grain Embargo'. *Foreign Affairs*, 59 (1980–1), pp. 142–62.

Pelkmans, Jacques and Peter Robson, 'The Aspiration of the White Paper'. *Journal of Common Market Studies*, XXV (1987), pp. 181–92.

Platel, Régis. 'L'Environnement International en 1980'. *Revue d'Économie Politique*, 91 (1981), pp. 836–56.

Pomeranz, Norton. 'Toward a New International Order in Government Procurement'. *Law and Policy in International Business*, 11 (1979), pp. 1263–300.

Rivers, Richard R. and John D. Greenwald. 'The Negotiations of a Code on Subsidies and Countervailing Measures: Bridging Fundamental Policy Differences'. *Law and Policy in International Business*, 11 (1979), pp. 1447–96.

Secret, Pierre. 'L'Activité Économique Française en 1974'. *Révue d'Économie Politique*, 85 (1975), pp. 1035–55.

Sherman, Saul L. 'Reflections on the New Customs Valuation Code'. *Law and Policy in International Business*, 12 (1980), pp. 119–58.

Spaventa, Luigi. 'The Political Economy of European Monetary Integration'. *PSL Quarterly Review*, 66 (2013), pp. 325–42.

Taake, Hans-Helmut and Dieter Weiss. 'The World Textile Agreement: The Exporter's Viewpoint'. *Journal of World Trade Law*, 8 (1974), pp. 624–54.

Thirlwall, A.P. 'The Balance of Payments Constraint as An Explanation of International Growth Rate Differences'. *Banca Nazionale del Lavoro Quarterly Review*, 32 (1979), pp. 45–53.

Van Bael Ivo. 'Ten Years of EEC Antidumping Enforcement'. *Journal of World Trade Law*, 13 (1979), pp. 395–408.

Vasey, Martin. 'Decision Making in the Agricultural Council and the Luxembourg Compromise'. *Common Market Law Review*, 25 (1988), pp. 725–32.

Vasey, Martin. 'The 1985 Farm Price Negotiations and the Reform of the Common Agricultural Policy'. *Common Market Law Review*, 22 (1985), pp. 649–72.

Volle, Michel. 'Synthèse de l'Évolution de l'Économie Française en 1980 et 1981'. *Revue d'Économie Politique*, 91 (1981), pp. 810–37.

Winham, Gilbert R. 'Robert Strauss, the MTN and the Control of Faction'. *Journal of World Trade Law*, 14 (1980), pp. 377–97.

Index

Page numbers in **bold** refer to figures, page numbers in *italic* refer to tables.